SPELL CHECK

CHECK

✔ ✔ ✔ ✔ ✔

based on

The American Heritage® Dictionary

of the English Language,

Third Edition

Houghton Mifflin Company

Boston   New York

Library of Congress Cataloging-in-Publication Data

Spell check : based on The American Heritage dictionary
    of the English language, third edition.
        p.   cm.
    ISBN 0-395-75691-X
    1. Spellers.   2. English language — Syllabication — Dictionaries.
    I. American Heritage dictionary of the English language.
PE1146.S78   1996   96-55
428.1 — dc20   CIP

For information about this and other Houghton Mifflin trade and reference books
and multimedia products, visit The Bookstore at Houghton Mifflin on the World
Wide Web at http://www.hmco.com/trade/.

Manufactured in the United States of America

QWT   10

CONTENTS

EDITORIAL AND PRODUCTION STAFF

Editorial Staff

Managing Editor
Marion Severynse

Senior Lexicographer
Joseph P. Pickett

Editor
Ann-Marie Imbornoni, *Project Director*

Associate Editor
James J. Boyle

Assistant Editors
Beth Anderson
Susan S. Chicoski

Production Staff

Production and Manufacturing Manager
Christopher Leonesio

Production Supervisor
Elizabeth Rubè

Senior Art & Production Coordinator
Margaret Anne Miles

Text Design
Melodie Wertelet

HOW TO USE THIS BOOK

Spell Check is a useful guide to spelling and dividing into syllables the most commonly used words in the English language. In addition, *Spell Check* also functions as a guide to basic pronunciation, showing which syllables are stressed when a word is pronounced. The body of the book comprises a list of approximately 40,000 words, the core of which was taken from *The American Heritage Student Dictionary,* including many new words and technical and scientific terms from *The American Heritage College Dictionary, Third Edition.*

Spell Check has several special features that will save you time and effort: an explanation of some basic rules of spelling; a section on forming plurals; a section on forming compounds and hyphenation. There is also a sound-spelling correspondence table to help those who know the pronunciation of a word but are having difficulty finding it under the correct spelling.

Although *Spell Check* is simple to use, the following guide will help you make the most of its special benefits and features.

Division of Words

Spell Check clearly shows how a word may be divided into syllables. Such divisions are indicated by a centered dot, a stress mark, or a hyphen:

com•put′er	screen′writ′er
dou′ble-check′	right′-an′gled

At the end of a line of type, a word may be broken wherever a syllable division is indicated. However, many editors, compositors, and typesetters observe the following general principles:

1. A syllable consisting of a single letter should not be separated from the rest of the word:

> abide, not a-bide
> stealthy, not stealth-y
> uto-pia, not u-topia or utopi-a

2. A syllable consisting of a single letter that is embedded in the word should not be separated from the preceding syllable:

> oxy-gen, not ox-ygen
> visi-tation, not vis-itation

3. The preceding rule does not apply to the suffixes *-able* and *-ible* or to words in which the vowel standing alone is the first syllable of a root word:

> account-able, not accounta-ble
> flex-ible, not flexi-ble
> un-aware, not una-ware

4. Compound words, if possible, are divided between their elements:

> any-body   over-estimate   type-writer

5. A hyphenated word should be divided only at the hyphen.

Stress

Spell Check indicates the relative degree of stress that a syllable has when it is pronounced. Two different stress marks are used. The first, a boldface stress, indicates the syllable that receives the primary stress in the word:

> cen′ter   in•ven′tion   sin•cere′

The second mark, a lighter stress, indicates syllables that are not as strong as the one marked with a primary stress, but are still stronger than unmarked syllables:

> bi′o•log′i•cal   dic′tion•ar′y

Inflected Forms

Inflected forms are given for every entry word exhibiting any irregularity or unpredictable stress or spelling changes in the inflected forms. These forms include the plurals of nouns; the past tense, past participle, and present participle of verbs; and comparative and superlative forms of adjectives. Many inflected forms have been cut back, or shortened, to save space:

fish *pl.* fish *or*
    fish'es

mad, mad'der,
    mad'dest

bake, baked,
    bak'ing

po'di•um *pl.* -di•a
    or -di•ums

shy, shi'er *or* shy'er,
    shi'est *or* shy'est

fly, flew, flown,
    fly'ing

Note that verbs may have two or three inflected forms. If only two forms are given, the first is both the past tense and the past participle (*baked*). If three forms are given, the first is the past tense (*flew*) and the second is the past participle (*flown*). Variant inflected forms are also shown (*shyer, shyest*).

If a word has more than one part of speech, usually only one part of speech is entered (the one with the most complicated spelling changes in the inflected forms):

cry, cried, cry'ing

slide, slid, slid'ing

If, however, a word's stress pattern changes depending on whether it is used as a noun or verb, both forms are entered:

rec'ord *n.*
re•cord' *v.*

Variants

Spell Check includes variant spellings of words whenever these are in common use. Such variant spellings appear only at the main entry for that word. If the variants are used almost equally, they are separated by an *or:*

> aes•thet′ic *or* es•thet′ic

When one form is preferred over another form, the preferred form is entered first and the two forms are separated by an *also:*

> ge′o•graph′ic *also* ge′o•graph′i•cal

Words Likely to Be Confused

In *Spell Check*, glosses, or brief definitions, are given for all pairs or sets of words that are likely to be confused, including homographs (words that are spelled the same but have different meanings), homophones (words that are pronounced the same but spelled differently), words that have similar spellings or pronunciations, and troublesome words that are often used incorrectly. A check mark precedes a cross-reference to the word or words with which the entry word may be confused:

> smelt *(fish)*, pl. smelts   smelt *(to melt)*
>   or smelt
>
> hoard *(cache)*   horde *(throng)*
>   ✔ *horde*   ✔ *hoard*
>
> ac•cept′ *(to receive)*   ex•cept′ *(to leave out)*
>   ✔ *except*   ✔ *accept*
>
> bi•week′ly *(once in*   sem′i•week′ly *(twice a*
>   *two weeks)*   *week)*
>   ✔ *semiweekly*   ✔ *biweekly*

Should such words fall in regular alphabetical order, only the gloss is shown:

> bloc *(group)*
> block *(solid substance)*

Although it would be impossible to formulate a set of rules that would cover the spelling of all English words, the seven basic rules given here are intended as an aid in learning and understanding the correct spelling of a large number of English words.

Seven Basic Rules of Spelling

1. Adding a suffix to a one-syllable word.

a. Words of one syllable that end in a single consonant preceded by a single vowel double the final consonant before a suffix beginning with a vowel: *bag, baggage; hop, hopper; red, redder; stop, stopped.* There are two notable exceptions to this rule: *bus* (*buses* or *busses; busing* or *bussing*) and *gas* (*gasses* or *gases; gassing; gassy*).

b. If a word ends with two or more consonants or if it ends with one consonant preceded by two or more vowels instead of one, the final consonant is not doubled: *debt, debtor; lick, licking; mail, mailed; sweet, sweetest.*

2. Adding a suffix to a word with two or more syllables.

a. Words of two or more syllables that have the accent on the last syllable and end in a single consonant preceded by a single vowel double the final consonant before a suffix beginning with a vowel: *admit, admitted; confer, conferring; control, controller; regret, regrettable.* There are a few exceptions: *chagrin, chagrined; transfer, transferred, transferring* but *transferable, transference.*

b. When the accent shifts to the first syllable of the word after the suffix is added, the final consonant is not doubled: *prefer, preference; refer, reference.*

c. If the word ends with two consonants or if the final consonant is preceded by more than one vowel, the final consonant is not doubled: *perform, performance; repeal, repealing.*

d. If the word is accented on any syllable except the last, the final consonant is not doubled: *develop, developed; market, marketed.* However, some words like *cobweb, handicap,* and *outfit* follow the models of *web, cap,* and *fit,* even though these words may not be true compounds. A few others ending in *g* double the final *g* so that it will not be pronounced like *j*: *zigzag, zigzagged.*

3. Adding a suffix beginning with a vowel to a word ending in a silent *e*. Words ending with a silent *e* usually drop the *e* before a suffix beginning with a vowel: *force, forcible; glide, gliding; operate, operator; trifle, trifler.* However, there are many exceptions to this rule:

a. Many words of this type have alternative forms: *blamable* or *blameable; bluish* or *blueish.* And in certain cases, alternative forms have different meanings: *linage* or *lineage* (number of lines) but *lineage* (ancestry).

b. Many words ending in *ce* or *ge* keep the *e* before the suffixes *-able* and *-ous: advantage, advantageous; trace, traceable.*

c. Words ending in a silent *e* keep the *e* if the word could be mistaken for another word: *dye, dyeing; singe, singeing.*

d. If the word ends in *ie*, the *e* is dropped and the *i* changed to *y* before the suffix *-ing.* A word ending in *i* remains unchanged before *-ing: die, dying; ski, skiing.*

e. *Mile* and *acre* do not drop the *e* before the suffix *-age: mileage, acreage.*

4. Adding a suffix beginning with a consonant to a word ending in a silent *e*. Words ending with a silent *e* generally retain the *e* before a suffix that begins with a consonant: *plate, plateful; shoe, shoeless; arrange, arrangement; white, whiteness.* However, there are many exceptions to this rule. Some of the most common are: *abridge, abridgment; acknowledge, acknowledgment; argue, argument; awe, awful; due, duly; judge, judgment; nine, ninth; true, truly; whole, wholly; wise, wisdom.*

5. Adding a suffix to a word ending in *y.*

a. Words ending in *y* preceded by a consonant generally change the *y* to *i* before the addition of a suffix, except when the suffix begins with an *i: accompany, accompaniment; beauty, beautiful; icy, icier, iciest, icily, iciness;* but *reply, replying.*

b. The *y* is retained in derivatives of *baby, city,* and *lady* and before the suffixes *-ship* and *-like: babyhood, cityscape, ladyship, ladylike.*

c. Adjectives of one syllable ending in *y* preceded by a consonant usually retain the *y* when a suffix beginning with a consonant is added: *shy, shyly, shyness; sly, slyly, slyness; wry, wryly, wryness;* but *dryly* or *drily, dryness.* These adjectives usually also retain the *y* when a suffix beginning with a vowel is added, although most have variants where the *y* has changed to *i: dry, drier* or *dryer, driest* or *dryest; shy, shier* or *shyer, shiest* or *shyest.*

d. Words ending in *y* preceded by a vowel usually retain the *y* before a suffix: *buy, buyer; key, keyless; coy, coyer, coyest; gay, gayer, gayest;* but *day, daily; gay, gaily* or *gayly.*

e. Some words drop the final *y* before the addition of the suffix *-eous: beauty, beauteous.*

6. Adding a suffix to a word ending in *c.* Words ending in *c* almost always have the letter *k* inserted after the *c* when a suffix beginning with *e, i,* or *y* is added: *panic, panicky; picnic, picnicker.*

7. The problem of "ie" or "ei."

a. When the two letters have a long *e* sound (as in *feet*), *i* generally comes before *e,* except after *c: believe, chief, grieve, niece, siege, shield;* but *either, leisure, neither, seize, sheik.*

b. After *c, e* generally comes before *i: ceiling, conceit, deceive, perceive, receive, receipt;* but *ancient, financier, specie.*

c. When the two letters have a long *a* sound (as in *cake*), a short *e* sound (as in *pet*), a short *i* sound (as in *fit*), or a long *i* sound (as in *mine*), *e* generally comes before *i*: *Fahrenheit, foreign, forfeit, height, neighbor, sleight, sovereign, surfeit;* but *friend, handkerchief, mischief, sieve.*

Many words spelled with *ie* or *ei* present no difficulties because the vowels are pronounced separately: *deity, piety.*

Forming Plurals

1. The plural of most nouns is formed by adding *s* to the singular: *apples, epochs, griefs, months, Georges, the Romanos.*

2. a. Common nouns ending in *ch* (soft), *sh, s, ss, x, z* or *zz* usually form their plurals by adding *es*: *churches, slashes, gases, classes, foxes, buzzes.*

b. Proper nouns of this type add *es*: *Charles, the Charleses; the Keaches; the Joneses; the Coxes.*

3. a. Common nouns ending in *y* preceded by a vowel usually form their plurals by adding *s*: *bays, guys, keys, toys.*

b. Common nouns ending in *y* preceded by a consonant or by *qu* change the *y* to *i* and add *es*: *baby, babies; city, cities; faculty, faculties; soliloquy, soliloquies.*

c. Proper nouns ending in *y* form their plurals regularly, and do not change the *y* to *i* as common nouns do: *the two Kathys; the Connallys; the two Kansas Citys.* There are a few well-known exceptions to this rule: *the Alleghenies, the Ptolemies, the Rockies, the Two Sicilies.*

4. Most nouns ending in *f, ff,* or *fe* form their plurals regularly by adding *s* to the singular: *chief, chiefs; proof, proofs; roof, roofs; sheriff, sheriffs; fife, fifes.* However, some nouns ending in *f* or *fe* change the *f* or *fe* to *v* and add *es*: *calf, calves; elf, elves; half, halves; knife, knives; life, lives; loaf, loaves; self, selves; shelf, shelves; thief, thieves; wife, wives; wolf, wolves.* A few nouns ending in *f* or *ff,* including *beef, dwarf, hoof, scarf, wharf,* and *staff* have two plural forms: *beefs, beeves; dwarfs* or *dwarves; hoofs* or *hooves; scarfs* or *scarves; wharfs* or *wharves; staffs* or *staves*. In this case, sometimes different forms have different meanings, as *beefs* (complaints) and *beeves* (animals) or *staffs* (people) and *staves* (long poles).

5. a. Nouns ending in *o* preceded by a vowel form their plurals by adding *s* to the singular: *cameos, duos, studios, zoos.*

b. Most nouns ending in *o* preceded by a consonant also usually add *s* to form the plural: *altos, casinos, egos, Latinos.* However, some nouns ending in *o* preceded by a consonant add *es*: *echoes, heroes, jingoes, noes, potatoes, tomatoes.* Some nouns ending in *o* preceded by a consonant have two plural forms: *buffaloes* or *buffalos; cargoes* or *cargos; desperadoes* or *desperados; halos* or *haloes; mosquitoes* or *mosquitos; zeros* or *zeroes.*

6. Most nouns ending in *i* form their plurals by adding *s: alibis, khakis, rabbis, skis.* Three exceptions are *alkali, taxi,* and *chili: alkalis* or *alkalies; taxis* or *taxies; chilies.*

7. a. A few nouns undergo a vowel change in the stem: *foot, feet; goose, geese; louse, lice; man, men; mouse, mice; tooth, teeth; woman, women.* Usually compounds in which one of these nouns is the final element form their plurals in the same way: *webfoot, webfeet; gentleman, gentlemen; dormouse, dormice; Englishwoman, Englishwomen.* Note, however, that *mongoose* and many words ending in *man,* such as *German* and *human,* are not compounds. These words forms their plurals by adding *s: mongooses; Germans, humans.*

b. Three nouns have plurals ending in *en: ox, oxen; child, children; brother, brothers* (of the same parent) or *brethren* (a fellow member).

8. a. Compounds written as a single word form their plurals the same way that the final element of the compound does: *cloths, dishcloths; brushes, hairbrushes; wives, midwives; men, anchormen; women, businesswomen.*

b. In rare cases both parts of the compound are made plural: *manservant, menservants.*

c. Compounds ending in *-ful* normally form their plurals by adding *s* at the end: *cupfuls, handfuls, tablespoonfuls.*

d. Compound words, written with or without a hyphen, that consist of a noun followed by an adjective or other qualifying expression form their plurals by making the same change in the noun as when the noun stands alone: *daughter-in-law, daughters-in-law; man-of-war, men-of-war; heir apparent, heirs apparent; notary public, notaries public.*

9. Some nouns, mainly names of birds, fishes, and mammals, have the same form in the plural as in the singular: *bison, deer, moose, sheep, swine.* Some words that follow this pattern, such as *antelope, cod, crab, elk, fish, flounder, grouse, herring, quail, reindeer, salmon, shrimp,* and *trout,* also have regular plurals ending in *-s: antelope, antelopes; fish, fishes; salmon, salmons.* Normally in such cases the unchanged plural denotes that the animal in question is being considered collectively, while the plural ending in *s* is used specifically to denote different varieties or species or kinds: *We caught six fish* but *Half a dozen fishes inhabit the lake.* By far, however, most animal names take a regular plural: *dogs, cats, lions, monkeys, whales.*

10. a. Many words indicating nationality or place of origin have the same form in the plural as in the singular: *Japanese, Milanese, Swiss.*

b. Similarly a few names of tribes or peoples have the same form in the plural as in the singular: *Iroquois; Sioux.* Many other such names have both an unchanged plural form and a regular plural form ending in *s: Apache* or *Apaches; Cherokee* or *Cherokees; Eskimo* or *Eskimos; Zulu* or *Zulus.*

11. Many nouns derived from a foreign language retain their foreign plurals: (from Latin) *alumna, alumnae; bacillus, bacilli; genus, genera; series, series;* (from Greek) *analysis, analyses; basis,* *bases; crisis, crises; criterion, criteria* or *criterions; phenomenon, phenomena* or *phenomenons;* (from French) *adieu, adieux* or *adieus; beau, beaux* or *beaus; madame, mesdames;* (from Italian) *paparazzo, paparazzi;* (from Hebrew) *cherub, cherubim* or *cherubs; kibbutz, kibbutzim.* As you can see, many words of this type also have a regular plural ending in *s* or *es,* in which case the English plural is usually the one used in everyday speech, and the foreign plural is reserved for a technical sense or for use by a specialist: *antennas* (TV or radio part) or *antennae* (physiological structure).

12. a. Usage with regard to forming the plurals of letters, numbers, and abbreviations varies. In some cases you have a choice between adding *s* or *'s: three As* or *three A's; the ABCs* or *the ABC's; the 1900s* or *the 1900's; PhDs* or *PhD's; several IOUs* or *several IOU's.* With lowercase letters, symbols, abbreviations with periods, and in cases where confusion might arise without an apostrophe, use *'s* to form the plural: *p's and q's; +'s; -'s; M.A.'s; A's and I's; 2's.*

b. The plural of a word being used as a word is indicated by *'s: underline all the but's.*

Word Compounding

A compound word is made up of two or more words that together express a single idea. There are three types of compound words. An *open compound* consists of two or more words written separately, such as *salad dressing* or *April Fools' Day.* A *hyphenated compound* has words connected by a hyphen, such as *mother-in-law* or *force-feed.* A *solid compound* is two words that are written as one word, such as *keyboard* or *typewriter.* In addition, a compound may be classified as permanent or temporary. A *permanent compound* is fixed by common usage and can usually be found in the dictionary, whereas a *temporary compound* consists of two or more words joined by a hyphen as needed, usually to modify another word or to avoid ambiguity. The following general rules apply to forming compounds.

Prefixes and suffixes

1. Normally, prefixes and suffixes are joined with a second element without a hyphen, unless doing so would double a vowel or triple a consonant: *antianxiety, anticrime, antiwar* but *anti-intellectual; childlike, taillike* but *bell-like.* Even so, many common prefixes, such as *co-, de-, pre-, pro-,* and *re-,* are added without a hyphen although a double vowel is the result: *coordinate, preeminent, reenter.*

2. A hyphen is also used when the element following a prefix is capitalized, or when the element preceding a suffix is a proper noun: *anti-American, America-like.*

3. The hyphen is usually retained in words that begin with *all-, ex-* (meaning "former"), *half-, quasi-* (in adjective constructions), and *self-: all-around; ex-governor; half-life* but *halfhearted, halfpenny, halftone, halfway; quasi-scientific* but *a quasi success; self-defense* but *selfhood, selfish, selfless, selfsame.*

4. Certain homographs require a hyphen to prevent mistakes in pronunciation and meaning: *recreation* (enjoyment), *re-creation* (new creation).

When the compound is a noun or adjective

5. In order to avoid confusion, compound modifiers are generally hyphenated: *fine-wine tasting; high-school teacher; hot-water bottle; minimum-wage worker; rare-book store; real-life experiences.* If there is no possibility of confusion, or if the hyphen would look clumsy, omit the hyphen: *bubonic plague outbreak, chemical engineering degree, temp agency employee.*

6. When a noun that is an open compound is preceded by an adjective, the compound is often hyphenated to avoid confusion: *wine cellar, damp wine-cellar; broom closet, tiny broom-closet; house cat, old house-cat.*

7. Compound adjectives formed with *high-* or *low-* are generally hyphenated: *high-quality programming; low-budget films.*

8. Compound adjectives formed with an adverb plus an adjective or a participle are often hyphenated when they occur before the noun they modify: *a well-known actor, an ill-advised move, best-loved poems, a much-improved situation, the so-called cure.* However, when these compounds occur after the noun, or when they are modified, the hyphen is usually omitted: *the actor is well known; an extremely well known actor.* Many compounds of this type are permanent hyphenated compounds: *a well-done steak; the steak was well-done.*

9. If the adverb ends in *-ly* in an adverb-adjective compound, the hyphen is omitted: *a finely tuned mechanism; a carefully worked canvas.*

10. Compound adjectives formed with a noun and a past participle are always hyphenated when they precede the noun they modify: *helium-filled balloons, snow-capped mountains.* Many compounds of this type have become permanent and are hyphenated whether they precede or follow the noun they modify: *the tongue-tied winner; She remained tongue-tied.*

11. Also hyphenate compound adjectives formed with an adjective and a noun to which *-d* or *-ed* has been added: *yellow-eyed cat, fine-grained wood, many-tiered cake, stout-limbed toddler.* Many such compounds have become permanent hyphenated or solid compounds: *middle-aged, old-fashioned, lightheaded, kindhearted.*

12. Compound adjectives formed with a noun, adjective, or adverb and a present participle are hyphenated when the compound precedes the noun it modifies: *a bone-chilling tale, two good-looking sons, long-lasting friendship.* Many such compounds have become permanent solid compounds: *earsplitting, farseeing.* Many such compounds have become permanent and are hyphenated whether they precede or follow the noun they modify: *far-reaching consequences; The consequences are far-reaching.*

13. Compound nouns formed with a noun and a gerund are generally open: *crime solving, house hunting, trout fishing.* Many such compounds, however, have become permanent solid compounds: *faultfinding, housekeeping.*

14. Compound modifiers formed of capitalized words should not be hyphenated: *Old English poetry; Iron Age manufacture; New World plants.*

15. Usage is divided with regard to compounds that are proper names used to designate ethnic groups. Under normal circumstances such terms when used as nouns or adjectives should appear without a hyphen: *a group of African Americans, many Native Americans, French Canadians in Boston; a Jewish American organization, Latin American countries.* However, many (but not all) compounds of this type are now frequently hyphenated: *African-Americans, French-Canadian music.*

16. Nouns or adjectives consisting of a short verb and a preposition are either hyphenated or solid depending on current usage. The same words used as verbs are written separately: *a breakup* but *break up a fight; a bang-up job* but *bang up the car.*

17. Two nouns of equal value are hyphenated when the person or thing is considered to have the characteristics of both nouns: *secretary-treasurer, city-state, time-motion study.*

18. Compound forms must always reflect meaning. Consequently, some compounds may change in form depending on how they are used: *Anyone may go* but *Any one of these will do; Everyone is here* but *Every one of these is good.*

19. Scientific compounds are usually not hyphenated: *carbon monoxide poisoning; dichromic acid solution.*

Phrases

20. Phrases used as modifiers are normally hyphenated: *a happy-go-lucky person; a here-today-gone-tomorrow attitude.*

21. A foreign phrase used as a modifier is not hyphenated: *a bona fide offer; a per diem allowance.*

Numbers

22. Numbers from twenty-one to ninety-nine and adjective compounds with a numerical first element (whether spelled out or written in figures) are hyphenated: *twenty-one, thirty-first, second-rate movie, third-story window, three-dimensional figure, six-sided polygon, 13-piece band, 19th-century novel, decades-old newspapers.*

23. Spelled-out numbers used with *-fold* are not hyphenated; figures and *-fold* are hyphenated: *tenfold; 20-fold.*

24. Compounds of a number and *-odd* are hyphenated: *four-odd, 60-odd.*

25. Modifying compounds consisting of a number and a possessive noun are not hyphenated: *one week's pay; 35 hours' work.*

26. Fractions used as modifiers are hyphenated unless the numerator or denominator of the fraction contains a hyphen: *three-eighths inch; twenty-four hundredths part; The pie was one-half eaten.* Fractions used as nouns are usually not hyphenated: *He ate one half of the pie.*

Color

27. Compound color adjectives are hyphenated: *a red-gold sunset; a cherry-red sweater.*

28. Color compounds whose first element ends in *-ish* are hyphenated when they precede the noun, but not when they follow the noun: *a reddish-gold sunset; The sky is reddish gold.*

SOUND-SPELLING CORRESPONDENCES

This table, which is designed to help the user find a word known only through its pronunciation, lists the speech sounds of English and matches them with their possible spellings. Note that the letter *x* spells six sounds in English: ks, as in box, exit; gz, as in exact; sh, as in anxious; gzh, as in luxury; ksh, also as in luxury; and z, as in anxiety, xerography.

SOUND	SPELLING	SAMPLE WORDS
a (as in **pat**)	ai	plaid
	au	laugh
a (as in **mane**)	ae	maelstrom
	ai	pain
	ao	gaol
	au	gauge
	ay	pay
	e	suede
	ea	break
	ee	matinee, melee
	ei	vein, feign
	ey	prey
a (as in **father**)	ah	**ah**
	e	sergeant
	ea	heart
b (as in **bib**)	bb	blubber
	pb	cupboard
ch (as in **church**)	c	cello
	Cz	**Cz**ech
	tch	pa**tch**, sti**tch**

SOUND	SPELLING	SAMPLE WORDS
ch (as in **church**)	ti	question
	tu	denture
d (as in **deed**)	dd	ladder
	ed	mailed
e (as in **pet**)	a	any
	ae	aesthetic
	ai	said
	ay	says
	ea	thread
	ei	heifer
	eo	leopard
	ie	friendly
	oe	roentgen
	u	burial
e (as in **be**)	ae	Caesar
	ay	quay
	ea	each, beach
	ee	beet
	ei	conceit
	eo	people
	ey	key
	i	piano, cardiac
	ie	siege
	oe	phoenix
	y	ichthyosis, city
er (as in **certain**)	ear	pearl, yearn
	eur	restaurateur
	ir	bird, first
	or	work
	our	journey
	ur	burden
	yr	myrtle

SOUND	SPELLING	SAMPLE WORDS
f (as in **f**i**f**e)	ff	sti**ff**
	gh	enou**gh**
	lf	ha**lf**
	ph	**ph**osphate
g (as in **g**a**g**)	gg	bra**gg**ed
	gh	**gh**ost
	gu	**gu**est
h (as in **h**at)	wh	**wh**ole
	g	**G**ila monster
	j	**j**ai alai
i (as in p**i**t)	a	vill**a**ge, clim**a**te
	e	**e**nough
	ee	b**ee**n
	ia	carr**ia**ge
	ie	s**ie**ve
	o	w**o**men
	u	b**u**sy
	ui	b**ui**lt
	y	c**y**st, phar**y**nx
i (as in **i**dle)	ai	gua**i**ac, **ai**sle
	ay	b**ay**ou
	ei	h**ei**ght, m**ei**osis
	ie	l**ie**
	uy	b**uy**
	y	sk**y**, l**y**re
	ye	r**ye**
j (as in **j**ar)	d	gra**d**ual
	dg	lo**dg**ing
	di	sol**di**er
	dj	a**dj**ective
	g	**g**eriatric
	gg	exa**gg**erate

SOUND	SPELLING	SAMPLE WORDS
k (as in **k**ite)	c	**c**all, e**c**stasy
	cc	a**cc**ount
	cch	sa**cch**arin
	ch	**ch**orus
	ck	a**ck**nowledge
	cqu	la**cqu**er
	cu	bis**cu**it
	lk	ta**lk**
	q	Ira**q**i
	qu	**qu**ay
	que	pla**que**
l (as in **l**id)	ll	ta**ll**, **ll**ama
	lh	**Lh**asa apso
m (as in **m**um)	chm	dra**chm**
	gm	paradi**gm**
	lm	ba**lm**
	mb	plu**mb**
	mm	ha**mm**er
	mn	sole**mn**
n (as in **n**o)	gn	**gn**at, ali**gn**
	kn	**kn**ife
	mn	**mn**emonic
	nn	ca**nn**y, i**nn**
	pn	**pn**eumonia
o (as in p**o**t)	a	w**a**ffle, w**a**tch
	ho	**ho**nest
	ou	tr**ou**gh
o (as in n**o**)	au	m**au**ve
	eau	b**eau**, bur**eau**
	eo	y**eo**man
	ew	s**ew**
	oa	f**oa**l, f**oa**m
	oe	f**oe**

SOUND	SPELLING	SAMPLE WORDS
o (as in no)	oh	**oh**m
	oo	br**oo**ch
	ou	sh**ou**lder
	ough	bor**ough**, d**ough**
	ow	l**ow**, r**ow**
	owe	**owe**
o (as in for)	a	**a**ll
	ah	Ut**ah**an
	au	c**au**ght, g**au**nt
	aw	**aw**ful
	oa	br**oa**d
	ough	b**ough**t
oi (as in noise)	oy	b**oy**
ou (as in out)	au	s**au**erkraut
	hou	**hou**r
	ough	b**ough**
	ow	sc**ow**l, s**ow**
oo (as in took)	o	w**o**man, w**o**lf
	ou	sh**ou**ld
	u	c**u**shion, f**u**ll
oo (as in boot)	eu	l**eu**kemia
	ew	shr**ew**
	ieu	l**ieu**tenant
	o	d**o**, m**o**ve, tw**o**
	oe	can**oe**
	ou	gr**ou**p, s**ou**p
	u	r**u**de
	ue	bl**ue**, fl**ue**
	ui	br**ui**se, fr**ui**t
p (as in pop)	pp	ha**pp**y
r (as in roar)	rh	**rh**ythm
	rr	che**rr**y

SOUND	SPELLING	SAMPLE WORDS
r (as in **r**oar)	rrh	ci**rrh**osis
	wr	**wr**ite
s (as in **s**ay)	c	**c**ellar, medi**c**ine
	ps	**ps**ychology
	sc	**sc**iatic, ab**sc**ess
	sch	**sch**ism
	ss	pa**ss**, sa**ss**afras
	sth	i**sth**mus
sh (as in **sh**ip)	ce	o**ce**anic
	ch	**ch**andelier
	ci	spe**ci**al
	s	**s**ugar
	sc	con**sc**ience
	sch	**sch**ist
	se	nau**se**ous
	si	pen**si**on
	ss	ti**ss**ue, mi**ss**ion
	ti	elec**ti**on, na**ti**on
t (as in **t**ie)	bt	de**bt**
	ed	stopp**ed**
	ght	cau**ght**
	pt	**pt**omaine, recei**pt**
	th	**th**yme
	tt	le**tt**er
u (as in c**u**t)	o	s**o**n, inc**o**me
	oe	d**oe**s
	oo	bl**oo**d
	ou	c**ou**ple, tr**ou**ble
u (as in **u**se)	eau	b**eau**tiful
	eu	f**eu**d, **eu**genic
	eue	qu**eue**
	ew	p**ew**
	ieu	adi**eu**

SOUND	SPELLING	SAMPLE WORDS
u (as in **u**se)	iew	v**iew**
	ue	c**ue**
	you	**you**th
	yu	**yu**le
v (as in **v**alve)	f	o**f**
w (as in **w**ith)	o	**o**ne
	u	g**u**anese, q**u**ick
y (as in **y**es)	i	on**i**on
	j	halle**l**ujah
z (as in **z**ebra)	cz	**cz**ar
	s	ri**s**e, her**s**
	ss	de**ss**ert
	x	**x**ylem
	zz	fu**zz**

SPELL
CHECK

A

aard'vark'
ab'a·ca'
a·back'
ab'a·cus *pl.* -cus·es
  or -ci'
a·baft'
ab'a·lo'ne
a·ban'don
a·ban'doned
a·base', a·based',
  a·bas'ing
a·base'ment
a·bash'
a·bate', a·bat'ed,
  a·bat'ing
a·bate'ment
ab'at·toir'
ab'bess
ab'bey *pl.* -beys
ab'bot
ab·bre'vi·ate',
  -at'ed, -at'ing
ab·bre'vi·a'tion
ab'di·cate', -cat'ed,
  -cat'ing
ab'di·ca'tion
ab'di·ca'tor
ab'do·men
ab·dom'i·nal
ab·duct'
ab·duc'tion
ab·duc'tor
a·beam'
a·bed'

Ab'e·na'ki *pl.* -ki *or*
  -kis
ab'er·rant
ab'er·ra'tion
a·bet', a·bet'ted,
  a·bet'ting
a·bet'tor *or*
  a·bet'ter
a·bey'ance
ab·hor', -horred',
  -hor'ring
ab·hor'rence
ab·hor'rent
a·bide', a·bode' *or*
  a·bid'ed, a·bid'ing
a·bil'i·ty
ab'ject'
ab'ju·ra'tion
ab·jure' *(to re-*
  nounce), -jured',
  -jur'ing
  ✓ *adjure*
ab·la'tion
a·blaze'
a'ble, a'bler, a'blest
a'ble-bod'ied
a·bloom'
ab·lu'tion
a'bly
ab'ne·gate',
  -gat'ed, -gat'ing
ab'ne·ga'tion
ab·nor'mal
ab'nor·mal'i·ty
a·board'
a·bode'

a·bol'ish
ab'o·li'tion
ab'o·li'tion·ist
A'-bomb'
a·bom'i·na·ble
a·bom'i·na·bly
a·bom'i·nate',
  -nat'ed, -nat'ing
a·bom'i·na'tion
ab'o·rig'i·nal
ab'o·rig'i·ne
a·bort'
a·bor'tion
a·bor'tive
a·bound'
a·bout'
a·bout'-face',
  -faced', -fac'ing
a·bove'
a·bove'board'
ab'ra·ca·dab'ra
a·brade', a·brad'ed,
  a·brad'ing
ab·ra'sion
ab·ra'sive
a·breast'
a·bridge',
  a·bridged',
  a·bridg'ing
a·bridg'ment *also*
  a·bridge'ment
a·broad'
ab'ro·gate', -gat'ed,
  -gat'ing
ab'ro·ga'tion
a·brupt'

ab'scess'
ab'scessed'
ab•scis'sa *pl.*
  -scis'sas *or* -scis'sae
ab•scis'sion
ab•scond'
ab'sence
ab'sent *adj.*
ab•sent' *v.*
ab'sen•tee'
ab•sen•tee'ism
ab'sent-mind'ed
ab'sinthe *also*
  ab'sinth
ab'so•lute'
ab'so•lute'ly
ab'so•lu'tion
ab'so•lut'ism
ab•solv'a•ble
ab•solve', -solved',
  -solv'ing
ab•sorb' *(to soak up)*
  ✔ adsorb
ab•sorbed'
ab•sorb'ent
ab•sorb'ing
ab•sorp'tion
ab•stain'
ab•ste'mi•ous
ab•sten'tion
ab'sti•nence
ab'sti•nent
ab'stract' *n.*
ab•stract' *v.*
ab•stract'ed
ab•strac'tion
ab•struse'

ab•surd'
ab•surd'i•ty
a•bun'dance
a•bun'dant
a•buse', a•bused',
  a•bus'ing
a•bus'er
a•bu'sive
a•but', a•but'ted,
  a•but'ting
a•but'ment
a•but'ter
a•buzz'
a•bys'mal *(deep,
  limitless, bad)*
  ✔ abyssal
a•byss'
a•bys'sal *(deep, relat-
  ing to ocean depths)*
  ✔ abysmal
a•ca'cia
ac'a•deme'
ac'a•de'mi•a
ac'a•dem'ic
ac'a•de•mi'cian
ac'a•dem'i•cism
  also a•cad'e•mism
a•cad'e•my
A•ca'di•an
a•can'thus *pl.*
  -thus•es *or* -thi'
a' cap•pel'la
ac•cede' *(to agree),*
  -ced'ed, -ced'ing
  ✔ exceed
ac•ced'ence
ac•cel'er•an'do

ac•cel'er•ant
ac•cel'er•ate',
  -at'ed, -at'ing
ac•cel'er•a'tion
ac•cel'er•a'tor
ac•cel'er•om'e•ter
ac'cent'
ac•cen'tu•al
ac•cen'tu•ate',
  -at'ed, -at'ing
ac•cen'tu•a'tion
ac•cept' *(to receive)*
  ✔ except
ac•cept'a•bil'i•ty
ac•cept'a•ble
ac•cept'a•bly
ac•cep'tance
ac•cep'tant
ac'cep•ta'tion
ac'cess *(entrance)*
  ✔ excess
ac•ces'si•bil'i•ty
ac•ces'si•ble
ac•ces'si•bly
ac•ces'sion
ac•ces•so'ri•al
ac•ces•so'ri•ly
ac•ces'so•rize',
  -ized', -iz'ing
ac•ces'so•ry
ac'ci•dent
ac'ci•den'tal
ac'ci•dent-prone'
ac•claim'
ac'cla•ma'tion
  (acclaim)
  ✔ acclimation

ac·clam'a·to'ry

ac'cli·mate',
-mat'ed, -mat'ing

ac'cli·ma'tion
(adaptation)
✔ *acclamation*

ac·cli'ma·ti·za'tion

ac·cli'ma·tize',
-tized', -tiz'ing

ac·cliv'i·ty

ac'co·lade'

ac·com'mo·date',
-dat'ed, -dat'ing

ac·com'mo·da'-
tion

ac·com'pa·ni·
ment

ac·com'pa·nist

ac·com'pa·ny,
-nied, -ny·ing

ac·com'plice

ac·com'plish

ac·com'plish·ment

ac·cord'

ac·cor'dance

ac·cord'ing·ly

ac·cor'di·on

ac·cost'

ac·count'

ac·count'a·bil'i·ty

ac·count'a·ble

ac·count'ant

ac·count'ing

ac·cou'ter *or*
ac·cou'tre, -tered *or*
-tred, -ter·ing *or*
-tre·ing

ac·cou'ter·ments
or ac·cou'tre·ments

ac·cred'it

ac·cred'i·ta'tion

ac·cre'tion

ac·cru'al

ac·crue', -crued',
-cru'ing

ac·cul'tur·ate'

ac·cul'tur·a'tion

ac·cu'mu·late',
-lat'ed, -lat'ing

ac·cu'mu·la'tion

ac·cu'mu·la'tive

ac·cu'mu·la'tor

ac'cu·ra·cy

ac'cu·rate

ac·curs'ed *also*
ac·curst'

ac'cu·sa'tion

ac·cu'sa·tive

ac·cuse', -cused',
-cus'ing

ac·cus'er

ac·cus'tom

ace, aced, ac'ing

a·cer'bic *also*
a·cerb'

a·cer'bi·ty

ac'e·tal'

ac'et·al'de·hyde'

a·cet'a·min'o·
phen

ac'e·tate'

a·ce'tic *(relating to
acetic acid)*
✔ *ascetic*

ac'e·tone'

a·ce'tyl

a·cet'y·lene'

a·ce'tyl·sal'i·cyl'ic
ac'id

ache, ached, ach'ing

a·chieve',
a·chieved',
a·chiev'ing

a·chiev'er

a·chieve'ment

A·chil'les' heel'

ach'ro·mat'ic

ach'y

ac'id

a·cid'ic

a·cid'i·fi·ca'tion

a·cid'i·fy', -fied',
-fy'ing

a·cid'i·ty

ac'i·do·phil'ic *also*
ac'i·doph'i·lus

a·cid'u·late',
-lat'ed, -lat'ing

a·cid'u·la'tion

a·cid'u·lous

ac·knowl'edge,
-edged, -edg·ing

ac·knowl'edge·
a·ble

ac·knowl'edg·
ment *or* ac·knowl'-
edge·ment

ac'me

ac'ne

ac'o·lyte'

ac'o·nite'

a'corn'
a·cous'tic *also*
  a·cous'ti·cal
a·cous'tics
ac·quaint'
ac·quain'tance
ac·quain'tance·
  ship'
ac·quaint'ed
ac'qui·esce',
  -esced', -esc'ing
ac'qui·es'cence
ac'qui·es'cent
ac·quir'a·ble
ac·quire', -quired',
  -quir'ing
ac·quire'ment
ac'qui·si'tion
ac·quis'i·tive
ac·quis'i·tor
ac·quit', -quit'ted,
  -quit'ting
ac·quit'tal
ac·quit'tance
ac·quit'ter
a'cre
a'cre·age
a'cre-foot'
ac'rid
ac'ri·mo'ni·ous
ac'ri·mo'ny
ac'ro·bat'
ac'ro·bat'ic
ac'ro·nym'
a·crop'o·lis
a·cross'
a·cros'tic

a·cryl'ic
ACTH
ac'tin
act'ing
ac·tin'ic
ac'ti·nide'
ac'ti·nism
ac·tin'i·um
ac'tion
ac'tion·a·ble
ac'ti·vate', -vat'ed,
  -vat'ing
ac'ti·va'tion
ac'ti·va'tor
ac'tive
ac'tive·ly
ac'tiv·ism
ac'tiv·ist
ac·tiv'i·ty
ac'tor
ac'tress
ac'tu·al
ac'tu·al'i·ty
ac'tu·al·ly
ac'tu·ar'y
ac'tu·ate', -at'ed,
  -at'ing
ac'tu·a'tion
ac'tu·a'tor
a·cu'i·ty
a·cu'men
ac'u·punc'ture
a·cute'
ad (*advertisement*)
  ✔ add
ad'age
a·da'gio

ad'a·mant
Ad'am's ap'ple
a·dapt' (*to adjust*)
  ✔ adept, adopt
a·dapt'a·bil'i·ty
a·dapt'a·ble
ad'ap·ta'tion
a·dapt'ed
a·dapt'er *also*
  a·dap'tor
a·dap'tive
add (*to combine*)
  ✔ ad
ad'dax'
ad'dend'
ad·den'dum *pl.* -da
add'er (*one that*
  adds)
ad'der (*snake*)
ad·dict' *v.*
ad'dict' *n.*
ad·dict'ed
ad·dic'tion
ad·dic'tive
ad·di'tion (*adding*)
  ✔ edition
ad·di'tion·al
ad'di·tive
ad'dle, -dled, -dling
ad·dress'
ad'dress·ee'
ad·duce', -duced',
  -duc'ing
ad·duct'
ad·duc'tion
ad'e·nine'
ad'e·noi'dal

ad'e•noids'
a•dept' *(skillful)*
  ✔ adapt, adopt
ad'ept' *(skilled person)*
ad'e•qua•cy
ad'e•quate
ad'e•quate•ly
ad•here' *(to stick)*,
  -hered', -her'ing
  ✔ cohere
ad•her'ence
ad•her'ent
ad•he'sion
ad•he'sive
ad hoc'
ad'i•a•bat'ic
a•dieu' *(farewell)*, pl.
  a•dieus' or a•dieux'
  ✔ ado
ad in'fi•ni'tum
ad'i•os'
ad'i•pose'
ad•ja'cent
ad'jec•ti'val
ad'jec•tive
ad•join'
ad•join'ing
ad•journ'
ad•journ'ment
ad•judge',
  -judged', -judg'ing
ad•ju'di•cate',
  -cat'ed, -cat'ing
ad•ju'di•ca'tion
ad•ju'di•ca'tive
ad•ju'di•ca'tor

ad•junct'
ad'ju•ra'tion
ad•jure' *(to command)*, -jured',
  -jur'ing
  ✔ abjure
ad•just'
ad•just'a•ble
ad•just'er
ad•just'ment
ad'ju•tant
ad-lib', -libbed',
  -lib'bing
ad•min'is•ter
ad•min'is•trate',
  -trat'ed, -trat'ing
ad•min'is•tra'tion
ad•min'is•tra'tive
ad•min'is•tra'tor
ad'mi•ra•ble
ad'mi•ra•bly
ad'mi•ral
ad'mi•ral•ty
ad'mi•ra'tion
ad•mire', -mired',
  -mir'ing
ad•mir'er
ad•mis'si•bil'i•ty
ad•mis'si•ble
ad•mis'si•bly
ad•mis'sion
ad•mit', -mit'ted,
  -mit'ting
ad•mit'tance
ad•mit'ted•ly
ad•mix'
ad•mix'ture

ad•mon'ish
ad•mon'ish•ment
ad'mo•ni'tion
ad•mon'i•to'ry
ad nau'se•am
a•do' *(fuss)*
  ✔ adieu
a•do'be
ad'o•les'cence
ad'o•les'cent
A•don'is or a•don'is
a•dopt' *(to take as one's own)*
  ✔ adapt, adept
a•dopt'a•ble
a•dop'tion
a•dop'tive
a•dor'a•ble
a•dor'a•bly
ad'o•ra'tion
a•dore', a•dored',
  a•dor'ing
a•dor'er
a•dorn'
ad•re'nal
a•dren'a•line
a•drift'
a•droit'
ad•sorb' *(to accumulate on a surface)*
  ✔ absorb
ad•sorp'tion
ad'u•late', -lat'ed,
  -lat'ing
ad'u•la'tion
ad'u•la'tor
ad'u•la•to'ry

a·dult'
a·dul'ter·ant
a·dul'ter·ate',
  -at'ed, -at'ing
a·dul'ter·a'tion
a·dul'ter·er
a·dul'ter·ess
a·dul'ter·ous
a·dul'ter·y
a·dult'hood'
ad·um'brate'
ad·um·bra'tion
ad·vance',
  -vanced', -vanc'ing
ad·vance'ment
ad·van'tage
ad'van·ta'geous
ad·vent'
Ad'vent·ism
Ad'vent·ist
ad·ven·ti'tious
ad·ven'ture, -tured,
  -tur'ing
ad·ven'tur·er
ad·ven'ture·some
ad·ven'tur·ous
ad'verb
ad·ver'bi·al
ad'ver·sar'y
ad·verse' (hostile)
  ✔ averse
ad·ver'si·ty
ad·vert'
ad'ver·tise', -tised',
  -tis'ing
ad'ver·tise'ment
ad'ver·tis'er

ad'ver·tis'ing
ad·vice' (guidance)
  ✔ advise
ad·vis'a·bil'i·ty
ad·vis'a·ble
ad·vis'a·bly
ad·vise' (to give
  advice), -vised',
  -vis'ing
  ✔ advice
ad·vis'ed·ly
ad·vise'ment
ad·vis'er or ad·vi'-
  sor
ad·vi'so·ry
ad'vo·ca·cy
ad'vo·cate', -cat'ed,
  -cat'ing
ad'vo·cate n.
ad'vo·ca'tion
ad'vo·ca'tor
adz or adze
ae'gis also e'gis
aer·ate', -at'ed,
  -at'ing
aer·a'tion
aer'a'tor
aer'i·al
aer'i·al·ist
aer'ie or aer'y also
  ey'rie or ey'ry
  (nest), pl. aer'ies
  also ey'ries
  ✔ airy, eerie
aer'obe'
aer·o'bic
aer'o·dy·nam'ic

  also aer'o·dy·
  nam'i·cal
aer·ol'o·gy
aer'o·nau'tic also
  aer'o·nau'ti·cal
aer'o·pause'
aer'o·sol'
aer'o·space'
aes'thete or
  es'thete
aes·thet'ic or
  es·thet'ic
aes·the·ti'cian or
  es·the·ti'cian
aes·thet'i·cism or
  es·thet'i·cism
aes·thet'ics or
  es·thet'ics
a·far'
af·fa·bil'i·ty
af'fa·ble
af'fa·bly
af·fair'
af·fect' (to influence,
  to pretend)
  ✔ effect
af'fec·ta'tion
af·fect'ed
af·fect'ing
af·fec'tion
af·fec'tion·ate
af·fec'tive
af'fer·ent
af·fi'ance, -anced,
  -anc'ing
af·fi·da'vit
af·fil'i·ate', -at'ed,

-at'ing
af•fil'i•a'tion
af•fin'i•ty
af•firm'
af'fir•ma'tion
af•fir'ma•tive
af•fix' *v.*
af'fix' *n.*
af•flict'
af•flic'tion
af•flu•ence
af•flu•ent
af•ford'
af•ford'a•ble
af•fray'
af•fright'
af•front'
Af'ghan' *(person, dog)*
af'ghan' *(blanket)*
a•fi'cio•na'do *pl.* -dos
a•field'
a•fire'
a•flame'
a•float'
a•flut'ter
a•foot'
a•fore'
a•fore'men'tioned
a•fore'said'
a•fore'thought'
a for'ti•o'ri
a•foul'
a•fraid'
A'-frame'
a•fresh'

Af'ri•can
Af'ri•can-
  A•mer'i•can *or*
  Af'ri•can
  A•mer'i•can
Af'ri•kaans'
Af'ri•ka'ner
Af'ro *pl.* -ros
Af'ro-A•mer'i•can
Af'ro-A'si•at'ic
af'ter
af'ter all' *also*
  af'ter•all'
af'ter•birth'
af'ter•burn'er
af'ter•care'
af'ter•deck'
af'ter•ef•fect'
af'ter•glow'
af'ter•im'age
af'ter•life'
af'ter•math'
af'ter•noon'
af'ter•shock'
af'ter•taste'
af'ter•thought'
af'ter•ward *also*
  af'ter•wards
af'ter•world'
a•gain'
a•gainst'
a•gape'
a'gar' *also*
  a'gar'-a'gar'
ag'ate
a•ga've
age, aged, ag'ing

aged *(of the age of)*
ag'ed *(elderly)*
age'ism *also* ag'ism
age'ist
age'less
a'gen•cy
a•gen'da *pl.* -das
a•gen'dum *pl.* -da
  also -dums
a'gent
age'-old'
ag•glom'er•ate',
  -at'ed, -at'ing
ag•glom'er•a'tion
ag•glu'ti•nate',
  -nat'ed, -nat'ing
ag•glu'ti•na'tion
ag•glu'ti•na'tive
ag•gran'dize',
  -dized', -diz'ing
ag•gran'dize•ment
ag•gran'diz'er
ag'gra•vate',
  -vat'ed, -vat'ing
ag'gra•va'tion
ag'gra•va'tor
ag'gre•gate',
  -gat'ed, -gat'ing
ag'gre•ga'tion
ag•gres'sion
ag•gres'sive
ag•gres'sor
ag•grieved'
a•ghast'
ag'ile
ag'ile•ly
a•gil'i•ty

ag′i•tate′, -tat′ed,
-tat′ing
ag′i•ta′tion
ag′i•ta′tor
a•gleam′
a•glit′ter
a•glow′
ag•nos′tic
ag•nos′ti•cal•ly
ag•nos′ti•cism
a•go′
a•gog′
ag′o•nize′, -nized′,
-niz′ing
ag′o•ny
ag′o•ra pl. -o•rae′ or
-o•ras
ag′o•ra•pho′bi•a
ag′o•ra•pho′bic
a•gou′ti pl. -tis
a•grar′i•an
a•gree′, a•greed′,
a•gree′ing
a•gree′a•ble
a•gree′a•bly
a•gree′ment
ag′ri•busi′ness
ag′ri•cul′tur•al
ag′ri•cul′ture
ag′ri•cul′tur•ist
ag′ro•nom′ic or
ag′ro•nom′i•cal
a•gron′o•mist
a•gron′o•my
a•ground′
a′gue
ah

a•ha′
a•head′
a•hem′
a•hoy′
aid (to help)
aide (assistant)
aide′-de-camp′ pl.
aides′-de-camp′
AIDS
ai•grette′ or ai•gret′
ai′ki•do′
ail (to be ill)
✔ ale
ai•lan′thus
ai′le•ron′
ail′ment
aim
aim′less
Ai′nu pl. -nu or -nus
air (gas)
✔ are, e′er, ere, heir
air′ bag′
air′ base′
air′ blad′der
air′borne′
air′ brake′
air′brush′
air′-con•di′tion
air′-con•di′tioned
air′ con•di′tion•er
air′ con•di′tion•ing
air′-cooled′
air′craft′ pl.
-craft
air′craft car′rier
air′drome′
air′drop′, -dropped′,

-drop′ping
Aire′dale′
air′field′
air′flow′
air′foil′
air′ force′
air′glow′
air′ gun′
air′ hammer′
air′ hole′
air′i•ly
air′i•ness
air′ing
air′ lane′
air′ let′ter
air′lift′
air′line′
air′lin′er
air′ lock′
air′mail′ v.
air′mail′ or air′
mail′ n.
air′man
air′plane′
air′port′
air′pow′er or air′
pow′er
air′ shaft′
air′ship′
air′sick′
air′sick′ness
air′space′ or air′
space′
air′ speed′
air′strip′
air′tight′
air′time′

air'-to-air'
air'-to-sur'face
air'waves'
air'way'
air'wor·thi·ness
air'wor'thy
air'y (relating to air)
  ✔ aerie
aisle (passageway)
  ✔ isle
a·jar'
a·kim'bo
a·kin'
Al'a·ba'mi·an or
  Al'a·bam'an
al'a·bas'ter
à' la carte' also a' la
  carte'
a·lack'
a·lac'ri·ty
al'a·me'da
à' la mode'
a·larm'
a·larm'ing
a·larm'ist
a·la'rum
a·las'
A·las'kan
alb
al'ba·core' pl. -core'
  or -cores'
Al·ba'ni·an
al'ba·tross' pl.
  -tross' or
  -tross'es
al·be'it
al'bi·nism

al·bi'no pl. -nos
al'bum
al·bu'men (egg
  white)
al·bu'min (protein)
al·chem'i·cal or
  al·chem'ic
al'che·mist
al'che·my
al'co·hol'
al'co·hol'ic
al'co·hol·ism
al'cove'
al'de·hyde'
al'der
al'der·man
ale (beverage)
  ✔ ail
a·lee'
a·lert'
A·leut' pl. A·leut' or
  A·leuts'
A·leu'tian
ale·wife' pl. -wives'
Al'ex·an'dri·an
al·fal'fa
al·fres'co
al'ga pl. -gae
al'ge·bra
al'ge·bra'ic
Al·ge'ri·an
Al·gon'quin pl.
  -quin or -quins
al'go·rithm
a'li·as
al'i·bi' pl. -bis'
a'li·en

al'ien·a·ble
al'ien·ate', -at'ed,
  -at'ing
al'ien·a'tion
al'ien·a'tor
a·light', a·light'ed
  or a·lit', a·light'ing
a·lign' also a·line',
  a·ligned' also
  a·lined', a·lign'ing
  also a·lin'ing
a·lign'ment also
  a·line'ment
a·like'
al'i·men'ta·ry
al'i·mo'ny
al'i·phat'ic
a·live'
al'ka·li' pl. -lis' or
  -lies'
al'ka·line
al'ka·line-earth'
  met'al
al'ka·lin'i·ty
al'ka·lize' also
  al'ka·lin·ize', -lized'
  also -lin·ized',
  -liz'ing also
  -lin·iz'ing
al'ka·loid'
all (total)
  ✔ awl
all'-A·mer'i·can
al·lan'to·is pl.
  al'lan·to'i·des'
all'-a·round' also
  all'-round'

al•lay′
al′le•ga′tion
al•leg′a•ble
al•lege′ -leged′,
  -leg′ing
al•leged′
al•leg′ed•ly
al•le′giance
al′le•gor′i•cal
al′le•gor′ist
al′le•go′ry
al′le•gret′to
al•le′gro
al•lele′
al•le′lic
al′le•lu′ia
al′ler•gen
al′ler•gen′ic
al•ler′gic
al′ler•gist
al′ler•gy
al•le′vi•ate′ -at′ed,
  -at′ing
al•le′vi•a′tion
al•le′vi•a′tor
al′ley *(passageway)*,
  pl. -leys
  ✔ *ally*
al′ley•way′
al•li′ance
al•lied′
al′li•ga′tor
all′-im•por′tant
al•lit′er•ate′ -at′ed,
  -at′ing
al•lit′er•a′tion
al•lit′er•a′tive

all′-night′
al′lo•cate′, -cat′ed,
  -cat′ing
al′lo•ca′tion
al•lot′, -lot′ted,
  -lot′ting
al•lot′ment
al′lo•trope′
al′lo•trop′ic
al•lot′ro•py
al•lot′ter
all′-out′ *adv.*
all′-out′ *adj.*
all′ o•ver *adv.*
all′-o•ver *also*
  all′o•ver *adj.*
al•low′
al•low′a•ble
al•low′a•bly
al•low′ance
al′loy′ *n.*
al•loy′ *v.*
all′-pur′pose
all read′y *(com-
  pletely prepared)*
  ✔ *already*
all′ right′
all′spice′
all′-star′ *adj. & n.*
all′-time′ *adj.*
all′ to•geth′er
  (collectively)
  ✔ *altogether*
al•lude′ *(to refer to)*,
  -lud′ed, -lud′ing
  ✔ *elude*
al•lure′, -lured′,

-lur′ing
al•lu′sion *(reference)*
  ✔ *illusion*
al•lu′sive *(sugges-
  tive)*
  ✔ *elusive, illusive*
al•lu′vi•al
al•lu′vi•um *pl.*
  -vi•ums *or* -vi•a
al•ly′, -lied′, -ly′ing
al′ly *(friend)*
  ✔ *alley*
al′ma ma′ter
al′ma•nac′
al•might′y
al′mond
al′mo•ner
al′most′
alms
alms′house′
al•ni′co′
al′oe
al′oe ver′a
a•loft′
a•lo′ha
a•lone′
a•long′
a•long′side′
a•loof′
a•loud′
alp
al•pac′a *pl.* -pac′a *or*
  -pac′as
al′pen•horn′
al′pen•stock′
al′pha
al′pha•bet′

al'pha•bet'i•cal
  also al'pha•bet'ic

al'pha•bet'i•za'-
tion

al'pha•bet•ize',
  -ized', -iz'ing

al'pha•bet•iz'er

al'pha•nu•mer'ic

al'pine' *(relating to high mountains)*

Al'pine' *(relating to the Alps)*

al•read'y *(by this time)*
  ✔ all ready

Al•sa'tian

al'so

al'so-ran'

al'tar *(religious table)*
  ✔ alter

al'tar•piece'

al'ter *(to change)*
  ✔ altar

al'ter•a•ble

al'ter•a•bly

al'ter•a'tion

al'ter•ca'tion

al'ter e'go

al'ter•nate',
  -nat'ed, -nat'ing

al'ter•nate *adj.*

al'ter•na'tion

al'ter•na•tive

al'ter•na'tor

al•though' *also*
  al•tho'

al•tim'e•ter

al'ti•tude'

al'to *pl.* -tos

al'to•cu'mu•lus

al'to•geth'er
  (completely)
  ✔ all together

al'to•stra'tus

al'tru•ism

al'tru•ist

al'tru•is'tic

al'um

a•lu'mi•na

a•lu'mi•num

a•lum'na *pl.* -nae'

a•lum'nus *pl.* -ni'

al•ve'o•lar

al•ve'o•lus *pl.* -li'

al'ways

a•lys'sum

Alz'heim•er's
  dis•ease'

a•mal'gam

a•mal'ga•mate',
  -mat'ed, -mat'ing

a•mal'ga•ma'tion

a•mal'ga•ma'tor

am'a•ni'ta

a•man'u•en'sis *pl.*
  -ses

am'a•ranth'

am'a•ryl'lis

a•mass'

a•mass'a•ble

a•mass'er

am'a•teur'

am'a•teur'ish

am'a•to'ry

a•maze', a•mazed',
  a•maz'ing

a•maz'ed•ly

a•maze'ment

Am'a•zon' *also*
  am'a•zon'

Am'a•zo'ni•an
  (relating to the Amazon River)

am'a•zo'ni•an
  (resembling an Amazon)

am•bas'sa•dor

am'ber

am'ber•gris'

am'bi•ance *also*
  am'bi•ence

am•bi•dex'ter'i•ty

am'bi•dex'trous

am'bi•ent

am'bi•gu'i•ty

am•big'u•ous

am•bi'tion

am•bi'tious

am•biv'a•lence

am•biv'a•lent

am'ble, -bled, -bling

am'bler

am•bro'sia

am•bro'sial

am'bu•lance

am'bu•la•to'ry

am'bus•cade',
  -cad'ed, -cad'ing

am'bush

a•me'lio•rate',
  -rat'ed, -rat'ing

a•me′lio•ra′tion
a•me′lio•ra′tor
a•men′
a•me′na•bil′i•ty *or*
  a•me′na•ble•ness
a•me′na•ble
a•me′na•bly
a•mend′ *(to improve)*
  ✔ emend
a•mend′ment
a•mends′
a•men′i•ty
Am′er•a′sian
A•mer′i•can
A•mer′i•ca′na
A•mer′i•can
  In′di•an *n.*
A•mer′i•can-
  In′di•an *adj.*
A•mer′i•can•ism
A•mer′i•can•i•za′-
  tion
A•mer′i•can•ize′,
  -ized′, -iz′ing
am′er•i′ci•um
Am′er•in′di•an *also*
  Am′er•ind′
am′e•thyst
a′mi•a•bil′i•ty
a′mi•a•ble
a′mi•a•bly
am′i•ca•bil′i•ty
am′i•ca•ble
am′i•ca•bly
a•mid′ *also* a•midst′
am′ide′
a•mid′ships′ *also*

a•mid′ship′
a•mi′go *pl.* -gos
a•mine′
a•mi′no ac′id
A′mish
a•miss′
am′i•ty
am′me′ter
am′mo
am•mo′nia
am•mo′ni•um
am′mu•ni′tion
am•ne′sia
am′nes•ty
am′ni•o•cen•te′sis
  pl. -ses
am′ni•on *pl.*
  -ni•ons *or* -ni•a
am′ni•ot′ic
a•moe′ba *also*
  a•me′ba *pl.* -bas *or*
  -bae
a•moe′bic
a•mong′ *also*
  a•mongst′
a•mor′al
a′mo•ral′i•ty
am′o•rous
a•mor′phous
am′or•ti•za′tion
am′or•tize′, -tized′,
  -tiz′ing
a•mount′
a•mour′
amp
am′per•age
am•pere′

am′per•sand′
am•phet′a•mine′
am•phib′i•an
am•phib′i•ous
am′phi•bole′
am′phi•the′a•ter
am•pho′ra *pl.*
  -pho•rae′ *or*
  -pho•ras
am′ple, -pler, -plest
am′pli•fi•ca′tion
am′pli•fi′er
am′pli•fy′, -fied′,
  -fy′ing
am′pli•tude′
am′ply
am′poule *also*
  am′pule *or* am′pul
am′pu•tate′,
  -tat′ed, -tat′ing
am′pu•ta′tion
am′pu•ta′tor
am′pu•tee′
a•muck′ *also*
  a•mok′
am′u•let
a•mus′a•ble
a•muse′, a•mused′,
  a•mus′ing
a•muse′ment
a•mus′ing
am′yl
am′y•lase′
An′a•bap′tist
an′a•bol′ic
a•nab′o•lism
a•nach′ro•nism

a•nach′ro•nis′tic
an′a•con′da
an′aer•obe′
an′aer•o′bic
an′a•gram′
a′nal
an′al•ge′si•a
an′al•ge′sic
a•na•log′
    com•pu′ter
a•nal′o•gous
an′a•logue′ *also*
    an′a•log′
a•nal′o•gy
a•nal′y•sis *pl.*
    -ses′
an′a•lyst
an′a•lyt′ic *or*
    an′a•lyt′i•cal
an′a•lyz′a•ble
an′a•ly•za′tion
an′a•lyze′, -lyzed′,
    -lyz′ing
an′a•lyz′er
an′a•pest′
an′a•phase′
an′a•phy•lac′tic
an′a•phy•lax′is
an•ar′chic *or*
    an•ar′chi•cal
an′ar•chism
an′ar•chist
an′ar•chis′tic
an′ar•chy
A′na•sa′zi *pl.* -zi
a•nath′e•ma *pl.*
    -mas

a•nath′e•ma•ti•za′-
    tion
a•nath′e•ma•tize′,
    -tized′, -tiz′ing
an′a•tom′i•cal *also*
    an′a•tom′ic
a•nat′o•mist
a•nat′o•mi•za′tion
a•nat′o•mize′,
    -mized′, -miz′ing
a•nat′o•my
an′ces•tor
an•ces′tral
an′ces•try
an′chor
an′chor•age
an′cho•rite′
an′chor•man
an′chor•per′son
an′chor•wom′an
an′cho′vy *pl.* -vy
an′cient
an′cil•lar′y
an•dan′te
and′i′ron
an′dro•gen
an•dro•gen′ic
an•drog′y•nous
an•drog′y•ny
an′droid′
an′ec•dot′al
an′ec•dote′
a•ne′mi•a *also*
    a•nae′mi•a
a•ne′mic *also*
    a•nae′mic
an′e•mom′e•ter

a•nem′o•ne
an′es•the′sia *also*
    an′aes•the′sia
an′es•the•si•ol′o•
    gist *also* an′aes•
    the′si•ol′o•gist
an′es•the•si•ol′o•
    gy *also* an′aes•
    the′si•ol′o•gy
an′es•thet′ic *also*
    an′aes•thet′ic
a•nes′the•tist *also*
    a•naes′the•tist
a•nes′the•ti•za′tion
a•nes′the•tize′ *also*
    a•naes′the•tize′,
    -tized′, -tiz′ing
an′eu•rysm *also*
    an′eu•rism
a•new′
an′gel
An′ge•le′no *pl.*
    -nos
an′gel•fish′
an′gel food′ cake′
an•gel′ic *also*
    an•gel′i•cal
an′ger
an•gi′na
an•gi′na pec′to•ris
an′gi•o•sperm′
an′gle, -gled, -gling
an′gler
an′gler•fish′
an′gle•worm′
An′gli•can
An′gli•can•ism

An'gli•cize', -cized',
-ciz'ing
an'gling
An'glo *pl.* -glos
An'glo-
A•mer'i•can
An'glo-French'
An'glo-Nor'man
An'glo-Sax'on
An•go'ra *(animal)*
an•go'ra *(yarn)*
an'gri•ly
an'gri•ness
an'gry
angst
ang'strom
an'guish
an'guished
an'gu•lar
an'gu•lar'i•ty
an•hy'dride
an•hy'drous
an'i•line *also*
   an'i•lin
an'i•mad•ver'sion
an'i•mal
an'i•mal'cule
an'i•mate', -mat'ed,
   -mat'ing
an'i•mat'ed•ly
an'i•ma'tion
a'ni•ma'to
an'i•ma'tor
an'i•mism
an'i•mos'i•ty
an'i•mus
an'i'on

an'ise
an'ise seed' *or*
   an'i•seed'
an'kle
an'kle•bone'
an'klet
an'nals
an•neal'
an'ne•lid
an•nex' *v.*
an'nex' *n.*
an'nex•a'tion
an•ni'hi•late',
   -lat'ed, -lat'ing
an•ni'hi•la'tion
an•ni'hi•la'tive
an•ni'hi•la'tor
an'ni•ver'sa•ry
an'no Dom'i•ni'
an'no•tate', -tat'ed,
   -tat'ing
an'no•ta'tion
an'no•ta'tive
an'no•ta'tor
an•nounce',
   -nounced',
   -nounc'ing
an•nounce'ment
an•nounc'er
an•noy'
an•noy'ance
an•noy'er
an•noy'ing
an•nu'al
an•nu'i•ty
an•nul', -nulled',
   -nul'ling

an'nu•lar
an•nul'ment
an'nu•lus *pl.*
   -lus•es *or* -li'
an•nun'ci•ate' *(to
   announce)*, -at'ed,
   -at'ing
   ✔ enunciate
an•nun'ci•a'tion
an'ode'
an'o•dyne'
a•noint'
a•noint'ment
a•nom'a•lous
a•nom'a•ly
a•non'
an'o•nym'i•ty
a•non'y•mous
a•noph'e•les'
an'o•rec'tic
an'o•rex'i•a
   nerv•o'sa
an'o•rex'ic
an•oth'er
an•ox'i•a
an'swer
an'swer•ing
   ma•chine'
ant *(insect)*
   ✔ aunt
ant•ac'id
an•tag'o•nism
an•tag'o•nist
an•tag'o•nis'tic
an•tag'o•nize',
   -nized', -niz'ing
Ant•arc'tic

an'te, -ted *or* -teed,
-te•ing
ant'eat'er
an'te•bel'lum
an'te•ce'dent
an'te•cham'ber
an'te•date', -dat'ed,
-dat'ing
an'te•di•lu'vi•an
an'te•lope' *pl.*
-lope' *or* -lopes'
an'te me•rid'i•em
an•ten'na *pl.* -nae
or -nas
an'te•pe'nult *n.*
an'te•pe•nul'ti•
mate *adj. & n.*
an•te'ri•or
an'te•room'
an'them
an'ther
ant'hill'
an•thol'o•gist
an•thol'o•gize',
-gized', -giz'ing
an•thol'o•gy
an'thra•cite'
an'thrax'
an'thro•po•cen'tric
an'thro•poid'
an'thro•po•log'i•
cal
an'thro•pol'o•gist
an'thro•pol'o•gy
an'thro•po•mor'-
phic
an'thro•po•mor'-

phism
an'ti•a•bor'tion
an'ti•air'craft'
an'ti•bal•lis'tic
mis'sile
an'ti•bi•ot'ic
an'ti•bod'y
an'tic
an'ti•christ'
an•tic'i•pate',
-pat'ed, -pat'ing
an•tic'i•pa'tion
an•tic'i•pa'tor
an•tic'i•pa•to'ry
an'ti•cler'i•cal
an'ti•cli•mac'tic
an'ti•cli'max
an'ti•cli'nal
an'ti•cline'
an'ti•co•ag'u•lant
an'ti•cy'clone'
an'ti•de•pres'sant
an'ti•do'tal
an'ti•dote'
an'ti•freeze'
an'ti•gen *also*
an'ti•gene'
an'ti•gen'ic
an'ti•grav'i•ty
an'ti•he'ro *pl.* -roes
an'ti•her'o•ine *or*
an'ti-her'o•ine
an'ti•his'ta•mine'
an'ti•knock'
an'ti•log'
an'ti•log'a•rithm
an'ti•ma•cas'sar

an'ti•mat'ter
an'ti•mis'sile
an'ti•mo'ny
an'ti•neu•tri'no *pl.*
-nos
an'ti•neu'tron'
an'ti•nu'cle•ar
an'ti•ox'i•dant
an'ti•par'ti•cle
an'ti•pas'to *pl.* -tos
or -ti
an•tip'a•thet'ic
also an•tip'a•thet'i•
cal
an•tip'a•thy
an'ti•per'spi•rant
an'ti•phon'
an•tiph'o•nal
an•tiph'o•ny
an•tip'o•dal
an•tip'o•des'
an'ti•pov'er•ty
an'ti•pro'ton
an'ti•py•ret'ic
an'ti•quar'i•an
an'ti•quar'y
an'ti•quate',
-quat'ed, -quat'ing
an•tique', -tiqued',
-tiqu'ing
an•tiq'ui•ty
an'ti-Se•mit'ic
an'ti-Sem'i•tism
an'ti•sep'tic
an'ti•slav'er•y
an'ti•so'cial
an'ti•tank'

an·tith'e·sis *pl.* -ses'
an'ti·thet'i·cal *also*
  an'ti·thet'ic
an'ti·tox'in
an'ti·trades'
an'ti·trust'
an'ti·ven'in
an'ti·vi'ral
an'ti·war'
ant'ler
an'to·nym'
ant'sy
a'nus *pl.* a'nus·es
an'vil
anx·i'e·ty
anx'ious
an'y
an'y·bod'y
an'y·how'
an'y·more'
an'y·one'
an'y·place'
an'y·thing'
an'y·time'
an'y·way'
an'y·where'
A'-OK'
A'-one'
a·or'ta *pl.* -tas *or* -tae
a·pace'
A·pach'e *pl.*
  A·pach'e *or* -es
a·part'
a·part'heid'
a·part'ment
ap'a·thet'ic
ap'a·thy

ape, aped, ap'ing
a·pé'ri·tif'
ap'er·ture
a'pex *pl.* a'pex·es *or*
  a'pi·ces'
a·pha'sia
a·pha'sic
a·phe'li·on *pl.* -li·a
a'phid
aph'o·rism
aph'o·ris'tic
aph'ro·dis'i·ac'
a'pi·ar'y
a'pi·cal
a·piece'
ap'ish
a·plen'ty
a·plomb'
a·poc'a·lypse'
a·poc'a·lyp'tic *also*
  a·poc'a·lyp'ti·cal
A·poc'ry·pha
  (Biblical books)
a·poc'ry·pha *(writ-
  ings of questionable
  authority)*
A·poc'ry·phal
  *(relating to the
  Apocrypha)*
a·poc'ry·phal *(of
  questionable
  authority)*
ap'o·gee
a·pol'o·get'ic
a·pol'o·gist
a·pol'o·gize',
  -gized', -giz'ing

a·pol'o·gy
ap'o·plec'tic
ap'o·plex'y
a·pos'ta·sy
a·pos'tate'
a·pos'tle
ap'os·tol'ic
a·pos'tro·phe
a·pos'tro·phize',
  -phized', -phiz'ing
a·poth'e·car'ies'
  meas'ure
a·poth'e·car'y
ap'o·thegm' *also*
  ap'o·phthegm'
  (maxim)
ap'o·them' *(geomet-
  ric distance)*
a·poth'e·o'sis *pl.*
  -ses'
ap·pall'
ap·pall'ing
ap'pa·loo'sa
ap'pa·ra'tus *pl.* -tus
  or -tus·es
ap·par'el, -eled *or*
  -elled, -el'ing *or*
  -el·ling
ap·par'ent
ap'pa·ri'tion
ap·peal'
ap·peal'ing
ap·pear'
ap·pear'ance
ap·pease', -peased',
  -peas'ing
ap·pease'ment

ap•pel′lant
ap•pel′late
ap′pel•la′tion
ap•pend′
ap•pend′age
ap′pen•dec′to•my
ap•pen′di•ci′tis
ap•pen′dix *pl.*
  -dix•es *or* -di•ces′
ap′per•tain′
ap′pe•tite′
ap′pe•tiz′er
ap′pe•tiz′ing
ap•plaud′
ap•plaud′a•ble
ap•plaud′er
ap•plause′
ap′ple
ap′ple but′ter
ap′ple•jack′
ap′ple•sauce′
ap•pli′ance
ap′pli•ca•bil′i•ty
ap′pli•ca•ble
ap′pli•ca•bly
ap′pli•cant
ap′pli•ca′tion
ap′pli•ca′tor
ap•plied′
ap•pli′er
ap′pli•qué′, -quéd′,
  -qué′ing
ap•ply′, -plied′,
  -ply′ing
ap•point′
ap•point′ee′
ap•point′ive

ap•point′ment
ap•por′tion
ap•por′tion•ment
ap•pose′ *(to juxta-*
  pose), -posed′,
  -pos′ing
  ✔ *oppose*
ap′po•site *(appro-*
  priate)
  ✔ *opposite*
ap′po•si′tion
ap•pos′i•tive
ap•prais′al
ap•praise′,
  -praised′, -prais′ing
ap•prais′er
ap•pre′cia•ble
ap•pre′cia•bly
ap•pre′ci•ate′,
  -at′ed, -at′ing
ap•pre′ci•a′tion
ap•pre′ci•a•tive
ap•pre′ci•a′tor
ap′pre•hend′
ap′pre•hen′sion
ap′pre•hen′sive
ap•pren′tice, -ticed,
  -tic•ing
ap•pren′tice•ship′
ap•prise′, -prised′,
  -pris′ing
ap•proach′
ap•proach′a•bil′i•
  ty
ap•proach′a•ble
ap′pro•ba′tion
ap•pro′pri•ate′,

  -at′ed, -at′ing
ap•pro′pri•ate•ly
ap•pro′pri•a′tion
ap•pro′pri•a′tor
ap•prov′al
ap•prove′, -proved′,
  -prov′ing
ap•prox′i•mate′,
  -mat′ed, -mat′ing
ap•prox′i•mate•ly
ap•prox′i•ma′tion
ap•pur′te•nance
a′pri•cot′
A′pril
a′pron
ap′ro•pos′
apse
ap′ti•tude′
apt′ly
aq′ua *pl.* -uae *or* -uas
aq′ua•cul′ture *also*
  aq′ui•cul′ture
aq′ua•ma•rine′
aq′ua•plane′,
  -planed′, -plan′ing
aq′ua re′gi•a
a•quar′i•um *pl.*
  -i•ums *or* -i•a
a•quat′ic
aq′ue•duct′
a′que•ous
aq′ui•fer
aq′ui•line′
Ar′ab
ar′a•besque′
A•ra′bi•an
Ar′a•bic

ar′a•ble
a•rach′nid
A•rap′a•ho′ *pl.* -ho′
  or -hos′
Ar′au•ca′ni•an
Ar′a•wak′ *pl.* -wak′
  or -waks′
Ar′a•wa′kan *pl.*
  -kan *or* -kans
ar′bi•ter
ar′bi•trage′
ar′bi•tra•geur′
ar′bit′ra•ment
ar′bi•trar′i•ly
ar′bi•trar′i•ness
ar′bi•trar′y
ar′bi•trate′, -trat′ed,
  -trat′ing
ar′bi•tra′tion
ar′bi•tra′tor
ar′bor
ar•bo′re•al
ar′bo•re′tum *pl.*
  -tums *or* -ta
ar′bor•vi′tae
ar•bu′tus
arc *(to curve),* arced
  or arcked, arc′ing *or*
  arck′ing
  ✔ *ark*
ar•cade′
arch
ar′chae•o•log′i•cal
  or ar′che•o•log′i•cal
ar′chae•ol′o•gist *or*
  ar′che•ol′o•gist
ar′chae•ol′o•gy *or*

ar′che•ol′o•gy
ar′chae•op′ter•yx
ar•cha′ic
ar•cha•ism
arch′an′gel
arch•bish′op
arch•dea′con
arch•di′o•cese
arch•duch′ess
arch•duke′
arched
arch•en′e•my
arch′er
arch′er•y
ar′che•type′
ar′chi•pel′a•go′ *pl.*
  -goes′ *or* -gos′
ar′chi•tect
ar′chi•tec′tur•al
ar′chi•tec′ture
ar′chi•trave′
ar•chi′val
ar′chive′
ar′chi•vist
arch′ly
arch′way′
arc′tic
ar′dent
ar′dor
ar′du•ous
are *form of* to be
are *(metric unit of*
  area)
  ✔ *air, e′er, ere, heir*
ar′e•a *(space)*
  ✔ *aria*
Ar′e•a Code′ *also*

ar′che•ol′o•gy
ar′chae•op′ter•yx
ar•e′a•way′
a•re′na
aren′t
Ar′gen•tine′ *or*
  Ar′gen•tin′e•an
ar′gon′
ar′go•sy
ar′got
ar′gu•a•ble
ar′gu•a•bly
ar′gue, -gued,
  -gu′ing
ar′gu•er
ar′gu•ment
ar′gu•men′ta•tive
ar′gu•men′ta•tive•
  ly
ar′gyle′ *also* ar′gyll′
a′ri•a *(melody)*
  ✔ *area*
ar′id
a•rid′i•ty
a•right′
A•rik′a•ra *pl.* -ra
a•rise′, a•rose′,
  a•ris′en, a•ris′ing
ar′is•toc′ra•cy
a•ris′to•crat′
a•ris′to•crat′ic
Ar′is•to•te′li•an
Ar′is•to•te′li•an•
  ism
a•rith′me•tic *n.*
ar′ith•met′ic *or*
  ar′ith•met′i•cal *adj.*
a•rith′me•ti′cian

Ar'i·zo'nan *or*
  Ar'i·zo'ni·an
ark *(boat)*
  ✔ *arc*
Ar·kan'san
armed
ar·ma'da
ar·ma·dil'lo *pl.* -los
Ar'ma·ged'don
ar'ma·ment
ar'ma·ture
arm'band'
arm'chair'
Ar·me'ni·an
arm'ful'
arm'hole'
ar'mi·stice
arm'let
arm'load'
ar·moire'
ar'mor
ar'mored
ar'mor·er
ar·mo'ri·al
ar'mor·y
arm'pit'
arm'rest'
ar'my
ar'ni·ca
a·ro'ma
ar'o·mat'ic
a·round'
a·rous'a·ble
a·rous'al
a·rouse', a·roused',
  a·rous'ing
ar·peg'gi·o *pl.* -os

ar'que·bus
ar·raign'
ar·raign'ment
ar·range', -ranged',
  -rang'ing
ar·range'ment
ar'rant
ar'ras *pl.* -ras
ar·ray'
ar·ray'er
ar·rears'
ar·rest'
ar·rest'ing
ar·rhyth'mi·a
ar·ri'val
ar·rive', -rived',
  -riv'ing
ar·ri've·der'ci
ar'ro·gance
ar'ro·gant
ar'ro·gate', -gat'ed,
  -gat'ing
ar'ro·ga'tion
ar'row
ar'row·head'
ar'row·root'
ar·roy'o *pl.* -os
ar'se·nal
ar'se·nic
ar'son
ar'son·ist
art' dec'o *also* Art'
  Dec'o
ar·te'ri·al
ar·te'ri·ole'
ar·te'ri·o·scle·ro'sis
ar'ter·y

ar·te'sian well'
art'ful
ar·thrit'ic
ar·thri'tis
ar'thro·pod'
ar'thro·scope'
Ar·thu'ri·an
ar'ti·choke'
ar'ti·cle
ar·tic'u·la·ble
ar·tic'u·lar
ar·tic'u·late',
  -lat'ed, -lat'ing
ar·tic'u·late·ly
ar·tic'u·la'tion
ar·tic'u·la'tor
ar'ti·fact' *also*
  ar'te·fact'
ar'ti·fice
ar·tif'i·cer
ar'ti·fi'cial
ar'ti·fi'ci·al'i·ty
ar·til'ler·y
ar·til'ler·y·man
ar'ti·san
art'ist
ar·tis'tic
art'ist·ry
art'less
art' nou·veau'
art'work'
ar'um
Ar'y·an
as'a·fet'i·da
as·bes'tos *also*
  as·bes'tus
as·cend'

as·cen'dan·cy *also*
as·cen'den·cy
as·cen'dant *also*
as·cen'dent
as·cend'ing
as·cen'sion
as·cent' *(upward slope)*
✔ assent
as'cer·tain'
as'cer·tain'a·ble
as'cer·tain'a·bly
as·cet'ic *(austere)*
✔ acetic
as·cet'i·cism
ASCII
a·scor'bic ac'id
as'cot
as·crib'a·ble
as·cribe', -cribed',
-crib'ing
as·crip'tion
a·sep'sis
a·sep'tic
a·sex'u·al
a·shamed'
a·sham'ed·ly
A·shan'ti *pl.* -ti *or*
-tis
ash'can' *or* ash'
can'
ash'en
a·shore'
ash'tray'
ash'y
A'sian
A'sian A·mer'i·

can *or* A'sian-
A·mer'i·can
A'si·at'ic
a·side'
as'i·nine'
ask
a·skance'
a·skew'
a·slant'
a·sleep'
asp
as·par'a·gus
as'par·tame'
as'pect
as'pen
as·per'i·ty
as·per'sion
as'phalt'
as'pho·del'
as·phyx'i·a
as·phyx'i·ate',
-at'ed, -at'ing
as·phyx'i·a'tion
as·phyx'i·a'tor
as'pic
as'pi·rant
as'pi·rate', -rat'ed,
-rat'ing
as'pi·ra'tion
as'pi·ra'tor
as·pire', -pired',
-pir'ing
as'pi·rin
ass *pl.* ass'es
as·sail'
as·sail'a·ble
as·sail'er

as·sail'ant
as·sas'sin
as·sas'si·nate',
-nat'ed, -nat'ing
as·sas'si·na'tion
as·sas'si·na'tor
as·sault'
as·sault'er
as·say' *n.*
as·say' *(to analyze)*
✔ essay
as·say'er
as'se·gai' *or*
as'sa·gai' *pl.* -gais'
as·sem'blage
as·sem'ble, -bled,
-bling
as·sem'bler
as·sem'bly
as·sem'bly line'
as·sem'bly·man
as·sem'bly·
woman
as·sent' *(agreement)*
✔ ascent
as·sert'
as·sert'er *or*
as·ser'tor
as·ser'tion
as·ser'tive
as·sess'
as·sess'a·ble
as·sess'ment
as·ses'sor
as·set
as·sev'er·ate',
-at'ed, -at'ing

as'si·du'i·ty
as·sid'u·ous
as·sign'
as·sign'a·ble
as'sig·na'tion
as·sign·ee'
as·sign'er
as·sign'ment
as·sim'i·la·ble
as·sim'i·late', -lat'ed, -lat'ing
as·sim'i·la'tion
as·sim'i·la'tive *also* as·sim'i·la·to'ry
as·sim'i·la'tor
As·sin'i·boin' *pl.* -boin' *or* -boins'
as·sist'
as·sis'tance
as·sis'tant
as·siz'es
as·so'ci·ate', -at'ed, -at'ing
as·so'ci·a'tion
as·so'ci·a'tive
as·so'ci·a'tor
as·so·nance
as·so·nant
as·sort'
as·sort'ed
as·sort'ment
as·suage', -suaged', -suag'ing
as·suage'ment
as·sum'a·ble
as·sum'a·bly
as·sume' *(to sup-*

pose, to undertake),
-sumed', -sum'ing
✔ presume
as·sump'tion
as·sur'ance
as·sure' *(to declare positively, to convince),* -sured', -sur'ing
✔ ensure, insure
as·sur'ed·ly
as'ta·tine'
as'ter
as'ter·isk'
a·stern'
as'ter·oid'
asth'ma
asth·mat'ic
as'tig·mat'ic
a·stig'ma·tism
a·stir'
a·ston'ish
a·ston'ish·ing
a·ston'ish·ment
a·stound'
a·stound'ing
a·strad'dle
as'tra·khan
as'tral
a·stray'
a·stride'
as·trin'gen·cy
as·trin'gent
as'tro·labe'
as'tro·log'i·cal *or* as'tro·log'ic
as·trol'o·ger

as·trol'o·gy
as·trom'e·try
as'tro·naut'
as'tro·nau'tic *or* as'tro·nau'ti·cal
as·tron'o·mer
as'tro·nom'i·cal *also* as'tro·nom'ic
as·tron'o·my
as'tro·phys'i·cal
as'tro·phys'i·cist
as'tro·phys'ics
as·tute'
as·tute'ly
a·sun'der
a·sy'lum
a'sym·met'ri·cal *also* a'sym·met'ric
a·sym'me·try
at'a·vism
at'a·vis'tic
a·tax'i·a *also* a·tax'y
a·tax'ic
at'el·ier'
a tem'po
Ath'a·bas'kan
a'the·ism
a'the·ist
a'the·is'tic
A·the'ni·an
ath'er·o·scle·ro'sis
a·thirst'
ath'lete'
ath'lete's foot'
ath·let'ic
a·thwart'
at'las *pl.* -las·es

at′mos•phere′
at′mos•pher′ic also
  at′mos•pher′i•cal
a′toll′
at′om
a•tom′ic
at′om•i•za′tion
at′om•ize′, -ized′,
  -iz′ing
at′om•iz′er
a•ton′al′i•ty
a•tone′, a•toned′,
  a•ton′ing
a•tone′ment
a•top′
ATP
a′tri•um *pl.* a′tri•a
  or -ums
a•tro′cious
a•troc′i•ty
at′ro•phy, -phied,
  -phy•ing
at′ro•pine′ *also*
  at′ro•pin
at•tach′
at•tach′a•ble
at′ta•ché′
at′ta•ché′ case′
at•tach′ment
at•tack′
at•tack′er
at•tain′
at•tain′a•bil′i•ty
at•tain′a•ble
at•tain′der
at•tain′ment

at•taint′
at•tar′
at•tempt′
at•tempt′a•ble
at•tend′
at•ten′dance
at•ten′dant
at•ten′tion
at•ten′tive
at•ten′tive•ly
at•ten′u•ate′,
  -at′ed, -at′ing
at•ten′u•a′tion
at•test′
at•test′ed
at′tic
at•tire′, -tired′,
  -tir′ing
at′ti•tude′
at•tor′ney *pl.* -neys
at•tor′ney at law′
  pl. at′torneys at
  law′
at•tor′ney
  gen′er•al *pl.*
  at•tor′neys
  gen′er•al *or*
  at•tor′ney
  gen′er•als
at•tract′
at•tract′er *or*
  at•trac′tor
at•trac′tion
at•trac′tive
at•trac′tive•ly
at•trib′ut•a•ble
at•trib′ute, -ut•ed,

  -ut•ing
at′tri•bute′ *n.*
at•trib′ut•er *or*
  at•trib′u•tor
at′tri•bu′tion
at•trib′u•tive
at•tri′tion
at•tune′, -tuned′,
  -tun′ing
at•tune′ment
a•typ′i•cal
au′burn
auc′tion
auc′tion•eer′
au•da′cious
au•dac′i•ty
au′di•bil′i•ty *or*
  au′di•ble•ness
au′di•ble
au′di•bly
au′di•ence
au′di•o′ *pl.* -di•os′
au′di•om′e•ter
au′di•o-vis′u•al
  also au′di•o•
  vis′u•al
au′dit
au•di′tion
au′di•tor
au′di•to′ri•um *pl.*
  -ri•ums *or* -ri•a
au′di•to′ry
auf Wie′der•
  seh′en
au′ger *(tool)*
  ✔ *augur*
aught *also* ought

(anything at all)
  ✔ ought
aught *also* ought
  (zero)
  ✔ ought
aug·ment′
aug·ment′a·ble
aug′men·ta′tion
aug·ment′er
au gra′tin
au′gur *(to predict)*
  ✔ auger
au′gu·ry
au·gust′ *(majestic)*
Au′gust *(month)*
au jus′
auk
auld′ lang syne′
aunt *(female relative)*
  ✔ ant
au′ra *pl.* -ras *or* -rae
au′ral *(relating to the ear)*
  ✔ oral
au′re·ole′
au′ re·voir′
au′ri·cle *(part of the ear)*
  ✔ oracle
au·ric′u·lar
au′rochs′ *pl.* -rochs′
au·ro′ra
au·ro′ra aus·tra′lis
au·ro′ra bo′re·al′is
aus′pi·ces
aus·pi′cious
aus·tere′, -ter′er,

-ter′est
aus·ter′i·ty
Aus·tra′lian
Aus′tri·an
au′tarch
au·teur′
au·teur′ism
au·then′tic
au·then′ti·cate′,
  -cat′ed, -cat′ing
au·then·tic′i·ty
au·then′ti·ca′tion
au·then′ti·ca′tor
au′thor
au·thor′i·tar′i·an
au·thor′i·tar′i·an·ism
au·thor′i·ta′tive
au·thor′i·ty
au′thor·i·za′tion
au′thor·ize′, -ized′,
  -iz′ing
au′thor·iz′er
au′thor·ship′
au′tism
au′to *pl.* -tos
au′to·bi·og′ra·pher
au′to·bi′o·graph′i·cal *or* au′to·bi′o·graph′ic
au′to·bi·og′ra·phy
au′to·clave′
au·toc′ra·cy
au′to·crat′
au′to·crat′ic
au′to·graph′
au′to·graph′ic *or*

au′to·graph′i·cal
au′to·im·mune′
au′to·im·mu′ni·ty
au′to·mak′er
au′to·mate′,
  -mat′ed, -mat′ing
au′to·mat′ed
  tel′ler ma·chine′
au′to·mat′ic
au′to·ma′tion
au·tom′a·ton *pl.*
  -tons *or* -ta
au′to·mo·bile′
au′to·mo′tive
au′to·nom′ic
au·ton′o·mous
au·ton′o·my
au′to·pi′lot
au′top·sy
au′tumn
au·tum′nal
aux·il′ia·ry
aux′in
a·vail′
a·vail′a·bil′i·ty *or*
  a·vail′a·ble·ness
a·vail′a·ble
a·vail′a·bly
av′a·lanche′
a·vant′-garde′
av′a·rice
av′a·ri′cious
a·vast′
av′a·tar′
a·venge′, a·venged′,
  a·veng′ing
a·veng′er

av'e•nue'
a•ver', a•verred',
  a•ver'ring
av'er•age, -aged,
  -ag•ing
a•verse' *(opposed,*
  reluctant)
  ✔ adverse
a•verse'ly
a•ver'sion
a•vert'
a•vert'a•ble *or*
  a•vert'i•ble
a'vi•an
a'vi•ar'y
a'vi•a'tion
a'vi•a'tor
av'id
a•vid'i•ty
a'vi•on'ics
av'o•ca'do *pl.* -dos
av'o•ca'tion
a•void'
a•void'a•ble
a•void'a•bly
a•void'ance
av'oir•du•pois'
  weight'
a•vouch'
a•vow'
a•vow'al
a•vun'cu•lar
aw *interj.*
  ✔ awe
a•wait'
a•wake', a•woke' *or*
  a•waked', a•waked'

or a•wok'en,
  a•wak'ing
a•wak'en
a•wak'en•er
a•wak'en•ing
a•ward'
a•ward'a•ble
a•ward'er
a•ware'
a•ware'ness
a•wash'
a•way' *(at a dis-*
  tance)
  ✔ aweigh
awe *(to fill with won-*
  der), awed, aw'ing
  ✔ aw
a•weigh' *(free of the*
  bottom)
  ✔ away
awe'some
awe'struck' *also*
  awe'strick'en
aw'ful *(horrible)*
  ✔ offal
aw'ful•ly
a•while'
awk'ward
awl *(tool)*
  ✔ all
awn'ing
AWOL
a•wry'
ax *or* axe, axed,
  ax'ing
ax'i•al
ax'i•om

ax'i•o•mat'ic
ax'is *pl.* ax'es
ax'le
ax'le•tree'
ax'on'
a'ya•tol'lah
aye *also* ay *(a vote of*
  yes)
  ✔ eye, I
Ay'ma•ra' *pl.* -ra'
Ay'ma•ran'
Ayr'shire
a•zal'ea
az'i•muth
AZT
Az'tec' *also*
  Az•tec'an
az'ure

B

baa, baaed, baa'ing
bab'bitt met'al
bab'ble, -bled,
  -bling
bab'bler
babe
ba'bel *also* Ba'bel
ba•boon'
ba•bush'ka
ba'by, -bied, -by•ing
ba'by•hood'
ba'by•ish
Bab'y•lo'ni•an
ba'by's breath'
ba'by-sit', -sat',

-sit'ting
bab'y sit'ter
bac'ca•lau're•ate
Bac'cha•na'lian
   also bac'cha•
   na'lian
bach'e•lor
bach'e•lor's but'-
   ton *pl.* bach'e•lor's
   but'tons
bach'e•lor's
   de•gree'
ba•cil'lus *pl.* -cil'li'
back
back'ache'
back'bite', -bit',
   -bit'ten, -bit'ing
back'bit'er
back'board'
back'bone'
back'break'ing
back'coun'try
back'drop'
back'er
back'field'
back'fire', -fired',
   -fir'ing
back'-for•ma'tion
   or back' for•ma'tion
back'gam'mon
back'ground'
back'hand'
back'hand'ed
back'hoe'
back'ing
back'lash'
back'list'

back'log'
back'pack'
back'pack'er
back'rest'
back'-seat' driv'er
back'side'
back'slide', -slid',
   -slid'ing
back'slid'er
back'space',
   -spaced', -spac'ing
back'spin'
back'stage'
back'stairs' *also*
   back'stair' *adj.*
back'stitch'
back'stop'
back'stretch'
back'stroke'
back' talk'
back'track'
back'up' *n. & adj.*
back'ward *or*
   back'wards *adv.*
back'wash'
back'wa'ter
back'woods'
back' yard' *also*
   back'yard'
ba'con
bac•te'ri•a *sing.*
   -ri•um
bac•te'ri•al
bac•te'ri•cid'al
bac•te'ri•cide'
bac•te'ri•o•log'i•cal
bac•te'ri•ol'o•gist

bac•te'ri•ol'o•gy
Bac'tri•an camel
bad, worse, worst
badge
badg'er
bad'i•nage'
bad'lands'
bad'min'ton
bad'mouth' *or*
   bad'-mouth'
baf'fle, -fled, -fling
baf'fler
bag, bagged,
   bag'ging
bag'a•telle'
ba'gel
bag'gage
bag'gi•ness
bag'gy
bag'pipe'
bag'pip'er
bah
Ba•ha'mi•an *or*
   Ba•ha'man
bail *(money, pail han-*
   dle)
   ✔ *bale*
bail *(to empty)*
   ✔ *bale*
bail'iff
bail'i•wick'
bail'out' *n.*
bails'man
bait *(lure)*
   ✔ *bate*
baize
bake, baked, bak'ing

bak'er
bak'er's doz'en
bak'er•y
bak'ing pow'der
bak'ing so'da
ba•kla•va'
bal'a•lai'ka
bal'ance, -anced,
 -anc•ing
bal•bo'a
bal•brig'gan
bal'co•ny
bald
bal'da•chin *also*
 bal'da•chi'no *pl.*
 -chins *also* -chi'nos
bal'der•dash
bald'-faced'
bald'head'ed
bald'ing
bald'pate'
bal'dric
bale (*to bundle
 tightly*), baled,
 bal'ing
 ✔ *bail*
ba•leen'
bale'ful
bal'er
balk
Bal'kan
balk'y
ball (*round object,
 dance*)
 ✔ *bawl*
bal'lad
ball'-and-sock'et

joint'
bal'last
ball' bear'ing
bal'le•ri'na
bal•let'
bal•lis'tic
bal•lis'tics
bal•loon'
bal•loon'ist
bal'lot
ball'park'
ball'play'er
ball'point' pen'
ball'room'
bal'ly•hoo' *pl.*
 -hoos'
bal'ly•hoo',
 -hooed', -hoo'ing
balm'y
ba•lo'ney (*nonsense*)
 ✔ *bologna*
bal'sa
bal'sam
Balt
Bal'tic
bal•us'ter
bal'us•trade'
bam•bi'no *pl.* -nos
 or -ni
bam•boo' *pl.* -boos
bam•boo'zle, -zled,
 -zling
bam•boo'zler
ban, banned, ban'-
 ning
ba•nal'
ba•nal'i•ty

ba•nan'a
band'age, -aged,
 -ag•ing
ban•dan'na *or*
 ban•dan'a
band'box'
ban'di•coot'
ban'dit
ban'di•try
band'mas'ter
ban'do•leer' *or*
 ban'do•lier'
band' saw'
band'stand'
band'wag'on
ban'dy, -died,
 -dy•ing
ban'dy-leg'ged
bane
bane'ber'ry
bane'ful
bang
ban'gle
bang'-up' *adj.*
ban'ish
ban'ish•ment
ban'is•ter *also*
 ban'nis•ter
ban'jo *pl.* -jos *or*
 -joes
bank'book'
bank'card'
bank'er
bank'ing
bank' note'
bank'roll'
bank'rupt'

bank′rupt•cy
ban′ner
banns *also* bans
ban′quet
ban′shee
ban′tam
ban′tam•weight′
ban′ter
ban′ter•er
Ban′tu *pl.* Ban′tu
ban′yan
ban•zai′
ba′o•bab′
bap′tism
bap•tis′mal
Bap′tist
bap′tis•ter•y *also*
   bap′tis•try
bap′tize′, -tized′,
   -tiz′ing
bar, barred, bar′ring
barb
bar•bar′i•an
bar•bar′ic
bar′ba•rism
bar•bar′i•ty
bar′ba•rous
bar′be•cue′, -cued′,
   -cu′ing
barbed
barbed′ wire′
bar′bel *(feeler)*
bar′bell′ *(weight)*
bar′ber
bar′ber•ry
bar′ber•shop′
bar′bi•can

bar•bi′tu•rate
bar′ca•role′ *also*
   bar′ca•rolle′
bar′ code′
bard *(poet)*
   ✔ barred
bare *(naked)*, bar′er,
   bar′est
   ✔ bear
bare *(to uncover)*,
   bared, bar′ing
   ✔ bear
bare′back′ *also*
   bare′backed′
bare′faced′
bare′foot′ *also*
   bare′foot′ed
bare′hand′ed
bare′head′ed
bare′leg′ged
bare′ly
bar′gain
barge, barged,
   barg′ing
bar′ite
bar′i•tone′
bar′i•um
bark *(sound, outer
   covering)*
bark *also* barque
   (ship)
bar′keep′er
bar′ken•tine′
bark′er
bar′ley
bar′ley•corn′
bar′maid′

bar′man
bar mitz′vah,
   -vahed, vah•ing
barn
bar′na•cle
barn′storm′
barn′storm′er
barn′yard′
bar′o•gram′
bar′o•graph′
ba•rom′e•ter
bar′o•met′ric *or*
   bar′o•met′ri•cal
ba•rom′e•try
bar′on *(nobleman)*
   ✔ bar′ren
bar′on•ess
bar′on•et
bar′on•et•age
bar′on•et•cy
bar′on•et•ess
ba•ro′ni•al
bar′o•ny
ba•roque′
ba•rouche′
bar′rack
bar′ra•cu′da *pl.* -da
   or -das
bar′rage *(dam)*
bar•rage′ *(to fire at)*,
   -raged′, -rag′ing
barred *(having bars
   or stripes)*
   ✔ bard
bar′rel, -reled *or*
   -relled, -rel•ing *or*
   -rel•ling

bar'ren *(sterile)*
  ✔ baron

bar'ren•ness

bar•rette' *(hair clasp)*
  ✔ burette

bar'ri•cade',
  -cad'ed, -cad'ing

bar'ri•er

bar'ri•o' *pl.* -os'

bar'ris•ter

bar'room'

bar'row

bar'tend'er

bar'ter

bas'al

ba•salt'

base *(to find a basis for)*, based, bas'ing
  ✔ bass

base *(contemptible)*,
  bas'er, bas'est
  ✔ bass

base'ball'

base'board'

base' hit'

base'less

base' line'

base'man

base'ment

base'ness

ba•sen'ji

base' run'ner

bash

bash'ful

ba'sic *(fundamental)*

BA'SIC *(computer language)*

ba'si•cal•ly

bas'il

ba•sil'i•ca

bas'i•lisk'

ba'sin

ba'sis *pl.* -ses'

bask *(to take pleasure in)*
  ✔ basque, Basque

bas'ket

bas'ket•ball'

bas'ket•ry

basque *(bodice)*
  ✔ bask

Basque *(people)*
  ✔ bask

bas'-re•lief'

bass *(fish), pl.* bass *or* bass'es

bass *(voice)*
  ✔ base

bas'set hound'

bas'si•net'

bas'so *pl.* -sos *or* -si

bas•soon'

bas•soon'ist

bass' vi'ol

bass'wood'

bast

bas'tard

baste, bast'ed,
  bast'ing

bas'ti•na'do *also*
  bas'ti•nade' *pl.*
  -na'does *also*
  -nades'

bas'tion

bat, bat'ted, bat'ting

bat'boy'

batch

bate *(to lessen)*,
  bat'ed, bat'ing
  ✔ bait

ba•teau' *pl.* -teaux'

bat'girl'

bath *n.*

bathe, bathed,
  bath'ing

bath'er

ba•thet'ic

bath'house'

bath'ing cap'

bath'ing suit'

bath'mat'

bath'o•lith'

ba'thos'

bath'robe'

bath'room'

bath'tub'

bath'y•scaph' *also*
  bath'y•scaphe'

bath'y•sphere'

ba•tik'

ba•tiste'

bat mitz'vah *or* bas
  mitz'vah, -vahed,
  -vah•ing

ba•ton'

bats'man

bat•tal'ion

bat'ten

bat'ter

bat'ter•ing ram'

bat′ter•y
bat′ting
bat′tle, -tled, -tling
bat′tle-ax′ or bat′tle-
   axe′
bat′tle cry′
bat′tle•dore′
bat′tle•field′
bat′tle•front′
bat′tle•ground′
bat′tle•ment
bat′tler
bat′tle roy′al *pl.*
   bat′tles roy′al
bat′tle•ship′
bat′ty
bau′ble
baud
baux′ite′
bawd′y
bawd′i•ness
bawl *(cry)*
   ✔ *ball*
bay *(water, recess,
   color, tree)*
   ✔ *bey*
bay *(to bark),* bayed,
   bay′ing
   ✔ *bey*
bay′ber′ry
bay′ leaf′
bay•′o•net, -net•ed
   or -net•ted,
   -net•ing *or* -net•ting
bay′ou
ba•zaar′ *also* ba•zar′
   (market)

✔ *bizarre*
ba•zoo′ka
BB gun
be *(to exist), singular
   present tense forms,*
   am, are, is *plural
   present tense form,*
   are *present participle,*
   be′ing *singular
   past tense forms,*
   was, were *plural
   past tense form,*
   were *past participle,*
   been
   ✔ *bee*
beach *(shore)*
   ✔ *beech*
beach′head′
bea′con
bead
bead′ing
bea′dle
bead′work′
bead′y
bea′gle
beak
beak′er
beam
bean
bean′bag′
bean′ curd′
bean′ie
bean′pole′
bean′ sprouts′
bean′stalk′
bear *(to hold up),*
   bore, borne *or*

born, bear′ing
   ✔ *bare*
bear *(animal)*
   ✔ *bare*
bear′a•ble
bear′a•bly
beard
bear′er
bear′ing
bear′ish
bé•ar•naise′ sauce′
bear′skin′
beast
beast′li•ness
beat *(to hit),* beat,
   beat′en *or* beat,
   beat′ing
   ✔ *beet*
beat′er
be′a•tif′ic
be•at′i•fy′, -fied′,
   -fy′ing
be•at′i•tude′
beat′nik′
beat′-up′ *adj.*
beau *(boyfriend), pl.*
   beaus *or* beaux
   ✔ *bow*
Beau′fort scale
beaut
beau′te•ous
beau•ti′cian
beau•ti•fi•ca′tion
beau′ti•fi′er
beau′ti•ful
beau′ti•fy′, -fied′,
   -fy′ing

beau'ty
beaux-arts'
bea'ver
bea'ver·board'
be·calmed'
be·cause'
beck'on
be·cloud'
be·come', -came',
  -come', -com'ing
bed, bed'ded, bed'-
  ding
bed'-and-break'-
  fast
be·daub'
be·daz'zle, -zled,
  -zling
bed'bug'
bed'cham'ber
bed'clothes'
bed'ding
be·deck'
be·dev'il, -iled or
  -illed, -il·ing or
  -il·ling
be·dev'il·ment
be·dew'
bed'fel'low
be·di'zen
bed'lam
Bed'ou·in *pl.* -in or
  -ins
bed'pan'
bed'post'
be·drag'gled
bed'rid'den
bed'rock'

bed'roll'
bed'room'
bed'side'
bed'sore'
bed'spread'
bed'spring'
bed'stead'
bed'time'
bee *(insect, gathering)*
  ✔ be
beech *(tree)*
  ✔ beach
beech'nut'
beef *(animal), pl.*
  beeves *or* beef
beef *(complaint), pl.*
  beefs
beef'i·ness
beef'steak'
beef'y
bee'hive'
bee'keep'er
bee'line'
beep'er
beer *(beverage)*
  ✔ bier
bees'wax'
beet *(plant)*
  ✔ beat
bee'tle *(insect, mal-
  let)*
  ✔ betel
bee'tle *(to overhang),*
  -tled, -tling
  ✔ betel
bee'tle-browed'
be·fall', -fell',

-fall'en, -fall'ing
be·fit', -fit'ted,
  -fit'ting
be·fog', -fogged',
  -fog'ging
be·fore'
be·fore'hand'
be·foul'
be·friend'
be·fud'dle, -dled,
  -dling
beg, begged,
  beg'ging
be·get', -got',
  -got'ten *or* -got',
  -get'ting
be·get'ter
beg'gar
beg'gar·ly
beg'gar·y
be·gin', -gan',
  -gun', -gin'ning
be·gin'ner
be·gone'
be·go'nia
be·grime',
  -grimed', -grim'ing
be·grudge',
  -grudged',
  -grudg'ing
be·guile', -guiled',
  -guil'ing
be·guile'ment
be·guil'er
be·guine'
be·half'
be·have', -haved',

-hav'ing
be•hav'ior
be•hav'ior•al
be•hav'ior•ism
be•hav'ior•ist
be•head'
be•he'moth
be•hest'
be•hind'
be•hind'hand'
be•hold', -held',
 -hold'ing
be•hold'en
be•hold'er
be•hoove',
 -hooved',
 -hoov'ing
beige
be'ing
be•jew'eled
bel *(unit of measure-*
 ment)
 ✔ bell, belle
be•la'bor
be•lat'ed
be•lay'
bel can'to
belch
bel'dam *or* bel'dame
be•lea'guer
bel'fry
Bel'gian
be•lie', -lied',
 -ly'ing
be•lief'
be•liev'a•ble
be•lieve', -lieved',

-liev'ing
be•liev'er
be•lit'tle, -tled,
 -tling
bell *(instrument)*
 ✔ bel, belle
bel'la•don'na
bell'-bot'toms
bell'boy'
belle *(woman)*
 ✔ bel, bell
belles-let'tres
bell'flow'er
bell'hop'
bel'li•cose'
bel'li•cos'i•ty
bel•lig'er•ence
bel•lig'er•en•cy
bel•lig'er•ent
bell' jar'
bel'low
bel'lows
bell'weth'er
bel'ly, -lied, -ly•ing
bel'ly•ache',
 -ached', -ach'ing
bel'ly•ach'er
bel'ly•band'
bel'ly•but'ton
bel'ly•land',
 -land'ed, -land'ing
bel'ly land'ing
bel'ly laugh'
be•long'
be•long'ings
be•lov'ed
be•low'

belt
belt'ing
belt'way'
be•lu'ga
bel've•dere'
be'ma *pl.* -ma•ta
be•moan'
be•mused'
bench
bench'mark'
bend, bent,
 bend'ing
be•neath'
Ben'e•dic'tine
ben'e•dic'tion
ben'e•fac'tor
be•nef'ic
ben'e•fice
be•nef'i•cence
be•nef'i•cent
ben'e•fi'cial
ben'e•fi'ci•ar'y
ben'e•fit', -fit•ed *also*
 -fit•ted, -fit•ing *or*
 -fit•ting
be•nev'o•lence
be•nev'o•lent
Ben•ga'li
be•night'ed
be•nign'
be•nig'nant
be•nig'ni•ty
ben'i•son
bent
be•numb'
ben'zene' *(hydrocar-*
 bon)

ben'zine' *(mixture of hydrocarbons)*
ben'zo•ate' of so'da
ben•zo'ic ac'id
ben'zo•in
ben'zol
be•queath'
be•quest'
be•rate', -rat'ed, -rat'ing
Ber'ber
be•reave', -reaved' or -reft', -reav'ing
be•reave'ment
be•reft'
be•ret'
berg *(iceberg)*
  ✔ *burg*
ber'i•ber'i
ber•ke'li•um
berm
Ber•mu'da shorts'
ber'ry *(fruit)*
  ✔ *bury*
ber•serk'
berth *(bed)*
  ✔ *birth*
ber'yl
be•ryl'li•um
be•seech', -sought' or -seeched', -seech'ing
be•set', -set', -set'ting
be•side' *(next to)*
be•sides' *(in addi-*

tion)
be•siege', -sieged', -sieg'ing
be•sieg'er
be•smirch'
be•sot', be•sot'ted, be•sot'ting
be•spat'ter
be•speak', -spoke', -spo'ken or -spoke', -speak'ing
be•spec'ta•cled
be•sprin'kle, -kled, -kling
Bes'semer proc'ess
best
bes'tial
bes'ti•al'i•ty
bes'ti•ar'y
be•stir', -stirred', -stir'ring
be•stow'
be•stow'al
be•strew', -strewed', -strewed' or -strewn', -strew'ing
be•stride', -strode', -strid'den, -strid'ing
best'sell'er
best'-sell'ing
bet, bet or bet'ted, bet'ting
be'ta
be•take', -took', -tak'en, -tak'ing
be'ta•tron'

be'tel *(plant)*
  ✔ *beetle*
be'tel nut'
bête noire'
be•think', -thought', -think'ing
be•tide', -tid'ed, -tid'ing
be•times'
be•to'ken
be•tray'
be•tray'al
be•tray'er
be•troth'
be•troth'al
be•trothed'
bet'ter *(greater)*
  ✔ *bettor*
bet'ter•ment
bet'tor *also* bet'ter *(one who bets)*
  ✔ *better*
be•tween'
be•twixt'
bev'el, -eled or -elled, -el'ing or -el'ling
bev'er•age
bev'y
be•wail'
be•ware', -wared', -war'ing
be•wil'der
be•witch'
be•witch'ing
bey *(governor)*
  ✔ *bay*

be•yond'
bi•a'ly *pl.* -lys
bi•an'nu•al *(twice a year)*
✔ biennial, biyearly, semiannual, semiyearly
bi'as, -ased *or* -assed, -as•ing *or* -as•sing
bi•ath'lon
bi•ax'i•al
bib
Bi'ble
bib'li•cal
bib'li•og'ra•pher
bib'li•o•graph'i•cal *or* bib'li•o•graph'ic
bib'li•og'ra•phy
bib'u•lous
bi•cam'er•al
bi•car'bon•ate'
bi•cen•ten'a•ry
bi•cen•ten'ni•al
bi'ceps' *pl.* -ceps' *or* -ceps'es
bi•chlo'ride'
bick'er
bick'er•er
bi•coast'al *or* bi-coast'al
bi•con•cave'
bi•con•vex'
bi•cul'tur•al
bi•cus'pid
bi•cy•cle, -cled, -cling
bi•cy•cler *or*

bi'cy•clist
bid *(to order, to invite)*, bade *or* bid, bid'den *or* bid, bid'ding
bid *(to make an offer)*, bid, bid'ding
bid'der
bid'dy
bide, bid'ed *or* bode, bid'ed, bid'ing
bi•det'
bi•en'ni•al *(lasting two years, once every two years)*
✔ biannual, biyearly, semiannual, semiyearly
bier *(coffin stand)*
✔ beer
bi•fo'cal *adj.*
bi•fo'cals *n.*
bi•fur•ca'tion
bi•fur•cate', -cat'ed, -cat'ing
big, big'ger, big'gest
big'a•mist
big'a•mous
big'a•my
big'-heart'ed
big'horn' *pl.* -horn' *or* -horns'
bight *(loop, curve, bay)*
✔ bite, byte
big' league' *n.*
big'-league' *adj.*

big'ot
big'ot•ed
big'ot•ry
big' shot'
big' time' *n.*
big'time' *or* big'-time' *adj.*
bike, biked, bik'ing
bik'er
bike'way'
bi•ki'ni
bi•lat'er•al
bile
bilge
bi•lin'gual
bil'ious
bilk
bill
bill'board'
bil'let
bil'let-doux' *pl.* bil'lets-doux'
bill'fold'
bil'liards
bill'ing
bil'lion
bil'lion•aire'
bil'lionth
bil'low
bil'ly
bil'ly club'
bil'ly goat'
bi•month'ly *(once every two months, twice a month)*
✔ semimonthly

bin
bi′na•ry
bin•au′ral
bind, bound,
  bind′ing
bind′er
bind′er•y
bind′ing
bind′weed′
binge, binged,
  bing′ing *or*
  binge′ing
bin′go *pl.* -goes
bin′na•cle
bin•oc′u•lar
bi•no′mi•al
bi′o•chem′i•cal
bi′o•chem′ist
bi′o•chem′is•try
bi′o•chip′
bi′o•com•pat′i•bil′-
  i•ty
bi′o•de•grad′a•ble
bi′o•di•ver′si•ty
bi′o•en′gi•neer′ing
bi′o•eth′ics
bi′o•feed′back′
bi′o•gen′e•sis
bi•og′ra•pher
bi′o•graph′i•cal
  also bi′o•graph′ic
bi•og′ra•phy
bi′o•haz′ard
bi′o•log′i•cal *also*
  bi′o•log′ic
bi•ol′o•gist
bi•ol′o•gy

bi′o•lu′mi•nes′-
  cence
bi′o•lu′mi•nes′-
  cent
bi′o•mass′
bi•ome′
bi′o•me•chan′ics
bi′o•med′i•cine
bi′o•met′rics
bi•on′ic
bi′o•phys′i•cist
bi′o•phys′ics
bi′op′sy
bi′o•rhythm
bi•os′co•py
bi′o•sphere′
bi′o•syn′the•sis
bi′o•syn•thet′ic
bi•o′ta
bi′o•tech′no•log′i•
  cal
bi′o•tech•nol′o•gy
bi•ot′ic
bi′o•tin
bi•par′ti•san
bi•par′ti•san•ism
bi•par′tite′
bi•ped′
bi′plane′
bi•po′lar
bi•ra′cial
birch
bird′bath′
bird′cage′
bird′call′
bird′ dog′
bird′er

bird′house′
bird′ie
bird′lime′
bird′ of par′a•dise′
  pl. birds′ of
  par′a•dise′
bird′seed′
bird′s′-eye′
bird′ watch′er
bird′ watch′ing
bi•ret′ta
birr *(whirring sound)*
  ✔ *bur*
birth *(beginning)*
  ✔ *berth*
birth′day′
birth′mark′
birth′place′
birth′rate′
birth′right′
birth′stone′
bis′cuit *pl.* -cuits
bi′sect′
bi•sec′tion
bi′sec′tor
bi•sex′u•al
bi•sex•u•al′i•ty
bish′op
bish′op•ric
bis′muth
bi′son
bisque
bis′tro *pl.* -tros
bit
bitch
bite *(to grip or tear
  with the teeth)*, bit,

bit'ten *or* bit,
bit'ing
✔ bight, byte
bit'er
bit'ter
bit'tern
bit'ter·root'
bit'ter·sweet'
bi·tu'men
bi·tu'mi·nous
bi·va'lent
bi'valve'
biv'ou·ac', -acked',
-ack'ing
bi·week'ly (once
every two weeks,
twice a week)
✔ semiweekly
biyearly (once every
two years, twice a
year)
✔ biannual, bien-
nial, semiannual,
semiyearly
bi·zarre' (strange)
✔ bazaar
blab, blabbed,
blab'bing
blab'ber·mouth'
black'-and-blue'
adj.
black'-and-white'
adj.
black'ball'
black'ber'ry
black'bird'
black'board'

black'bod'y
black' box'
black'damp'
black'en
black' eye'
black'-eyed' pea'
black'-eyed'
Su'san
Black'foot' pl. -foot'
or -feet'
black'guard
black'head'
black' hole'
black'ing
black'ish
black'jack'
black'list'
black'mail'
black'mail'er
black' mar'ket n.
black'-mar'ket adj.
& v.
black'-mar'ket·er
or black'-mar'ke·
teer'
black'out'
black'smith'
black'snake'
black'thorn'
black'-tie' adj.
black'top',
-topped', -top'ping
blad'der
blade
blah
blam'a·ble also
blame'a·ble

blame, blamed,
blam'ing
blame'less
blame'wor'thi·
ness
blame'wor'thy
blanch also blench
(to whiten)
✔ blench
bland
blan'dish
blank
blan'ket
blare, blared,
blar'ing
blar'ney
bla·sé'
blas·pheme',
-phemed,
-phem'ing
blas·phem'er
blas'phe·mous
blas'phe·my
blast
blas'to·coel' or
blas'to·coele'
blas'to·derm'
blast'off' also
blast'-off'
blas'tu·la pl. -las or
-lae'
bla'tan·cy
bla'tant
blaze, blazed,
blaz'ing
blaz'er
bla'zon

bleach
bleach'ers
bleak
blear
blear'i•ness
blear'y
bleat
bleat'er
bleed, bled,
  bleed'ing
bleed'er
bleed'ing heart' *n.*
bleed'ing-heart'
  adj.
bleep
blem'ish
blench (to shy away)
  ✔ *blanch*
blend, blend'ed *or*
  blent, blend'ing
blend'er
bless, blessed *or*
  blest, bless'ing
bless'ed *also* blest
  adj.
bless'ing
blight
blimp
blind
blind'ers
blind'fold'
blind'fold'ed
blind'man's buff'
blink'er
blintz *also* blin'tze
blip
bliss

bliss'ful
blis'ter
blis'ter•y
blis'ter•ing
blithe, blith'er,
  blith'est
blithe'ly
blithe'some
blitz
blitz'krieg'
bliz'zard
bloat
blob
bloc (*group*)
block (*solid sub-
  stance*)
block•ade', -ad'ed,
  -ad'ing
block•ad'er
block•ade'-run'ner
block'age
block'bust'er
block'head'
block'house'
bloke
blond *also* blonde
blood
blood' bank'
blood'bath'
blood' count'
blood'cur'dling
blood'ed
blood'hound'
blood'i•ness
blood'less
blood'let'ting
blood'line'

blood'mo•bile'
blood'root'
blood'shed'
blood'shot'
blood'stained'
blood'stone'
blood'stream' *also*
  blood' stream'
blood'suck'er
blood'thirst'i•ness
blood'thirst'y
blood'y, -ied, -y•ing
bloom
bloom'ers
bloom'ing
bloop'er
blos'som
blot, blot'ted,
  blot'ting
blotch
blotch'y
blot'ter
blouse
blow, blew, blown,
  blow'ing
blow'-dry', -dried',
  -dry'ing
blow' dry'er
blow'er
blow'fish' *pl.* -fish'
  or -fish'es
blow'fly'
blow'gun'
blow'hard'
blow'hole'
blow'off' *n.*
blow'out' *n.*

blow'pipe'
blow'torch'
blow'up' *n.*
blow'zy *also*
  blow'sy
blub'ber
bludg'eon
blue, blu'er, blu'est
blue, blued, blu'ing
blue' ba'by
blue'bell' *also*
  blue'bells'
blue'ber'ry
blue'bird'
blue' blood' *(noble descent)*
blue' blood' *(a person of noble descent)*
blue'bon'net
blue'bot'tle
blue' cheese'
blue'-col'lar *adj.*
blue'fish' *pl.* -fish'
  or -fish'es
blue'grass'
blue' jay'
blue'print'
blue'-rib'bon *adj.*
blues
blu'ets
bluff
bluff'er
blu'ing *also*
  blue'ing
blu'ish *also* blue'ish
blun'der
blun'der•buss'

blunt
blur, blurred,
  blur'ring
blurb
blur'ry
blurt
blush
blush'er
blus'ter
blus'ter•er
blus'ter•ous
blus'ter•y
bo'a
boar *(animal)*
  ✔ Boer, bore
board
board'er *(lodger)*
  ✔ border
board'ing house'
board'ing school'
board'walk'
boast
boast'er
boast'ful
boat
boat'house'
boat'man
boat' peo'ple
boat'swain *also*
  bo's'n *or* bo'sun
bob, bobbed,
  bob'bing
bob'bin
bob'ble, -bled,
  -bling
bob'by
bob'by pin'

bob'by socks' *also*
  bob'by sox'
bob'cat'
bob'o•link'
bob'sled', -sled'ded,
  -sled'ding
bob'tail'
bob'white'
bode, bod'ed,
  bod'ing
bo•de'ga
bod'ice
bod'i•less
bod'i•ly
bod'kin
bod'y
bod'y•build'ing
bod'y•guard'
Boer *(Dutch South African)*
  ✔ boar, bore
bog, bogged,
  bog'ging
bo'gey *also* bo'gy *or*
  bo'gie *pl.* -geys *also*
  -gies
bo'gey•man'
bog'gle, -gled,
  -gling
bo'gus
bo•he'mi•an
boil
boil'er
boil'ing point'
bois'ter•ous
bo'la *also* bo'las
bold

bold′face′ *n. & adj.*
bold′-faced′ *adj.*
bole *(tree trunk)*
✔ *boll, bowl*
bo•le′ro *pl.* -ros
bo•li′var *pl.* -vars *or*
-var•es′
Bo•liv′i•an
boll *(seed pod)*
✔ *bole, bowl*
bol′lix *also* bol′lox
bo•lo′gna *also*
ba•lo′ney *or*
bo•lo′ney *(meat)*
✔ *baloney*
Bol′she•vik′ *pl.* -viks′
or Bol′she•vi′ki
Bol′she•vism
Bol′she•vist
bol′ster
bolt
bo′lus *pl.* -lus•es
bomb
bom•bard′
bom•bar•dier′
bom•bard′ment
bom′bast′
bom•bas′tic
bom•ba•zine′
bomb′er
bomb′shell′
bomb′sight′
bo′na fide′
bo•nan′za
bon′bon′
bond′age
bond′hold′er

bond′man
bond′ser′vant
bonds′man
bond′wom′an
bone, boned,
bon′ing
bone′black′ *also*
bone′ black′
bone′-dry′
bone′fish′ *pl.* -fish′
or -fish′es
bone′head′
bone′ meal′
bon′er
bon′fire′
bon′go drums′
bon′gos
bon•ho•mie′
bo•ni′to *pl.* -to *or*
-tos
bon mot′ *pl.* bons
mots′
bon′net
bon′ny *also* bon′nie
bon•sai′ *pl.* bon•sai′
bo′nus *pl.* -nus•es
bon′ vi•vant′ *pl.*
bons′ vi•vants′
bon′ voy•age′
bon′i•ness
bon′y *or* bon′ey,
-i•er *or* -ey•er, -i•est
or -ey′est
boo *pl.* boos
boo, booed, boo′ing
boob
boo′-boo *also* boo′-

boo *pl.* -boos
boo′by
boo′by prize′
boo′by trap′
boog′ie-woog′ie
book
book′bind′er
book′bind′er•y
book′bind′ing
book′case′
book′ club′
book′end′
book′ie
book′ing
book′ish
book′keep′er
book′keep′ing
book′let
book′mak′er
book′mak′ing
book′mark′
book′mo•bile′
book′plate′
book′sell′er
book′shelf′
book′shop′
book′stand′
book′store′
book′worm′
Bool′e•an
al′ge•bra
boom
boo′mer•ang′
boom′town′
boon
boon′docks′
boor

boor′ish
boost
boost′er
boot′black′
boot′ camp′
boot′ed
boo′tee *also* boo′tie
(baby shoe)
    ✔ *booty*
booth
boot′jack′
boot′leg′, -legged′,
    -leg′ging
boot′leg′ger
boot′lick′
boot′lick′er
boot′strap′
boo′ty (plunder)
    ✔ *bootee*
booze, boozed,
    booz′ing
booz′er
bop, bopped,
    bop′ping
bo′rate
bo′rax′
Bor·deaux′ *pl.*
    -deaux′
bor′der (boundary)
    ✔ *boarder*
bor′der·land′
bor′der·line′
bore (to drill, to
weary), bored,
bor′ing
    ✔ *boar, Boer*
bore (wave)

    ✔ *boar, Boer*
bore′dom
bor′er
bo′ric ac′id
bor′ing
born (brought into
life)
    ✔ *bourn*
born′-a·gain′
bo′ron
bor′ough (town)
    ✔ *burro, burrow*
bor′row
bor′row·er
bor′row·ing
borscht *also* borsch
bor′zoi′
bosk′y
bos′om
boss
boss′ism
boss′y
Bos′ton ter′ri·er
bo·tan′i·cal *also*
    bo·tan′ic
bot′a·nist
bot′a·ny
botch
bot′fly′ *also* bot′ fly′
both
both′er
both′er·some
bot′tle, -tled, -tling
bot′tle·neck′
bot′tler
bot′tom
bot′tom·land′

bot′tom·less
bot′u·lism
bou′doir′
bouf·fant′
bou′gain·vil′le·a
    also bou′gain·
    vil′lae·a
bough (branch)
    ✔ *bow*
bouil′la·baisse′
bouil′lon′ (broth)
    ✔ *bullion*
boul′der
boul′e·vard′
bounce, bounced,
    bounc′ing
bounc′er
bounc′i·ly
bounc′y
bound
bound′a·ry
bound′en
bound′less
boun′te·ous
boun′ti·ful
boun′ty
bou·quet′
bour′bon
bour·geois′ *pl.*
    -geois′
bour′geoi·sie′
bourn *also* bourne
(stream)
    ✔ *born*
bourn *also* bourne
(limit)
    ✔ *born*

bour·rée'

bout

bou·tique'

bou'ton·niere' *also*
  bou'ton·nière'

bo'vine'

bow *(front of a ship, bending)*
  ✔ *bough*

bow *(weapon)*
  ✔ *beau*

bowd'ler·ism

bowd'ler·i·za'tion

bowd'ler·ize'

bow'el

bow'er

bow'ie knife'

bowl *(dish, ball)*
  ✔ *bole, boll*

bow'leg'

bow'leg'ged

bowl'er

bow'line

bowl'ing

bow'man

bow'sprit'

bow'string'

bow' tie'

box *(container, slap),*
  pl. box'es

box *(shrub), pl.* box
  or box•es

box'car'

box'er

box'ing

box'wood'

box'y

boy *(boy child)*
  ✔ *buoy*

boy'cott'

boy'friend'

boy'hood'

boy'ish

Boy' Scout'

boy'sen•ber'ry

bra

brace, braced,
  brac'ing

brace'let

brac'er

bra'chi·o·pod'

brack'en

brack'et

brack'ish

bract

brad, brad'ded,
  brad'ding

brag, bragged,
  brag'ging

brag'ga·do'ci·o'

brag'gart

brag'ger

Brah'ma *(deity)*

Brah'man *also*
  Brah'ma *also*
  Brah'min *(cattle)*

Brah'man·ism

Brah'min *also*
  Brah·man *(class)*

braid

braid'er

Braille *or* braille

brain

brain'child'

brain'-dead'

brain' death'

brain'less

brain'pan'

brain' stem' *also*
  brain'stem'

brain'storm'

brain'wash'

brain'wash'ing

brain' wave'

brain'y

braise *(to cook),*
  braised, brais'ing
  ✔ *braze*

brake *(to slow or
  stop),* braked,
  brak'ing
  ✔ *break*

brake *(fern)*
  ✔ *break*

brake'man

bram'ble

bram'bly

bran

branch

brand

brand'er

bran'dish

brand'-new'

bran'dy, -died,
  -dy·ing

brant *pl.* brant *or*
  brants

brash

brass

bras'se·rie'

bras·siere'

brass′y

brat

brat′ty

brat′wurst′

bra•va′do *pl.* -dos *or*
  -does

brave, brav′er,
  brav′est

brave, braved,
  brav′ing

brave′ly

brav′er•y

bra′vo *pl.* -vos

bra•vu′ra

brawl

brawl′er

brawn

brawn′i•ness

brawn′y

bray

braze *(to solder),*
  brazed, braz′ing
  ✔ *braise*

bra′zen, -zened,
  -zen•ing

bra′zier

Bra•zil′ian

Bra•zil′ nut′

breach *(gap, viola-*
  tion)
  ✔ *breech*

bread

bread′-and-but′ter
  adj.

bread′bas′ket

bread′fruit′

bread′ line′

bread′stuff′

breadth

bread′win′ner

break *(to make unus-*
  able), broke,
  bro′ken, break′ing
  ✔ *brake*

break′a•ble

break′age

break′down′ *n.*

break′er

break′fast

break′front′

break′neck′

break′point′

break′through′ *n.*

break′up′ *n.*

break′wa′ter

bream *pl.* bream *or*
  breams

breast

breast′bone′

breast′-feed′, -fed′,
  -feed′ing

breast′plate′

breast′stroke′

breast′work′

breath *n.*

breathe, breathed,
  breath′ing

breath′er

breath′less

breath′tak′ing

breath′y

breech *(buttocks)*
  ✔ *breach*

breech′cloth′

breech′es buoy′

breech′load′er

breed, bred,
  breed′ing

breed′er

breed′ing

breeze, breezed,
  breez′ing

breeze′way′

breez′i•ly

breez′y

breth′ren

Bret′on

breve

bre′vi•ar′y

brev′i•ty

brew

brew′er•y

brew′ing

bri′ar *also* bri′er
  (shrub, pipe)
  ✔ *brier*

bri′ar•wood′

bribe, bribed,
  brib′ing

brib′er•y

bric′-a-brac′

brick *pl.* bricks *or*
  brick

brick′bat′

brick′lay′er

brick′lay′ing

brick′work′

brick′yard′

bri′dal *(relating to a*
  bride)
  ✔ *bridle*

bride
bride'groom'
brides'maid'
bridge'a·ble
bridge, bridged,
　bridg'ing
bridge'head'
bridge'work'
bri'dle (to restrain),
　-dled, -dling
　✔ bridal
bri'dle path'
brief
brief'case'
brief'ing
bri'er also bri'ar
　(thorny shrub)
　✔ briar
brig
bri·gade'
brig'a·dier'
brig'a·dier'
　gen'er·al pl.
　brig'a·dier'
　gen'er·als
brig'and
brig'an·tine'
bright
bright'en
bril'liance
bril'lian·cy
bril'liant
brim, brimmed,
　brim'ming
brim'ful
brim'stone'
brin'dle

brin'dled
brine
bring, brought,
　bring'ing
brink
brin'y
bri·quette' also
　bri·quet'
brisk
bris'ket
bris'ling
bris'tle, -tled, -tling
bris'tly
britch'es
Brit'i·cism
Brit'ish
Brit'ish·er
Brit'on
brit'tle, -tler, -tlest
broach (to begin to
　discuss)
　✔ brooch
broad
broad'ax' or
　broad'axe'
broad'cast', -cast'
　or -cast'ed, -cast'ing
broad'cast'er
broad'cloth'
broad'en
broad'loom'
broad'-mind'ed
broad'side'
broad'sword'
bro·cade', -cad'ed,
　-cad'ing
broc'co·li

bro·chure'
bro'gan
brogue
broil
broil'er
broke
bro'ken
bro'ken-down'
bro'ken·heart'ed
bro'ker
bro'ker·age
bro'mide'
bro'mine'
bron'chi·a sing.
　-chi·um
bron'chi·al
bron'chi·ole'
bron·chit'ic
bron·chi'tis
bron'cho·scope'
bron'chus pl. -chi'
bron'co pl. -cos
bron'to·saur' or
　bron'to·sau'rus
bronze, bronzed,
　bronz'ing
bronz'y
brooch (pin)
　✔ broach
brood
brood'er
brook
brook'let
broom (implement
　for sweeping)
　✔ brougham
broom'corn'

broom'stick'
broth
broth'er
broth'er•hood'
broth'er-in-law' *pl.*
  broth'ers-in-law'
broth'er•li•ness
broth'er•ly
brougham *(carriage)*
  ✔ broom
brow
brow'beat', -beat',
  -beat'en, -beat'ing
brown
brown' Bet'ty
brown'ie
brown'ish
brown'out'
brown'stone'
browse, browsed,
  brows'ing
brows'er
bru'in
bruise, bruised,
  bruis'ing
bruis'er
bruit *(to spread news)*
  ✔ brute
brunch
bru•nette' *also*
  bru•net'
brunt
brush
brush'fire' *also*
  brush' fire'
brush'land'
brush'off' *also*

brush'-off' *n.*
brush'wood'
brush'work'
brusque
brusque'ly
brusque'ness
Brus'sels sprouts'
bru'tal
bru•tal'i•ty
bru'tal•ize', -ized',
  -iz'ing
brute *(beast)*
  ✔ bruit
brut'ish
bub'ble, -bled, -bling
bub'ble gum'
bub'bly
bu'bo *pl.* -boes
bu•bon'ic plague'
buc'ca•neer'
buck
buck'a•roo' *pl.*
  -roos'
buck'board'
buck'et
buck'et•ful'
buck'et seat'
buck'eye'
buck'le, -led, -ling
buck'ler
buck'ram
buck'saw'
buck'shot'
buck'skin'
buck'tooth' *pl.*
  -teeth'
buck'toothed'

buck'wheat'
bu•col'ic
bud, bud'ded,
  bud'ding
Bud'dhism
Bud'dhist
bud'dy
budge, budged,
  budg'ing
budg'er•i•gar'
budg'et
bud'get•ar'y
budg'ie
buff
buf'fa•lo' *pl.* -lo' or
  -loes' or -los'
buff'er
buf•fet' *(furniture,
  meal)*
buf'fet *(blow)*
buf•foon'
buf•foon'er•y
bug, bugged,
  bug'ging
bug'a•boo' *pl.*
  -boos'
bug'bear'
bug'gy
bu'gle, -gled, -gling
bu'gler
build, built,
  build'ing
build'er
build'ing
build'up' *also*
  build'-up' *n.*
built'-in'

built'-up'
bulb
bul'bous
Bul·gar'i·an
bulge, bulged,
   bulg'ing
bulg'i·ness
bulg'y
bulk
bulk'head'
bulk'i·ness
bulk'y
bull
bull'dog'
bull'doze', -dozed',
   -doz'ing
bull'doz'er
bul'let
bul'le·tin
bul'le·tin board'
bul'let·proof'
bull'fight'
bull'fight'er
bull'fight'ing
bull'finch'
bull'frog'
bull'head'
bull'head'ed
bull'horn'
bul'lion (gold or
   silver bars)
   ✔ bouillon
bull'ish
bul'lock
bull'pen'
bull'ring'
bull's'-eye' or bull's'

eye'
bul'ly, -lied, -ly•ing
bul'rush'
bul'wark'
bum, bummed,
   bum'ming
bum'ble·bee'
bum'mer
bump
bump'er
bump'er stick'er
bump'i·ness
bump'kin
bump'y
bun
bunch
bun'dle, -dled,
   -dling
bung
bun'ga·low'
bung'hole'
bun'gle, -gled,
   -gling
bun'gler
bun'ion
bunk
bun'ker
bunk'house'
bun'ny
Bun'sen burn'er
bunt
bunt'er
bunt'ing
buoy (float)
   ✔ boy
buoy'an·cy
buoy'ant

bur also burr (prickly
   seed)
   ✔ birr
bur'ble, -bled,
   -bling
bur'den
bur'den·some
bur'dock'
bu'reau pl. -reaus or
   -reaux
bu·reauc'ra·cy
bu'reau·crat'
bu'reau·crat'ic
bu·rette' also
   bu·ret' (glass tube)
   ✔ barrette
burg (city or town)
   ✔ berg
bur'geon
burg'er (hamburger)
   ✔ burgher
bur'gess
burgh'er (citizen)
   ✔ burger
bur'glar
bur'glar·ize', -ized',
   -iz'ing
bur'gla·ry
bur'gle, bur'gled,
   bur'gling
bur'go·mas'ter
bur'gun·dy (color)
Bur'gun·dy (wine)
bur'i·al
burl
bur'lap'
bur·lesque',

-lesqued', -les'quing
bur'li•ness
bur'ly
Bur•mese' *pl.* -mese'
burn, burned *or*
 burnt, burn'ing
burn'a•ble
burn'er
burn'ing
bur'nish
bur•noose' *also*
 bur•nous'
burn'out' *n.*
burp
burr *(rough spot)*
burr *also* bur *(trill)*
bur•ri'to *pl.* -tos
bur'ro *(donkey), pl.*
 -ros
 ✔ borough
bur'row *(hole)*
 ✔ borough
bur'row•er
bur'sa *pl.* -sae *or* -sas
bur'sar
bur•si'tis
burst
bur'y *(to put in the*
 ground), -ied, -y•ing
 ✔ berry
bus *(vehicle), pl.*
 bus'es *or* bus'ses
bus *(to transport),*
 bused *or* bussed,
 bus'ing *or* bus'sing
bus'boy' *also* bus'
 boy'

bush
bushed
bush'el
bush'i•ness
bush'ing
Bush'man
bush'mas'ter
bush'whack'
bush'whack'er
bush'y
bus'i•ly
busi'ness
busi'ness•like'
busi'ness•man
busi'ness•per'son
busi'ness•wom'an
bus'load'
bust
bus'tard
bust'er
bus•tier'
bus'tle, -tled, -tling
bust'y
bus'y, -ied, -y•ing
bus'y•bod'y
bus'y•ness
bus'y•work'
but *conj.*
 ✔ butt
bu'ta•di•ene'
bu'tane'
butch'er
butch'er•y
but'ler
butt *(to hit or push)*
 ✔ but
butt *(target)*

✔ but
butte
but'ter
but'ter bean'
but'ter•cup'
but'ter•fat'
but'ter•fin'gers
but'ter•fish' *pl.*
 -fish' *or* -fish'es
but'ter•fly'
but'ter•milk'
but'ter•nut'
but'ter•scotch'
but'ter•y
but'tock
but'ton
but'ton•hole',
 -holed', -hol'ing
but'ton•wood'
but'tress
bu'tyl
bu•tyr'ic
bux'om
buy *(to purchase),*
 bought, buy'ing
 ✔ by
buy'er
buzz
buz'zard
buzz'er
buzz' saw'
by *prep.*
 ✔ buy
by' and by' *adv.*
by'-and-by' *n.*
bye'-bye'
by'gone'

by'law'
by'line'
by'pass' *also*
  by'-pass'
by'-path'
by'-play'
by'prod'uct *or*
  by'-prod'uct
by'road'
by'stand'er
byte *(computer unit)*
  ✔ *bight, bite*
by'way'
by'word'
Byz'an•tine'

C

cab
ca•bal', -balled',
  -bal'ling
cab'al•le'ro *pl.* -ros
ca•ban'a *also*
  ca•ba'ña
cab'a•ret'
cab'bage
cab'by *or* cab'bie
cab'driv'er
cab'in
cab'i•net'
cab'i•net•mak'er
cab'i•net•work'
ca'ble, -bled, -bling
ca'ble car'
ca'ble•gram'
ca•boose'

cab'ri•o•let'
ca•ca'o *pl.* -os
cach'a•lot'
cache *(to hide)*,
  cached, cach'ing
  ✔ *cash*
ca•chet'
cack'le, -led, -ling
ca•coph'o•nous
ca•coph'o•ny
cac'tus *pl.* -ti' *or*
  -tus•es
cad
ca•dav'er
ca•dav'er•ous
cad'die *also* cad'dy
  (to carry golf clubs),
  -died, -dy•ing
  ✔ *caddy*
cad'dis fly' *also*
  cad'dice fly'
Cad'do *pl.* Cad'do
  or -dos
Cad'do•an
cad'dy *(small con-
  tainer)*
  ✔ *caddie*
ca'dence
ca•den'za
ca•det'
cad'mi•um
cad're
ca•du'ce•us *pl.*
  -ce•i'
cae'sar *also* Cae'sar
cae•su'ra *pl.* -su'ras
  -su'rae

ca•fé' *also* ca•fe'
caf'e•te'ri•a
caf•feine' *also*
  caf•fein'
caf'tan' *or* kaf'tan'
cage, caged, cag'ing
ca'gey *also* ca'gy,
  -gi•er, -gi•est
cag'i•ness
ca•hoots'
cai'man *also*
  cay'man *pl.* -mans
cairn
cais'son'
ca•jole', -joled',
  -jol'ing
ca•jol'er•y
Ca'jun *also* Ca'jan
cake, caked, cak'ing
cake'walk'
cake'walk'er
cal'a•bash'
cal'a•boose'
cal'a•mine'
ca•lam'i•tous
ca•lam'i•ty
cal•car'e•ous
cal'ci•fi•ca'tion
cal'ci•fy', -fied',
  -fy'ing
cal'ci•mine',
  -mined', -min'ing
cal'ci•na'tion
cal'cine', -cined',
  -cin'ing
cal'cite'
cal'ci•um

cal'cu·la·bil'i·ty
cal'cu·la·ble
cal'cu·late', -lat'ed,
 -lat'ing
cal'cu·la'tion
cal'cu·la'tor
cal'cu·lus *pl.* -li' or
 -lus·es
cal'dron *also*
 caul'dron
cal'en·dar *(time
 chart)*
cal'en·der *(press)*
calf *pl.* calves
calf'skin'
cal'i·ber
cal'i·brate',
 -brat'ed, -brat'ing
cal'i·bra'tion
cal'i·co' *pl.* -coes' or
 -cos'
Cal'i·for'nian
cal'i·for'ni·um
cal'i·per *also*
 cal'li·per
ca'liph *also* ca'lif
ca'liph·ate'
cal'is·then'ics
call
cal'la
call'er
cal·lig'ra·pher
cal·lig'ra·phy
call'ing
cal·li'o·pe'
cal·los'i·ty
cal'lous *(having*

calluses, unfeeling)
 ✔ *callus*
cal'low
call'-up' *n.*
cal'lus *(hard tissue),*
 pl. -lus·es
 ✔ *callous*
calm
cal'o·mel'
ca·lor'ic
cal'o·rie
cal'o·rif'ic
cal'o·rim'e·ter
cal'u·met'
ca·lum'ni·ate',
 -at'ed, -at'ing
ca·lum'ni·a'tion
ca·lum'ni·a'tor
ca·lum'ni·ous
cal'um·ny
calve, calved,
 calv'ing
Cal'vin·ism
Cal'vin·ist
Cal'vin·is'tic
Ca·lyp'so *or*
 ca·lyp'so
ca'lyx *pl.* -lyx·es *or*
 -ly·ces'
cal·zo'ne
cam
ca'ma·ra·der'ie
cam'ber
cam'bi·um
Cam'bri·an
Cam·bo'di·an
cam'bric

cam'cord'er
cam'el
ca·mel'lia
cam'el's hair'
Cam'em·bert'
cam'e·o' *pl.* -os'
cam'er·a
cam'er·a·man'
cam'er·a·wom'an
cam'i·sole'
cam'ou·flage',
 -flaged', -flag'ing
camp
cam·paign'
cam·paign'er
cam'pa·ni'le *pl.* -les
 or -li
camp'er
camp'fire'
Camp' Fire' Girl'
camp'ground'
cam'phor
camp'site'
cam'pus *pl.* -pus·es
cam'shaft'
can *aux. v., past tense*
 could
can *(to preserve),*
 canned, can'ning
Ca'naan·ite'
Ca·na'di·an
ca·nal'
ca·nard'
ca·nar'y
can'cel, -celed *also*
 -celled, -cel'ing
 also -cel·ling

can'cel•la'tion
can'cer
can'cer•ous
can•del'a
can•de•la'bra *pl.*
  -bras
can•de•la'brum *pl.*
  -bra *or* -brums
can'did
can'di•da•cy
can'di•date'
can'died
can'dle
can'dle•hold'er
can'dle•light'
can'dle•pin'
can'dle•pow'er
can'dle•snuff'er
can'dle•stick'
can'dle•wick'
can'dor
can'dy, -died, -dy•ing
can'dy strip'er
cane, caned, can'ing
cane'brake'
ca'nine
can'is•ter
can'ker
can'ker•ous
can'ker sore'
can'ker•worm'
can'na
can'na•bis
can'ner•y
can'ni•bal
can'ni•bal•ism
can'ni•bal•is'tic

can'ni•bal•ize',
  -ized', -iz'ing
can'ni•ly
can'non *(gun), pl.*
  -non
  ✔ *canon*
can'non•ade',
  -ad'ed, -ad'ing
can'non ball' *also*
  can'non ball'
can'non•eer'
can'not
can'ny
ca•noe', -noed',
  -noe'ing
ca•noe'ist
can'on *(church law,*
  cleric)
  ✔ *cannon*
ca•non'i•cal *also*
  ca•non'ic
can'on•i•za'tion
can'on•ize', -ized',
  -iz'ing
can'o•py, -pied,
  -py•ing
cant *(slope, jargon)*
can't *contraction*
can'ta•loupe' *also*
  can'ta•loup'
can•tan'ker•ous
can•ta'ta
can•teen'
can'ter *(gallop)*
  ✔ *cantor*
can'ti•cle
can'ti•le'ver

can'tle
can'to *pl.* -tos
can'ton
Can'ton•ese'
can•ton'ment
can'tor *(singer)*
  ✔ *canter*
can'vas *(cloth)*
  ✔ *canvass*
can'vas•back'
can'vass *(to ask for*
  votes)
  ✔ *canvas*
can'vass•er
can'yon *also* ca'ñon
caou'tchouc'
cap, capped,
  cap'ping
ca'pa•bil'i•ty
ca'pa•ble
ca'pa•bly
ca•pa'cious
ca•pac'i•tance
ca•pac'i•tate',
  -tat'ed, -tat'ing
ca•pac'i•tive
ca•pac'i•tor
ca•pac'i•ty
ca•par'i•son
cape
ca'per
cap'il•lar'y
cap'i•tal *(city,*
  wealth, letter)
  ✔ *capitol*
cap'i•tal•ism
cap'i•tal•ist

cap′i•tal•is′tic
cap′i•tal•i•za′tion
cap′i•tal•ize′, -ized′,
 -iz′ing
cap′i•tal
 pun′ish•ment
cap′i•tol *(building)*
 ✔ *capital*
ca•pit′u•late′,
 -lat′ed, -lat′ing
ca•pit′u•la′tion
cap′let
ca′pon′
cap′puc•ci′no *pl.*
 -nos
ca•price′
ca•pri′cious
cap′size′, -sized′,
 -siz′ing
cap′stan
cap′stone′
cap′su•lar
cap′su•late′ *also*
 cap′su•lat′ed
cap′su•la′tion
cap′sule
cap′sul•ize′, -ized′,
 -iz′ing
cap′tain
cap′tain•cy
cap′tion
cap′tious
cap′ti•vate′,
 -vat′ed, -vat′ing
cap′ti•va′tion
cap′ti•va′tor
cap′tive

cap•tiv′i•ty
cap′tor
cap′ture, -tured,
 -tur•ing
cap′u•chin
car
ca•rafe′
car′a•mel
car′a•pace′
car′at *(unit of weight)*
 ✔ *caret, carrot, karat*
car′a•van′
car′a•van•sa′ry *also*
 car′a•van′se•rai′ *pl.*
 -ries *also* -rais
car′a•vel′
car′a•way′
car′bide′
car′bine′
car′bo•hy′drate′
car′bo•lat′ed
car•bol′ic ac′id
car′bon
car′bo•na′ceous
car′bon•ate′, -at′ed,
 -at′ing
car′bon•a′tion
car′bon•a′tor
car•bon′ic
car′bon•if′er•ous
 (containing carbon)
Car′bon•if′er•ous
 (geologic period)
car′bon•i•za′tion
car′bon•ize′, -ized′,
 -iz′ing
car′bon•yl

car•box′yl
car′box•yl′ic
car′bun′cle
car′bu•re′tor
car′cass
car•cin′o•gen
car•cin′o•gen′ic
car•ci•no′ma *pl.*
 -mas *or* -ma•ta
car′da•mom *or*
 car′da•mon
card′board′
car′di•ac′
car′di•gan
car′di•nal
car′di•o•gram′
car′di•o•graph′
car′di•ol′o•gist
car′di•ol′o•gy
car′di•o•pul′mo•
 nar′y
car′di•o•vas′cu•lar
card′sharp′ *also*
 card′sharp′er
care, cared, car′ing
ca•reen′ *(to swerve,
 to tilt)*
ca•reer′ *(to rush)*
ca•reer′ *(profession)*
care′free′
care′ful
care′giv′er
care′less
ca•ress′
car′et *(proofreading
 mark)*
 ✔ *carat, carrot, karat*

care′tak′er
care′worn′
car′fare′
car′go *pl.* -goes *or*
  -gos
car′hop′
Car′ib *pl.* -ib *or* -ibs
Car′i•ban *pl.* -ban *or*
  -bans
Car′ib•be′an
car′i•bou′ *pl.* -bou′
  or -bous′
car′i•ca•ture′,
  -tured′, -tur′ing
car′i•ca•tur′ist
car′ies *pl.* -ies
car′il•lon′
car′jack′ *or*
  car′-jack′
car′load′
Car′mel•ite′
car′mine
car′nage
car′nal
car•nal′i•ty
car•na′tion
car•nel′ian
car′ni•val
car′ni•vore′
car•niv′o•rous
car′ob
car′ol *(song),* -oled
  also -olled, -ol•ing
  or -ol•ling
  ✔ *carrel*
car′ol•er *or*
  car′ol•ler

Car′o•lin′i•an
car′om
car′o•tene′
ca•rot′id
ca•rous′al *(revelry)*
  ✔ *carousel*
ca•rouse′, -roused′,
  -rous′ing
car′ou•sel′ *or*
  car′rou•sel′ *(merry-*
  go-round)
  ✔ *carousal*
ca•rous′er
carp *(to complain)*
carp *(fish), pl.* carp *or*
  carps
car′pal *(relating to*
  the carpus)
car′pel *(flower part)*
car′pen•ter
car′pen•try
car′pet
car′pet•bag′
car′pet•bag′ger
car′pet•ing
car′pool′ *n.*
car′-pool′ *v.*
car′-pool′er
car′port′
car′pus *pl.* -pi′
car′rel *also* car′rell
  (library nook)
  ✔ *carol*
car′riage
car′ri•er
car′ri•on
car′rot *(plant)*

✔ *carat, caret, karat*
car′ry, -ried, -ry•ing
car′ry•all′
car′ry•on′ *adj. & n.*
car′ry•out′ *adj.*
car′ry•o′ver *n.*
car′sick′
cart′age
carte blanche′ *pl.*
  cartes blanches′
car•tel′
Car•te′sian
car′ti•lage
car′ti•lag′i•nous
car•tog′ra•pher
car′to•graph′ic *or*
  car′to•graph′i•cal
car•tog′ra•phy
car′ton
car•toon′
car•toon′ist
car′tridge
cart′wheel′
carve, carved,
  carv′ing
carv′er
car′ wash′
car′y•at′id *pl.* -ids *or*
  -i•des′
ca•sa′ba *also*
  cas•sa′ba
cas•cade′, -cad′ed,
  -cad′ing
cas•car′a
case, cased, cas′ing
ca′sein′
case′load′

case'ment
case'work'
case'work'er
cash (money)
  ✔ cache
cash'ew
cash•ier' (person
  who receives money)
ca•shier' (to dismiss)
cash'mere'
ca•si'no (gambling
  house), pl. -nos
ca•si'no also
  cas•si'no (card
  game)
cask (barrel)
  ✔ casque
cas'ket
casque (helmet, cask)
  ✔ cask
cas•sa'va
cas'se•role'
cas•sette'
cas'sia
cas'sock
cas'so•war'y
cast (to throw), cast,
  cast'ing
  ✔ caste
cas'ta•nets'
cast'a•way'
caste (social class)
  ✔ cast
cas'tel•lat'ed
cast'er (person who
  casts)
cast'er also cas'tor

(wheel, bottle)
  ✔ castor
cas'ti•gate', -gat'ed,
  -gat'ing
cas'ti•ga'tion
cas'ti•ga'tor
Cas•tile' soap'
Cas•til'ian
cast' i'ron n.
cast'-i'ron adj.
cas'tle, -tled, -tling
cast'off' n.
cas'tor (oil)
  ✔ caster
cas'trate', -trat'ed,
  -trat'ing
cas•tra'tion
ca'su•al
ca'su•al•ty
ca'su•ist
ca'su•is'tic or
  ca'su•is'ti•cal
ca'su•ist•ry
cat
cat'a•bol'ic
ca•tab'o•lism
cat'a•clysm
cat'a•clys'mic
cat'a•combs'
cat'a•falque'
Cat'a•lan'
cat'a•lep'sy
cat'a•lep'tic
cat'a•log' or
  cat'a•logue',
  -loged' or -logued',
  -log'ing or

-logu'ing
cat'a•log'er or
  cat'a•logu'er
ca•tal'pa
ca•tal'y•sis pl. -ses'
cat'a•lyst
cat'a•lyt'ic
cat'a•lyze', -lyzed',
  -lyz'ing
cat'a•ma•ran'
cat'a•mount'
cat'a•pult'
cat'a•ract'
ca•tarrh'
ca•tas'tro•phe
cat'a•stroph'ic
cat'a•to'ni•a
cat'a•ton'ic
Ca•taw'ba pl. -ba or
  -bas
cat'bird'
cat'boat'
cat'call'
catch, caught,
  catch'ing
catch'all'
catch'er
catch'word'
catch'y
cat'e•chism
cat'e•chist
cat'e•chi•za'tion
cat'e•chize',
  -chized', -chiz'ing
cat'e•chu'men
cat'e•gor'i•cal
cat'e•go•ri•za'tion

cat'e•go•rize',
-rized', -riz'ing
cat'e•go'ry
cat'e•nate', -nat'ed,
-nat'ing
cat'e•na'tion
ca'ter
cat'er-cor'nered
also cat'er-cor'ner
or cat'ty-cor'nered
or cat'ty-cor'ner *or*
kit'ty-cor'nered *or*
kit'ty-cor'ner
ca'ter•er
cat'er•pil'lar
cat'er•waul'
cat'fish' *pl.* -fish' *or*
-fish'es
cat'gut'
ca•thar'sis
ca•thar'tic
ca•the'dral
cath'e•ter
cath'ode'
cath'ode-ray'
tube'
cath'o•lic *(universal)*
Cath'o•lic *(relating
to the Catholic
Church)*
Ca•thol'i•cism
cat'i'on
cat'kin
cat'nap', -napped',
-nap'ping
cat'nip'
cat'-o'-nine'-tails'

pl. cat'-o'-nine'-
tails'
CAT' scan'
cat's'-eye'
cat's'-paw' *also*
cats'paw'
cat'tail'
cat'ti•ness
cat'tle
cat'tle•man
cat'ty
cat'walk'
Cau•ca'sian
Cau'ca•soid'
cau'cus *pl.* -cus•es *or*
-cus•ses
cau'cus, -cused *or*
-cussed, -cus•ing *or*
-cus•sing
cau'dal
cau'li•flow'er
caulk *also* calk
caulk'er
caus'al
cau•sal'i•ty
cau•sa'tion
caus'a•tive
cause, caused,
caus'ing
cause cé•lè'bre *pl.*
causes cé•lè'bres
cause'way'
caus'tic
cau'ter•i•za'tion
cau'ter•ize', -ized',
-iz'ing
cau'tion

cau'tion•ar'y
cau'tious
cav'al•cade'
cav'a•lier'
cav'al•ry
cave, caved, cav'ing
ca've•at'
cave'-in' *n.*
cave'man' *also*
cave' man'
cav'ern
cav'ern•ous
cav'i•ar' *also*
cav'i•are'
cav'il, -iled *also*
-illed, -il'ing *or*
-il•ling
cav'i•ta'tion
cav'i•ty
ca•vort'
ca'vy
caw
cay *(islet)*
✔ key, quay
cay•enne' pep'per
Ca•yu'ga *pl.* -ga *or*
-gas
cay•use'
Cay•use' *pl.* -use' *or*
-us'es
CD/ROM
cease, ceased,
ceas'ing
cease'-fire' *or*
cease'fire'
cease'less
ce'cum *also*

cae'cum *pl.* -ca
ce'dar
ce'dar wax'wing'
cede *(to yield)*,
  ced'ed, ced'ing
  ✔ seed
ce·dil'la
ceil'ing
cel'an·dine'
cel'e·brant
cel'e·brate',
  -brat'ed, -brat'ing
cel'e·bra'tion
cel'e·bra'tor
cel'e·bra·to'ry
ce·leb'ri·ty
ce·ler'i·ty
cel'er·y
ce·les'ta *also*
  ce·leste'
ce·les'tial
cel'i·ba·cy
cel'i·bate
cell *(room, basic unit*
  of living matter)
  ✔ sell
cel'lar *(storage room)*
  ✔ seller
cell'block'
cel'list
cel'lo *pl.* -los
cel'lo·phane'
cel'lu·lar
cel'lu·lite'
cel'lu·loid'
cel'lu·lose'
Cel'si·us

Celt *also* Kelt
Celt'ic
ce·ment'
cem'e·ter'y
cen'o·bite'
cen'o·taph'
Ce'no·zo'ic
cen'ser *(container for*
  incense)
cen'sor *(examiner)*
cen·so'ri·ous
cen'sor·ship'
cen'sur·a·ble
cen'sure, -sured,
  -sur·ing
cen'sus
cent *(coin)*
  ✔ scent, sent
cen'taur'
cen·ta'vo *pl.* -vos
cen·te·nar'i·an
cen·ten'a·ry
cen·ten'ni·al
cen'ter
cen'ter·board'
cen'ter·fold'
cen'ter·piece'
cen·tes'i·mal
cen'ti·grade'
cen'ti·gram'
cen'ti·li'ter
cen'ti·me'ter
cen'ti·pede'
cen'tral
cen·tral'i·ty
cen'tral·i·za'tion

cen'tral·ize', -ized',
  -iz'ing
cen·trif'u·gal
cen·trif'u·ga'tion
cen'tri·fuge',
  -fuged', -fug'ing
cen'tri·ole'
cen·trip'e·tal
cen'trist
cen'tro·some'
cen·tu'ri·on
cen'tu·ry
ce·phal'ic
ceph'a·lo·pod'
ceph'a·lo·tho'rax'
Ce'phe·id
ce·ram'ic
ce·ram'ist
ce're·al *(grain)*
  ✔ serial
cer'e·bel'lum *pl.*
  -bel'lums *or* -bel'la
cer'e·bral
cer'e·bro·spi'nal
cer'e·brum *pl.*
  -brums *or* -bra
cere'cloth'
cer'e·ment
cer'e·mo'ni·al
cer'e·mo'ni·ous
cer'e·mo'ny
ce·rise'
ce'ri·um
cer'tain
cer'tain·ty
cer'ti·fi'a·ble
cer'ti·fi'a·bly

cer•tif′i•cate
cer′ti•fi•ca′tion
cer′ti•fy′, -fied′,
 -fy′ing
cer′ti•tude′
ce•ru′le•an
cer′vi•cal
cer′vix *pl.* -vix•es *or*
 -vi•ces′
ce•sar′e•an *also*
 cae•sar′e•an
ce′si•um *also*
 cae′si•um
ces•sa′tion
ces′sion *(surrender-*
 ing of territory)
 ✔ *session*
cess′pool′
ce•ta′cean
chafe *(to irritate)*,
 chafed, chaf′ing
chaff *(husks of grain)*
chaff *(to tease)*
chaff′er *(person who*
 teases)
chaf′fer *(to bargain)*
chaf′finch
chaf′ing dish′
cha•grin′
chain
chain′-re•act′
chain′ re•ac′tion
chain′ saw′
chain′-smoke′,
 -smoked′,
 -smok′ing
chair

chair′ lift′
chair′man
chair′per′son
chair′wom′an
chaise
chaise longue′ *pl.*
 chaise longues′ *or*
 chaises longues′
chaise lounge′
chal•ced′o•ny
cha•let′
chal′ice *(cup)*
 ✔ *challis*
chalk
chalk′board′
chalk′i•ness
chalk′y
chal′lah
chal′lenge, -lenged,
 -leng•ing
chal′leng•er
chal′lis *(fabric)*
 ✔ *chalice*
cham′ber
cham′ber•lain
cham′ber•maid′
cham′bray′
cha•me′leon
cham′ois *(antelope)*,
 pl. -ois
cham′ois *also*
 cham′my *or*
 sham′my *(soft*
 leather), *pl.* -ois *also*
 -mies
cham′o•mile′ *or*
 cam′o•mile′

champ
cham•pagne′
cham′pi•on
cham′pi•on•ship′
chance, chanced,
 chanc′ing
chan′cel
chan′cel•ler•y *or*
 chan′cel•lor•y
chan′cel•lor
chan′cer•y
chan′cre
chanc′y
chan′de•lier′
chan′dler
change, changed,
 chang′ing
change′a•bil′i•ty *or*
 change′a•ble•ness
change′a•ble
change′a•bly
change′ling
change′o′ver *n.*
chang′er
chan′nel, -neled
 also -nelled,
 -nel′ing *also*
 -nel′ling
chant
chant′er
chan•teuse′
chan′tey *also*
 chan′ty *or* shan′tey
 or shan′ty *(song)*,
 pl. -teys *also* -ties
 ✔ *shanty*
chan′ti•cleer′

cha•os'
cha•ot'ic
chap, chapped,
    chap'ping
chap'ar•ral'
cha•peau' *pl.*
    -peaus' *or* -peaux'
chap'el
chap'er•on' *or*
    chap'er•one',
    -oned', -on'ing
chap'lain
chap'let
chaps
chap'ter
char, charred,
    char'ring
char'ac•ter
char'ac•ter•is'tic
char'ac•ter•i•za'-
    tion
char•ac•ter•ize',
    -ized', -iz'ing
cha•rade'
char'coal'
chard *(Swiss chard)*
    ✔ *shard*
char'don•nay' *also*
    Char'don•nay'
charge, charged,
    charg'ing
charge'a•ble
char•gé'
    d'af•faires' *pl.*
    char•gés' d'af•faires'
charg'er
char'i•ness

char'i•ot
char'i•o•teer'
cha•ris'ma
char•is•mat'ic
char'i•ta•ble
char'i•ta•bly
char'i•ty
char'la•tan
Charles'ton
char'ley horse'
charm
charm'er
charm'ing
char'nel house'
chart
char'ter
char'ter•er
char'treuse'
char'wom'an
char'y
chase, chased,
    chas'ing
chas'er
chasm
chas'sis *pl.* -sis
chaste, chast'er,
    chast'est
chas'ten
chas•tise', -tised',
    -tis'ing
chas•tise'ment
chas•tis'er
chas'ti•ty
chas'u•ble
chat, chat'ted,
    chat'ting
cha•teau' *also*

châ•teau' *pl.*
    -teaus' *or* -teaux'
chat'e•laine'
chat'tel
chat'ter
chat'ter•box'
chat'ty
chat'ti•ness
chauf'feur
chau'vin•ism
chau'vin•ist
chau'vin•is'tic
cheap *(inexpensive)*
    ✔ *cheep*
cheap'en
cheap'skate'
cheat
cheat'er
check *(restraint, veri-*
    fication, bank order)
    ✔ *Czech*
check'book'
checked
check'er
check'er•board'
check'ered
check'list'
check'mate',
    -mat'ed, -mat'ing
check'out' *n.*
check'point'
check'rein'
check'room'
check'up' *n.*
Ched'dar
cheek
cheek'bone'

cheek'y
cheep *(chirp)*
  ✔ *cheap*
cheer'ful
cheer'lead'er
cheer'less
cheer'y
cheese'burg'er
cheese'cake'
cheese'cloth'
chees'i•ness
chees'y
chee'tah
chef
chef-d'oeu'vre *pl.*
  chefs-d'oeu'vre
che'la *pl.* -lae
chem'i•cal
che•mise'
chem'ist
chem'is•try
che'mo•syn'the•sis
chem'o•syn•thet'ic
che'mo•ther'a•
  peu'tic
che'mo•ther'a•py
che•nille'
cher'ish
Cher'o•kee' *pl.*
  -kee' *or* -kees'
che•root' *also*
  she•root'
cher'ry
cher'ry•stone'
cher'ub *pl.* -u•bim
  or -ubs
che•ru'bic

chess'board'
chess'man
chest
ches'ter•field'
chest'nut'
chev'a•lier'
Chev'i•ot
chev'ron
chew
chew'i•ness
chew'ing gum'
che•wink'
chew'y
Chey•enne' *pl.*
  -enne' *or* -ennes'
Chi•an'ti
chic *(stylish)*, chic'er,
  chic'est
  ✔ *sheik*
Chi•ca'na *pl.* -nas
chi•can'er•y
Chi•ca'no *pl.* -nos
chick
chick'a•dee'
Chick'a•saw' *pl.*
  -saw' *or* -saws'
chick'en
chick'en-heart'ed
chick'en-liv'ered
chick'en•pox' *or*
  chick'en pox'
chick'en wire'
chick'pea'
chick'weed'
chic'le
chic'o•ry
chide, chid'ed *or*

chid, chid'ed *or*
  chid *or* chid'den,
  chid'ing
chief
chief'tain
chif•fon'
chif'fo•nier'
chig'ger
chi•gnon'
chig'oe
Chi•hua'hua
chil'blain'
child *pl.* chil'dren
child'bear'ing
child'birth'
child'hood'
child'ish
child'like'
child'proof'
Chil'e•an
chil'i *(pepper)*, *pl.*
  -ies
  ✔ *chilly*
chil'i con car'ne
chill
chill'i•ness
chill'y *(cold)*
  ✔ *chili*
chime, chimed,
  chim'ing
chi•me'ra *also*
  chi•mae'ra
chi•mer'i•cal
chim'i•chan'ga
chim'ney *pl.* -neys
chimp
chim'pan•zee'

chin, chinned,
  chin'ning
chi'na
chi'na•ber'ry
Chi'na•town'
chi'na•ware'
chinch
chin•chil'la
chine
Chi•nese' *pl.* -nese'
chink
chi'no *pl.* -nos
Chi•nook' *pl.*
  -nook' *or* -nooks'
chin'qua•pin'
chintz
chintz'y
chin'-up' *n.*
chip, chipped,
  chip'ping
Chip'e•wy'an *pl.*
  -an *or* -ans
chip'munk'
chip'per
Chip'pe•wa *pl.* -wa'
  or -was'
chi•rop'o•dist
chi•rop'o•dy
chi'ro•prac'tic
chi'ro•prac'tor
chirp
chir'rup
chis'el, -eled *or*
  -elled, -el•ing *or*
  -el•ling
chis'el•er
chit'chat',

-chat'ted,
  -chat'ting
chi'tin (*horny sub-
  stance*)
  ✔ chiton
chi'tin•ous
chi'ton (*mollusk,
  tunic*)
  ✔ chitin
chit'ter•lings *also*
  chit'lins *or*
  chit'lings
chiv'al•rous
chiv'al•ry
chive
chlo'ral
chlo'rate'
chlor'dane' *also*
  chlor'dan'
chlo'ride'
chlo'ri•nate',
  -nat'ed, -nat'ing
chlo'ri•na'tion
chlo'rine'
chlo'rite'
chlo'ro•fluo'ro•
  car'bon
chlo'ro•form'
chlo'ro•phyll' *also*
  chlo'ro•phyl'
chlo'ro•plast' *also*
  chlo'ro•plas'tid
chock
chock'-full'
choc'o•late
Choc'taw *pl.* -taw
  or -taws

choice, choic'er,
  choic'est
choir (*singers*)
  ✔ quire
choir'boy'
choir'girl'
choke, choked,
  chok'ing
choke'cher'ry
choke'damp'
choke'hold'
chok'er
chol'er (*anger*)
  ✔ collar
chol'er•a
chol'er•ic
cho•les'ter•ol'
chomp
choose, chose,
  cho'sen, choos'ing
choos'er
choos'y *also*
  choos'ey
chop, chopped,
  chop'ping
chop'per
chop'pi•ness
chop'py
chops
chop'sticks'
chop' su'ey
cho'ral (*relating to a
  chorus*)
  ✔ coral
cho•rale' *also*
  cho•ral' (*hymn*)
  ✔ corral

chord (*musical tones,
  line segment*)
  ✔ *cord*
chord′al
chor′date′
chore
cho·re′a
cho′re·o·graph′
cho′re·og′ra·pher
cho′re·o·graph′ic
cho′re·og′ra·phy
cho′ric
cho′ri·on′
cho′ri·on′ic
cho′ris·ter
cho′roid′
chor′tle, -tled,
  -tling
cho′rus *pl.* -rus·es
cho′rus, -rused *or*
  -russed, -rus·ing *or*
  -rus·sing
cho′sen
chow
chow′der
chow′ mein′
chrism
chris′ten
Chris′ten·dom
chris′ten·ing
Chris′tian
Chris′ti·an′i·ty
Christ′mas
chro′mate′
chro·mat′ic
chro·ma·tin
chro′ma·tog′ra·

phy
chrome
chro′mic
chro′mite′
chro′mi·um
chro′mo·so′mal
chro′mo·some′
chro′mo·sphere′
chron′ic
chron′i·cle, -cled,
  -cling
chron′i·cler
chron′o·log′i·cal
chro·nol′o·gy
chro·nom′e·ter
chrys′a·lid
chrys′a·lis *pl.* -lis·es
  or chry·sal′i·des′
chry·san′the·mum
chub′bi·ness
chub′by
chuck
chuck′le, -led, -ling
chuck′wal′la
chug, chugged,
  chug′ging
chuk′ka
chum, chummed,
  chum′ming
chum′my
chump
chunk
chunk′i·ness
chunk′y
church
church′go′er
church′man

church′war′den
church′wom′an
church′yard′
churl
churl′ish
churn
chute (*vertical
  trough*)
  ✔ *shoot*
chut′ney
chutz′pah
chyle
chyme
ci·ca′da *pl.* -das *or*
  -dae′
ci′der
ci′gar′
cig′a·rette′
cil′i·a *sing.* -i·um
cil′i·ar′y
cil′i·ate
cinch
cin·cho′na
Cin′co de Ma′yo
cinc′ture
cin′der
cin′der block′ *or*
  cin′der·block′
cin′e·ma
cin′e·mat′ic
cin′e·ma·tog′ra·
  pher
cin′e·ma·tog′ra·
  phy
cin′na·bar′
cin′na·mon
ci′pher *also* cy′pher

cir'ca
cir·ca'di·an
cir'cle, -cled, -cling
cir'clet
cir'cuit
cir·cu'i·tous
cir'cuit·ry
cir'cu·lar
cir'cu·lar'i·ty
cir'cu·lar·ize',
  -ized', -iz'ing
cir'cu·late', -lat'ed,
  -lat'ing
cir'cu·la'tion
cir'cu·la·to'ry
cir·cum·cise',
  -cised', -cis'ing
cir·cum·ci'sion
cir·cum'fer·ence
cir·cum·flex'
cir·cum·lo·cu'tion
cir·cum·nav'i·
  gate', -gat'ed,
  -gat'ing
cir·cum·nav'i·ga'-
  tion
cir·cum·scribe',
  -scribed', -scrib'ing
cir·cum·scrip'tion
cir·cum·spect'
cir·cum·spec'tion
cir·cum·stance
cir'cum·stan'tial
cir'cum·stan'ti·ate'
cir'cum·stan'ti·a'-
  tion
cir'cum·vent'

cir'cum·ven'tion
cir'cus
cir·rho'sis
cir'ro·cu'mu·lus
cir'ro·stra'tus
cir'rus *pl.* -ri'
cis'tern
cit'a·del
ci·ta'tion
cite *(to quote)*, cit'ed,
  cit'ing
  ✔ *sight, site*
cit'i·zen
cit'i·zen·ry
cit'i·zen·ship'
cit'rate'
cit'ric ac'id
cit'ron
cit'ro·nel'la
cit'rus *pl.* cit'rus
cit'y
cit'y-state'
cit'y·wide'
civ'et
civ'ic
civ'il
ci·vil'ian
ci·vil'i·ty
civ'i·li·za'tion
civ'i·lize', -lized',
  -liz'ing
clab'ber
clack *(noise)*
  ✔ *claque*
clad, clad, clad'ding
claim
claim'ant

clair·voy'ance
clair·voy'ant
clam, clammed,
  clam'ming
clam'bake'
clam'ber
clam'mi·ness
clam'my
clam'or
clam'or·ous
clamp
clam'shell'
clan
clan·des'tine
clang
clan'gor
clank
clan'nish
clans'man
clans'wom'an
clap, clapped,
  clap'ping
clap'board
clap'per
clap'trap'
claque *(group)*
  ✔ *clack*
clar'et
clar'i·fi·ca'tion
clar'i·fy', -fied',
  -fy'ing
clar'i·net'
clar'i·net'ist *or*
  clar'i·net'tist
clar'i·on
clar'i·ty
clash

clasp
class
clas'sic
clas'si•cal
clas'si•cism
clas'si•cist
clas'si•fi'a•ble
clas'si•fi•ca'tion
clas'si•fi'er
clas'si•fy', -fied',
  -fy'ing
class'mate'
class'room'
class'y
clat'ter
clause
claus'tro•pho'bi•a
clav'i•chord'
clav'i•cle
cla•vier'
claw
clay
clay'ey *or* clay'ish
clean
clean'-cut'
clean'er
clean'li•ness
cleanse, cleansed,
  cleans'ing
cleans'er
clean'-shav'en
clean'up' *n. & adj.*
clear
clear'ance
clear'-cut'
clear'-eyed'
clear'ing

clear'ing-house' *or*
  clear'ing•house'
clear'-sight'ed
cleat
cleav'age
cleave *(to split)*, cleft
  or cleaved *or* clove,
  cleft *or* cleaved *or*
  clo'ven, cleav'ing
cleave *(to adhere)*,
  cleaved, cleav'ing
cleav'er
clef
cleft
clem'a•tis
clem'en•cy
clem'ent
clench
cler'gy
cler'gy•man
cler'gy•wom'an
cler'ic
cler'i•cal
clerk
clev'er
clew *(ball of yarn)*
  ✔ *clue*
clew *also* clue *(corner
  of a sail)*
  ✔ *clue*
cli•ché'
click *(sound)*
  ✔ *clique*
cli'ent
cli'en•tele'
cliff
cliff' dwell'er

cliff'hang'er
cli•mac'ter•ic
cli•mac'tic *also*
  cli•mac'ti•cal *(relat-
  ing to a climax)*
  ✔ *climatic*
cli'mate
cli•mat'ic *(relating
  to climate)*
  ✔ *climactic*
cli'ma•tol'o•gy
cli'max'
climb *(ascent)*
  ✔ *clime*
climb'a•ble
climb'er
clime *(climate)*
  ✔ *climb*
clinch
clinch'er
cling, clung,
  cling'ing
cling'stone'
clin'ic
clin'i•cal
cli•ni'cian
clink
clink'er
clip, clipped,
  clip'ping
clip'board'
clip'per
clique *(group)*
  ✔ *click*
cliqu'ey *or* cliqu'y
  or cliqu'ish
clit'o•ris

clo•a′ca *pl.* -cae′
cloak
cloak′room′
clob′ber
clock
clock′wise′
clock′work′
clod
clod′hop′per
clog, clogged,
  clog′ging
clois′ter
clomp
clone, cloned,
  clon′ing
clop, clopped,
  clop′ping
close, clos′er,
  clos′est
close *(to shut)*,
  closed, clos′ing
  ✔ *clothes*
closed′-cap′tioned
closed′ cir′cuit
close′-fist′ed
close′-knit′
close′ly
close′-mouthed′
close′out′
clos′et
close′-up′ *n.*
clo′sure
clot, clot′ted,
  clot′ting
cloth *n.*
clothe, clothed *or*
  clad, cloth′ing

clothes *(garments)*
  ✔ *close*
clothes′horse′
clothes′line′
clothes′pin′
cloth′ier
cloth′ing
clo′ture
cloud
cloud′burst′
cloud′i•ness
cloud′y
clout
clove
clo′ven
clo′ver
clo′ver•leaf′
clown
cloy
club, clubbed,
  club′bing
club′foot′
club′foot′ed
club′house′
cluck
clue *(to give informa-*
  tion), clued,
  clue′ing *or* clu′ing
  ✔ *clew*
clump
clump′y
clum′si•ly
clum′si•ness
clum′sy
clunk′y
clus′ter
clutch

clut′ter
coach
coach′man
co•ag′u•lant
co•ag′u•late′,
  -lat′ed, -lat′ing
co•ag′u•la′tion
coal *(fuel)*
  ✔ *kohl*
co•a•lesce′, -lesced′,
  -lesc′ing
co′a•les′cence
co′a•les′cent
co′a•li′tion
co-an′chor *or*
  co•an′chor *n.*
co-an′chor *v.*
coarse *(rough)*,
  coars′er, coars′est
  ✔ *course*
coars′en
coast
coast′al
coast′er
coast′line′
coat *(garment)*
  ✔ *cote*
co•a′ti
co•a′ti•mun′di
coat′ing
coat′room′
coat′tail′
co•au′thor
coax
co•ax′i•al
cob
co′balt′

cob'ble, -bled,
    -bling
cob'bler
cob'ble•stone'
CO'BOL'
co'bra
cob'web'
co'ca
co•caine'
coc'cus *pl.* -ci
coc'cyx *pl.*
    coc•cy'ges
coch'i•neal'
coch'le•a *pl.* -le•ae'
    also -le•as
cock
cock•ade'
cock'a•too' *pl.*
    -toos'
cock'a•trice
cock'er•el
cock'er span'iel
cock'eyed'
cock'fight'
cock'horse'
cock'i•ness
cock'le
cock'le•bur'
cock'le•shell'
cock'ney *pl.* -neys
cock'pit'
cock'roach'
cocks'comb'
cock'sure'
cock'tail'
cock'y
co'coa

co'coa but'ter
co'co•nut' *also*
    co'coa•nut'
co•coon'
cod *pl.* cod *or* cods
co'da
cod'dle, -dled,
    -dling
code, cod'ed,
    cod'ing
co'de•fen'dant
co'deine'
co'dex' *pl.* -di•ces'
cod'fish'
codg'er
cod'i•cil
cod'i•fi•ca'tion
cod'i•fi'er
cod'i•fy', -fied',
    -fy'ing
cod'-liv'er oil'
co•ed' *or* co'-ed'
co•ed'u•ca'tion
co•ef•fi'cient
coe'la•canth'
coe•len'ter•ate'
co•en'zyme
co•e'qual
co•erce', -erced',
    -erc'ing
co•erc'er
co•erc'i•ble
co•er'cion
co•er'cive
co•e'val
co'ex•ist'
co'ex•is'tence

co'ex•is'tent
co'ex•tend'
co'ex•ten'sive
cof'fee
cof'fee break'
cof'fee•cake'
cof'fee•house'
cof'fee•mak'er *also*
    cof'fee mak'er
cof'fee•pot'
cof'fee shop'
cof'fer
cof'fin
co•found'
co'func'tion
cog
co'gen•cy
co'gent
cog'i•tate', -tat'ed,
    -tat'ing
cog'i•ta'tion
co'gnac'
cog'nate'
cog•ni'tion
cog'ni•tive
cog'ni•zance
cog'ni•zant
cog•no'men *pl.*
    -no'mens *or*
    -nom'i•na
co'gno•scen'te *pl.*
    -ti
cog'wheel'
co•hab'it
co•hab'i•tant
co•hab'i•ta'tion
co•here' *(to stick to-*

gether), -hered',
-her'ing
✔ adhere
co•her'ence
co•her'en•cy
co•her'ent
co•he'sion
co•he'sive
co'hort'
coif
coif•feur' (hair-
dresser)
coif•fure' (hairstyle)
coil
coin (money)
✔ quoin
coin'age
co•in'cide', -cid'ed,
-cid'ing
co•in'ci•dence
co•in'ci•dent
co•in'ci•den'tal
co'i•tus
coke
co'la
col'an•der
cold
cold'-blood'ed
cold'-call' or cold'
call' v.
cold'-heart'ed
cole'slaw'
co'le•us
col'ic
col'ick•y
col•i'se•um also
col'os•se'um

co•li'tis
col•lab'o•rate',
-rat'ed, -rat'ing
col•lab'o•ra'tion
col•lab'o•ra'tor
col•lage'
col'la•gen
col•lapse', -lapsed',
-laps'ing
col•laps'i•ble
col'lar (neck band)
✔ choler
col'lar•bone'
col'lard
col•late', -lat'ed,
-lat'ing
col•lat'er•al
col•la'tion
col'league'
col•lect'
col•lect'a•ble or
col•lect'i•ble
col•lect'ed
col•lec'tion
col•lec'tive
col•lec'tiv•ism
col•lec'tiv•ist
col•lec'tiv•i•za'-
tion
col•lec'tiv•ize',
-ized', -iz'ing
col•lec'tor
col'lege
col•le'gian
col•le'giate
col•lide', -lid'ed,
-lid'ing

col'lie
col'lier
col'lier•y
col•lin'e•ar
col•li'sion
col'lo•cate'
col'lo•ca'tion
col'loid'
col•loi'dal
col•lo'qui•al
col•lo'qui•al•ism
col•lo'qui•um pl.
-qui'ums or -qui•a
col'lo•quy pl.
col'lo•quies
col•lude', -lud'ed,
-lud'ing
col•lu'sion
col•lu'sive
co•logne'
Co•lom'bi•an (re-
lating to Colombia)
✔ Columbian
co'lon (punctuation
mark), pl. -lons
co'lon (intestine), pl.
-lons or -la
colo'nel (officer)
✔ kernel
co•lo'ni•al
co•lo'ni•al•ism
col'o•nist
col'o•ni•za'tion
col'o•nize', -nized',
-niz'ing
col'o•niz'er
col'on•nade'

col'o·ny
col'o·phon'
col'or
Col'o·ra'dan
col'or·a'tion
col'or·a·tu'ra
col'or·blind' *or*
  col'or-blind'
col'or·blind'ness
col'or-code',
  -cod'ed, -cod'ing
col'ored
col'or·er
col'or·fast'
col'or·ful
col'or·im'e·ter
col'or·ing
col'or·i·za'tion
col'or·ize', -ized',
  -iz'ing
col'or·less
co·los'sal
co·los'sus *pl.* -los'si'
  or -los'sus·es
colt
colt'ish
Co·lum'bi·an *(re-
lating to the U. S.)*
  ✔ Colombian
col'um·bine'
col'umn
co·lum'nar
col'um·nist
co'ma *(state of un-
consciousness), pl.*
  -mas
co'ma *(gas cloud), pl.*

-mae
Co·man'che *pl.*
  -che *or* -ches
co'ma·tose'
comb
com·bat', -bat'ed *or*
  -bat'ted, -bat'ing *or*
  -bat'ting
com'bat' *n.*
com·bat'ant
com·bat'ive
comb'er
com·bi·na'tion
com·bine', -bined',
  -bin'ing
com'bine' *n.*
com'bo *pl.* -bos
com·bus'ti·bil'i·ty
com·bus'ti·ble
com·bus'ti·bly
com·bus'tion
come, came, come,
  com'ing
come'back' *n.*
co·me'di·an
co·me'dic
co·me'di·enne'
come'down' *n.*
com'e·dy
come'li·ness
come'ly
come'-on' *n.*
com'er
co·mes'ti·ble
com'et
com'fit
come'up'pance

com'fort
com'fort·a·ble
com'fort·a·bly
com'fort·er
com'fy
com'ic
com'i·cal
com'ing
com'ing-out' *n.*
com'ma
com·mand'
com'man·dant'
com'man·deer'
com·mand'er
com·mand'er in
  chief' *pl.*
  com·mand'ers in
  chief'
com·mand'ing
com·mand'ment
com·man'do *pl.*
  -dos *or* -does
com·mem'o·rate',
  -rat'ed, -rat'ing
com·mem'o·ra'-
  tion
com·mem'o·ra·
  tive
com·mem'o·ra'tor
com·mem'o·ra·
  to'ry
com·mence',
  -menced',
  -menc'ing
com·mence'ment
com·mend'
com·mend'a·ble

com·mend′a·bly
com′men·da′tion
com·men′da·to·ry
com·men′sal
com·men′sal·ism
com·men′su·ra·ble
com·men′su·ra·bly
com·men′su·rate
com′ment
com′men·tar′y
com′men·tate′,
  -tat′ed, -tat′ing
com′men·ta′tor
com′merce
com·mer′cial
com·mer′cial·ism
com·mer′cial·i·za′-
tion
com·mer′cial·ize′,
  -ized′, -iz′ing
com·min′gle,
  -gled, -gling
com·mis′er·ate′,
  -at′ed, -at′ing
com·mis′er·a′tion
com·mis′er·a′tive
com·mis′er·a′tor
com′mis·sar
com′mis·sar′i·at
com′mis·sar′y
com·mis′sion
com·mis′sion·er
com·mit′, -mit′ted,
  -mit′ting
com·mit′ta·ble
com·mit′tal
com·mit′ment

com·mit′tee
com·mit′tee·man
com·mit′tee·
  wom′an
com·mix′
com·mix′ture
com·mode′
com·mo′di·ous
com·mod′i·ty
com′mo·dore′
com′mon
com·mon·al′i·ty
com′mon·al·ty
com′mon·er
com′mon-law′ *adj.*
com′mon·place′
com′mon sense′ *n.*
com′mon·sense′
  adj.
com′mon·sen′si·
ble
com′mon·weal′
com′mon·wealth′
com·mo′tion
com·mu′nal
com·mu·nal′i·ty
com·mune′,
  -muned′, -mun′ing
com′mune′ *n.*
com·mu′ni·ca·
bil′i·ty
com·mu′ni·ca·ble
com·mu′ni·ca·bly
com·mu′ni·cant
com·mu′ni·cate′,
  -cat′ed, -cat′ing
com·mu′ni·ca′tion

com·mu′ni·ca′tive
com·mu′ni·ca′tor
com·mun′ion
com·mu′ni·qué′
com′mu·nism *also*
  Com′mu·nism
Com′mu·nist *also*
  com′mu·nist
com·mu·nis′tic
com·mu′ni·ty
com·mu·ta′tion
com′mu·ta′tive
com′mu·ta′tor
com·mute′,
  -mut′ed, -mut′ing
com·mut′er
com·pact′ *adj. & v.*
com′pact′ *n.*
com·pact disk′ *or*
  com′pact disc′
com·pac′tor *or*
  com·pact′er
com·pan′ion
com·pan′ion·a·
bil′i·ty
com·pan′ion·a·ble
com·pan′ion·a·bly
com·pan′ion·ship′
com·pan′ion·way′
com′pa·ny
com′pa·ra·ble
com′pa·ra·bly
com·par′a·tive
com·pare′, -pared′,
  -par′ing
com·par′i·son
com·part′ment

com'part·men'tal·
 ize', -ized', -iz'ing
com'pass
com·pas'sion
com·pas'sion·ate
com·pat'i·bil'i·ty
com·pat'i·ble
com·pat'i·bly
com·pa'tri·ot
com·pel', -pelled',
 -pel'ling
com·pen'di·ous
com·pen'di·um *pl.*
 -di·ums *or* -di·a
com'pen·sate',
 -sat'ed, -sat'ing
com'pen·sa'tion
com'pen·sa'tor
com·pen'sa·to'ry
com·pete', -pet'ed,
 -pet'ing
com'pe·tence
com'pe·ten·cy
com'pe·tent
com'pe·ti'tion
com·pet'i·tive
com·pet'i·tor
com'pi·la'tion
com·pile', -piled',
 -pil'ing
com·pil'er
com·pla'cence
com·pla'cen·cy
com·pla'cent *(self-
 satisfied)*
 ✔ complaisant
com·plain'

com·plain'ant
com·plaint'
com·plai'sance
com·plai'sant
 (willing)
 ✔ complacent
com'ple·ment
 *(something that
 completes)*
 ✔ compliment
com'ple·men'ta·ry
 (completing)
 ✔ complimentary
com·plete', -plet'er,
 -plet'est
com·plete',
 -plet'ed, -plet'ing
com·ple'tion
com·plex' *adj.*
com'plex' *n.*
com·plex'ion
com·plex'i·ty
com·pli'ance
com·pli'an·cy
com·pli'ant
com'pli·cate',
 -cat'ed, -cat'ing
com'pli·ca'tion
com·plic'it
com·plic'i·ty
com'pli·ment
 (praise)
 ✔ complement
com'pli·men'ta·ry
 (praising)
 ✔ complementary
com·ply', -plied',

-ply'ing
com·po'nent
com·port'
com·port'ment
com·pose', -posed',
 -pos'ing
com·pos'ed·ly
com·pos'er
com·pos'ite
com'po·si'tion
com·pos'i·tor
com·post'
com·po'sure
com'pote
com·pound' *v.*
com'pound' *adj.
 & n.*
com·pound'a·ble
com·pound'er
com'pre·hend'
com'pre·hend'i·
 ble
com'pre·hen'si·
 bil'i·ty
com'pre·hen'si·ble
com'pre·hen'si·bly
com'pre·hen'sion
com'pre·hen'sive
com·press'
com·pressed'
com·press'i·bil'i·ty
com·press'i·ble
com·pres'sion
com·pres'sor
com·prise',
 -prised', -pris'ing
com'pro·mise',

-mised', -mis'ing
com·pul'sion
com·pul'sive
com·pul'so·ry
com·punc'tion
com·put'a·ble
com·pu·ta'tion
com·pute', -put'ed,
-put'ing
com·put'er
com·put'er·i·za'-
tion
com·put'er·ize',
-ized', -iz'ing
com'rade
com'rade·ship'
con, conned,
con'ning
con·cat'e·nate',
-nat'ed, -nat'ing
con·cat'e·na'tion
con·cave'
con·cav'i·ty
con·ceal'
con·ceal'a·ble
con·ceal'er
con·ceal'ment
con·cede', -ced'ed,
-ced'ing
con·ceit'
con·ceit'ed
con·ceiv'a·bil'i·ty
con·ceiv'a·ble
con·ceive',
-ceived', -ceiv'ing
con·ceiv'er
con'cen·trate',

-trat'ed, -trat'ing
con'cen·tra'tion
con'cen·tra'tor
con·cen'tric
con'cept'
con·cep'tion
con·cep'tu·al
con·cep'tu·al·ism
con·cep'tu·al·ist
con·cep'tu·al·i·za'-
tion
con·cep'tu·al·ize',
-ized', -iz'ing
con·cern'
con·cerned'
con·cern'ing
con'cert
con·cert'ed
con·cer'ti'na
con·cer'to *pl.* -tos
or -ti
con·ces'sion
con·ces'sion·aire'
conch *(mollusk), pl.*
conchs *or* conch'es
✔ conk
con·cierge'
con·cil'i·ate',
-at'ed, -at'ing
con·cil'i·a'tion
con·cil'i·a'tor
con·cil'i·a·to'ry
con·cise'
con·cise'ly
con'clave'
con·clude',
-clud'ed, -clud'ing

con·clud'er
con·clu'sion
con·clu'sive
con·clu'sive·ly
con·clu'so·ry
con·coct'
con·coc'tion
con·com'i·tance
con·com'i·tant
con'cord'
con·cor'dance
con'course'
con·cres'cence
con·cres'cent
con·crete' *adj.*
con'crete' *n.*
con·crete'ly
con·cu'bine'
con·cur', -curred',
-cur'ring
con·cur'rence
con·cur'rent
con·cus'sion
con·demn'
con'dem·na'tion
con·dens'a·ble *or*
con·dens'i·ble
con'den·sate'
con'den·sa'tion
con·dense',
-densed', -dens'ing
con·dens'er
con'de·scend'
con'de·scend'ing
con'de·scen'sion
con·di·ment
con·di'tion

con·di′tion·al
con·di′tioned
con·di′tion·er
con·di′tion·ing
con′do pl. -dos
con·dole′, -doled′,
  -dol′ing
con·do′lence
con′dom
con·do·min′i·um
con·done′,
  -doned′, -don′ing
con′dor
con·duce′, -duced′,
  -duc′ing
con·du′cive
con·du′cive·ness
con·duct′ v.
con′duct′ n.
con·duc′tance
con·duct′i·bil′i·ty
con·duct′i·ble
con·duc′tion
con·duc′tive
con′duc·tiv′i·ty
con·duc′tor
con′du·it
cone
Con′es·to′ga
  wag′on
co′ney also co′ny pl.
  -neys also -nies
con·fab′ n.
con·fab′, -fabbed′,
  -fab′bing
con·fab′u·late′,
  -lat′ed, -lat′ing

con·fab′u·la′tor
con·fec′tion
con·fec′tion·er
con·fec′tion·er′y
con·fed′er·a·cy
con·fed′er·ate′,
  -at′ed, -at′ing
con·fed′er·a′tion
con·fer′, -ferred′,
  -fer′ring
con′fer·ence
con·fess′
con·fes′sion
con·fes′sion·al
con·fes′sor
con·fet′ti
con′fi·dant′ (friend)
  ✓ confident
con′fi·dante′ (fe-
  male friend)
  ✓ confident
con·fide′, -fid′ed,
  -fid′ing
con′fi·dence
con′fi·dent (certain)
  ✓ confidant, confi-
  dante
con′fi·den′tial
con′fi·den′ti·al·i·
  ty
con·fid′er
con·fid′ing
con·fig′u·ra′tion
con·fig′u·ra′tive or
  con·fig′u·ra′tion·al
con·fig′ure
con·fine′, -fined′,

-fin′ing
con·fine′ment
con′fines′
con·firm′
con′fir·ma′tion
con·firmed′
con·firm′ed·ly
con·fis·cate′,
  -cat′ed, -cat′ing
con′fis·ca′tion
con′fis·ca′tor
con′fla·gra′tion
con′flict′ n.
con·flict′ v.
con·flic′tive
con′flu·ence
con′flu·ent
con·form′
con·form′a·ble
con′for·ma′tion
con·form′er
con·form′ist
con·form′i·ty
con·found′
con′fra·ter′ni·ty
con·front′
con′fron·ta′tion
Con·fu′cian
Con·fu′cian·ism
con·fuse′, -fused′,
  -fus′ing
con·fus′ed·ly
con·fu′sion
con′fu·ta′tion
con·fute′, -fut′ed,
  -fut′ing
con·fut′er

con·geal′
con·geal′ment
con·gen′ial
con·ge′ni·al′i·ty
con·gen′i·tal
con′ger
con·gest′
con·ges′tion
con·ges′tive
con·glom′er·ate′,
 -at′ed, -at′ing
con·glom′er·a′-
 tion
Con′go·lese′ *pl.*
 -lese′
con·grat′u·late′,
 -lat′ed, -lat′ing
con·grat′u·la′tion
con·grat′u·la·to′ry
con′gre·gate′,
 -gat′ed, -gat′ing
con′gre·ga′tion
con′gre·ga′tion·al
con′gre·ga′tion·al·
 ism *also* Con′gre·
 ga′tion·al·ism
con′gre·ga′tion·al·
 ist *also* Con′gre·
 ga′tion·al·ist
con′gre·ga′tor
con′gress *also*
 Con′gress
con·gres′sion·al
con′gress·man
con′gress·wom′an
con′gru·ence
con′gru·en·cy

con′gru·ent
con·gru′i·ty
con′ic
con′i·cal
con′i·fer
co·nif′er·ous
con·jec′tur·al
con·jec′ture,
 -tured, -tur·ing
con·join′
con·join′er
con·joint′
con′ju·gal
con′ju·gate′,
 -gat′ed, -gat′ing
con′ju·ga′tion
con·junc′tion
con·junc′ti·va *pl.*
 -vas *or* -vae
con·junc′tive
con·junc′ti·vi′tis
con′jure, -jured,
 -jur′ing
con′jur·er *also*
 con′jur·or
conk (*hit*)
 ✓ conch
con·nect′
con·nect′er *or*
 con·nec′tor
con·nect′i·ble
con·nec′tion
con·nec′tive
con·niv′ance
con·nive′, -nived′,
 -niv′ing
con′nois·seur′

con′no·ta′tion
con′no·ta·tive
con·note′, -not′ed,
 -not′ing
con·nu′bi·al
con′quer
con′quer·a·ble
con′quer·or *or*
 con′quer·er
con′quest′
con·quis′ta·dor′ *pl.*
 -dors′ *or* -dor·es
con·san·guin′e·ous
con·san·guin′i·ty
con′science
con′sci·en′tious
con′scious
con′script′ *n.*
con·script′ *v.*
con·scrip′tion
con′se·crate′,
 -crat′ed, -crat′ing
con′se·cra′tion
con′se·cra·tor
con·sec′u·tive
con·sec′u·tive·ly
con·sen′sus
con·sent′
con′se·quence
con′se·quent
con′se·quen′tial
con·serv′a·ble
con′ser·va′tion
con′ser·va′tion·ist
con·ser′va·tism
con·ser′va·tive
con·ser′va·tor

con•ser′va•to•ry
con•serve′,
  -served′, -serv′ing
con•sid′er
con•sid′er•a•ble
con•sid′er•a•bly
con•sid′er•ate
con•sid′er•ate•ly
con•sid′er•a′tion
con•sid′ered
con•sid′er•ing
con•sign′
con•sign′a•ble
con•sign′ment
con•sist′
con•sis′ten•cy
con•sis′tent
con•sis′to•ry
con•sol′a•ble
con′so•la′tion
con•sole′, -soled′,
  -sol′ing
con′sole′ *n.*
con•sol′i•date′,
  -dat′ed, -dat′ing
con•sol′i•da′tor
con•sol′i•da′tion
con′som•mé′
con′so•nance
con′so•nant
con′so•nan′tal
con′sort′ *n.*
con•sort′ *v.*
con•sor′ti•um *pl.*
  -ti•a
con•spec′tus
con•spic′u•ous

con•spir′a•cy
con•spir′a•tor
con•spir′a•to′ri•al
con•spire′, -spired′,
  -spir′ing
con•spir′er
con•sta•ble
con•stab′u•lar′y
con′stan•cy
con′stant
con′stel•la′tion
con′ster•na′tion
con′sti•pate′,
  -pat′ed, -pat′ing
con′sti•pa′tion
con•stit′u•en•cy
con•stit′u•ent
con′sti•tute′,
  -tut′ed, -tut′ing
con′sti•tu′tion
con′sti•tu′tion•al
con′sti•tu′tion•
  al′i•ty
con′sti•tu′tion•al•
  ize′, -ized′, -iz′ing
con′sti•tu′tive
con•strain′
con•strain′ed•ly
con•strain′er
con•straint′
con•strict′
con•stric′tion
con•stric′tive
con•stric′tor
con•struct′
con•struc′tion
con•struc′tion•al

con•struc′tive
con•struc′tive•ly
con•struc′tive•ness
con•struc′tor
con•strue′, -strued′,
  -stru′ing
con′sul
con′su•lar
con′su•late
con•sult′
con•sult′ant
con′sul•ta′tion
con•sul′ta•tive
con•sum′a•ble
con•sume′,
  -sumed′, -sum′ing
con•sum′er
con•sum′er•ism
con′sum•mate′,
  -mat′ed, -mat′ing
con′sum•mate•ly
con′sum•ma′tion
con•sump′tion
con•sump′tive
con′tact′
con•ta′gion
con•ta′gious
con•tain′
con•tain′a•ble
con•tain′er
con•tain′er•ize′,
  -ized′, -iz′ing
con•tain′ment
con•tam′i•nant
con•tam′i•nate′,
  -nat′ed, -nat′ing
con•tam′i•na′tion

con•tam′i•na′tor
con•temn′
con′tem•plate′,
   -plat′ed, -plat′ing
con′tem•pla′tive
con′tem′pla•tive
con′tem′pla•tive•ly
con′tem′pla•tor
con•tem′po•ra′ne•
   ous
con•tem′po•rar′y
con•tempt′
con•tempt′i•ble
con•tempt′i•bly
con•temp′tu•ous
con•tend′
con•tend′er
con•tent′ *n.*
con•tent′ *adj. & v.*
con•tent′ed
con•ten′tion
con•ten′tious
con•tent′ment
con′test′ *n.*
con•test′ *v.*
con•test′a•ble
con•tes′tant
con′text′
con•tex′tu•al
con•tex′tu•al•i•
   za′tion
con•tex′tu•al•ize′,
   -ized′, -iz′ing
con′ti•gu′i•ty
con•tig′u•ous
con′ti•nence
con′ti•nent

con′ti•nen′tal
con•tin′gen•cy
con•tin′gent
con•tin′u•al
con•tin′u•ance
con•tin′u•a′tion
con•tin′ue, -ued,
   -u•ing
con′ti•nu′i•ty
con•tin′u•ous
con•tin′u•um *pl.*
   -u•a *or* -u•ums
con•tort′
con•tor′tion
con•tor′tion•ist
con′tour
con′tra•band′
con′tra•bass′
con′tra•bas•soon′
con′tra•cep′tion
con′tra•cep′tive
con′tract′ *n.*
con•tract′ *v.*
con•tract′i•ble
con•trac′tile′
con•trac′tion
con•trac′tor
con•trac′tu•al
con′tra•dict′
con′tra•dic′tion
con′tra•dic′to•ri•ly
con′tra•dic′tor•i•
   ness
con′tra•dic′to•ry
con′tra•dis•tinc′-
   tion
con•tral′to *pl.* -tos

con•trap′tion
con′tra•pun′tal
con′tra•pun′tist
con′trar′i•ly
con′trar′i•ness
con′trar′i•wise′
con•trar′y *(com-
   pletely different)*
con•trar′y *(willful)*
con′tra•vene′,
   -vened′, -ven′ing
con′tra•ven′tion
con′tre•danse′ *also*
   con′tre•dance′ *or*
   con′tra•dance′ *or*
   con′tra•danse′
con′tre•temps′ *pl.*
   -temps′
con•trib′ute′,
   -ut′ed, -ut′ing
con′tri•bu′tion
con•trib′u•tive
con•trib′u•tor
con•trib′u•to′ry
con•trite′
con•tri′tion
con•tri′vance
con•trive′, -trived′,
   -triv′ing
con•triv′er
con•trol′, -trolled′,
   -trol′ling
con•trol′la•ble
con•trol′ler *also*
   comp•trol′ler

con'tro·ver'sial
con'tro·ver'sy
con'tro·vert'
con'tro·vert'i·ble
con'tu·ma'cious
con'tu·ma·cy
con'tu·me'li·ous
con'tu·me·ly
con·tuse', -tused',
  -tus'ing
con·tu'sion
co·nun'drum
con'va·lesce',
  -lesced', -lesc'ing
con'va·les'cence
con'va·les'cent
con·vect'
con·vec'tion
con·vene', -vened',
  -ven'ing
con·ven'ience
con·ven'ient
con'vent
con·ven'tion
con·ven'tion·al
con·ven'tion·al'i·
  ty
con·verge',
  -verged', -verg'ing
con·ver'gence
con·ver'gent
con·ver'sant
con'ver·sa'tion
con'ver·sa'tion·al
con'ver·sa'tion·al·
  ist
con·verse',

-versed', -vers'ing
con'verse' n.
con·verse'ly
con·ver'sion
con·vert' v.
con'vert' n.
con·vert'er
con·vert'i·bil'i·ty
con·vert'i·ble
con·vert'i·bly
con·vex'
con·vex'i·ty
con·vey'
con·vey'ance
con·vey'er also
  con·vey'or
con·vict' v.
con'vict' n.
con·vic'tion
con·vince',
  -vinced', -vinc'ing
con·vinc'i·ble
con·viv'i·al
con·viv'i·al'i·ty
con'vo·ca'tion
con·voke', -voked',
  -vok'ing
con'vo·lut'ed
con'vo·lu'tion
con'voy'
con·vulse',
  -vulsed', -vuls'ing
con·vul'sion
con·vul'sive
coo (to murmur),
  cooed, coo'ing
  ✔ coup

cook
cook'book'
cook'er
cook'er·y
cook'ie also cook'y
  pl. -ies
cook'out'
cool
cool'ant
cool'er
cool'-head'ed
cool'ly (in a cool
  manner)
  ✔ coulee
coon'skin'
coop (cage)
  ✔ coupe
co'-op' n.
coop'er
co·op'er·ate',
  -at'ed, -at'ing
co·op'er·a'tion
co·op'er·a·tive
co·op'er·a·tive·ly
co-opt'
co·or'di·nate adj.
co·or'di·nate',
  -nat'ed, -nat'ing
co·or'di·na'tion
co·or'di·na'tor
coot
coo'tie
cop
cope, coped, cop'ing
co'pe·pod'
Co·per'ni·can
cop'i·er

co'pi'lot
cop'ing
co'pi•ous
co•pla'nar
co•pol'y•mer
cop'-out' *also* cop'out'
cop'per
cop'per•as
cop'per•head'
cop'per•plate'
cop'per•smith'
cop'per•y
cop'pice
co'pra
copse
Copt
cop'ter
Cop'tic
cop'u•la
cop'u•late', -lat'ed, -lat'ing
cop'u•la'tion
cop'y, -ied, -y•ing
cop'y•book'
cop'y•cat'
cop'y•ed'it *or* cop'y-ed'it
cop'y•ed'i•tor
cop'y•ist
cop'y•right'
cop'y•writ'er
co'quet•ry
co•quette'
co•quet'tish
co•qui'na
cor'a•cle

cor'al *(stony sub-stance)*
  ✔ *choral*
cor'bel
cord *(rope)*
  ✔ *chord*
cord'age
cord'ed
cor'dial
cor•dial'i•ty
cor'dil•le'ra
cord'ite'
cord'less
cor'do•ba
cor'don
cor'do•van
cor'du•roy'
cord'wood'
core *(to remove the center)*, cored, cor'ing
  ✔ *corps*
cor'er
co'ri•an'der
Co•rin'thi•an
cork
cork'er
cork'screw'
cork'y
corm
cor'mo•rant
corn
corn' bread' *or* corn'bread'
corn'cob'
corn'crib'
cor'ne•a

cor'ner
cor'ner•stone'
cor•net'
cor•net'ist *also* cor•net'tist
corn'field'
corn' flakes'
corn'flow'er
corn'husk'
cor'nice
Cor'nish
corn'meal' *also* corn' meal'
corn'pone' *or* corn' pone'
corn'stalk'
corn'starch'
cor'nu•co'pi•a
corn'y
co•rol'la
cor'ol•lar'y
co•ro'na *pl.* -nas *or* -nae
cor'o•nar'y
cor'o•na'tion
cor'o•ner
cor'o•net'
cor'po•ral
cor'po•rate
cor'po•ra'tion
cor•po're•al
corps *(military unit)*, *pl.* corps
  ✔ *core, corpse*
corps' de bal•let'
corpse *(body)*
  ✔ *corps*

corps'man
cor'pu·lence
cor'pu·lent
cor'pus *pl.* -po·ra
cor'pus·cle
cor·ral' *(enclosed area)*, -ralled', -ral'ling
  ✔ *chorale*
cor·rect'
cor·rec'tion
cor·rec'tive
cor're·late', -lat'ed, -lat'ing
cor're·la'tion
cor·rel'a·tive
cor're·spond'
cor're·spon'dence
cor're·spon'dent
cor're·spond'ing
cor'ri·dor
cor·rob'o·rate', -rat'ed, -rat'ing
cor·rob'o·ra'tion
cor·rob'o·ra'tive
cor·rob'o·ra'tor
cor·rode', -rod'ed, -rod'ing
cor·ro'sion
cor·ro'sive
cor'ru·gate', -gat'ed, -gat'ing
cor'ru·ga'tion
cor·rupt'
cor·rupt'er
cor·rupt'i·ble
cor·rupt'i·bil'i·ty

cor·rupt'i·bly
cor·rup'tion
cor·sage'
cor'sair'
cor'se·let
cor'set
Cor'si·can
cor'tege'
cor'tex' *pl.* -ti·ces' *or* -tex'es
cor'ti·cal
cor'ti·sone'
co·run'dum
cor·us·cate', -cat'ed, -cat'ing
cor·us·ca'tion
cor·vette'
cor'ymb
co·se'cant'
co·sign' *(to sign jointly)*
co'sine' *(mathematical function)*
cos·met'ic
cos'me·tol'o·gist
cos'me·tol'o·gy
cos'mic
cos·mog'o·ny
cos·mog'ra·phy
cos'mo·log'i·cal
cos·mol'o·gist
cos·mol'o·gy
cos'mo·naut'
cos'mo·pol'i·tan
cos'mos
Cos'sack
cos'set

cost
cos'tal
co'star' *also* co'-star'
Cos'ta Ri'can
cost'-ef·fec'tive
cost'li·ness
cost'ly
cos'tume', -tumed', -tum'ing
cos'tum'er
cot
co·tan'gent
cote *(shed)*
  ✔ *coat*
co'ter·ie
co·til'lion *also* co·til'lon
cot'tage
cot'tag·er
cot'ter pin'
cot'ton
cot'ton·mouth'
cot'ton·seed'
cot'ton·tail'
cot'ton·wood'
cot'ton·y
cot'y·le'don
couch
cou'gar
cough
could
could'n't
cou'lee *(ravine)*
  ✔ *coolly*
cou'lomb'
coul'ter
coun'cil *(group)*

✔ *counsel*

coun'cil•man

coun'cil•or *also*
coun'cil•lor *(member of a council)*
✔ *counselor*

coun'cil•wom'an

coun'sel *(to advise)*,
-seled *or* -selled,
-sel•ing *or* -sel•ling
✔ *council*

coun'sel•or *also*
coun'sel•lor *(adviser)*
✔ *councilor*

count

count'a•ble

count'down'

coun'te•nance,
-nanced, -nanc•ing

coun'ter *(contrary)*

count'er *(flat surface, small object, one that counts)*

coun'ter•act'

coun'ter•at•tack'

coun'ter•bal'ance
n.

coun'ter•bal'ance,
-anced, -anc•ing

coun'ter•claim' *n.*

coun'ter•claim' *v.*

coun'ter•clock'-
wise'

coun'ter•cul'ture

coun'ter•cur'rent

coun'ter•dem'on•
stra'tion

coun'ter•es'pi•o•
nage'

coun'ter•feit'

coun'ter•feit'er

coun'ter•in•tel'li•
gence

coun'ter•mand'

coun'ter•march' *n.*

coun'ter•meas'ure
n.

coun'ter•mine' *v.*

coun'ter•move' *n.*

coun'ter•of•fen'-
sive

coun'ter•of'fer *n.*

coun'ter•pane'

coun'ter•part'

coun'ter•point'

coun'ter•poise',
-poised', -pois'ing

coun'ter•pro•duc'-
tive

coun'ter•rev'o•lu'-
tion

coun'ter•rev'o•lu'-
tion•ar'y

coun'ter•sign'

coun'ter•sink',
-sunk', -sink'ing

coun'ter•spy'

coun'ter•ten'or

coun'ter•weight'

count'ess

count'less

coun'tri•fied'

coun'try

coun'try•man

coun'try•side'

coun'try•wom'an

coun'ty

coup *(stratagem)*, *pl.*
coups
✔ *coo*

coup' d'é•tat' *pl.*
coups' d'é•tat' *or*
coup' d'é•tats'

coupe *(dessert)*
✔ *coop*

cou•pé' *also* coupe
(car)

cou'ple, -pled,
-pling

cou'pler

cou'plet

cou'pling

cou'pon'

cour'age

cou•ra'geous

cou'ri•er

course *(to flow)*,
coursed, cours'ing
✔ *coarse*

cours'er

court

cour'te•ous

cour'te•san

cour'te•sy

court'house'

court'i•er

court'li•ness

court'ly

court'-mar'tial *pl.*
courts'-mar'tial

court'-mar'tial,
  -tialed *also* -tialled,
  -tial•ing *or* -tial•ling
court'room'
court'ship'
court'yard'
cous'in *(relative)*
  ✔ *cozen*
co•va'lence
co•va'lent
cove
cov'en
cov'e•nant
cov'er
cov'er•age
cov'er•alls'
cov'er•ing
cov'er•let
cov'ert
cov'er-up' *or*
  cov'er•up' *n.*
cov'et
cov'et•ous
cov'ey *pl.* -eys
cow
cow'ard
cow'ard•ice
cow'ard•li•ness
cow'ard•ly
cow'bell'
cow'bird'
cow'boy'
cow'catch'er
cow'er
cow'girl'
cow'hand'
cow'herd'

cow'hide'
cowl
cow'lick'
cowl'ing
cow'man
co'work'er
cow'poke'
cow'pox'
cow'punch'er
cow'rie *or* cow'ry *pl.*
  -ries
cow'slip'
cox'comb'
cox'swain
coy
coy•o'te
coy'pu *pl.* -pus
coz'en *(to deceive)*
  ✔ *cousin*
coz'en•er
co'zi•ly
co'zi•ness
co'zy
crab, crabbed,
  crab'bing
crab'bed *adj.*
crab'ber
crab'bi•ly
crab'by
crab'grass' *or* crab'
  grass'
crack
crack'down' *n.*
cracked
crack'er
crack'er•jack'
crack'ing

crack'le, -led, -ling
crack'pot'
crack'up' *or*
  crack'-up' *n.*
cra'dle, -dled, -dling
craft *(skill)*, *pl.* crafts
craft *(boat or plane)*,
  pl. craft
craft'i•ly
crafts'man
crafts'man•ship'
crafts'wom'an
craft'y
crag
crag'gi•ness
crag'gy
cram, crammed,
  cram'ming
cramp
cramped
cram'pon'
cran'ber'ry
crane, craned,
  cran'ing
cra'ni•al
cra'ni•um *pl.*
  -ni•ums *or* -ni•a
crank
crank'case'
crank'shaft'
crank'y
cran'ny
crape
crap'pie *pl.* -pies
craps
crash
crash'-land'

crass

crate, crat'ed,
 crat'ing

cra'ter

cra·vat'

crave, craved,
 crav'ing

cra'ven

craw

crawl

crawl'er

cray'fish' also
 craw'fish' pl. -fish'
 or -fish'es

cray'on'

craze, crazed,
 craz'ing

cra'zi·ly

cra'zi·ness

cra'zy

creak (squeak)
 ✔ creek

creak'i·ness

creak'y

cream

cream'er

cream'er·y

cream'i·ness

cream'y

crease, creased,
 creas'ing

cre·ate', -at'ed,
 -at'ing

cre·a'tion

cre·a'tion·ism

cre·a'tive

cre·a'tive·ly

cre·a·tiv'i·ty or
 cre·a'tive·ness

cre·a'tor

crea'ture

crèche

cre'dence

cre·den'tial

cred'i·bil'i·ty

cred'i·ble

cred'i·bly

cred'it

cred'it·a·bil'i·ty or
 cred'it·a·ble·ness

cred'it·a·ble

cred'it·a·bly

cred'i·tor

cre'do pl. -dos

cre·du'li·ty

cred'u·lous

Cree pl. Cree or
 Crees

creed

creek (stream)
 ✔ creak

Creek pl. Creek or
 Creeks

creel

creep, crept,
 creep'ing

creep'er

creep'i·ness

creep'y

cre·mate', -mat'ed,
 -mat'ing

cre·ma'tion

cre·ma'to'ri·um pl.
 -ri·ums or -ri·a

cre'ma·to'ry

Cre'ole'

cre'o·sol'

cre'o·sote', -sot'ed,
 -sot'ing

crepe also crêpe

crepe' pap'er

cre·pus'cu·lar

cres·cen'do pl. -dos
 or -di

cres'cent

cress

cres'set

crest

crest'fall'en

Cre·ta'ceous

Cre'tan (relating to
 Crete)
 ✔ cretin

cre'tin (person with
 cretinism)
 ✔ Cretan

cre'tin·ism

cre·tonne'

cre·vasse' (chasm)

crev'ice (narrow
 crack)

crew

crew' cut' or
 crew'cut'

crew'el (yarn)
 ✔ cruel

crew'el·work'

crib, cribbed,
 crib'bing

crib'bage

crick

crick'et
crick'et•er
cri'er
crime
Cri•me'an
crim'i•nal
crim'i•nal•ist
crim'i•nal•is'tics
crim'i•no•log'i•cal
crim'i•nol'o•gist
crim'i•nol'o•gy
crimp
crimp'y
crim'son
cringe, cringed,
  cring'ing
cring'er
crin'kle, -kled,
  -kling
crin'kly
cri'noid'
crin'o•line
crip'ple, -pled,
  -pling
crip'pler
cri'sis pl. -ses
crisp
crisp'i•ness
crisp'y
criss'cross'
cri•te'ri•on pl. -ri•a
  or -ri•ons
crit'ic
crit'i•cal
crit'i•cism
crit'i•cize', -cized',
  -ciz'ing

crit'i•ciz'er
cri•tique', -tiqued',
  -tiqu'ing
crit'ter
croak
Croat
Cro•a'tian
cro•chet'
crock
crock'er•y
croc'o•dile'
cro'cus pl. -cus•es
croft
croft'er
crois•sant'
Cro-Mag'non
crone
cro'ny
crook
crook'ed
croon
croon'er
crop, cropped,
  crop'ping
crop'-dust'ing
crop'land'
crop'per
cro•quet' *(game)*
cro•quette' *(small
  cake)*
cro'sier or cro'zier
cross
cross'bar'
cross'beam'
cross'bill'
cross'bones'
cross'bow'

cross'breed', -bred',
  -breed'ing
cross'-coun'try
cross'-cul'tur•al
cross'cur'rent
cross'cut', -cut',
  -cut'ting
cross'-ex•am'i•na'-
  tion
cross'-ex•am'ine,
  -ined, -in'ing
cross'-ex•am'in•er
cross'-eyed'
cross'-fer'til•i•za'-
  tion
cross'-fer'til•ize',
  -ized', -iz'ing
cross'fire'
cross'-grained'
cross'hatch'
cross'ing
cross'-leg'ged
cross'o'ver *n.*
cross'piece'
cross'-pol'li•nate',
  -nat'ed, -nat'ing
cross'-pol'li•na'-
  tion
cross'-pur'pose'
cross'-re•fer',
  -ferred', -fer'ring
cross'-ref'er•ence
cross'road'
cross' sec'tion
cross'-stitch'
cross'-town' or
  cross'town'

cross'walk'
cross'way'
cross'wise' *also*
cross'ways'
cross'word' puz'-
zle
crotch
crotch'et
crotch'et•i•ness
crotch'et•y
crouch
croup
croup'y
crou'ton'
crow
Crow *pl.* Crow *or*
Crows
crow'bar'
crowd
crown
crown' prince'
crown' prin'cess
crow's'-feet'
crow's'-nest'
cru'cial
cru'ci•ble
cru'ci•fi'er
cru'ci•fix'
cru'ci•fix'ion
cru'ci•form'
cru'ci•fy', -fied',
-fy'ing
crud'dy
crude, crud'er,
crud'est
crude'ly
cru'di•ty

cru'el *(merciless)*,
-el•er *or* -el•ler,
-el•est *or* -el•lest
✔ crewel
cru'el•ty
cru'et
cruise *(travel)*,
cruised, cruis'ing
✔ cruse
cruise' mis'sile
cruis'er
crul'ler
crumb
crum'ble, -bled,
-bling
crum'bli•ness
crum'bly
crum'my
crum'pet
crum'ple, -pled,
-pling
crunch
crunch'y
cru•sade', -sad'ed,
-sad'ing
cru•sad'er
cruse *(small bottle)*
✔ cruise
crush
crush'a•ble
crush'er
crust
crus•ta'cean
crust'i•ness
crust'y
crutch
crux *pl.* crux'es *or*

cru'ces
cry, cried, cry'ing
cry'ba'by
cry'o•bank'
cry'o•gen
cry'o•gen'ic
cry'o•gen'ics
cry•on'ics
crypt
cryp'tic
cryp'to•gram'
cryp'to•graph'
cryp•tog'ra•pher
cryp•to•graph'ic
cryp•tog'ra•phy
crys'tal
crys'tal•line
crys'tal•li•za'tion
crys'tal•lize',
-lized', -liz'ing
crys'tal•log'ra•phy
cub
Cu'ban
cub'by•hole'
cube, cubed,
cub'ing
cu'bic
cu'bi•cal *(cubic)*
cu'bi•cle *(small room)*
cub'ism
cub'ist
cu'bit
Cub' Scout'
cuck'old
cuck'old•ry
cuck'oo *pl.* -oos

cu'cum·ber

cud

cud'dle, -dled,
 -dling

cud'dly

cudg'el, -eled or
 -elled, -el·ing or
 -el·ling

cue *(stick, signal)*
 ✔ *queue*

cue *(to strike with a
 stick, to signal)*,
 cued, cu'ing
 ✔ *queue*

cue' ball'

cuff

cuff' link' or
 cuff'link'

cui·rass'

cui·sine'

cul'-de-sac' *pl.*
 culs'-de-sac' or
 cul'-de-sacs'

cu'li·nar'y

cull

culm

cul'mi·nate',
 -nat'ed, -nat'ing

cul'mi·na'tion

cu'lottes'

cul'pa·bil'i·ty

cul'pa·ble

cul'pa·bly

cul'prit

cult

cul'ti·vate', -vat'ed,
 -vat'ing

cul'ti·va'tion

cul'ti·va'tor

cul'tur·al

cul'ture, -tured,
 -tur·ing

cul'vert

cum'ber

cum'ber·some

cum'brous

cum'in

cum lau'de

cum'mer·bund'

cu'mu·la'tive

cu'mu·lo·nim'bus
 pl. -bus·es or -bi

cu'mu·lus *pl.* -li'

cu'ne·i·form'

cun'ning

cup, cupped,
 cup'ping

cup'board

cup'cake'

cup'ful'

cu'pid

cu·pid'i·ty

cu'po·la

cu'pric

cu'prous

cur

cur'a·bil'i·ty

cur'a·ble

cu·ra're *also* cu·ra'ri

cu'rate

cu'ra·tive

cu·ra'tor

curb

curb'ing

curb'side' *n.* & *adj.*

curb'stone'

curd

cur'dle, -dled,
 -dling

cure, cured, cur'ing

cu·ré'

cure'-all'

cu'ret·tage'

cu·rette' *also* cu·ret'

cur'few

cu'rie

cu'ri·o' *pl.* -os'

cu'ri·os'i·ty

cu'ri·ous

cu'ri·um

curl

curl'er

cur'lew

curl'i·cue'

curl'i·ness

curl'ing

curl'y

cur·mudg'eon

cur'rant *(fruit)*
 ✔ *current*

cur'ren·cy

cur'rent *(present-
 day)*
 ✔ *currant*

cur'rent *(electric
 charge)*
 ✔ *currant*

cur·ric'u·lar

cur·ric'u·lum *pl.* -la
 or -lums

cur'ry, -ried, -ry·ing

cur′ry•comb′

curse, cursed *or*
curst, curs′ing

curs′ed *also* curst
adj.

curs′er *(person who
curses)*
✔ cursor

cur′sive

cur′sor *(indicator)*
✔ curser

cur•so′ri•al

cur′so•ri•ly

cur′so•ry

curt

cur•tail′

cur•tail′ment

cur′tain

curt′sy *or* curt′sey
pl. -sies *or* -seys

curt′sy *or* curt′sey,
-sied *or* -seyed,
-sy•ing *or* -sey•ing

cur•va′ceous

cur′va•ture

curve, curved,
curv′ing

curve′ ball′ *or*
curve′ball′

cur′vi•lin′e•ar

cush′ion

cush′y

cusp

cus′pid

cus′pi•dor′

cuss

cus′tard

cus•to′di•al

cus•to′di•an

cus′to•dy

cus′tom

cus′tom•ar′i•ly

cus′tom•ar′y

cus′tom-built′

cus′tom•er

cus′tom•house′
also cus′toms•
house′

cus′tom•ize′, -ized′,
-iz′ing

cus′tom-made′

cut, cut, cut′ting

cut′-and-dried′
also cut′-and-dry′

cu•ta′ne•ous

cut′a•way′

cute, cut′er, cut′est

cu′ti•cle

cut′ie *also* cut′ey

cu′tin

cut′lass *also* cut′las

cut′ler•y

cut′let

cut′off′ *n.*

cut′out′ *n.*

cut′-rate′

cut′ter

cut′throat′

cut′ting

cut′tle•bone′

cut′tle•fish′

cut′up′ *n.*

cut′worm′

cy′an′

cy′a•nide′

cy′a•no′sis

cy′a•not′ic

cy′ber•net′ic

cy′ber•punk′

cy′ber•space′

cy′cad′

cy′cla•mate′

cy′cla•men

cy′cle, -cled, -cling

cy′clic *or* cy′cli•cal

cy′clist

cy′clone′

cy•clon′ic

Cy′clops *pl.*
Cy•clo′pes

cy′clo•ram′a

cy′clo•tron′

cyg′net *(young
swan)*
✔ signet

cyl′in•der

cy•lin′dri•cal *also*
cy•lin′dric

cym′bal *(instru-
ment)*
✔ symbol

cyn′ic

cyn′i•cal

cyn′i•cism

cy′no•sure′

cy′press

Cyp′ri•ot *also*
Cyp′ri•ote′

Cy•ril′lic

cyst

cys'tic
cys'tic fi·bro'sis
cys·ti'tis
cy·to·log'i·cal
cy·tol'o·gist
cy·tol'o·gy
cy'to·plasm
cy'to·plas'mic
cy'to·plast'
cy'to·sine'
czar *also* tsar *or* tzar
czar'e·vitch'
cza·rev'na
cza·ri'na
czar'ist
cza·rit'za
Czech (*relating to the Czech Republic*)
  ✔ *check*
Czech'o·slo'vak *or* Czech'o·slo·va'ki·an

D

dab, dabbed, dab'bing
dab'ble, -bled, -bling
dab'bler
da ca'po
dace *pl.* dace *or* dac'es
dachs'hund'
dac'tyl
dac·tyl'ic

dad'dy
daddy long'legs'
  pl. daddy long'legs'
da'do *pl.* -does
daf'fo·dil
daf'fy
dag'ger
da·guerre'o·type'
dahl'ia
dai'ly
dain'ty
dai·qui'ri *pl.* -ris
dair'y
dair'y·ing
dair'y·maid'
dair'y·man
dair'y·wom'an
da'is
dai'sy
Da·ko'tan
dale
dal'li·ance
dal'ly, -lied, -ly·ing
Dal·ma'tian
dam (*barrier, to restrain*), dammed, dam'ming
  ✔ *damn*
dam (*female animal*)
  ✔ *damn*
dam'age, -aged, -ag·ing
dam'ask
dame
damn (*to condemn*)
  ✔ *dam*
dam'na·ble

dam·na'tion
damned
damp'en
damp'er
dam'sel
dam'sel·fly'
dam'son
dance, danced, danc'ing
danc'er
dance'wear'
dan·de·li'on
dan'der
dan'di·fy', -fied', -fy'ing
dan'dle, -dled, -dling
dan'druff
dan'dy
Dane (*native of Denmark*)
  ✔ *deign*
dan'ger
dan'ger·ous
dan'gle, -gled, -gling
Dan'ish
dap'per
dap'ple, -pled, -pling
dare, dared, dar'ing
dare'dev'il
dare'say'
dar'ing
dark'en
dar'kling
dark'room'

dar'ling
darn
Dar·win'i·an
Dar'win·ism
dash'board'
dash'ing
das'tard
da'ta
da'ta·base'
dat'a·ble *or*
   date'a·ble
da'ta proc'ess·ing
date, dat'ed, dat'ing
date'line'
da'tive
da'tum *pl.* -ta *also*
   -tums
daub
daugh'ter
daugh'ter-in-law'
   pl. daugh'ters-in-
   law'
daunt
dau'phin
dav'en·port'
dav'it
daw
daw'dle, -dled,
   -dling
dawn
day'break'
day'care' *or* day'
   care'
day'dream',
   -dreamed' *or*
   -dreamt',
   -dream'ing

day'light'
day'light-sav'ing
   time'
day'long'
day'school'
day'star'
day'time'
day'-to-day'
daze, dazed, daz'ing
daz'zle, -zled, -zling
dea'con
dea'con·ess
dea'con·ry
de·ac'ti·vate',
   -vat'ed, -vat'ing
de·ac'ti·va'tion
dead
dead'beat'
dead'en
dead'end' *n.*
dead'-end' *adj.*
dead'head'
dead'line'
dead'lock'
dead'pan'
dead'wood'
deaf'en
deal, dealt, deal'ing
deal'er
deal'er·ship'
dean
dean'er·y
dear *(beloved)*
   ✔ *deer*
dearth
death
death'bed'

death'blow'
death's'-head'
death'trap'
de·ba'cle
de·bar', -barred',
   -bar'ring
de·bark'
de·bar·ka'tion
de·base', -based',
   -bas'ing
de·base'ment
de·bat'a·ble
de·bate', -bat'ed,
   -bat'ing
de·bauch'
de·bauch'er·y
de·bil'i·tate',
   -tat'ed, -tat'ing
de·bil'i·ta'tion
de·bil'i·ta'tive
de·bil'i·ty
de·bone', -boned',
   -bon'ing
deb'it
deb'o·nair' *also*
   deb'o·naire'
de·brief'
de·bris' *also* dé·bris'
debt
debt'or
de·bug', -bugged',
   -bug'ging
de·bunk'
de·but' *also* dé·but'
deb'u·tante'
dec'ade'
dec'a·dence

dec'a·dent
de·caf'fein·at'ed
dec'a·gon'
dec'a·he'dron *pl.*
 -drons *or* -dra
de'cal'
de·cal'ci·fi·ca'tion
de·cal'ci·fy', -fied',
 -fy'ing
dec'a·li'ter
de·camp'
de·cant'
de·cant'er
de·cap'i·tate',
 -tat'ed, -tat'ing
de·cap'i·ta'tion
de·car'bon·ate',
 -at'ed, -at'ing
de·cath'lon
de·cay'
de·cease', -ceased',
 -ceas'ing
de·ce'dent
de·ceit'
de·ceit'ful
de·ceive', -ceived',
 -ceiv'ing
de·ceiv'er
de·cel'er·ate',
 -at'ed, -at'ing
de·cel'er·a'tion
de·cel'er·a'tor
De·cem'ber
de'cen·cy
de'cent *(proper)*
 ✔ *descent, dissent*
de·cen'tral·i·za'-

tion
de·cen'tral·ize',
 -ized', -iz'ing
de·cep'tion
de·cep'tive
dec'i·bel
de·cide', -cid'ed,
 -cid'ing
de·cid'u·ous
dec'i·gram'
dec'i·li'ter
dec'i·mal
dec'i·mate',
 -mat'ed, -mat'ing
dec'i·ma'tion
dec'i·me'ter
de·ci'pher
de·ci'pher·a·ble
de·ci'sion
de·ci'sive
de·claim'
dec'la·ma'tion
de·clam'a·to'ry
de·clar'a·ble
dec'la·ra'tion
de·clar'a·tive
de·clare', -clared',
 -clar'ing
de·class'i·fi·ca'tion
de·class'i·fy', -fied',
 -fy'ing
de·claw'
de·clen'sion
dec'li·na'tion
de·cline', -clined',
 -clin'ing
de·cliv'i·ty

de·coct'
de·coc'tion
de·code', -cod'ed,
 -cod'ing
de·cod'er
dé·colle·tage'
dé·colle·té'
de'com·mis'sion
de'com·pos'a·ble
de'com·pose',
 -posed', -pos'ing
de'com·po·si'tion
de'com·press'
de'com·pres'sion
de'con·gest'
de'con·ges'tant
de'con·tam'i·nate',
 -nat'ed, -nat'ing
de'con·tam'i·na'-
 tion
de'con·trol',
 -trolled', -trol'ling
dé'cor' *or* de·cor'
dec'o·rate', -rat'ed,
 -rat'ing
dec'o·ra'tion
dec'o·ra'tive
dec'o·ra'tor
dec'o·rous
de·co'rum
de'coy'
de·crease',
 -creased',
 -creas'ing
de'crease' *n.*
de·cree', -creed',
 -cree'ing

dec're•ment
de•crep'it
de•crep'i•tude'
de'cre•scen'do *pl.*
  -dos
de•crim'i•nal•i•za'-
  tion
de•crim'i•nal•ize',
  -ized', -iz'ing
de•cry', -cried',
  -cry'ing
ded'i•cate, -cat'ed,
  -cat'ing
ded'i•ca'tion
ded'i•ca•to'ry
de•duce', -duced',
  -duc'ing
de•duc'i•ble
de•duct'
de•duct'i•ble
de•duc'tion
de•duc'tive
deed
dee'jay'
deem
deep
deep'en
deep'-fry', -fried',
  -fry'ing
deep' fry'er
deep'-root'ed
deep'-sea' *adj.*
deep'-seat'ed
deer *(animal), pl.*
  deer
  ✔ *dear*
deer'skin'

de-es'ca•late',
  -lat'ed, -lat'ing
de-es'ca•la'tion
de•face', -faced',
  -fac'ing
de•face'ment
de fac'to
def'a•ma'tion
de•fam'a•to'ry
de•fame', -famed',
  -fam'ing
de•fault'
de•feat'
de•feat'ism
de•feat'ist
def'e•cate', -cat'ed,
  -cat'ing
def'e•ca'tion
de'fect' *n.*
de•fect' *v.*
de•fec'tion
de•fec'tive
de•fec'tor
de•fend'
de•fen'dant
de•fense'
de•fense'less
de•fen'si•ble
de•fen'sive
de•fer', -ferred',
  -fer'ring
de•fer'ra•ble
def'er•ence *(submis-
  sion)*
  ✔ *difference*
def'er•en'tial
de•fer'ment

de•fi'ance
de•fi'ant
de•fib'ril•late',
  -lat'ed, -lat'ing
de•fi'cien•cy
de•fi'cient
def'i•cit
de•file', -filed',
  -fil'ing
de•file'ment
de•fine', -fined',
  -fin'ing
def'i•nite *(clear)*
  ✔ *definitive*
def'i•ni'tion
de•fin'i•tive *(final)*
  ✔ *definite*
de•flate', -flat'ed,
  -flat'ing
de•fla'tion
de•flect'
de•flec'tion
de•flec'tive
de•flec'tor
de•fog', -fogged',
  -fog'ging
de•fog'ger
de•fo'li•ant
de•fo'li•ate', -at'ed,
  -at'ing
de•fo'li•a'tion
de•for'est
de•for'es•ta'tion
de•form'
de'for•ma'tion
de•formed'
de•for'mi•ty

de•fraud'
de•fray'
de•frost'
de•frost'er
de•funct'
de•fuse', -fused',
  -fus'ing
de•fy', -fied', -fy'ing
de•gen'er•a•cy
de•gen'er•ate *adj.*
de•gen'er•ate',
  -at'ed, -at'ing
de•gen'er•a'tion
de•gen'er•a•tive
de•glu'ti'tion
de•grad'a•ble
deg'ra•da'tion
de•grade', -grad'ed,
  -grad'ing
de•gree'
de•hisce', -hisced',
  -hisc'ing
de•his'cence
de•his'cent
de•hu'man•i•za'-
  tion
de•hu'man•ize',
  -ized', -iz'ing
de'hu•mid'i•fi•ca'-
  tion
de'hu•mid'i•fi'er
de'hu•mid'i•fy',
  -fied', -fy'ing
de•hy'drate',
  -drat'ed, -drat'ing
de'hy•dra'tion
de•ice', -iced',

-ic'ing
de•ic'er
de'i•fi•ca'tion
de'i•fy', -fied',
  -fy'ing
deign *(to condescend)*
  ✔ Dane
de•i'on•ize', -ized',
  -iz'ing
de'ism
de'ist
de•is'tic
de'i•ty
de•ject'ed
de•jec'tion
de ju're
Del'a•war'e•an
de•lay'
de•lec'ta•ble
del'e•gate', -gat'ed,
  -gat'ing
del'e•ga'tion
de•lete', -let'ed,
  -let'ing
del'e•te'ri•ous
de•le'tion
delft
del'i *pl.* -is
de•lib'er•ate *adj.*
de•lib'er•ate',
  -at'ed, -at'ing
de•lib'er•a'tion
de•lib'er•a•tive
del'i•ca•cy
del'i•cate
del'i•ca•tes'sen
de•li'cious

de•light'
de•light'ed
de•light'ful
de•lim'it
de•lin'e•ate', -at'ed,
  -at'ing
de•lin'e•a'tion
de•lin'e•a•tive
de•lin'e•a'tor
de•lin'quen•cy
de•lin'quent
del'i•quesce',
  -quesced',
  -quesc'ing
del'i•ques'cence
del'i•ques'cent
de•lir'i•ous
de•lir'i•um *pl.*
  -i•ums *or* -i•a
de•liv'er
de•liv'er•a•ble
de•liv'er•ance
de•liv'er•y
dell
de•louse', -loused',
  -lous'ing
Del'phic
del•phin'i•um
del'ta
del'toid'
de•lude', -lud'ed,
  -lud'ing
del'uge, -uged,
  -ug'ing
de•lu'sion
de•lu'sive
de luxe' *also*

de•luxe'
delve, delved,
  delv'ing
de•mag'net•ize',
  -ized', -iz'ing
dem'a•gog'ic
dem'a•gogue'
dem'a•gogu'er•y
dem'a•gog'y
de•mand'
de•mand'ing
de•mar'cate',
  -cat•ed, -cat'ing
de'mar•ca'tion
de•mean'
de•mean'or
de•ment'ed
de•mer'it
de•mesne'
dem'i•god'
dem'i•god'dess
dem'i•john'
de•mil'i•ta•ri•za'-
  tion
de•mil'i•ta•rize',
  -rized', -riz'ing
de•mise'
dem'i•tasse'
dem'o *pl.* -os
de•mo'bi•li•za'-
  tion
de•mo'bil•ize',
  -ized', -iz'ing
de•moc'ra•cy
dem'o•crat'
dem'o•crat'ic
de•moc'ra•ti•za'-

tion
de•moc'ra•tize',
  -tized', -tiz'ing
de•mog'ra•pher
dem'o•graph'ic
de•mog'ra•phy
de•mol'ish
dem'o•li'tion
de'mon
de•mon'ic
de•mon'stra•ble
dem'on•strate',
  -strat'ed, -strat'ing
dem'on•stra'tion
de•mon'stra•tive
dem'on•stra'tor
de•mor'al•i•za'-
  tion
de•mor'al•ize',
  -ized', -iz'ing
de•mote', -mot'ed,
  -mot'ing
de•mo'tion
de•mur' *(to object)*,
  -murred',
  -mur'ring
de•mure' *(modest)*
de•mur'ral
de•mur'rer
de•mys'ti•fi•ca'-
  tion
de•mys'ti•fy',
  -fied', -fy'ing
de•na'tur•a'tion
de•na'ture, -tured,
  -tur•ing
den'drite'

de•ni'al
de•ni'er
den'i•grate',
  -grat•ed, -grat'ing
den'i•gra'tion
den'im
den'i•zen
de•nom'i•nate',
  -nat•ed, -nat'ing
de•nom'i•na'tion
de•nom'i•na'tion•
  al
de•nom'i•na'tor
de•no•ta'tion
de•no'ta•tive
de•note', -not'ed,
  -not'ing
de'noue•ment' *also*
  dé'noue•ment'
de•nounce',
  -nounced',
  -nounc'ing
dense, dens'er,
  dens'est
den'si•ty
den'tal
den'ti•frice'
den'tin *or* den'tine'
den'tist
den'tist•ry
den•ti'tion
den'ture
de•nude', -nud'ed,
  -nud'ing
de•nun'ci•a'tion
de•ny', -nied',
  -ny'ing

de•o'dor•ant
de•o'dor•i•za'tion
de•o'dor•ize',
  -ized', -iz'ing
de•o'dor•iz'er
de•ox'i•dize',
  -dized', -diz'ing
de•ox'i•diz'er
de•ox'y•ri'bo•nu•
  cle'ic ac'id
de•part'
de•part'ed
de•part'ment
de'part•men'tal
de•par'ture
de•pend'
de•pend'a•bil'i•ty
de•pend'a•ble
de•pend'ence
de•pend'en•cy
de•pend'ent
de•pict'
de•pic'tion
de•pil'a•to'ry
de•plane', -planed',
  -plan'ing
de•plet'a•ble
de•plete', -plet'ed,
  -plet'ing
de•ple'tion
de•plor'a•ble
de•plore', -plored',
  -plor'ing
de•ploy'
de•po'nent
de•pop'u•late',
  -lat'ed, -lat'ing

de•pop'u•la'tion
de•port'
de'por•ta'tion
de'port•ee'
de•port'ment
de•pose', -posed',
  -pos'ing
de•pos'it
dep'o•si'tion
de•pos'i•tor
de•pos'i•to'ry
de'pot
dep'ra•va'tion
  (corruption)
  ✔ deprivation
de•prave', -praved',
  -prav'ing
de•prav'i•ty
dep're•cate',
  -cat'ed, -cat'ing
dep're•ca'tion
de•pre'ci•ate',
  -at'ed, -at'ing
de•pre'ci•a'tion
de•pre'ci•a'tor
de•pre'ci•a'to'ry
dep're•da'tion
de•press'
de•pres'sant
de•pressed'
de•press'ing
de•pres'sion
de•pres'sive
de•pres'sor
dep'ri•va'tion *(loss)*
  ✔ depravation
de•prive', -prived',

-priv'ing
depth
dep'u•ta'tion
de•pute', -put'ed,
  -put'ing
dep'u•tize', -tized',
  -tiz'ing
dep'u•ty
de•rail'
de•rail'leur
de•range', -ranged',
  -rang'ing
der'by
de•reg'u•late',
  -lat'ed, -lat'ing
de•reg'u•la'tion
de•reg'u•la'tor
de•reg'u•la'to'ry
der'e•lict'
der'e•lic'tion
de•ride', -rid'ed,
  -rid'ing
de•ri'sion
de•ri'sive
de•riv'a•ble
der'i•va'tion
de•riv'a•tive
de•rive', -rived',
  -riv'ing
der'ma
der'mal
der'ma•ti'tis
der'ma•tol'o•gist
der'ma•tol'o•gy
der'mis
der'o•gate', -gat'ed,
  -gat'ing

der'o•ga'tion
de•rog'a•tive
de•rog'a•to'ry
der'rick
der'ring-do'
der'rin•ger
der'vish
de•sal'i•nize',
 -nized', -niz'ing
des'cant
de•scend'
de•scen'dant *(off-
 spring)*
de•scen'dent *also*
 de•scen'dant
 (descending)
de•scent' *(downward
 incline, ancestry)*
 ✔ decent, dissent
de•scrib'a•ble
de•scribe',
 -scribed', -scrib'ing
de•scrip'tion
de•scrip'tive
de•scry', -scried',
 -scry'ing
des'e•crate',
 -crat'ed, -crat'ing
des'e•cra'tion
de•seg're•gate',
 -gat'ed, -gat'ing
de•seg're•ga'tion
des'ert *(barren re-
 gion)*
de•sert' *(punish-
 ment)*
 ✔ dessert

de•sert' *(to abandon)*
 ✔ dessert
de•ser'tion
de•serve', -served',
 -serv'ing
de•serv'ed•ly
des'ic•cate', -cat'ed,
 -cat'ing
des'ic•ca'tion
de•sign'
des'ig•nate',
 -nat'ed, -nat'ing
des'ig•na'tion
des'ig•na'tive
des'ig•na'tor
des'ig•nee'
de•sign'er
de•sign'ing
de•sir'a•bil'i•ty
de•sir'a•ble
de•sir'a•bly
de•sire', -sired',
 -sir'ing
de•sir'ous
de•sist'
desk'top'
des'o•late *adj.*
des'o•late', -lat'ed,
 -lat'ing
des'o•la'tion
de•spair'
de•spair'ing
des'per•a'do *pl.*
 -does *or* -dos
des'per•ate *(despair-
 ing)*
 ✔ disparate

des'per•a'tion
des'pi•ca•ble
des'pi•ca•bly
de•spise', -spised',
 -spis'ing
de•spite'
de•spoil'
de•spo'li•a'tion
de•spon'dence *also*
 de•spon'den•cy
de•spon'dent
des'pot
des•pot'ic
des'pot•ism
des•sert' *(food)*
 ✔ desert
des'ti•na'tion
des'tine, -tined,
 -tin'ing
des'ti•ny
des'ti•tute'
des'ti•tu'tion
de•stroy'
de•stroy'er
de•struct'
de•struc'ti•ble
de•struc'tion
de•struc'tive
des'ul•to'ry
de•tach'
de•tach'a•bil'i•ty
de•tach'a•ble
de•tach'a•bly
de•tached'
de•tail'
de•tailed'
de•tain'

de•tect′
de•tect′a•ble also
  de•tect′i•ble
de•tec′tion
de•tec′tive
de•tec′tor
dé•tente′
de•ten′tion
de•ter′, -terred′,
  -ter′ring
de•ter′gent
de•te′ri•o•rate′,
  -rat′ed, -rat′ing
de•te′ri•o•ra′tion
de•ter′min•a•ble
de•ter′mi•nant
de•ter′mi•nate′,
  -nated′, -nat′ing
de•ter′mi•na′tion
de•ter′mine,
  -mined, -min•ing
de•ter′min•er
de•ter′rence
de•ter′rent
de•test′
de•test′a•ble
de•test′a•bly
de′tes•ta′tion
de•throne′,
  -throned′,
  -thron′ing
de•throne′ment
det′o•nate′,
  -nat′ed, -nat′ing
det′o•na′tion
det′o•na′tor
de′tour′

de•tox′i•fi•ca′tion
de•tox′i•fy′, -fied′,
  -fy′ing
de•tract′
de•trac′tion
de•trac′tor
det′ri•ment
det′ri•men′tal
de•tri′tus pl. -tus
deuce
deu•te′ri•um
de•val′u•a′tion
de•val′ue, -ued,
  -u•ing
dev′as•tate′, -tat′ed,
  -tat′ing
dev′as•ta′tion
de•vel′op
de•vel′op•er
de•vel′op•ing
de•vel′op•ment
de•vel′op•men′tal
de′vi•ance
de′vi•ant
de′vi•ate′, -at′ed,
  -at′ing
de′vi•a′tion
de•vice′ (con-
  trivance)
  ✔ devise
dev′il, -iled or -illed,
  -il•ing or -il•ling
dev′il•fish′
dev′il•ish
dev′il-may-care′
dev′il•ment
dev′il•try or

dev′il•ry
de′vi•ous
de•vise′ (to invent),
  -vised′, -vis′ing
  ✔ device
de•void′
de•volve′, -volved′,
  -volv′ing
De•vo′ni•an
de•vote′, -vot′ed,
  -vot′ing
dev′o•tee′
de•vo′tion
de•vour′
de•vout′
dew (moisture)
  ✔ do, due
dew′ber′ry
dew′claw′
dew′drop′
dew′lap′
dew′y
dew′i•ness
dex•ter′i•ty
dex′ter•ous also
  dex′trous
dex′trose′
di′a•be′tes
di′a•bet′ic
di′a•bol′i•cal also
  di′a•bol′ic
di′a•crit′ic
di′a•crit′i•cal
di′a•dem′
di′ag•nose′,
  -nosed′, -nos′ing
di′ag•no′sis pl. -ses

di·ag·nos'tic
di·ag·nos·ti'cian
di·ag'o·nal
di'a·gram',
 -grammed' *or*
 -gramed',
 -gram'ming *or*
 -gram'ing
di'a·gram·mat'ic
di'al, -aled *or* -alled,
 -al·ing *or* -al·ling
di'a·lect'
di'a·lec'tal
di'a·lec'tic
di'a·lec'ti·cal
di'a·logue' *or*
 di'a·log'
di·al'y·sis *pl.* -ses'
di·am'e·ter
di'a·met'ri·cal *also*
 di'a·met'ric
di'a·mond
di'a·mond·back'
di'a·pa'son
di'a·per
di·aph'a·nous
di'a·phragm'
di'ar·rhe'a
di'a·rist
di'a·ry
Di·as'po·ra *also*
 di·as'po·ra
di·as'to·le
di'a·stol'ic
di'a·tom'
di'a·tom'ic
di'a·ton'ic scale'

di'a·tribe'
dice *sing.* die
dice, diced, dic'ing
di·chot'o·my
dick'ens
dick'er
dick'ey *pl.* -eys
di'cot'
di'cot'y·le'don
di'cot'y·le'don·ous
dic·tate', -tat'ed,
 -tat'ing
dic·ta'tion
dic·ta'tor
dic·ta'to·ri·al
dic·ta'tor·ship'
dic'tion
dic'tion·ar'y
dic'tum *pl.* -ta *or*
 -tums
di·dac'tic
did'n't
die *(to become dead)*,
 died, dy'ing
 ✔ *dye*
die *(tool for stamp-*
 ing), *pl.* dies
 ✔ *dye*
die *(small cube)*, *pl.*
 dice
 ✔ *dye*
die'-hard' *also*
 die'hard'
di·er'e·sis *or*
 di·aer'e·sis *pl.* -ses'
die'sel
di'et

di'et·er
di'e·tar'y
di'e·tet'ic
di'e·ti'tian *or*
 di'e·ti'cian
dif'fer
dif'fer·ence *(dissim-*
 ilarity)
 ✔ *deference*
dif'fer·ent
dif'fer·en'tial
dif'fer·en'ti·ate',
 -at'ed, -at'ing
dif'fer·en'ti·a'tion
dif'fi·cult'
dif'fi·cul'ty
dif'fi·dence
dif'fi·dent
dif·fract'
dif·frac'tion
dif·fuse', -fused',
 -fus'ing
dif·fu'sion
dig, dug, dig'ging
di·gest' *v.*
di'gest' *n.*
di·gest'i·bil'i·ty
di·gest'i·ble
di·ges'tion
di·ges'tive
dig'ger
dig'gings
dig'it
dig'i·tal
dig'i·tal·is
dig'ni·fy', -fied',
 -fy'ing

dig′ni•tar′y
dig′ni•ty
di•gress′
di•gres′sion
di•he′dral
dike, diked, dik′ing
di•lap′i•dat′ed
di•lap′i•da′tion
di•lat′a•ble
dil′a•ta′tion
di•late′, -lat′ed,
  -lat′ing
di•la′tion
dil′a•to′ry
di•lem′ma
dil′et•tante′ pl.
  -tantes also -tan′ti
dil′et•tan′tism
dil′i•gence
dil′i•gent
dill
dil′ly-dal′ly,
  -dal′lied, -dal′ly•ing
di•lute′, -lut′ed,
  -lut′ing
di•lu′tion
dim, dim′mer,
  dim′mest
dim, dimmed,
  dim′ming
dime
di•men′sion
di•men′sion•al
di•min′ish
di•min′ish•ing
di•min′u•en′do
dim′i•nu′tion

di•min′u•tive
dim′i•ty
dim′mer
dim′ple, -pled,
  -pling
dine *(to eat)*, dined,
  din′ing
  ✔ dyne
din′er
di•nette′
ding′-dong′
din′ghy *(small*
  boat)
  ✔ dingy
din′gle
din′go pl. -goes
din′gy *(dirty)*
  ✔ dinghy
din′gi•ness
din′ing room′
din′ky
din′ner
din′ner•time′
di′no•flag′el•late
di′no•saur′
dint
di′o•cese
di′ode′
di′o•ram′a
di•ox′ide
dip, dipped,
  dip′ping
diph•the′ri•a
diph′thong′
dip′loid′
di•plo′ma
di•plo′ma•cy

dip′lo•mat′
dip′lo•mat′ic
dip′per
dip′stick′
dip′ter•ous
dip′tych
dire, dir′er, dir′est
di•rect′
di•rec′tion
di•rec′tion•al
di•rec′tive
di•rec′tor
di•rec′tor•ate
di•rec′to′ri•al
di•rec′to•ry
dirge
dir•ham′
dir′i•gi•ble
dirn′dl
dirt
dirt′-cheap′
dirt′y, -ied, -y•ing
dis′a•bil′i•ty
dis•a′ble, -bled,
  -bling
dis′a•buse′, -bused′,
  -bus′ing
dis′ad•van′tage
dis•ad•van′taged
dis•ad′van•ta′-
  geous
dis′af•fect′
dis′af•fect′ed
dis′af•fec′tion
dis′a•gree′, -greed′,
  -gree′ing
dis′a•gree′a•ble

dis·a·gree′a·bly
dis′a·gree′ment
dis′al·low′
dis′ap·pear′
dis′ap·pear′ance
dis′ap·point′
dis′ap·point′ed
dis′ap·point′ing
dis′ap·prov′al
dis′ap·prove′,
 -proved′, -prov′ing
dis·arm′
dis·ar′ma·ment
dis·arm′ing
dis′ar·range′,
 -ranged′, -rang′ing
dis′ar·ray′
dis′as·sem′ble,
 -bled, -bling
dis′as·so′ci·ate′,
 -at′ed, -at′ing
dis′as·so′ci·a′tion
dis·as′ter
dis·as′trous
dis′a·vow′
dis′a·vow′al
dis·band′
dis·bar′, -barred′,
 -bar′ring
dis·be·lief′
dis·be·lieve′,
 -lieved′, -liev′ing
dis·be·liev′er
dis·bur′den
dis·burse′ *(to pay out)*, -bursed′,
 -burs′ing

 ✔ *disperse*
dis·burse′ment
dis·card′ *v.*
dis′card′ *n.*
disc′ brake′ *also*
 disk′ brake′
dis·cern′
dis·cern′i·ble
dis·cern′i·bly
dis·cern′ing
dis·cern′ment
dis·charge′,
 -charged′,
 -charg′ing
dis′charge′ *n.*
dis·ci′ple
dis′ci·pli·nar′i·an
dis′ci·pli·nar′y
dis′ci·pline,
 -plined, -plin′ing
disc′ jock′ey
dis·claim′
dis·claim′er
dis·close′, -closed′,
 -clos′ing
dis·clo′sure
dis′co *pl.* -cos
dis′co, -coed,
 -co′ing
dis·cog′ra·phy
dis′coid′
dis′col′or
dis·col′or·a′tion
dis′com·bob′u·
 late′, -lat′ed,
 -lat′ing
dis′com·bob′u·la′-

tion
dis·com′fit *(to make uneasy)*
 ✔ *discomfort*
dis·com′fi·ture′
dis·com′fort *(uneasiness)*
 ✔ *discomfit*
dis′com·pose′,
 -posed′, -pos′ing
dis′com·po′sure
dis′con·cert′
dis′con·nect′
dis′con·nect′ed
dis′con·nec′tion
dis·con′so·late
dis′con·tent′
dis′con·tent′ed
dis′con·tin′u·ance
dis′con·tin′u·a′-
 tion
dis′con·tin′ue,
 -ued, -u′ing
dis′con·tin′u·ous
dis′cord′
dis·cor′dance
dis·cor′dant
dis′co·theque′
dis′count′
dis′count′a·ble
dis·cour′age, -aged,
 -ag·ing
dis·course′ *n.*
dis·course′,
 -coursed′,
 -cours′ing
dis·cour′te·ous

dis·cour'te·sy
dis·cov'er
dis·cov'er·a·ble
dis·cov'er·y
dis·cred'it
dis·cred'it·a·ble
dis·cred'it·a·bly
dis·creet' *(prudent)*
  ✔ discrete
dis·crep'an·cy
dis·crep'ant
dis·crete' *(distinct)*
  ✔ discreet
dis·cre'tion
dis·cre'tion·ar'y
dis·crim'i·nate',
  -nat'ed, -nat'ing
dis·crim'i·na'tion
dis·crim'i·na'tor
dis·crim'i·na·to'ry
dis·cur'sive
dis'cus *pl.* -cus·es
dis·cuss'
dis·cuss'i·ble
dis·cus'sion
dis·dain'
dis·ease'
dis·eased'
dis'em·bark'
dis'em·bar·ka'tion
dis'em·bod'ied
dis'em·bod'i·ment
dis'em·bod'y, -ied,
  -y'ing
dis'em·bow'el,
  -eled *or* -elled,
  -el'ing *or* -el·ling

dis'en·chant'
dis'en·cum'ber
dis'en·fran'chise',
  -chised', -chis'ing
dis'en·gage',
  -gaged', -gag'ing
dis'en·gage'ment
dis'en·tan'gle,
  -gled, -gling
dis'en·tan'gle·
  ment
dis·fa'vor
dis·fig'ure, -ured,
  -ur'ing
dis·fran'chise',
  -chised', -chis'ing
dis·gorge',
  -gorged', -gorg'ing
dis·grace',
  -graced', -grac'ing
dis·grace'ful
dis·grun'tle, -tled,
  -tling
dis·guise', -guised',
  -guis'ing
dis·gust'
dis·gust'ed
dis·gust'ing
dish
dis'ha·bille' *also*
  des'ha·bille'
dis'har·mo'ni·ous
dis·har'mo·ny
dish'cloth'
dis·heart'en
di·shev'eled *or*
  di·shev'elled

dis·hon'est
dis·hon'es·ty
dis·hon'or
dis·hon'or·a·ble
dis·hon'or·a·bly
dish'pan'
dish'rag'
dish'tow'el
dish'wash'er
dish'wa'ter
dis·il·lu'sion
dis·in'cli·na'tion
dis'in·clined'
dis'in·fect'
dis'in·fec'tion
dis'in·fec'tant
dis'in·her'it
dis·in'te·grate',
  -grat'ed, -grat'ing
dis·in'te·gra'tion
dis'in·ter', -terred',
  -ter'ring
dis'in·ter'ment
dis·in'ter·est·ed
dis·joint'
dis·joint'ed
disk *also* disc
disk' drive'
disk·ette'
dis·like', -liked',
  -lik'ing
dis'lo·cate', -cat·ed,
  -cat'ing
dis'lo·ca'tion
dis·lodge',
  -lodged', -lodg'ing
dis·loy'al

dis•loy'al•ty
dis'mal
dis•man'tle, -tled,
  -tling
dis•may'
dis•mem'ber
dis•miss'
dis•miss'al
dis•mount'
dis'o•be'di•ence
dis'o•be'di•ent
dis'o•bey'
dis'o•blige',
  -bliged', -blig'ing
dis•or'der
dis•or'der•li•ness
dis•or'der•ly
dis•or'gan•i•za'tion
dis•or'gan•ize',
  -ized', -iz'ing
dis•o'ri•ent
dis•o'ri•en•ta'tion
dis•own'
dis•par'age, -aged,
  -ag'ing
dis'pa•rate *(differ-
  ent)*
  ✔ desperate
dis•par'i•ty
dis•pas'sion•ate
dis•patch' *also*
  des•patch'
dis•patch'er
dis•pel', -pelled',
  -pel'ling
dis•pen'sa•bil'i•ty
dis•pen'sa•ble

dis•pen'sa•ry
dis•pen•sa'tion
dis•pense',
  -pensed', -pens'ing
dis•pens'er
dis•per'sal
dis•perse' *(to
  scatter)*, -persed',
  -pers'ing
  ✔ disburse
dis•per'sion
dis•pir'it
dis•pir'it•ed
dis•place', -placed',
  -plac'ing
dis•place'ment
dis•play'
dis•please',
  -pleased',
  -pleas'ing
dis•pleas'ure
dis•port'
dis•pos'a•ble
dis•pos'al
dis•pose', -posed',
  -pos'ing
dis•po•si'tion
dis•pos•sess'
dis•pos•ses'sion
dis•proof'
dis'pro•por'tion
dis'pro•por'tion•
  ate
dis•prove',
  -proved', -prov'ing
dis•put'a•bil'i•ty
dis•put'a•ble

dis•pu'tant
dis•pu•ta'tion
dis•pute', -put'ed,
  -put'ing
dis•qual'i•fi•ca'-
  tion
dis•qual'i•fy',
  -fied', -fy'ing
dis•qui'et
dis•qui'e•tude'
dis'qui•si'tion
dis're•gard'
dis're•pair'
dis•rep'u•ta•ble
dis're•pute'
dis're•spect'
dis're•spect'ful
dis•robe', -robed',
  -rob'ing
dis•rupt'
dis•rup'tion
dis•rup'tive
dis•sat'is•fac'tion
dis•sat'is•fy', -fied',
  -fy'ing
dis•sect'
dis•sec'tion
dis•sem'ble, -bled,
  -bling
dis•sem'bler
dis•sem'i•nate',
  -nat'ed, -nat'ing
dis•sem'i•na'tion
dis•sen'sion
dis•sent' *(disagree-
  ment)*
  ✔ decent, descent

dis•sent′er
dis′ser•ta′tion
dis•serv′ice
dis•sev′er
dis′si•dence
dis′si•dent
dis•sim′i•lar
dis•sim′i•lar′i•ty
dis•sim′u•late′,
　-lat′ed, -lat′ing
dis•sim′u•la′tion
dis′si•pate′, -pat′ed,
　-pat′ing
dis′si•pa′tion
dis•so′ci•ate′,
　-at′ed, -at′ing
dis•so′ci•a′tion
dis•sol′u•ble
dis′so•lute′
dis′so•lu′tion
dis•solv′a•ble
dis•solve′, -solved′,
　-solv′ing
dis′so•nance
dis′so•nant
dis•suade′,
　-suad′ed, -suad′ing
dis•sua′sion
dis′taff′
dis′tance
dis′tant
dis•taste′
dis•taste′ful
dis•tem′per
dis•tend′
dis•ten′tion *also*
　dis•ten′sion

dis•till′ *also* dis•til′,
　-tilled′, -till′ing
dis′til•late′
dis′til•la′tion
dis•till′er
dis•till′er•y
dis•tinct′
dis•tinc′tion
dis•tinc′tive
dis•tin′guish
dis•tin′guish•a•ble
dis•tin′guished
dis•tort′
dis•tor′tion
dis•tract′
dis•trac′tion
dis•traught′
dis•tress′
dis•trib′ute, -ut•ed,
　-ut′ing
dis′tri•bu′tion
dis•trib′u•tive
dis•trib′u•tor
dis′trict′
dis•trust′
dis•turb′
dis•tur′bance
di•sul′fide′
dis•un′ion
dis′u•nite′, -nit′ed,
　-nit′ing
dis′u•ni′ty
dis•use′
ditch
dith′er
dit′to *pl.* -tos
dit′ty

di′u•ret′ic
di•ur′nal
di′va
di•va′lent
di•van′
dive, dived *or* dove,
　dived, div′ing
dive′-bomb′
div′er
di•verge′, -verged′,
　-verg′ing
di•ver′gence
di•ver′gent
di′vers *(various)*
di•verse′ *(different)*
di•ver′si•fi•ca′tion
di•ver′si•fy′, -fied′,
　-fy′ing
di•ver′sion
di•ver′si•ty
di•vert′
di•ver′ti•men′to *pl.*
　-tos *or* -ti
di•vest′
di•ves′ti•ture
di•vid′a•ble
di•vide′, -vid′ed,
　-vid′ing
div′i•dend′
di•vid′er
div′i•na′tion
di•vine′, -vined′,
　-vin′ing
div′ing board′
div′ing suit′
di•vin′ing rod′
di•vin′i•ty

di•vis'i•bil'i•ty
di•vis'i•ble
di•vis'i•bly
di•vi'sion
di•vi'sive
di•vi'sor
di•vorce', -vorced',
  -vorc'ing
di•vor•cé'
di•vor•cée'
div'ot
di•vulge', -vulged',
  -vulg'ing
div'vy, -vied,
  -vy•ing
Dix'ie•land'
diz'zy, -zied,
  -zy•ing
diz'zi•ness
DNA
do *(to perform)*, did,
  done, do'ing, does
  ✔ dew, due
do *(what should be
  done, party)*, pl. do's
  or dos
  ✔ dew, due
do *(musical tone)*
  ✔ doe, dough
dob'bin
Do'ber•man
  pin'scher
doc'ile
do•cil'i•ty
dock
dock'et
dock'yard'

doc'tor
doc'tor•al
doc'tor•ate
doc'tri•naire'
doc'tri•nal
doc'trine
doc'u•dra'ma
doc'u•ment
doc'u•men'ta•ry
doc'u•men•ta'tion
dod'der
dod'der•ing
do•dec'a•gon'
do'dec•a•he'dron
  pl. -drons *or* -dra
dodge, dodged,
  dodg'ing
dodg'er
do'do *pl.* -does *or*
  -dos
doe *(female deer)*, pl.
  doe *or* does
  ✔ do, dough
do'er
doe'skin'
does'n't
doff
dog, dogged,
  dog'ging
dog'cart'
dog'catch'er
doge
dog'-ear'
dog'-eared'
dog'fight'
dog'fish'
dog'ged

dog'ger•el
dog'gy *or* dog'gie
dog'gy bag'
dog'house'
dog'ma
dog•mat'ic
dog'ma•tism
do'-good'er
dog'sled'
dog'trot'
dog'watch'
dog'wood'
doi'ly
do'ings
do'-it-your•self'
dol'drums
dole, doled, dol'ing
dole'ful
doll
dol'lar
doll'house'
dol'lop
dol'ly
dol'man *(garment)*
dol'men *(stone
  structure)*
dol'o•mite'
do'lor
do'lor•ous
dol'phin
dolt
do•main'
dome, domed,
  dom'ing
do•mes'tic
do•mes'ti•cate',
  -cat'ed, -cat'ing

do•mes'ti•ca'tion
do'mes•tic'i•ty
dom'i•cile', -ciled',
 -cil'ing
dom'i•nance
dom'i•nant
dom'i•nate',
 -nat'ed, -nat'ing
dom'i•na'tion
dom'i•neer'
dom'i•neer'ing
Do•min'i•can
do•min'ion
dom'i•no' *pl.* -noes'
 or -nos'
don, donned,
 don'ning
do'nate', -nat'ed,
 -nat'ing
do•na'tion
done *(finished)*
 ✔ *dun*
don'jon *(tower)*
 ✔ *dungeon*
don'key *pl.* -keys
don'nish
don'ny•brook'
do'nor
do'-no'thing
don't
doo'dad'
doo'dle, -dled,
 -dling
doo'dler
doo'dle•bug'
doom
dooms'day'

door
door'bell'
door'jamb'
door'knob'
door'man
door'mat'
door'nail'
door'sill'
door'step'
door'stop'
door'way'
door'yard'
doo'zy *or* doo'zie
do'pa•mine'
dope, doped,
 dop'ing
dop'ey, dop'i•er,
 dop'i•est
Dop'pler ef•fect'
Dor'ic
dor'man•cy
dor'mant
dor'mer
dor'mi•to'ry
dor'mouse'
dor'sal
do'ry
dos'age
dose, dosed, dos'ing
dos'si•er'
dot, dot'ted, dot'-
 ting
dot'age
do'tard
dote, dot'ed,
 dot'ing
dot'ty

dou'ble, -bled,
 -bling
dou'ble-bar'reled
dou'ble-breast'ed
dou'ble-check' *v.*
dou'ble-cross'
dou'ble-deal'er
dou'ble-deal'ing
dou'ble-deck'er
dou'ble-dig'it
 adj.
dou'ble-edged'
dou'ble-en•ten'-
 dre
dou'ble-head'er
 also dou'ble•head'-
 er
dou'ble-joint'ed
dou'ble knit' *also*
 dou'ble-knit'
dou'ble-park'
dou'ble-quick'
dou'ble-space',
 -spaced', -spac'ing
dou'blet
dou'ble talk' *or*
 dou'ble-talk' *or*
 dou'ble•talk'
dou'ble time' *n.*
dou'ble-time' *v.*
dou•bloon'
dou'bly
doubt
doubt'ful
doubt'less
douche, douched,
 douch'ing

dough *(bread mixture, money)*
  ✔ do, doe
dough'i•ness
dough'nut' *also*
  do'nut'
dough'ti•ness
dough'ty
dough'y
dour
douse *(to immerse, to extinguish)*, doused, dous'ing
  ✔ dowse
dove
dove'cote' *also*
  dove'cot'
dove'tail'
dow'a•ger
dow'dy
dow'el, -eled *or*
  -elled, -el•ing *or*
  -el•ling
dow'er
down
down'beat'
down'cast'
down'er
down'fall'
down'grade',
  -grad'ed, -grad'ing
down'heart'ed
down'hill' *adv.*
down'hill' *adj.*
down'load'
down'play'
down'pour'

down'right'
down'scale',
  -scaled', -scal'ing
down'shift'
down'side'
down'stage'
down'stairs' *adv.*
down'stairs' *adj.*
down'stream' *adj.*
down'stream' *adv.*
down'swing'
down'time'
down'-to-earth'
down'town' *adj.*
down'town' *adv.*
down'trod'den
down'turn'
down'ward
down'wind'
down'y
dow'ry
dowse *(to divine)*,
  dowsed, dows'ing
  ✔ douse
dows'er
dox•ol'o•gy
doze, dozed, doz'ing
doz'en *pl.* doz'en *or*
  doz'ens
doz'enth
drab, drab'ber,
  drab'best
drach'ma *pl.* -mas
  or -mae
draft•ee'
drafts'man
drafts'man•ship'

drafts'per'son
drafts'wom'an
draft'y
drag, dragged,
  drag'ging
drag'gle, -gled,
  -gling
drag'net'
drag'on
drag'on•fly'
dra•goon'
drain
drain'age
drain'pipe'
drake
dram
dra'ma
dra•mat'ic
dram'a•tis
  per•so'nae'
dram'a•tist
dram'a•ti•za'tion
dram'a•tize',
  -tized', -tiz'ing
drape, draped,
  drap'ing
drap'er
drap'er•y
dras'tic
Dra•vid'i•an *or*
  Dra•vid'ic
draw, drew, drawn,
  draw'ing
draw'back'
draw'bridge'
draw'er *(one who draws)*

drawer *(compartment)*
draw'ing
draw'ing room'
draw'knife'
drawl
draw'string'
dread
dread'ful
dread'locks'
dread'nought'
dream, dreamed *or* dreamt, dream'ing
dream'land'
dream'y
drear'i·ness
drear'y
dredge, dredged, dredg'ing
dregs
drench
drenched
dress
dres·sage'
dress'er
dress'ing
dress'mak'er
dress'mak'ing
dress'y
drib'ble, -bled, -bling
drib'bler
drib'let
dri'er *also* dry'er *(one that dries)*
  ✔ *dryer*
drift'er

drift'wood'
drink, drank, drunk, drink'ing
drip, dripped, drip'ping
drip'-dry', -dried', -dry'ing
drive, drove, driv'en, driv'ing
drive'-in' *n.*
driv'el, -eled *or* -elled, -el·ing *or* -el·ling
driv'el·er *or* driv'el·ler
driv'er
drive' shaft'
drive'way'
driz'zle, -zled, -zling
driz'zly
droll
drom'e·dar'y
drone, droned, dron'ing
drool
droop *(to sag)*
  ✔ *drupe*
droop'y
drop, dropped, drop'ping
drop' cloth'
drop' kick'
drop' leaf'
drop'let
drop'out' *n.*
drop'per
drop'pings

drop'sy
dross
drought
drove
drov'er
drown
drowse, drowsed, drows'ing
drows'y
drub, drubbed, drub'bing
drudge, drudged, drudg'ing
drudg'er·y
drug, drugged, drug'ging
drug'gist
drug'store'
dru'id
drum, drummed, drum'ming
drum'beat'
drum'lin
drum'mer
drum'stick'
drunk'ard
drunk'en
drupe *(fruit)*
  ✔ *droop*
druth'ers
dry, dri'er *or* dry'er, dri'est *or* dry'est
dry, dried, dry'ing
dry'ad
dry'-clean'
dry' clean'er
dry' clean'ing

dry′ dock′ *n.*

dry′-dock′ *v.*

dry′er *(appliance that dries)*
  ✔ drier

dry′ly

dry′ wall′ *or* dry′wall′

du′al *(double)*
  ✔ duel

du·al′i·ty

dub, dubbed, dub′bing

du′bi·ous

du′cal

duc′at

duch′ess

duch′y

duck′bill′

duck′ling

duck′weed′

duct

duc′tile

duc·til′i·ty

dude

dudg′eon

due *(owed as a debt)*
  ✔ dew, do

du′el *(to fight),* -eled *or* -elled, -el•ing *or* -el•ling
  ✔ dual

du′el•er *or* du′el•ler *or* du′el•ist *or* du′el•list

du•et′

duf′fel *or* duf′fle

duf′fle bag′ *or* duf′fel bag′

dug′out′ *n.*

duke

duke′dom

dul′cet

dul′ci•mer

dull

dull′ard

du′ly

dumb

dumb′bell′

dumb′found′ *also* dum′found′

dumb′wait′er

dum′my

dump′ling

dump′site′

dump′y

dun *(to ask for payment),* dunned, dun′ning
  ✔ done

dun *(grayish brown)*
  ✔ done

dunce

dune

dung

dun′ga•ree′

dun′geon *(prison)*
  ✔ donjon

dunk

du′o *pl.* -os

du′o•dec′i•mal

du′o•de′nal

du′o•de′num *pl.* -na *or* -nums

dupe, duped, dup′ing

du′ple

du′plex′

du′pli•cate *adj. & n.*

du′pli•cate′, -cat′ed, -cat′ing

du′pli•ca′tion

du′pli•ca′tor

du•plic′i•ty

du′ra•bil′i•ty

du′ra•ble

du′ra•bly

du′rance

du•ra′tion

du•ress′

dur′ing

du′rum

dusk′y

dust′ bowl′

dust′er

dust′ jack′et

dust′pan′

dust′y

Dutch

Dutch′man

Dutch′ ov′en

Dutch′ treat′

Dutch′wom′an

du′te•ous

du′ti•a•ble

du′ti•ful

du′ty

dwarf *pl.* dwarfs *or* dwarves

dwell, dwelt *or* dwelled, dwell′ing

dwin'dle, -dled,
  -dling
dye *(to color)*, dyed,
  dye'ing
  ✔ *die*
dyed'-in-the-wool'
dy'er
dye'stuff'
dy•nam'ic
dy'na•mism
dy'na•mite',
  -mit'ed, -mit'ing
dy'na•mo' *pl.* -mos'
dy•nas'tic
dy'nas•ty
dyne *(unit of force)*
  ✔ *dine*
dys•en•ter'y
dys•func'tion
dys•gen'ic
dys•lex'i•a
dys•lex'ic
dys•pep'sia
dys•pep'tic
dys•pro'si•um
dys•troph'ic
dys'tro•phy *also*
  dis•tro'phi•a

E

each
ea'ger
ea'gle
ea'gle-eyed'
ea'glet

ear
ear'ache'
ear'drum'
eared
ear'flap'
earl
earl'dom
ear'lobe'
ear'ly
ear'mark'
ear'muff'
earn *(to gain)*
  ✔ *urn*
earn'er
ear'nest
earn'ings
ear'phone'
ear'piece'
ear'plug'
ear'ring'
ear'shot'
ear'split'ting
earth
earth'bound' *also*
  earth'-bound'
earth'en
earth'en•ware'
earth'ling
earth'ly *(relating to
  the earth, not heav-
  enly)*
  ✔ *earthy*
earth'quake'
earth'shak'ing
earth'ward *adv. &
  adj.*
earth'wards *adv.*

earth'work'
earth'worm'
earth'y *(relating to
  the soil, natural)*
  ✔ *earthly*
ear'wax'
ear'wig'
ease, eased, eas'ing
ea'sel
eas'i•ly
eas'i•ness
east
east'bound'
Eas'ter
east'er•ly
east'ern
east'ern•er
east'ern•most'
east'ward *adv. &
  adj.*
east'wards *adv.*
eas'y
eas'y chair'
eas'y•go'ing *also*
  eas'y-go'ing
eat, ate, eat'en,
  eat'ing
eat'a•ble
eat'er
eat'er•y
eats
eau' de co•logne'
  pl. eaux' de
  co•logne'
eaves
eaves'drop',
  -dropped',

-drop'ping
eaves'drop'per
ebb
eb'on•ite'
eb'on•y
e•bul'lience
e•bul'lient
ec•cen'tric
ec'cen•tric'i•ty
ec•cle'si•as'tic
ec•cle'si•as'ti•cal
ech'e•lon'
e•chid'na
e•chi'no•derm'
ech'o *pl.* -oes
ech'o, -oed, -o•ing
ech'o•car'di•o•
  gram'
ech'o•car'di•o•
  graph'
e•cho'ic
ech'o•lo•ca'tion
é•clair'
é•clat'
e•clec'tic
e•clec'ti•cism
e•clipse', e•clipsed',
  e•clips'ing
e•clip'tic
ec'o•cide'
ec'o•log'i•cal
e•col'o•gist
e•col'o•gy
e•con'o•met'rics
ec'o•nom'ic
ec'o•nom'i•cal
ec'o•nom'ics

e•con'o•mist
e•con'o•mize',
  -mized', -miz'ing
e•con'o•my
ec'o•sys'tem
ec'ru
ec•sta•sy
ec•stat'ic
ec'to•derm'
ec'to•plasm
Ec'ua•dor'i•an
ec'u•men'i•cal
ec'ze•ma
E'dam
ed'dy, -died, -dy•ing
e'del•weiss'
e•de'ma
E'den
edge, edged, edg'ing
edge'wise' *also*
  edge'ways'
edg'i•ness
edg'y
ed'i•ble
e'dict'
ed'i•fi•ca'tion
ed'i•fice
ed'i•fy', -fied',
  -fy'ing
ed'it
e•di'tion *(publica-
  tion)*
  ✔ addition
ed'i•tor
ed'i•to'ri•al
ed'i•to'ri•al•ize',
  -ized', -iz'ing

ed'u•ca•ble
ed'u•cate', -cat'ed,
  -cat'ing
ed'u•ca'tion
ed'u•ca'tion•al
ed'u•ca'tor
e•duce', e•duced',
  e•duc'ing
e•duc'i•ble
eel *pl.* eel *or* eels
e'en *(evening)*
e'en *(even)*
e'er *(ever)*
  ✔ air, are, ere, heir
ee'rie *or* ee'ry *(weird)*
  ✔ aerie
ee'ri•ly
ef•face', -faced',
  -fac'ing
ef•face'ment
ef•fac'er
ef•fect' *(result)*
  ✔ affect
ef•fec'tive
ef•fec'tive•ness
ef•fec'tu•al
ef•fec'tu•ate',
  -at'ed, -at'ing
ef•fem'i•na•cy *or*
  ef•fem'i•nate•ness
ef•fem'i•nate
ef'fer•ent
ef'fer•vesce',
  -vesced', -vesc'ing
ef'fer•ves'cence
ef'fer•ves'cent
ef•fete'

ef•fete'ness
ef•fi•ca'cious
ef•fi'ca•cy
ef•fi'cien•cy
ef•fi'cient
ef'fi•gy
ef'flo•resce'
ef'flo•res'cence
ef'flo•res'cent
ef•flu'ence
ef'flu•ent
ef•flu'vi•um *pl.*
-vi•a *or* -vi•ums
ef'fort
ef•front'er•y
ef•ful'gence
ef•ful'gent
ef•fu'sion
ef•fu'sive
ef•fu'sive•ly
eft
e•gal'i•tar'i•an
e•gal'i•tar'i•an•ism
egg
egg'beat•er
egg'head'
egg'nog'
egg'plant'
egg'shell'
eg'lan•tine'
e'go *pl.* e•gos
e'go•cen'tric
e'go•ism
e'go•ist
e'go•is'tic *or*
e'go•is'ti•cal
e'go•tism

e'go•tist
e'go•tis'tic *or*
e'go•tis'ti•cal
e'go trip' *n.*
e'go-trip', -tripped',
-trip'ping
e•gre'gious
e'gress'
e'gret
E•gyp'tian
E'gyp•tol'o•gist
E'gyp•tol'o•gy
eh
ei'der
ei'der•down'
eight
eight•een'
eight•eenth'
eighth
eight'i•eth
eight'y
ein•stein'i•um
ei'ther
e•jac'u•late',
-lat'ed, -lat'ing
e•jac'u•la'tion
e•ject'
e•jec'tion
e•jec'tor
eke, eked, ek'ing
e•lab'o•rate
e•lab'o•rate',
-rat'ed, -rat'ing
e•lab'o•rate•ly
e•lab'o•ra'tion
e'land *pl.* e'land
also e'lands

e•lapse', e•lapsed',
e•laps'ing
e•las'tic
e•las•tic'i•ty
e•las'ti•cized'
e•late', e•lat'ed,
e•lat'ing
e•la'tion
el'bow
el'bow•room'
eld'er *(older)*
el'der *(shrub)*
el'der•ber'ry
eld'er•li•ness
eld'er•ly
eld'est
El' Do•ra'do
e•lect'
e•lec'tion
e•lec'tion•eer'
e•lec'tive
e•lec'tor
e•lec'tor•al
e•lec'tor•ate
e•lec'tric *also*
e•lec'tri•cal
e•lec•tri'cian
e•lec•tric'i•ty
e•lec'tri•fi•ca'tion
e•lec'tri•fy', -fied',
-fy'ing
e•lec'tro•car'di•o•
gram'
e•lec'tro•car'di•o•
graph'
e•lec'tro•chem'i•
cal

e·lec'tro·chem'is·try

e·lec'tro·con·vul'·sive

e·lec'tro·cute', -cut'ed, -cut'ing

e·lec'tro·cu'tion

e·lec'trode'

e·lec'tro·en·ceph'·a·lo·gram'

e·lec'tro·en·ceph'·a·lo·graph'

e·lec·trol'y·sis

e·lec'tro·lyte'

e·lec'tro·lyt'ic

e·lec'tro·lyze', -lyzed', -lyz'ing

e·lec'tro·mag'net

e·lec'tro·mag·net'·ic

e·lec'tro·mag'net·ism

e·lec'tro·mo'tive

e·lec'tron

e·lec·tron'ic

e·lec'tro·plate', -plat'ed, -plat'ing

e·lec'tro·scope'

e·lec'tro·scop'ic

e·lec'tro·shock'

e·lec'tro·stat'ic

e·lec'tro·ther'a·py

e·lec'tro·va'lence

e·lec'tro·va'len·cy

e·lec'tro·va'lent

el'e·gance

el'e·gant

el'e·gi'ac

el'e·gize', -gized', -giz'ing

el'e·gy

el'e·ment

el'e·men'tal

el'e·men'ta·ry

el'e·phant

el'e·phan'tine'

el'e·vate', -vat'ed, -vat'ing

el'e·va'tion

el'e·va'tor

e·lev'en

e·lev'enth

elf *pl.* elves

elf'in

elf'ish

e·lic'it *(to bring out)* ✔ illicit

e·lide', e·lid'ed, e·lid'ing

el'i·gi·bil'i·ty

el'i·gi·ble

e·lim'i·nate', -nat'ed, -nat'ing

e·lim'i·na'tion

e·li'sion

e·lite' *or* é·lite'

e·lit'ism *or* é·lit'ism

e·lit'ist

e·lix'ir

E·liz'a·be'than

elk *pl.* elk *or* elks

elk'hound'

ell

el·lipse'

el·lip'sis *pl.* -ses

el·lip'soid'

el·lip'soi'dal

el·lip'tic *or* el·lip'ti·cal

elm

el'o·cu'tion

e·lon'gate', -gat'ed, -gat'ing

e·lon'ga'tion

e·lope', e·loped', e·lop'ing

e·lope'ment

el'o·quence

el'o·quent

else

else'where'

e·lu'ci·date', -dat'ed, -dat'ing

e·lu'ci·da'tion

e·lude' *(to escape from)*, e·lud'ed, e·lud'ing ✔ allude

e·lu'sive *(tending to escape)* ✔ allusive, illusive

el'ver

el'y·tron' *pl.* -tra

e·ma'ci·ate', -at'ed, -at'ing

e·ma'ci·a'tion

E'-mail' *or* e'-mail'

em'a·nate', -nat'ed, -nat'ing

em'a·na'tion

em'a·na'tive

e·man′ci·pate′,
  -pat′ed, -pat′ing
e·man′ci·pa′tion
e·man′ci·pa′tor
e·mas′cu·late′,
  -lat′ed, -lat′ing
e·mas′cu·la′tion
em·balm′
em·balm′er
em·bank′ment
em·bar′go pl. -goes
em·bar′go, -goed,
  -go′ing
em·bark′
em·bar·ka′tion
em·bar′rass
em·bar′rass·ment
em·bas·sy
em·bat′tled
em·bed′ also
  im·bed′, -bed′ded,
  -bed′ding
em·bel′lish
em′ber
em·bez′zle, -zled,
  -zling
em·bez′zle·ment
em·bez′zler
em·bit′ter
em·bla′zon
em′blem
em·blem·at′ic or
  em′blem·at′i·cal
em·bod′i·ment
em·bod′y, -bod′ied,
  -bod′y·ing
em·bold′en

em′bo·lism
em′bo·lus pl. -li′
em·boss′
em·brace′, -braced′,
  -brac′ing
em·bra′sure
em·broi′der
em·broi′der·y
em·broil′
em′bry·o′ pl. -os′
em′bry·o·log′i·cal
  or em′bry·o·log′ic
em′bry·ol′o·gist
em′bry·ol′o·gy
em′bry·on′ic
e·mcee′, -ceed′,
  -cee′ing
e·mend′ *(to correct
  by editing)*
  ✔ *amend*
e·men′da′tion
e·men′da·tor
e·men′da·to′ry
em′er·ald
e·merge′,
  e·merged′,
  e·merg′ing
e·mer′gence
e·mer′gen·cy
e·mer′gent
e·mer′i·ta
e·mer′i·tus
em′er·y
e·met′ic
em′i·grant *(one who
  leaves one's native
  land)*

✔ *immigrant*
em′i·grate′ *(to leave
  one's native land)*,
  -grat′ed, -grat′ing
  ✔ *immigrate*
em′i·gra′tion *(leav-
  ing one's own
  land)*
  ✔ *immigration*
é′mi·gré′
em′i·nence
em′i·nent *(promi-
  nent)*
  ✔ *immanent, immi-
  nent*
e·mir′
e·mir′ate
em′is·sar′y
e·mis′sion
e·mis′sive
e·mit′, e·mit′ted,
  e·mit′ting
e·mit′ter
e·mol′lient
e·mol′u·ment
e·mote′, e·mot′ed,
  e·mot′ing
e·mo′tion
e·mo′tion·al
e·mo′tive
em·pa·thet′ic
em·path′ic
em′pa·thize′,
  -thized′, -thiz′ing
em′pa·thy
em′per·or
em′pha·sis pl. -ses′

em′pha·size′,
-sized′, -siz′ing
em·phat′ic
em·phy·se′ma
em′pire
em·pir′i·cal
em·pir′i·cism
em·pir′i·cist
em·place′ment
em·ploy′
em·ploy′ee *also*
em·ploy′e
em·ploy′er
em·ploy′ment
em·po′ri·um *pl.*
-ri·ums *or* -ri·a
em·pow′er
em′press
emp′ti·ness
emp′ty, -tied,
-ty′ing
emp′ty-hand′ed
em′py·re′al
em′py·re′an
e′mu
em·u·late′, -lat′ed,
-lat′ing
em·u·la′tion
em·u·la′tor
em·u·lous
e·mul′si·fi·ca′tion
e·mul′si·fy′, -fied′,
-fy′ing
e·mul′sion
en·a′ble, -bled,
-bling
en·act′

en·ac′tor
en·act′ment
e·nam′el, -eled *or*
-elled, -el·ing *or*
-el·ling
e·nam′el·ware′
en·am′or, -ored,
-or·ing
en·camp′
en·camp′ment
en·cap′su·late′ *also*
in·cap′su·late′,
-lat′ed, -lat′ing
en·cap′su·la′tion
en·case′, -cased′,
-cas′ing
en′ce·phal′ic
en·ceph′a·li′tis
en·ceph′a·lo·gram′
en·ceph′a·lo·
graph′
en·ceph′a·log′ra·
phy
en·ceph′a·lon′
en·chant′
en·chant′er
en·chant′ing
en·chant′ment
en′chi·la′da
en·ci′pher
en·cir′cle, -cled,
-cling
en·cir′cle·ment
en′clave′
en·close′ *also*
in·close′, -closed′,
-clos′ing

en·clo′sure
en·code′, -cod′ed,
-cod′ing
en·cod′er
en·co′mi·um *pl.*
-mi·ums *or* -mi·a
en·com′pass
en·core′, -cored′,
-cor′ing
en·coun′ter
en·cour′age, -aged,
-ag·ing
en·cour′age·ment
en·croach′
en·crust′ *also*
in·crust′
en′crus·ta′tion
en·cum′ber
en·cum′brance
en·cyc′li·cal
en·cy′clo·pe′di·a
en·cy′clo·pe′dic
end
en·dan′ger
en·dan′gered
en·dear′
en·deav′or
en·dem′ic
end′game′ *also*
end′ game′
end′ing
en′dive′
end′less
end′most′
end′note′
en′do·car′di·um
pl. -di·a

en•do•carp'
en•do•crine
en•do•cri•nol'o•gist
en•do•cri•nol'o•gy
en•do•derm' *also*
  en•to•derm'
en•do•don'tia
en•do•don'tics
en•do•me•tri•o'sis
en•do•me'tri•um
en•do•morph'
en•do•mor'phic
en•do•plasm
en•dor'phin
en•dorse', -dorsed',
  -dors'ing
en•dorse'ment
en•dors'er
en'do•scope'
en'do•skel'e•ton
en'do•sperm'
en'do•ther'mic
en•dow'
en•dow'ment
end'pa'per *also*
  end' pa'per
end' plate'
end'play'
end'point' *or*
  end' point' *also*
  end'-point'
en•due' *also*
  in•due', -dued',
  -du'ing
en•dur'a•ble
en•dur'a•bly

en•dur'ance
en•dure', -dured',
  -dur'ing
end'wise' *also*
  end'ways'
en•e•ma *pl.* -mas
en'e•my
en'er•get'ic
en'er•gize', -gized',
  -giz'ing
en'er•giz'er
en'er•gy
en'er•vate', -vat'ed,
  -vat'ing
en'er•va'tion
en•fee'ble, -bled,
  -bling
en•fee'ble•ment
en'fi•lade', -lad'ed,
  -lad'ing
en•fold'
en•force', -forced',
  -forc'ing
en•force'a•ble
en•force'ment
en•forc'er
en•fran'chise',
  -chised', -chis'ing
en•fran'chise•ment
en•gage', -gaged',
  -gag'ing
en•gage'ment
en•gag'ing
en•gen'der
en'gine
en'gi•neer'
en'gi•neer'ing

Eng'lish
Eng'lish•man
Eng'lish•wom'an
en•gorge', -gorged',
  -gorg'ing
en•gorge'ment
en•graft'
en•grave', -graved',
  -grav'ing
en•grav'er
en•gross'
en•gross'ing
en•gulf'
en•hance',
  -hanced',
  -hanc'ing
en•hance'ment
e•nig'ma
en'ig•mat'ic *or*
  en'ig•mat'i•cal
en•join'
en•joy'
en•joy'a•ble
en•joy'ment
en•kin'dle, -dled,
  -dling
en•large', -larged',
  -larg'ing
en•large'ment
en•larg'er
en•light'en
en•light'en•ment
en•list'
en•list'ment
en•liv'en
en masse'
en•mesh'

en'mi•ty
en•no'ble, -bled,
  -bling
en•nui'
e•nor'mi•ty
e•nor'mous
e•nough'
en•plane' *also*
  em•plane'
en•rage', -raged',
  -rag'ing
en•rap'ture, -tured,
  -tur•ing
en•rich'
en•rich'ment
en•roll' *also* en•rol',
  -rolled', -roll'ing
en•roll'ment *also*
  en•rol'ment
en route'
en•sconce',
  -sconced',
  -sconc'ing
en•sem'ble
en•shrine' *also*
  in•shrine',
  -shrined',
  -shrin'ing
en•shrine'ment
en•shroud'
en'sign
en'si•lage
en•slave', -slaved',
  -slav'ing
en•slave'ment
en•snare', -snared',
  -snar'ing

en•snarl'
en•sue', -sued',
  -su'ing
en•sure' *(to make
  sure)*, -sured',
  -sur'ing
  ✔ assure, insure
en•tab'la•ture'
en•tail'
en•tan'gle, -gled,
  -gling
en•tan'gle•ment
en'ter
en•ter'ic
en'ter•i'tis
en'ter•prise'
en'ter•pris'ing
en'ter•tain'
en'ter•tain'er
en'ter•tain'ment
en•thrall'
en•throne',
  -throned',
  -thron'ing
en•throne'ment
en•thuse', -thused',
  -thus'ing
en•thu'si•asm
en•thu'si•ast
en•thu'si•as'tic
en•tice', -ticed',
  -tic'ing
en•tice'ment
en•tire'
en•tire'ly
en•tire'ty
en•ti'tle, -tled,

  -tling
en•ti'tle•ment
en'ti•ty
en•tomb'
en•tomb'ment
en'to•mo•log'ic *or*
  en'to•mo•log'i•cal
en'to•mol'o•gist
en'to•mol'o•gy
en'tou•rage'
en'trails
en'train'
en'trance *n.*
en•trance',
  -tranced',
  -tranc'ing
en'trant
en•trap', -trapped',
  -trap'ping
en•trap'ment
en•treat' *also*
  in•treat'
en•treat'y
en•trée *or* en'tree
en•trench' *also*
  in•trench'
en'tre•pre•neur'
en'tro•py
en•trust' *also*
  in•trust'
en'try
en'try•way'
en•twine' *also*
  in•twine',
  -twined', -twin'ing
e•nu'mer•ate',
  -at'ed, -at'ing

e•nu′mer•a′tion
e•nu′mer•a′tive
e•nu′mer•a′tor
e•nun′ci•ate′ *(to ar-*
  ticulate), -at′ed,
  -at′ing
  ✔ *annunciate*
e•nun′ci•a′tion
e•nun′ci•a′tor
en•vel′op *v.*
en′ve•lope′ *n.*
en•vel′op•ment
en•ven′om
en′vi•a•ble
en′vi•a•bly
en′vi•ous
en•vi′ron•ment
en•vi′ron•men′tal
en•vi′rons
en•vis′age, -aged,
  -ag•ing
en•vi′sion
en′voy′
en′vy, -vied, -vy•ing
en•wrap′,
  -wrapped′,
  -wrap′ping
en′zy•mat′ic
en′zyme
E′o•cene′
e′o•hip′pus
E′o•lith′ic
e′on′
ep•au′let′ *also*
  ep′au•lette′
e•phed′rine
e•phem′er•al

E•phe′sian
ep′ic *(poem)*
  ✔ *epoch*
ep′i•cen′ter
ep′i•cure′
ep′i•cu•re′an
ep′i•dem′ic
ep′i•de′mi•o•log′ic
  or ep′i•de′mi•o•
  log′i•cal
ep′i•de′mi•ol′o•gist
ep′i•de′mi•ol′o•gy
ep′i•der′mis
ep′i•glot′tis *pl.*
  -glot′tis•es *or*
  -glot′ti•des′
ep′i•gram′
ep′i•gram•mat′ic
ep′i•graph′
ep′i•lep′sy
ep′i•lep′tic
ep′i•logue′ *also*
  ep′i•log′
ep′i•neph′rine *also*
  ep′i•neph′rin
e•piph′a•ny
ep′i•phyte′
ep′i•phyt′ic
e•pis′co•pa•cy
e•pis′co•pal
E•pis′co•pa′lian
e•pis′co•pate
ep′i•sode′
ep′i•sod′ic
e•pis′te•mol′o•gy
e•pis′tle
e•pis′to•lar′y

ep′i•taph′
ep′i•the′li•al
ep′i•the′li•um *pl.*
  -li•ums *or* -li•a
ep′i•thet′
e•pit′o•me
e•pit′o•mize′,
  -mized′, -miz′ing
ep′och *(period of*
  time)
  ✔ *epic*
ep′och•al
ep′o•nym′
e•pon′y•mous
ep•ox′y
ep′si•lon′
Ep′som salts′
eq′ua•bil′i•ty
eq′ua•ble
eq′ua•bly
e′qual, e′qualed *or*
  e′qualled,
  e′qual•ing *or*
  e′qual•ling
e•qual′i•ty
e′qual•i•za′tion
e′qual•ize′, -ized′,
  -iz′ing
e′qual•ize′
e′qua•nim′i•ty
e•quate′, e•quat′ed,
  e•quat′ing
e•qua′tion
e•qua′tor
e′qua•to′ri•al
eq′uer•ry
e•ques′tri•an

e·qui·an'gu·lar
e·qui·dis'tant
e·qui·lat'er·al
e·qui·lib'ri·um
e'quine'
e·qui·noc'tial
e'qui·nox'
e·quip', e·quipped',
    e·quip'ping
eq'ui·page
e·quip'ment
e'qui·poise'
eq'ui·ta·ble
eq'ui·ta·bly
eq'ui·ty
e·quiv'a·lence
e·quiv'a·lent
e·quiv'o·cal
e·quiv'o·cate',
    -cat·ed, -cat·ing
e·quiv'o·ca'tion
e·quiv'o·ca'tor
e'ra
e·rad'i·ca·ble
e·rad'i·cate',
    -cat·ed, -cat·ing
e·rad'i·ca'tion
e·ras'a·ble
e·rase', e·rased',
    e·ras'ing
e·ras'er
e·ra'sure
er'bi·um
ere *(before)*
    ✔ air, are, e'er, heir
e·rect'
e·rec'tion

e·rec'tor
erg
er'go
er·go·nom'ics
er'got
er'got·ism
E'rie *pl.* E'rie *or*
    E'ries
er'mine
e·rode', e·rod'ed,
    e·rod'ing
e·rog'e·nous
e·ro'sion
e·ro'sive
e·rot'ic
e·rot'i·cism
err
er'rand
er'rant
er·rat'ic
er·ra'tum *pl.* -ta
er·ro'ne·ous
er'ror
er'satz'
erst'while'
e·ruct'
e·ruc·ta'tion
er'u·dite'
er'u·di'tion
e·rupt' *(to explode)*
    ✔ irrupt
e·rup'tion
e·rup'tive
e·ryth'ro·blast'
e·ryth'ro·cyte'
es·ca·late', -lat·ed,
    -lat'ing

es'ca·la'tion
es'ca·la'tor
es·cap'a·ble
es'ca·pade'
es·cape', -caped',
    -cap'ing
es·cap·ee'
es·cape'ment
es·cap'ism
es·cap'ist
es'car·got'
es'ca·role'
es·carp'ment
es·chew'
es'cort' *n.*
es·cort' *v.*
es'crow'
es·cutch'eon
es'ker
Es·ki·mo' *pl.* -mo'
    or -mos'
e·soph'a·ge'al
e·soph'a·gus *also*
    oe·soph'a·gus *pl.*
    -gi'
es'o·ter'ic
es'pa·drille'
es·pe'cial
es·pe'cial·ly
es'pi·o·nage'
es'pla·nade'
es·pous'al
es·pouse', -poused',
    -pous'ing
es·pres'so *pl.* -sos
es·prit'
es·prit' de corps'

es·py', -pied',
 -py'ing
es'quire'
es'say' n.
es'say' (to attempt)
 ✔ assay
es'say·ist
es'sence
es·sen'tial
es·tab'lish
es·tab'lish·ment
es·tate'
es·teem'
es'ter
es'ti·ma·ble
es'ti·ma·bly
es'ti·mate',
 -mat'ed, -mat'ing
es'ti·ma'tion
es'ti·vate', -vat'ed,
 -vat'ing
Es·to'ni·an
es·trange',
 -tranged',
 -trang'ing
es·trange'ment
es·tro'gen
es'trous adj.
es'trus n.
es'tu·ar'y
e'ta
et cet'er·a
etch
etch'ing
e·ter'nal
e·ter'ni·ty
eth'ane'

eth'a·nol'
e'ther
e·the're·al
eth'ic
eth'i·cal
eth'i·cist
eth'ics
E'thi·o'pi·an
eth'nic
eth·nic'i·ty
eth·no·cen'tric
eth·no·cen'trism
eth·nog'ra·pher
eth·no·graph'ic or
 eth·no·graph'i·cal
eth·nog'ra·phy
eth·no·log'ic or
 eth·no·log'i·cal
eth·nol'o·gist
eth·nol'o·gy
e'thos'
eth'yl
eth'yl·ene'
e'ti·o·log'ic or
 e'ti·o·log'i·cal
e'ti·ol'o·gist
e'ti·ol'o·gy also
 ae'ti·ol'o·gy
et'i·quette'
E·trus'can
e'tude'
et'y·mo·log'i·cal
et'y·mol'o·gist
et'y·mol'o·gy
eu·ca·lyp'tus pl.
 -tus·es or -ti'
Eu'cha·rist

Eu·clid'e·an or
 Eu·clid'i·an
eu·gen'ics
eu·gle'na
eu'lo·gist
eu'lo·gize', -gized',
 -giz'ing
eu'lo·gy
eu'nuch
eu'phe·mism
eu'phe·mis'tic
eu·pho'ni·ous
eu·pho'ni·um
eu·pho'ny
eu·pho'ri·a
eu·phor'ic
Eur·a'sian
eu·re'ka
Eu'ro-A·mer'i·can
Eu'ro·pe'an
eu·ro'pi·um
eu·sta'chian tube'
 or Eu·sta'chian
 tube'
eu·tha·na'sia
e·vac'u·ate', -at'ed,
 -at'ing
e·vac'u·a'tion
e·vac'u·ee'
e·vade', e·vad'ed,
 e·vad'ing
e·val'u·ate', -at'ed,
 -at'ing
e·val'u·a'tion
ev'a·nes'cence
ev'a·nes'cent
e'van·gel'i·cal also

e′van•gel′ic
e•van′gel•ism
e•van′gel•ist
e•van′gel•ize′,
  -ized′, -iz′ing
e•vap′o•rate′,
  -rat′ed, -rat′ing
e•vap′o•ra′tion
e•va′sion
e•va′sive
eve
e′ven
e′ven•hand′ed
eve′ning
e′ven•ly
e′ven•ness
e′ven•song′
e•vent′
e•vent′ful
e•ven′tide′
e•ven′tu•al
e•ven′tu•al′i•ty
e•ven′tu•al•ly
e•ven′tu•ate′,
  -at′ed, -at′ing
ev′er
ev′er•glade′
ev′er•green′
ev′er•last′ing
ev′er•more′
e•ver′sion
e•vert′
eve′ry
eve′ry•bod′y
eve′ry•day′
eve′ry•one′
eve′ry•place′

eve′ry•thing′
eve′ry•where′
e•vict′
e•vic′tion
ev′i•dence,
  -denced, -denc•ing
ev′i•dent
e′vil
e′vil•do′er
e′vil-mind′ed
e•vince′, e•vinced′,
  e•vinc′ing
e•vinc′i•ble
e•vis′cer•ate′,
  -at′ed, -at′ing
e•vis′cer•a′tion
ev′o•ca′tion
e•voc′a•tive
e•voke′, e•voked′,
  e•vok′ing
ev′o•lu′tion
ev′o•lu′tion•ar′y
ev′o•lu′tion•ism
ev′o•lu′tion•ist
e•volve′, e•volved′,
  e•volv′ing
ewe *(female sheep)*
  ✔ yew, you
ew′er
ex•ac′er•bate′,
  -bat′ed, -bat′ing
ex•ac′er•ba′tion
ex•act′
ex•act′ing
ex•ac′tion
ex•ac′ti•tude′
ex•act′ly

ex•ac′tor
ex•ag′ger•ate′,
  -at′ed, -at′ing
ex•ag′ger•a′tion
ex•ag′ger•a′tor
ex•alt′
ex•al′ta′tion
ex•alt′ed
ex•am′
ex•am′i•na′tion
ex•am′ine, -ined,
  -in•ing
ex•am′in•er
ex•am′ple
ex•as′per•ate′,
  -at′ed, -at′ing
ex•as′per•a′tion
ex′ca•vate′, -vat′ed,
  -vat′ing
ex′ca•va′tion
ex′ca•va′tor
ex•ceed′ *(to surpass)*
  ✔ accede
ex•ceed′ing
ex•cel′, -celled′,
  -cel′ling
ex′cel•lence
Ex′cel•len•cy
ex′cel•lent
ex•cept′ *(to leave
  out)*
  ✔ accept
ex•cept′ing
ex•cep′tion
ex•cep′tion•a•ble
ex•cep′tion•al
ex′cerpt′ *n.*

ex•cerpt' v.
ex•cess' (surplus)
  ✔ access
ex•ces'sive
ex•change',
  -changed',
  -chang'ing
ex•change'a•ble
ex•chang'er
ex'cheq'uer
ex'cise' (tax)
ex•cise' (to cut),
  -cised', -cis'ing
ex•ci'sion
ex•cit'a•bil'i•ty or
  ex•cit'a•ble•ness
ex•cit'a•ble
ex•cit'a•bly
ex'ci•ta'tion
ex•ci'ta•tive or
  ex•ci'ta•to'ry
ex•cite', -cit'ed,
  -cit'ing
ex•cite'ment
ex•claim'
ex'cla•ma'tion
ex•clam'a•to'ry
ex•clud'a•ble or
  ex•clud'i•ble
ex•clude', -clud'ed,
  -clud'ing
ex•clu'sion
ex•clu'sion•ar'y
ex•clu'sive
ex'com•mu'ni•
  cate', -cat'ed,
  -cat'ing

ex•com•mu'ni•ca'-
  tion
ex•co'ri•ate', -at'ed,
  -at'ing
ex•co'ri•a'tion
ex'cre•ment
ex•cres'cence
ex•cres'cent
ex•cre'ta
ex•crete', -cret'ed,
  -cret'ing
ex•cre'tion
ex'cre•to'ry
ex•cru'ci•at'ing
ex'cul•pate'
ex'cul•pa'tion
ex•cul'pa•to'ry
ex•cur'sion
ex•cus'a•ble
ex•cus'a•bly
ex•cuse', -cused',
  -cus'ing
ex•cus'er
ex'e•cra•ble
ex'e•crate', -crat'ed,
  -crat'ing
ex'e•cra'tion
ex'e•cute', -cut'ed,
  -cut'ing
ex'e•cu'tion
ex'e•cu'tion•er
ex•ec'u•tive
ex•ec'u•tor
ex•ec'u•trix'
ex'e•ge'sis pl. -ses
ex•em'plar
ex•em'plar'i•ly

ex•em'pla•ry
ex•em'pli•fi•ca'-
  tion
ex•em'pli•fy',
  -fied', -fy'ing
ex•empt'
ex•empt'i•ble
ex•emp'tion
ex'er•cise' (to make
  use of), -cised',
  -cis'ing
  ✔ exorcise
ex'er•cis'er
ex•ert'
ex•er'tion
ex•fo'li•ate'
ex•fo'li•a'tion
ex'ha•la'tion
ex•hale', -haled',
  -hal'ing
ex•haust'
ex•haust'i•ble
ex•haus'tion
ex•haus'tive
ex•hib'it
ex'hi•bi'tion
ex'hi•bi'tion•ism
ex'hi•bi'tion•ist
ex•hib'i•tor or
  ex•hib'it•er
ex•hil'a•rate',
  -rat'ed, -rat'ing
ex•hil'a•ra'tion
ex•hort'
ex'hor•ta'tion
ex•hor'ta•tive also
  ex•hor'ta•to'ry

ex'hu·ma'tion
ex·hume',
  -humed', -hum'ing
ex'i·gence
ex'i·gen·cy
ex'i·gent
ex'ile', -iled', -il'ing
ex·ist'
ex·is'tence
ex·is'tent
ex'is·ten'tial
ex'is·ten'tial·ism
ex'is·ten'tial·ist
ex'it
ex'o·bi·ol'o·gy
ex'o·bi·ol'o·gist
ex'o·crine
ex'o·dus
ex' of·fi'ci·o'
ex·on'er·ate',
  -at'ed, -at'ing
ex·on'er·a'tion
ex·or'bi·tance
ex·or'bi·tant
ex'or·cise' *(to drive
  away)*, -cised',
  -cis'ing
  ✔ exercise
ex'or·cism
ex'or·cist
ex'o·skel'e·ton
ex'o·sphere'
ex'o·spher'ic
ex'o·ther'mic *also*
  ex'o·ther'mal
ex·ot'ic
ex·ot'i·ca

ex·pand'
ex·pand'a·ble
ex·panse'
ex·pan'sion
ex·pan'sion·ism
ex·pan'sion·ist
ex·pan'sive
ex·pa'ti·ate', -at'ed,
  -at'ing
ex·pa'ti·a'tion
ex·pa'tri·ate',
  -at'ed, -at'ing
ex·pa'tri·a'tion
ex·pect'
ex·pec'tan·cy
ex·pec'tant
ex·pec'ta'tion
ex·pec'to·rant
ex·pec'to·rate',
  -rat'ed, -rat'ing
ex·pec'to·ra'tion
ex·pe'di·ence
ex·pe'di·en·cy
ex·pe'di·ent
ex·pe·dite', -dit'ed,
  -dit'ing
ex'pe·dit'er *or*
  ex'pe·di'tor
ex'pe·di'tion
ex'pe·di'tion·ar'y
ex'pe·di'tious
ex·pel', -pelled',
  -pel'ling
ex·pend'
ex·pend'a·ble
ex·pen'di·ture
ex·pense'

ex·pen'sive
ex·pen'sive·ly
ex·pe'ri·ence,
  -enced', -enc'ing
ex·per'i·ment
ex·per'i·men'tal
ex·per'i·men·ta'-
  tion
ex·per'i·ment'er
ex'pert'
ex'per·tise'
ex'pi·ate', -at'ed,
  -at'ing
ex'pi·a'tion
ex'pi·a'tor
ex'pi·ra'tion
ex·pire', -pired',
  -pir'ing
ex·plain'
ex·plain'a·ble
ex·plain'er
ex'pla·na'tion
ex·plan'a·to'ry
ex'ple·tive
ex'pli·ca·ble
ex'pli·cate', -cat'ed,
  -cat'ing
ex'pli·ca'tion
ex'pli·ca'tor
ex·plic'it
ex·plode', -plod'ed,
  -plod'ing
ex·plod'er
ex·ploit' *n.*
ex·ploit' *v.*
ex·ploit'a·ble
ex'ploi·ta'tion

ex·ploit'er
ex'plo·ra'tion
ex·plor'a·to'ry
ex·plore', -plored',
  -plor'ing
ex·plor'er
ex·plo'sion
ex·plo'sive
ex·plo'sive·ly
ex·po'nent
ex'po·nen'tial
ex·port' *v.*
ex'port' *n.*
ex·port'a·ble
ex'por·ta'tion
ex·port'er
ex·pose', -posed',
  -pos'ing
ex'po·sé'
ex·pos'er
ex'po·si'tion
ex·pos'i·tor
ex' post fac'to
ex·pos'tu·late',
  -lat'ed, -lat'ing
ex·pos'tu·la'tion
ex·po'sure
ex·pound'
ex·pound'er
ex·press'
ex·press'i·ble
ex·pres'sion
ex·pres'sion·ism
ex·pres'sion·ist
ex·pres'sive
ex·pres'sive·ly
ex·press'way'

ex·pro'pri·ate',
  -at'ed, -at'ing
ex·pro'pri·a'tion
ex·pro'pri·a'tor
ex·pul'sion
ex·punge',
  -punged',
  -pung'ing
ex'pur·gate',
  -gat'ed, -gat'ing
ex'pur·ga'tion
ex'pur·ga'tor
ex'qui·site
ex'tant *(existing)*
  ✔ extent
ex·tem'po·ra'ne·
  ous
ex·tem'po·rar'i·ly
ex·tem'po·rar'y
ex·tem'po·re
ex·tem'po·rize',
  -rized', -riz'ing
ex·tend'
ex·tend'ed
ex·tend'i·ble
ex·ten'si·ble
ex·ten'sion
ex·ten'sive
ex·ten'sor
ex·tent' *(size)*
  ✔ extant
ex·ten'u·ate',
  -at'ed, -at'ing
ex·ten'u·a'tion
ex·ten'u·a'tor
ex·ten'u·a·to'ry
ex·te'ri·or

ex·ter'mi·nate',
  -nat'ed, -nat'ing
ex·ter'mi·na'tion
ex·ter'mi·na'tor
ex·ter'nal
ex·ter'nal·i·za'·
  tion
ex·ter'nal·ize'
ex·tinct'
ex·tinc'tion
ex·tin'guish
ex·tin'guish·a·ble
ex·tin'guish·er
ex'tir·pate', -pat'ed,
  -pat'ing
ex'tir·pa'tion
ex·tol' *also* ex·toll',
  -tolled', -tol·ling
ex·tol'ler
ex·tort'
ex·tort'er
ex·tor'tion
ex·tor'tion·ate
ex·tor'tion·ist
ex'tra
ex·tract' *v.*
ex'tract' *n.*
ex·trac'tion
ex·trac'tor
ex'tra·cur·ric'u·lar
ex'tra·dite', -dit'ed,
  -dit'ing
ex'tra·di'tion
ex'tra·mar'i·tal
ex'tra·ne·ous
ex·traor'di·naire'
ex·traor'di·nar'i·ly

ex•traor'di•nar'y
ex•trap'o•late',
 -lat'ed, -lat'ing
ex•trap'o•la'tion
ex'tra•sen'so•ry
ex'tra•ter•res'tri•al
ex•trav'a•gance
ex•trav'a•gant
ex•trav'a•gan'za
ex•treme'
ex•trem'ism
ex•trem'ist
ex•trem'i•ty
ex'tri•cate', -cat'ed,
 -cat'ing
ex'tri•ca'tion
ex•trin'sic
ex'tra•ver'sion
ex'tro•vert'
ex•trude', -trud'ed,
 -trud'ing
ex•tru'sion
ex•u'ber•ance
ex•u'ber•ant
ex'u•da'tion
ex•ude', -ud'ed,
 -ud'ing
ex•ult'
ex•ul'tant
ex'ul•ta'tion
eye (organ or sight),
 eyed, eye'ing or
 ey'ing
 ✔ aye, I
eye'ball'
eye'brow'
eye'cup'

eye'drop'per
eye'glass'
eye'lash'
eye'let (small hole)
 ✔ islet
eye'lid'
eye' o'pen•er
eye'piece'
eye' shad'ow
eye'sight'
eye' sock'et
eye'sore'
eye'spot'
eye'stalk'
eye'strain'
eye'tooth'
eye'wash'
eye'wit'ness

F

fa'ble
fa'bled
fab'ric
fab'ri•cate', -cat'ed,
 -cat'ing
fab'ri•ca'tion
fab'u•list
fab'u•lous
fa•çade' also
 fa•cade'
face, faced, fac'ing
face'down' n.
face'down' adv.
face'less

face'-lift'
face'mask'
face'-off' n.
fac'et
fa•ce'tious
face'up' adv.
fa'cial
fac'ile
fa•cil'i•tate',
 -tat'ed, -tat'ing
fa•cil'i•ta'tion
fa•cil'i•ty
fac•sim'i•le
fact
fact'find'ing
fac'tion
fac'tion•al•ism
fac'tious
fac•ti'tious (artifi-
 cial)
 ✔ fictitious
fac'toid
fac'tor
fac•to'ri•al
fac'to•ry
fac'to•tum
fac'tu•al
fac'ul•ty
fad
fad'dish
fade, fad'ed, fad'ing
fade'-in' or fade'in'
 n.
fade'-out' or
 fade'out' n.
fa'er•ie also fa'er•y
 pl. -ies

fag, fagged, fag'ging
fag'ot also fag'got
Fahr'en•heit'
fail (to be unsuccess-
  ful)
  ✔ faille
fail'ing
faille (silk)
  ✔ fail, file
fail'-safe'
fail'ure
fain (willingly)
  ✔ feign
faint (pass out)
  ✔ feint
faint'-heart'ed
fair (just, lovely, light)
  ✔ fare
fair (market)
  ✔ fare
fair'ground'
fair'-haired'
fair'-mind'ed
fair'way'
fair'-weath'er adj.
fair'y
fair'y•land'
fait' ac•com•pli' pl.
  faits' ac•com•plis'
faith
faith'ful
faith'less
fa•ji'ta
fake, faked, fak'ing
fak'er (impostor)
  ✔ fakir
fak'er•y

fa•kir' (beggar)
  ✔ faker
fal'con
fal'con•er
fal'con•ry
fall, fell, fall'en,
  fall'ing
fal•la'cious
fal'la•cy
fal•li•bil'i•ty
fal'li•ble
fal'li•bly
fall'ing-out' pl.
  fall'ings-out' or
  fall'ing-outs'
fal•lo'pi•an
fall'out' n.
fal'low
false, fals'er, fals'est
false'hood'
false'ly
fal•set'to pl. -tos
fal'si•fi•ca'tion
fal'si•fi'er
fal'si•fy', -fied',
  -fy'ing
fal'si•ty
fal'ter
fal'ter•ing•ly
fame
famed
fa•mil'ial
fa•mil'iar
fa•mil'iar'i•ty
fa•mil'iar•ize',
  -ized', -iz'ing
fam'i•ly

fam'ine
fam'ished
fa'mous
fan, fanned,
  fan'ning
fa•nat'ic
fa•nat'i•cal
fa•nat'i•cism
fan'ci•er
fan'ci•ful
fan'cy, -cied, -cy•ing
fan'cy-free'
fan'cy•work'
fan•dan'go pl. -gos
fan'fare'
fang
fan'tail'
fan•ta'sia
fan•ta•size', -sized',
  -siz'ing
fan•tas'tic
fan•tas'ti•cal•ly
fan'ta•sy
far, far'ther or
  fur'ther, far'thest
  or fur'thest
far'ad
far'a•day'
far'a•way'
farce
far'ci•cal
fare (to get along),
  fared, far'ing
  ✔ fair
fare (money charged)
  ✔ fair
fare•well'

far'-fetched'
far'-flung'
fa•ri'na
far'i•na'ceous
farm
farm'er
farm' hand'
farm'house'
farm'land'
farm'stead'
farm' team'
farm'yard'
far'-off'
far'-out'
far•ra'go *pl.* -goes
far-reach'ing
far'ri•er
far'row
far•see'ing
Far'si
far'sight'ed *or*
  far'-sight'ed
far'ther (*to a greater*
  distance)
  ✔ *further*
far'ther•most'
far'thest (*to the most*
  distant point)
  ✔ *furthest*
far'thing
far'thin•gale'
fas'ci•a *pl.* -ci•ae'
fas'ci•cle
fas'ci•nate',
  -nat'ed, -nat'ing
fas'ci•na'tion
fas'cism

fas'cist
fash'ion
fash'ion•a•ble
fash'ion•a•bly
fast
fast'ball'
fas'ten
fas'ten•er
fas'ten•ing
fast' food' *n.*
fast'-food' *adj.*
fas•tid'i•ous
fat, fat'ter, fat'test
fa'tal
fa'tal•ism
fa'tal•ist
fa'tal•is'tic
fa•tal'i•ty
fa'tal•ly
fat'back'
fate (*destiny*)
  ✔ *fete*
fat'ed
fate'ful
fa'ther
fa'ther•hood'
fa'ther-in-law' *pl.*
  fa'thers-in-law'
fa'ther•land'
fa'ther•less
fa'ther•li•ness
fa'ther•ly
fath'om *pl.* -om *or*
  -oms
fath'om•a•ble
fa•tigue', -tigued',
  -tigu'ing

fat'ten
fat'ti•ness
fat'ty
fa•tu'i•ty
fat'u•ous
fau'cet
fault
fault'find'er
fault'find'ing
fault'i•ness
fault'y
faun (*deity*)
  ✔ *fawn*
fau'na *pl.* -nas *or*
  -nae'
faux pas' *pl.* faux
  pas'
fa'vor
fa'vor•a•ble
fa'vor•a•bly
fa'vor•ite
fa'vor•it•ism
fawn (*to flatter*)
  ✔ *faun*
fawn (*young deer*)
  ✔ *faun*
fax
fax' ma•chine'
fay
faze (*to upset*), fazed,
  faz'ing
  ✔ *phase*
fe'al•ty
fear
fear'ful
fear'less
fear'some

fea′si·bil′i·ty
fea′si·ble
fea′si·bly
feast
feat *(exploit)*
   ✔ *feet*
feath′er
feath′er bed′
feath′er·bed′ding
feath′er·brain′
feath′er·brained′
feath′ered
feath′er·weight′
feath′er·y
fea′ture
feb′rile
Feb′ru·ar′y
fe′cal
fe′ces
feck′less
fe′cund
fe·cun′di·ty
fed′er·al
fed′er·al·ism
fed′er·al·ist
fed′er·ate′, -at′ed,
   -at′ing
fed′er·a′tion
fe·do′ra
fee
fee′ble, -bler, -blest
fee′ble-mind′ed
fee′bly
feed, fed, feed′ing
feed′back′
feed′bag′
feed′er

feel, felt, feel′ing
feel′er
feel′ing·ly
feet *sing.* foot
   ✔ *feat*
feign *(to pretend)*
   ✔ *fain*
feint *(deceptive action)*
   ✔ *faint*
feist′y
feld′spar *also*
   fel′spar
fe·lic′i·tate′,
   -tat′ed, -tat′ing
fe·lic′i·ta′tion
fe·lic′i·tous
fe·lic′i·ty
fe′line′
fell
fel′lah *pl.* fel′la·hin′
   or fel′la·heen′
fel′low
fel′low·ship′
fel′on
fe·lo′ni·ous
fel′o·ny
felt
fe′male′
fem′i·nine
fem′i·nin′i·ty
fem′i·nism
fem′i·nist
femme′ fa·tale′ *pl.*
   femmes′ fa·tales′
fem′o·ral
fe′mur *pl.* -murs *or*
   fem′o·ra

fen
fence, fenced,
   fenc′ing
fenc′er
fend
fend′er
fend′er-bend′er *or*
   fend′er bend′er
fen′nel
fe′ral
fer′-de-lance′ *pl.*
   fer′-de-lance′
fer′ment′ *n.*
fer·ment′ *v.*
fer′men·ta′tion
fer′mi·um
fern
fe·ro′cious
fe·roc′i·ty
fer′ret *(animal, to
   hunt)*
fer′ret *also*
   fer′ret·ing *(tape)*
fer′ric
Fer′ris wheel′ *also*
   fer′ris wheel′
fer′rous
fer′rule *(metal ring)*
   ✔ *ferule*
fer′ry, -ried, -ry·ing
fer′ry·boat′
fer′tile
fer·til′i·ty
fer′til·i·za′tion
fer′til·ize′, -ized′,
   -iz′ing
fer′til·iz′er

fer′ule *(stick)*
  ✔ ferrule
fer′ven·cy
fer′vent
fer′vid
fer′vor
fes′tal
fes′ter
fes′ti·val
fes′tive
fes·tiv′i·ty
fes·toon′
fet′a
fe′tal *also* foe′tal
fetch
fete *also* fête *(festival)*
  ✔ fate
fete *also* fête *(to honor)*, fet′ed *also* fêt′ed, fet′ing *or* fêt′ing
  ✔ fate
fet′id
fet′ish
fet′ish·ism
fet′ish·ist
fet′lock′
fet′ter
fet′tle
fet′tuc·ci′ne
fe′tus *also* foe′tus *pl.* -tus·es
feud
feu′dal
feu′dal·ism
feu′dal·is′tic
fe′ver

fe′ver·ish
few
fez *pl.* fez′zes
fi′an·cé′ *(male)*
fi′an·cée′ *(female)*
fi·as′co *pl.* -coes *or* -cos
fi′at′
fib, fibbed, fib′bing
fib′ber
fi′ber
fi′ber·board′
fi′ber·glass′
fib′ril·la′tion
fi′brin
fi·brin′o·gen
fi′broid′
fi′brous
fib′u·la *pl.* -lae′ *or* -las
fick′le
fic′tion
fic′tion·al
fic′tion·al·ize′, -ized′, -iz′ing
fic·ti′tious *(imaginary)*
  ✔ factitious
fic′tive
fid′dle, -dled, -dling
fid′dler
fid′dle·sticks′
fi·del′i·ty
fidg′et
fidg′et·y
fie
fief

fief′dom
field
field′er
field′stone′
field′ test′ *n.*
field′-test′ *v.*
field′ trip′
field′work′
fiend
fiend′ish
fierce, fierc′er, fierc′est
fier′i·ness
fier′y
fi·es′ta
fife
fif·teen′
fif·teenth′
fifth
fif′ti·eth
fif′ty
fif′ty-fif′ty
fig
fight, fought, fight′ing
fight′er
fig′ment
fig′u·ra·tive
fig′ur·a·tive·ly
fig′ure, -ured, -ur·ing
fig′ure·head′
fig′u·rine′
Fi′ji·an
fil′a·ment
fil′bert
filch

filch′er
file *(folder, tool)*
  ✔ faille
file *(to put in order, to
  smooth)*, filed,
  fil′ing
  ✔ faille
fi·let′ *(lace)*
  ✔ fillet
fi·let′ mi·gnon′ *pl.*
  fi·lets′ mi·gnons′
fil′i·al
fil′i·bus′ter
fil′i·gree′, -greed′,
  -gree′ing
fil′ing
Fil′i·pi′no *pl.* -nos
fill′er
fil′let *(ribbon)*
fil·let′ *also* fi·let′
  *(piece of meat or
  fish)*
  ✔ filet
fil·let′ *also* fi·let′ *(to
  slice)*, fil·let′ed *also*
  fi·let′ed, fil·let′ing
  or fi·let′ing
  ✔ filet
fill′-in′
fill′ing
fil′lip
fil′ly
film
film′mak′er
film′mak′ing
film′strip′
film′y

fil′ter *(strainer)*
  ✔ philter
fil′ter·a·ble *also*
  fil′tra·ble
filth
filth′i·ness
filth′y
fil′trate′, -trat′ed,
  -trat′ing
fil·tra′tion
fin
fi·na′gle, -gled,
  -gling
fi·na′gler
fi′nal
fi′nal·e
fi′nal·ist
fi·nal′i·ty
fi′nal·i·za′tion
fi′nal·ize′, -ized′,
  -iz′ing
fi′nal·iz′er
fi′nal·ly
fi·nance′, -nanced′,
  -nanc′ing
fi·nan′cial
fin′an·cier′
finch
find, found, find′ing
find′er
fine, fin′er, fin′est
fine, fined, fin′ing
fine′-drawn′
fine′-grained′
fin′er·y
fi·nesse′, -nessed′,
  -ness′ing

fin′ger
fin′ger·board′
fin′ger hole′
fin′ger·ing
fin′ger·nail′
fin′ger-paint′
fin′ger paint′ing
fin′ger·print′
fin′ger·spell′
fin′ger·spell′ing
fin′ger·tip′
fin′i·cal
fin′ick·y
fin′is
fin′ish
fin′ished
fin′ish·er
fi′nite′
Finn
fin′nan had′die
finned
Finn′ish
fin′ny
fir *(tree)*
  ✔ fur
fire, fired, fir′ing
fire′arm′
fire′ball′
fire′boat′
fire′bomb′
fire′box′
fire′brand′
fire′break′
fire′bug′
fire′crack′er
fire′damp′
fire′dog′

fire′ drill′
fire′fight′er *also* fire′ fight′er
fire′fight′ing
fire′fly′
fire′house′
fire′ hy′drant
fire′light′
fire′man
fire′place′
fire′plug′
fire′pow′er
fire′proof′
fire′ screen′
fire′side′
fire′ sta′tion
fire′storm′
fire′ tow′er
fire′trap′
fire′ truck′
fire′wall′
fire′wood′
fire′work′
firm
fir′ma•ment
first
first′ aid′ *n.*
first′-aid′ *adj.*
first′ base′
first′ base′man
first′-born′
first′ class′ *n.*
first′-class′ *adj.*
first′-de•gree′ burn′
first′hand′
first′-rate′ *adj.*

first′-string′ *adj.*
firth
fis′cal
fish *pl.* fish *or* fish′es
fish′bowl′
fish′er *(one that fishes)*
    ✔ *fissure*
fish′er•man
fish′er•y
fish′hook′
fish′i•ness
fish′ing
fish′ing rod′
fish′meal′
fish′mon′ger
fish′net′
fish′pond′
fish′ stick′
fish′tail′
fish′wife′
fish′y
fis′sion
fis′sure *(crack)*
    ✔ *fisher*
fist′fight′
fist′ful′
fist′i•cuffs′
fis′tu•la *pl.* -las *or* -lae′
fit, fit′ted *or* fit, fit′ted, fit′ting
fit, fit′ter, fit′test
fitch
fit′ful
fit′ness
five

five′-and-dime′
five′-and-ten′
five′fold′
fix
fix′a•ble
fix′ate′, -at′ed, -at′ing
fix•a′tion
fix′a•tive
fixed
fix′ed•ly
fix′er
fix′ings
fix′ture
fizz
fiz′zle, -zled, -zling
fizz′y
fjord *or* fiord
flab
flab′ber•gast′
flab′bi•ness
flab′by
flac′cid
flac•cid′i•ty *or* flac′cid•ness
flack *(press agent)*
    ✔ *flak*
flac′on
flag, flagged, flag′ging
flag′el•late′, -lat′ed, -lat′ing
flag′el•la′tion
fla•gel′lum *pl.* -gel′la
flag′eo•let′
flag′man

flag'on
flag'pole'
fla'grance *or*
  fla'gran•cy
fla'grant
flag'ship'
flag'staff'
flag'stone'
flail
flair (*knack*)
  ✔ *flare*
flak (*artillery, criticism*)
  ✔ *flack*
flake, flaked,
  flak'ing
flak'i•ness
flak'y
flam•boy'ance *or*
  flam•boy'an•cy
flam•boy'ant
flame, flamed,
  flam'ing
fla•men'co *pl.* -cos
flame'throw'er
fla•min'go *pl.* -gos
  or -goes
flam'ma•bil'i•ty
flam'ma•ble (*easily ignited*)
  ✔ *inflammable,
  nonflammable*
flange
flank
flank'er
flan'nel
flan'nel•ette'

flap, flapped,
  flap'ping
flap'jack'
flap'per
flare (*to flame up*),
  flared, flar'ing
  ✔ *flair*
flare'-up' *n.*
flash'back' *n.*
flash'bulb' *or* flash'bulb'
flash'er
flash'i•ness
flash'light'
flash'y
flask
flat, flat'ter, flat'test
flat'bed'
flat'boat'
flat'car'
flat'fish' *pl.* -fish' *or* -fish'es
flat'foot' (*fallen arch*), *pl.* -feet'
flat'foot' (*police officer*), *pl.* -foots
flat'-foot'ed
Flat'head' *pl.* -head' *or* -heads'
flat'i'ron'
flat'land'
flat'ten
flat'ter
flat'ter•er
flat'ter•y
flat'top'
flat'u•lence

flat'u•lent
flat'ware'
flat'worm'
flaunt (*to show off*)
  ✔ *flout*
flau'tist
fla'vor
fla'vor•ful *or*
  fla'vor•some
flaw
flax
flax'en
flax'seed'
flay
flea (*insect*)
  ✔ *flee*
flea'bag'
flea'-bit'ten
fleck
fledge, fledged,
  fledg'ing
fledg'ling *also*
  fledge'ling
flee (*to run away*),
  fled, flee'ing
  ✔ *flea*
fleece, fleeced,
  fleec'ing
fleec'i•ness
fleec'y
fleet
fleet'ing
Flem'ing
Flem'ish
flesh'ly (*physical*)
flesh'y (*plump*)
fleur'-de-lis' *or*

fleur'-de-lys' *pl.*
fleurs'-de-lis' *or*
fleurs'-de-lys'

flew *past tense of*
fly
✔ *flu, flue*

flex'i•bil'i•ty

flex'i•ble

flex'i•bly

flex'ion

flex'or *(muscle)*
✔ *flexure*

flex'time'

flex'ure *(bend)*
✔ *flexor*

flick'er

fli'er *also* fly'er

flight

flight'i•ness

fight'-test' *v.*

flight'wor'thy

flight'y

flim'si•ly

flim'si•ness

flim'sy

flinch

fling, flung,
fling'ing

flint'lock'

flint'y

flip, flipped,
flip'ping

flip, flip'per,
flip'pest

flip'-flop'

flip'pan•cy

flip'pant

flip'per

flirt

flir•ta'tion

flir•ta'tious

flit, flit'ted, flit'ting

float

float'er

flock

floe *(floating ice)*
✔ *flow*

flog, flogged,
flog'ging

flog'ger

flood

flood'gate'

flood'light',
-light'ed *or* -lit',
-light'ing

flood'plain'

flood'wa'ter

floor

floor'board'

floor'ing

floor'show'

floor'walk'er

flop, flopped,
flop'ping

flop'pi•ness

flop'py

flop'py disk'

flo'ra *pl.* -ras *or*
-rae'

flo'ral

Flor'en•tine'

flo•res'cence
(flowering)
✔ *fluorescence*

flo'ret

flor'id

flor'in

flo'rist

floss

floss'y

flo•til'la

flot'sam

flounce, flounced,
flounc'ing

floun'der *v.*

floun'der *pl.* -der *or*
-ders

flour *(powdery meal)*
✔ *flower*

flour'ish

flout *(to scorn)*
✔ *flaunt*

flout'er

flow *(stream)*
✔ *floe*

flow' chart' *also*
flow'chart'

flow'er *(blossom)*
✔ *flour*

flow'er•i•ness

flow'er•pot'

flow'er•y

flu *(influenza)*
✔ *flew, flue*

flub, flubbed,
flub'bing

fluc'tu•ate', -at'ed,
-at'ing

fluc'tu•a'tion

flue *(pipe)*
✔ *flew, flu*

flu•en•cy
flu•ent
fluff
fluff'i•ness
fluff'y
flu'id
flu•id'i•ty
fluke
flume
flum'mox
flunk
flun'ky *also*
  flun'key *pl.* -kies
  also -keys
fluo•resce',
  -resced', -resc'ing
fluo•res'cence *(giv-
  ing off of light)*
  ✔ *florescence*
fluo•res'cent
fluor'i•date',
  -dat'ed, -dat'ing
fluor'i•da'tion
fluor'ide'
fluor'ine'
fluor'o•car'bon
fluor'o•scope'
fluor'o•scop'ic
fluo•ros'co•py
flur'ry, -ried, -ry•ing
flush
flus'ter
flute, flut'ed,
  flut'ing
flut'ist
flut'ter
flux

fly *(to move through
  the air)*, flew, flown,
  fly'ing
fly *(to hit a baseball)*,
  flied, fly'ing
fly *(insect)*
fly' ball'
fly'-by-night'
fly'catch'er
fly'er
fly'-fish'ing
fly'leaf'
fly'pa'per
fly'speck'
fly' swat'ter
fly'way'
fly'weight'
fly'wheel'
f'-num'ber
foal
foam
foam'y
fob, fobbed,
  fob'bing
fo'cal
fo'cus *pl.* -cus•es *or*
  -ci
fo'cus, -cused *or*
  -cussed, -cus•ing *or*
  -cus•sing
fod'der
foe
fog, fogged, fog'ging
fog'gi•ness
fog'gy
fog'horn'
fo'gy *also* fo'gey *pl.*

-gies *also* -geys
foi'ble
foil
foist
fold
fold'er
fo'li•age
fo'lic
fo'li•o' *pl.* -os'
folk *pl.* folk *or* folks
folk' dance'
folk' danc'ing
folk'lore'
folk'lor'ist
folk'-rock'
folk'sing'er
folk' sing'ing
folk'song'
folk'sy
folk'tale'
fol'li•cle
fol'low
fol'low•er
fol'low•ing
fol'low-up' *or*
  fol'low•up' *n.*
fol'ly
fo•ment'
fond
fon'dle, -dled,
  -dling
fon•due' *also*
  fon•du'
font
food
food'stuff'
fool

fool′er•y
fool′har′di•ness
fool′har′dy
fool′ish
fool′proof′
foot *pl.* feet
foot′age
foot′-and-mouth′
  dis•ease′
foot′ball′
foot′board′
foot′bridge′
foot′-can′dle
foot′ed
foot′fall′
foot′hill′
foot′hold′
foot′ing
foot′lights′
foot′lock′er
foot′loose′
foot′man
foot′note′
foot′path′
foot′-pound′
foot′print′
foot′race′ *or* foot′
  race′
foot′rest′
foot′sore′
foot′step′
foot′stool′
foot′wear′
foot′work′
fop
fop′per•y
fop′pish

for *prep. & conj.*
  ✔ *fore, four*
for′age, -aged,
  -ag•ing
for′ag•er
for′as•much′ as
for′ay′
for•bear′ *(to resist),*
  -bore′, -borne′,
  -bear′ing
  ✔ *forebear*
for•bear′ance
for•bid′, -bade′ *or*
  -bad′, -bid′den *or*
  -bid′, -bid′ding
force, forced,
  forc′ing
force′a•ble *(able to
  be forced, forcible)*
  ✔ *forcible*
force′ful
for′ceps *pl.* -ceps
forc′er
forc′i•ble *(accom-
  plished by force)*
  ✔ *forceable*
for′ci•bly
ford
ford′a•ble
fore *(forward)*
  ✔ *for, four*
fore′-and-aft′ *adj.*
fore•arm′ *v.*
fore•arm′ *n.*
fore′bear′ *also*
  for′bear′ *(ancestor)*
  ✔ *forbear*

fore•bode′,
  -bod′ed, -bod′ing
fore•bod′er
fore′brain′
fore′cast′, -cast′ *or*
  -cast′ed, -cast′ing
fore′cast′er
fore′cas′tle *also*
  fo′c's'le
fore•close′,
  -closed′, -clos′ing
fore•clo′sure
fore′court′
fore•doom′
fore′fa′ther
fore′fin′ger
fore′foot′
fore′front′
fore•go′ *(to precede),*
  -went′, -gone′,
  -go′ing
  ✔ *forgo*
fore′ground′
fore′hand′
fore′head′
for′eign
for′eign•er
fore•know′,
  -knew′, -known′,
  -know′ing
fore•knowl′edge
fore′leg′
fore′limb′
fore′lock′
fore′man
fore′mast′
fore′most′

fore′named′
fore′noon′
fo·ren′sic
fore′or·dain′
fore′part′
fore′paw′
fore′quar′ter
fore′run′ner
fore′sail
fore·see′, -saw′,
  -seen′, -see′ing
fore·see′a·ble
fore·se′er
fore·shad′ow
fore·short′en
fore′sight′
fore′sight′ed
fore′skin′
for′est
fore·stall′
fore·stall′er
for′es·ta′tion
for′est·er
for′est·ry
fore′taste′
fore·tell′, -told′,
  -tell′ing
fore′thought′
for·ev′er
for·ev′er·more′
fore·warn′
fore′wing′
fore′wom′an
fore′word′ (*preface*)
  ✔ *forward*
for′feit

for′fei·ture′
for·gath′er *also*
  fore·gath′er
forge, forged,
  forg′ing
forg′er
for′ger·y
for·get′, -got′,
  -got′ten *or* -got′,
  -get′ting
for·get′ful
for·get′-me-not′
for·get′ta·ble
for·get′ter
for·giv′a·ble
for·give′, -gave′,
  -giv′en, -giv′ing
for·giv′er
for·give′ness
for·go′ *also* fore·go′
  (*to do without*),
  -went′, -gone′,
  -go′ing
  ✔ *forego*
fork
forked
fork′lift′
for·lorn′
form
for′mal
for′mal′de·hyde′
for′mal·ism
for·mal′i·ty
for′mal·ize′, -ized′,
  -iz′ing
for′mal·iz′er

for′mal·ly (*in a for-
  mal manner*)
  ✔ *formerly*
for′mat′, -mat′ted,
  -mat′ting
for·ma′tion
for′ma·tive
form′er (*one that
  forms*)
for′mer (*earlier*)
for′mer·ly (*once*)
  ✔ *formally*
form′fit′ting
for′mi·da·bil′i·ty
for′mi·da·ble
for′mi·da·bly
for′mu·la *pl.* -las *or*
  -lae′
for′mu·la′ic
for′mu·late′,
  -lat′ed, -lat′ing
for′mu·la′tion
for′ni·cate′, -cat′ed,
  -cat′ing
for′ni·ca′tion
for·sake′, -sook′,
  -sak′en, -sak′ing
for·sooth′
for·swear′, -swore′,
  -sworn′, -swear′ing
for·syth′i·a
fort (*fortified place*)
forte (*strong point*)
for′te′ (*musical direc-
  tion*)
forth (*forward*)

✔ fourth
forth•com′ing
forth′right′
forth•with′
for′ti•eth
for′ti•fi•ca′tion
for′ti•fi′er
for′ti•fy′, -fied′,
   -fy′ing
for•tis′si•mo′
for′ti•tude′
fort′night′
FOR′TRAN′
for′tress
for•tu′i•tous
for′tu•nate
for′tune
for′tune•tell′er
for′tune•tell′ing
for′ty
for′ty-nin′er
fo′rum pl. -rums
for′ward (at or near
   the front)
   ✔ foreword
for′wards
fos′sil
fos′sil•i•za′tion
fos′sil•ize′, -ized′,
   -iz′ing
fos′ter
foul (rotten)
   ✔ fowl
fou•lard′
foul′-mouthed′
foul′-up′ n.

found
foun•da′tion
foun′der (to sink)
found′er (person
   who founds)
found′ling
foun′dry
fount
foun′tain
foun′tain•head′
four (number)
   ✔ for, fore
Four′-H′ Club′
four′-leaf′ clo′ver
four′-post′er
four′score′
four′some
four′square′
four′teen′
four′teenth′
fourth (number)
   ✔ forth
four′-wheel′ drive′
fowl (bird), pl. fowl
   or fowls
   ✔ foul
fox pl. fox′es also
   fox
fox′glove′
fox′hole′
fox′hound′
fox′ ter′ri•er
fox′trot′, -trot′ted,
   -trot′ting
fox′ trot′ n.
fox′y

foy′er
fra′cas
frac′tion
frac′tion•al
frac′tious
frac′ture, -tured,
   -tur•ing
frag′ile
frag′ile•ly
fra•gil′i•ty
frag′ment
frag′men•tar′y
frag′men•ta′tion
fra′grance
fra′grant
frail
frail′ty
frame, framed,
   fram′ing
fram′er
frame′-up′ n.
frame′work′
franc (money)
   ✔ frank
fran′chise′
Fran•cis′can
fran′ci•um
fran′gi•ble
frank (sincere)
   ✔ franc
frank (frankfurter)
   ✔ franc
frank′furt•er
frank′in•cense′
Frank′ish
fran′tic

fran'ti•cal•ly
frap•pé' *also* frappe
fra•ter'nal
fra•ter'ni•ty
frat'er•ni•za'tion
frat'er•nize',
  -nized', -niz'ing
frat'ri•cid'al
frat'ri•cide'
Frau *pl.* Frau'en
fraud
fraud'u•lence
fraud'u•lent
fraught
Fräu'lein' *pl.* -lein'
fray
fraz'zle, -zled, -zling
freak
freak'ish
freck'le, -led, -ling
free, fre'er, fre'est
free, freed, free'ing
free'bie *also* free'bee
free'boot'er
free'born'
freed'man
free'dom
freed'wom'an
free' fall' *or*
  free'-fall'
free'-for-all'
free'form' *adj.*
free'hand'
free'hand'ed
free'lance',
  -lanced', -lanc'ing
free'lanc'er

free'load'
free'load'er
free'man
Free'ma'son
Free'ma'son•ry
free'stand'ing
free'stone'
free'style'
free'think'er
free'think'ing
free' throw' *n.*
free'way'
free'wheel'ing
free'will' *adj.*
free' will' *n.*
freeze *(to form ice),*
  froze, fro'zen,
  freez'ing
  ✔ *frieze*
freeze'-dry', -dried',
  -dry'ing
freez'er
freight
freight'er
French
French'-
  Ca•na'di•an *also*
  French'-
  Ca•na'di•an
French' fry' *n.*
French'-fry' *v.*
French'man
French'wom'an
fre•net'ic
fre•net'i•cal•ly
fren'zied
fren'zy

fre'quen•cy
fre'quent *adj.*
fre•quent' *v.*
fres'co *pl.* -coes *or*
  -cos
fresh'en
fresh'et
fresh'man
fresh'wa'ter *adj.*
fret, fret'ted,
  fret'ting
fret'ful
fret'work'
Freud'i•an
fri'a•bil'i•ty *or*
  fri'a•ble•ness
fri'a•ble
fri'ar *(member of a*
  religious order)
  ✔ *fryer*
fric'as•see', -seed',
  -see'ing
fric'tion
Fri'day
friend
friend'li•ness
friend'ly
friend'ship'
frieze *(horizontal*
  band)
  ✔ *freeze*
frig'ate
fright
fright'en
fright'en•ing
fright'ful
frig'id

fri·gid'i·ty *or*
  frig'id·ness
fri·jol' *also* fri·jo'le
  pl. fri·jo'les
frill
frill'y
fringe, fringed,
  fring'ing
frip'per·y
Fri'sian
frisk
frisk'i·ly
frisk'y
frit'ter
fri·vol'i·ty
friv'o·lous
frizz
friz'zle, -zled, -zling
friz'zly
friz'zy
fro
frock
frog'man'
frol'ic, -icked,
  -ick·ing
frol'ic·some
from
frond
front
front'age
fron'tal
fron·tier'
fron·tiers'man
fron·tiers'wom·an
fron'tis·piece'
front'line'
front'-run'ner *also*

front'run'ner
frost'bite', -bit',
  -bit'ten, -bit'ing
frost'ing
frost'y
froth
froth'y
frown
frow'zi·ness
frow'zy *also* frow'sy
fruc'tose'
fru'gal
fru·gal'i·ty
fruit *pl.* fruit *or* fruits
fruit'cake'
fruit'ful
fruit'i·ness
fru·i'tion
fruit'less
fruit'y
frump'ish
frump'y
frus'trate', -trat'ed,
  -trat'ing
frus·tra'tion
frus'tum *pl.* -tums
  or -ta
fry, fried, fry'ing
fry'er *also* fri'er
  *(young chicken, one
  that fries)*
  ✓ friar
fry'ing pan'
f'-stop'
fuch'sia
fud'dle, -dled,
  -dling

fudge
fu'el, -eled *also*
  -elled, -el'ing *or*
  -el·ling
fu'gi·tive
fugue
ful'crum *pl.* -crums
  or -cra
ful·fill' *also* ful·fil',
  -filled', -fill'ing
ful·fill'ment
full'back'
full'-blood'ed
full'-blown'
full'-bod'ied
ful'ler·ene'
full'-fledged'
full'-length'
full'ness
full'-scale'
full'-size'
full'-time'
ful'ly
ful'mi·nate',
  -nat'ed, -nat'ing
ful'mi·na'tion
ful'some
fum'ble, -bled,
  -bling
fume, fumed,
  fum'ing
fu'mi·gant
fu'mi·gate', -gat'ed,
  -gat'ing
fu'mi·ga'tion
fu'mi·ga'tor
fun

func'tion
func'tion•al
func'tion•ar'y
fund
fun'da•men'tal
fun'da•men'tal•
  ism
fun'da•men'tal•ist
fu'ner•al
fu'ner•ar'y
fu•ne're•al
fun'gal *also*
  fun'gous
fun'gi•cide'
fun'gus *pl.* -gi *or*
  -gus•es
funk'y
fun'nel, -neled *or*
  -nelled, -nel•ing *or*
  -nel'ling
fun'nies
fun'ny
fur *(pelt)*
  ✔ fir
fur'bish
fur'bish•er
fu'ri•ous
furl
fur'long'
fur'lough
fur'nace
fur'nish
fur'nish•er
fur'nish•ing
fur'ni•ture
fu'ror'
furred

fur'ri•er
fur'ri•ness
fur'row
fur'ry *(having fur)*
  ✔ fury
fur'ther *(to a greater
  extent)*
  ✔ farther
fur'ther•ance
fur'ther•more'
fur'ther•most'
fur'thest *(to the
  greatest extent)*
  ✔ farthest
fur'tive
fu'ry *(rage)*
  ✔ furry
furze
fuse *also* fuze *(light-
  ing device)*
fuse *(to melt),* fused,
  fus'ing
fu'se•lage'
fu'si•bil'i•ty
fu'si•ble
fu'sil•lade'
fu'sion
fuss'i•ness
fuss'y
fus'ti•ness
fus'ty
fu'tile
fu'tile•ly
fu•til'i•ty
fu'ton *pl.* -ton *or*
  -tons
fu'ture

fu'tur•is'tic
fu•tu'ri•ty
fuzz'i•ly
fuzz'i•ness
fuzz'y

G

gab, gabbed,
  gab'bing
gab'ar•dine'
gab'ber
gab'bi•ness
gab'by
ga'ble
ga'bled
gad, gad'ded,
  gad'ding
gad'a•bout'
gad'fly'
gadg'et
gad'o•lin'i•um
Gael *(Celt)*
  ✔ gale
Gael'ic
gaff *(hook)*
gaffe *(error)*
gaf'fer
gag, gagged,
  gag'ging
gage *(pledge)*
  ✔ gauge
gag'gle
gai'e•ty *also*
  gay'e•ty
gai'ly *also* gay'ly

gain
gain'er
gain'ful
gain•say', -said',
  -say'ing
gait *(way of walking)*
  ✔ gate
gai'ter
ga'la
ga•lac'tic
Ga•la'tians
gal'ax•y
gale *(wind)*
  ✔ Gael
ga•le'na
Gal'i•le'an
gall
gal'lant
gal'lant•ry
gall'blad'der *also*
  gall' blad'der
gal'le•on
gal'ler•y
gal'ley *pl.* -leys
gall'fly'
Gal'lic
gall'ing
gal'li•um
gal'li•vant'
gal'lon
gal'lop
gal'lows *pl.* -lows *or*
  -lows•es
gall'stone'
ga•lore'
ga•losh'
gal•van'ic

gal'va•nism
gal'va•ni•za'tion
gal'va•nize',
  -nized', -niz'ing
gal'va•nom'e•ter
gam'bit
gam'ble *(bet)*, -bled,
  -bling
  ✔ gambol
gam'bler
gam'bol *(frolic)*,
  -boled *or* -bolled,
  -bol•ing *or*
  -bol•ling
  ✔ gamble
game, gamed,
  gam'ing
game, gam'er,
  gam'est
game'cock'
game'keep'er
game'ster
gam'ete'
gam'in
gam'ma
gam'ut
gam'y
gan'der
gang
gan'gling
gan'gli•on *pl.* -gli•a
  or -gli•ons
gang'plank'
gan'grene',
  -grened', -gren'ing
gan'gre•nous
gang'ster

gang'way'
gan'net
gant'let *(track)*
  ✔ gauntlet
gap, gapped,
  gap'ping
gape, gaped, gap'ing
gar
ga•rage', -raged',
  -rag'ing
garb
gar'bage
gar•ban'zo *pl.* -zos
gar'ble, -bled,
  -bling
gar'den
gar'den•er
gar•de'nia
gar'fish' *pl.* -fish' *or*
  -fish'es
gar•gan'tu•an
gar'gle, -gled,
  -gling
gar'goyle'
gar'ish
gar'land
gar'lic
gar'lick•y
gar'ment
gar'ner
gar'net
gar'nish
gar'nish•ee', -eed',
  -ee'ing
gar'ni•ture
gar'ret
gar'ri•son

gar•rote' or
  gar•rotte', -rot'ed
  or -rot'ted, -rot'ing
  or -rot'ting
gar•ru'li•ty
gar'ru•lous
gar'ter
gas *pl.* gas'es or
  gas'ses
gas, gassed, gas'sing
gas'e•ous
gas'-guz'zler
gash
gas'ket
gas'light'
gas'o•hol'
gas'o•line'
gasp
gas'sy
gas'tric
gas•tro•in•tes'ti•nal
gas'tro•nom'ic *also*
  gas'tro•nom'i•cal
gas•tron'o•my
gas'tro•pod'
gas•tru'la *pl.* -las or
  -lae'
gate (*entrance*)
  ✔ *gait*
gate'crash'er
gate'house'
gate'keep'er
gate'post'
gate'way'
gath'er
gath'er•ing
Gat'ling gun'

gauche
gau'cho *pl.* -chos
gaud'i•ly
gaud'y
gauge *also* gage (*to
  measure*), gauged
  also gaged,
  gaug'ing *also*
  gag'ing
  ✔ *gage*
gauge'a•ble
Gaul
Gaul'ish
gaunt
gaunt'let *also*
  gant'let (*glove,
  punishment*)
  ✔ *gantlet*
gauze
gauz'i•ness
gauz'y
gav'el
ga•votte'
gawk'y
gay
gaze, gazed, gaz'ing
ga•ze'bo *pl.* -bos or
  -boes
ga•zelle'
ga•zette'
gaz'et•teer'
gaz•pa'cho
gear
gear'ing
gear'shift'
gear'wheel' *also*
  gear' wheel'

geck'o *pl.* -os or
  -oes
gee
gee'zer
ge•fil'te fish'
Gei'ger count'er
gei'sha *pl.* -sha or
  -shas
gel (*jellylike mixture*),
  gelled, gel'ling
  ✔ *jell*
gel'a•tin *also*
  gel'a•tine
ge•lat'i•nous
ge•la'to *pl.* -ti
geld'ing
gel'id
gem, gemmed,
  gem'ming
gem'stone'
gen'darme'
gen'der
gene
ge'ne•a•log'i•cal
ge'ne•al'o•gist
ge'ne•al'o•gy
gen'er•al
gen'er•al•ist
gen'er•al'i•ty
gen'er•al•i•za'tion
gen'er•al•ize',
  -ized', -iz'ing
gen'er•al•ly
gen'er•al•ship'
gen'er•ate', -at'ed,
  -at'ing
gen'er•a'tion

gen′er•a•tive
gen′er•a′tor
ge•ner′ic
gen′er•os′i•ty
gen′er•ous
gen′e•sis *pl.* -ses′
gene′-splic′ing
ge•net′ic
ge•net′i•cist
ge•net′ics
gen′ial
ge′ni•al′i•ty
ge′nie
gen′i•tal
gen′i•ta′li•a
gen′i•tals
gen′i•tive
gen′ius *(gifted person)*, *pl.* -ius•es
gen′ius *(guardian spirit)*, *pl.* ge′ni•i′
gen′o•cid′al
gen′o•cide′
Gen′o•ese′
ge′nome
gen′o•type′
gen′re
gent
gen•teel′
gen′tian
gen′tile′ *also* Gen′tile′
gen•til′i•ty
gen′tle, -tler, -tlest
gen′tle•folk′
gen′tle•man
gen′tle•wom′an

gen′tly
gen′tri•fi•ca′tion
gen′tri•fy′, -fied′, -fy′ing
gen′try
gen•u•flect′
gen′u•flec′tion
gen′u•ine
ge′nus *pl.* gen′er•a
ge′o•cen′tric
ge′o•chem′is•try
ge′ode′
ge′o•des′ic
ge•od′e•sy
ge′o•det′ic
ge•og′ra•pher
ge′o•graph′ic *also* ge′o•graph′i•cal
ge•og′ra•phy
ge′o•log′ic *or* ge′o•log′i•cal
ge•ol′o•gist
ge•ol′o•gy
ge′o•mag•net′ic
ge′o•mag′ne•tism
ge′o•met′ric *also* ge′o•met′ri•cal
ge•om′e•try
ge′o•mor′phic
ge′o•mor′pho•log′ic *or* ge′o•mor′-pho•log′i•cal
ge′o•mor•phol′o•gy
ge′o•phys′i•cal
ge′o•phys′i•cist
ge′o•phys′ics

ge′o•po•lit′i•cal
ge′o•pol′i•tics
Geor′gian
ge′o•tac′tic
ge′o•tax′is
ge′o•ther′mal
ge′o•trop′ic
ge•ot′ro•pism
ge•ra′ni•um
ger′bil
ger′i•at′ric
germ
Ger′man
ger•mane′
Ger•man′ic
ger•ma′ni•um
ger′mi•cid′al
ger′mi•cide′
ger′mi•nal
ger′mi•nate′, -nat′ed, -nat′ing
ger′mi•na′tion
ger′mi•na′tor
ger′ry•man′der
ger′und
Ge•sta′po
ges•ta′tion
ges•tic′u•late′, -lat′ed, -lat′ing
ges•tic′u•la′tion
ges′ture, -tured, -tur′ing
get, got, got′ten *or* got, get′ting
get′a•way′ *n.*
get′-to•geth′er *n.*
get′up′ *n.*

get'-up'-and-go' *n.*
gew'gaw'
gey'ser
ghast'li•ness
ghast'ly
gher'kin
ghet'to *pl.* -tos *or*
    -toes
ghost
ghost'li•ness
ghost'ly
ghost' town'
ghost'write',
    -wrote', -writ'ten,
    -writ'ing
ghost'writ'er
ghoul
ghoul'ish
GI *pl.* GIs *or* GI's
gi'ant
gib'ber
gib'ber•ish
gib'bet, -bet•ed *or*
    -bet•ted, -bet•ing *or*
    -bet•ting
gib'bon
gib'bous
gibe *also* jibe *(tease)*,
    gibed *also* jibed,
    gib'ing *also* jib'ing
    ✔ *jibe*
gib'lets
gid'di•ness
gid'dy
gift
gift'ed
gift'-wrap',

-wrapped',
    -wrap'ping
gig, gigged, gig'ging
gig'a•bit'
gig'a•byte'
gig'a•hertz'
gi•gan'tic
gi•gan'tism
gig'a•watt'
gig'gle, -gled, -gling
gig'gler
gig'gly
Gi'la mon'ster
gild *(to cover with*
    gold), gild'ed *or*
    gilt, gild'ing
    ✔ *guild*
gill
gill' net'
gil'ly•flow'er
gilt *(gold)*
    ✔ *guilt*
gim'crack'
gim'let
gim'mick
gim'mick•ry
gim'mick•y
gimp'y
gin, ginned, gin'ning
gin'ger
gin'ger ale'
gin'ger•bread'
gin'ger•ly
gin'ger•snap'
ging'ham
gin'gi•val
gin'gi•vi'tis

gink'go *also* ging'ko
    pl. -goes *also* -koes
gin'seng'
gi•raffe' *pl.* -raffes'
    or -raffe'
gird, gird'ed *or* girt,
    gird'ing
gird'er
gir'dle, -dled, -dling
girl
girl'friend' *also* girl'
    friend'
Girl' Guide'
girl'hood'
girl'ish
Girl' Scout'
girth
gist
give, gave, giv'en,
    giv'ing
give'-and-take'
    also give' and take'
give'a•way'
giv'er
giz'mo *also* gis'mo
    pl. -mos
giz'zard
gla'cial
gla'cier *(ice mass)*
    ✔ *glazier*
gla'ci•ol'o•gy
glad, glad'der,
    glad'dest
glad'den
glade
glad'-hand' *v.*
glad'i•a'tor

glad'i•o'lus *also*
  glad'i•o'la *pl.* -li *or*
  -lus•es *also* -las
glad'some
glam'or•ize' *also*
  glam'our•ize',
  -ized', -iz'ing
glam'or•ous *also*
  glam'our•ous
glam'our *also*
  glam'or
glance, glanced,
  glanc'ing
glan'du•lar
glare, glared,
  glar'ing
glar'y
glass
glass'ful'
glass'ware'
glass'y
glau•co'ma
glaze, glazed,
  glaz'ing
glaz'er *(one that
  glazes)*
gla'zier *(one that
  cuts glass)*
  ✔ glacier
gleam
glean
glean'er
glee
glen
glib, glib'ber,
  glib'best
glide, glid'ed,

glid'ing
glid'er
glim'mer
glimpse, glimpsed,
  glimps'ing
glint
glis•sade', -sad'ed,
  -sad'ing
glis•san'do *pl.* -di *or*
  -dos
glis'ten
glis'ter
glitch
glit'ter
glit'te•ra'ti
glit'ter•y
gloam'ing
gloat
glob
glob'al
globe
globe'fish' *pl.* -fish'
  or -fish'es
globe'trot'ter
glob'u•lar
glob'ule
glob'u•lin
glock'en•spiel'
gloom'i•ly
gloom'i•ness
gloom'y
glo'ri•fi•ca'tion
glo'ri•fi'er
glo'ri•fy', -fied',
  -fy'ing
glo'ri•ous
glo'ry, -ried, -ry•ing

gloss
glos'sa•ry
gloss'i•ness
gloss'y
glot'tal
glot'tis *pl.* -tis•es *or*
  -ti•des'
glove, gloved,
  glov'ing
glow
glow'er
glow'ing
glow'worm'
glu'cose'
glue, glued, glu'ing
glum, glum'mer,
  glum'mest
glut, glut'ted, glut'-
  ting
glu'ten
glu'ten•ous *(relating
  to gluten)*
glu'ti•nous *(sticky)*
glut'ton
glut'ton•ous
glut'ton•y
glyc'er•in *also*
  glyc'er•ine
glyc'er•ol
gly'co•gen
gly'col'
glyph
G'-man'
gnarl
gnarled
gnash
gnat

gnaw
gneiss (rock)
✔ nice
gnoc'chi
gnome
gnu (antelope)
✔ knew, new
go, went, gone,
go'ing, goes
go pl. goes
goad
go'-a•head'
goal
goal'ie
goal'keep'er
goal' post'
goat
goat•ee'
goat'skin'
gob
gob'ble, -bled,
-bling
gob'ble•dy•gook'
also gob'ble•de•
gook'
gob'bler
go'-be•tween'
gob'let
gob'lin
go'-cart'
god'child'
god'daugh'ter
god'dess
god'fa'ther
god'for•sak'en also
God'for•sak'en
god'head'

god'hood'
god'less
god'like'
god'li•ness
god'ly
god'moth'er
god'par'ent
god'send'
god'son'
God'speed'
go'fer also go'-fer
(employee)
✔ gopher
go'-get'ter
gog'gle, -gled,
-gling
gog'gle-eyed'
gog'gles
go'ing
goi'ter
gold'brick'
gold'brick'er
gold'en
gold'en•rod'
gold'-filled'
gold'finch'
gold'fish' pl.
-fish' or -fish'es
gold'smith'
golf
golf'er
go'nad'
gon'do•la
gon'do•lier'
gon'er
gong
gon'or•rhe'a

goo
goo'ber
good, bet'ter, best
good-bye' or
good•bye' also
good-by' pl. -byes
also -bys
good'-for-
noth'ing
good'heart'ed
good'-hu'mored
good'-look'ing
good'-na'tured
good'ness
Good' Sa•mar'i•tan
good'-sized'
good'-tem'pered
good'will' also
good' will'
good'y also good'ie
goo'ey, -i•er, -i•est
goof'ball' or goof'
ball'
goof'i•ness
goof'off' n.
goof'y
goo'gol'
goo'gol•plex'
goon
goose pl. geese
goose'ber'ry
goose'neck'
goose'-step',
-stepped',
-step'ping
go'pher (animal)
✔ gofer

gore, gored, gor'ing

gorge, gorged,
  gorg'ing

gor'geous

go•ril'la *(animal)*
  ✓ guerrilla

gorse

gor'y

gosh

gos'hawk'

gos'ling

gos'pel

gos'sa•mer

gos'sip

gos'sip•er

Goth

Goth'ic

gouache

gouge, gouged,
  goug'ing

goug'er

gou'lash

gourd

gour•mand'

gour•met'

gout

gout'i•ness

gout'y

gov'ern

gov'ern•a•ble

gov'er•ness

gov'ern•ment

gov'ern•men'tal

gov'er•nor

gown

grab, grabbed,
  grab'bing

grace, graced,
  grac'ing

grace'ful

grace'less

gra'cious

grack'le

gra'date', -dat'ed,
  -dat'ing

gra•da'tion

grade, grad'ed,
  grad'ing

grad'er

gra'di•ent

grad'u•al

grad'u•ate', -at'ed,
  -at'ing

grad'u•a'tion

graf•fi'ti

graft

gra'ham

grail *or* Grail

grain

grain'y

gram

gram'mar

gram•mar'i•an

gram•mat'i•cal

gram'o•phone'

gram'pus

gran'a•ry

grand'aunt'

grand'child'

grand'dad'

grand'dad'dy

grand'daugh'ter

gran•dee'

gran'deur

grand'fa'ther

gran•dil'o•quence

gran•dil'o•quent

gran'di•ose'

gran'di•os'i•ty *or*
  gran'di•ose'ness

grand'ma'

grand'moth'er

grand'neph'ew

grand'niece'

grand'pa'

grand'par'ent

grand'son'

grand'stand'

grand'un'cle

gran'ite

gran'ny *or* gran'nie

gra•no'la

grant•ee'

gran'tor

gran'u•lar

gran'u•late',
  -lat'ed, -lat'ing

gran'u•la'tion

gran'ule

grape

grape'fruit'

grape'shot'

grape'vine'

graph

graph'eme'

graph'ic *also*
  graph'i•cal

graph'ite'

grap'nel

grap'ple, -pled,
  -pling

grasp
grasp'ing
grass
grass'hop'per
grass'land'
grass'roots'
grass'y
grate *(to shred)*,
  grat'ed, grat'ing
  ✔ great
grate *(framework)*
  ✔ great
grate'ful
grat'er
grat'i•fi•ca'tion
grat'i•fi'er
grat'i•fy', -fied',
  -fy'ing
grat'is
grat'i•tude'
gra•tu'i•tous
gra•tu'i•ty
grave, grav'er,
  grav'est
grave, graved,
  grav'en *or* graved,
  grav'ing
grave'dig'ger
grav'el, -eled *or*
  -elled, -el•ing *or*
  -el•ling
grave'side'
grave'site'
grave'stone'
grave'yard'
grav'id

grav'i•tate', -tat'ed,
  -tat'ing
grav'i•ta'tion
grav'i•ty
gra•vure'
gra'vy
gray *also* grey
gray'beard'
gray'ish
gray'ling *pl.* -ling *or*
  -lings
graze, grazed,
  graz'ing
grease, greased,
  greas'ing
grease'paint' *also*
  grease' paint'
greas'i•ness
greas'y
great *(large)*
  ✔ grate
great'-aunt' *or*
  great' aunt'
great'coat'
Great' Dane'
great'-grand'child'
great'-
  grand'daugh'ter
great'-grand'fa'ther
great'-
  grand'moth'er
great'-
  grand'par'ent
great'-grand'son'
great'heart'ed
great'neph'ew

great'niece'
great'-un'cle *or*
  great' un'cle
greave
grebe
Gre'cian
Grec'o-Ro'man
greed'i•ly
greed'i•ness
greed'y
Greek
green'back'
green'er•y
green'-eyed'
green'gage'
green'gro'cer
green'horn'
green'house'
green'ish
green'mail'
green'room'
green'sward'
green'wood'
greet
greet'ing
gre•gar'i•ous
Gre•go'ri•an
grem'lin
gre•nade'
gren'a•dier'
gren'a•dine'
grey'hound'
grid
grid'dle
grid'dle•cake'
grid'i'ron

grid'lock'

grief

griev'ance

grieve, grieved,
    griev'ing

griev'ous

grif'fin *also* grif'fon
    or gryph'on

grill *(cooking utensil)*

grille *also* grill *(grat-
    ing)*

grill'work'

grim, grim'mer,
    grim'mest

grim'ace, -aced,
    -ac•ing

grime

grim'i•ness

grim'y

grin, grinned,
    grin'ning

grind, ground,
    grind'ing

grind'er

grind'stone'

grip *(to grasp)*,
    gripped, grip'ping
    ✔ grippe

gripe *(to complain)*,
    griped, grip'ing

grippe *also* grip
    (influenza)
    ✔ grip

gris'ly *(gruesome)*
    ✔ grizzly

grist

gris'tle

gris'tly

grist'mill'

grit, grit'ted,
    grit'ting

grits

grit'ti•ness

grit'ty

griz'zled

griz'zly *(flecked with
    gray, bear)*
    ✔ grisly

groan

groan'er

groats

gro'cer

gro'cer•y

grog

grog'gi•ness

grog'gy

groin

grom'met

groom

grooms'man

groove

groov'y

grope, groped,
    grop'ing

gros'beak'

gros'grain'

gross *pl.* gross

gro•tesque'

grot'to *pl.* -toes *or*
    -tos

grouch

grouch'i•ly

grouch'i•ness

grouch'y

ground

ground' ball'

ground'break'ing

ground'er

ground'hog'

ground'less

ground'nut'

ground'out' *n.*

grounds'keep'er

ground' speed'
    also ground'speed'

ground'swell'

ground' wa'ter *also*
    ground'wa'ter

ground'work'

group

grou'per *pl.* -per *or*
    -pers

group'ie

group'ing

grouse *pl.* grouse *or*
    grous'es

grouse, groused,
    grous'ing

grout

grove

grov'el, -eled *also*
    -elled, -el•ing *or*
    -el•ling

grov'el•er *or*
    grov'el•ler

grow, grew, grown,
    grow'ing

grow'er

growl
grown'up' *also*
  grown'-up' *n.*
grown'-up' *adj.*
growth
grub, grubbed,
  grub'bing
grub'bi•ly
grub'bi•ness
grub'by
grub'stake',
  -staked', -stak'ing
grudge, grudged,
  grudg'ing
gru'el
gru'el•ing *also*
  gru'el•ling
grue'some
gruff
grum'ble, -bled,
  -bling
grum'bler
grump'i•ly
grump'i•ness
grump'y
grunt
gua'ca•mo'le
gua•na'co *pl.* -cos *or*
  -co
gua'nine'
gua'no *pl.* -nos
gua'no•sine'
Gua'ra•ni' *pl.* -ni' *or*
  -nis'
guar'an•tee', -teed',
  -tee'ing
guar'an•tor'

guar'an•ty, -tied,
  -ty•ing
guard
guard'ed
guard'house'
guard'i•an
guard'rail'
guard'room'
guards'man
Gua•te•ma'lan
gua'va
gu'ber•na•to'ri•al
gudg'eon
Guern'sey *pl.* -seys
guer•ril'la *or*
  gue•ril'la *(soldier)*
  ✔ *gorilla*
guess
guess'er
guess'ti•mate
guess'work'
guest
guf•faw'
guid'a•ble
guid'ance
guide, guid'ed,
  guid'ing
guide'book'
guide'line'
guide'post'
guid'er
guide'word'
guild *(association)*
  ✔ *gild*
guild'hall'
guile
guile'ful

guile'less
guil'lo•tine',
  -tined', -tin'ing
guilt *(remorse)*
  ✔ *gilt*
guilt'i•ly
guilt'i•ness
guilt'y
guin'ea
guin'ea fowl'
guin'ea pig'
guise
gui•tar'
gui•tar'ist
gu'lag'
gulch
gulf
gull
gul'let
gul'li•bil'i•ty
gul'li•ble
gul'ly
gulp
gum, gummed,
  gum'ming
gum' ar'a•bic
gum'ball'
gum'bo *pl.* -bos
gum'drop'
gum'mi•ness
gum'my
gump'tion
gum'shoe'
gun, gunned,
  gun'ning
gun'boat'
gun'cot'ton

gun'fight'
gun'fire'
gung' ho'
gun'lock'
gun'man
gun'ner
gun'ner•y
gun'ny
gun'ny•sack'
gun'pow'der
gun'shot'
gun'-shy'
gun'sling'er
gun'smith'
gun'wale *also*
  gun'nel
gup'py
gur'gle, -gled, -gling
gu'ru *pl.* -rus
gush
gush'er
gush'i•ness
gush'y
gus'set
gust
gus'ta•to'ry
gust'i•ness
gus'to *pl.* -toes
gust'y
gut, gut'ted, gut'ting
guts'y
gut'ter
gut'tur•al
guy
guz'zle, -zled, -zling
guz'zler
gym

gym•na'si•um *pl.*
  -si•ums *or* -si•a
gym'nast
gym•nas'tics
gym'no•sperm'
gy'ne•co•log'i•cal
  or gy'ne•co•log'ic
gy'ne•col'o•gist
gy'ne•col'o•gy
gyp *also* gip, gypped
  or gipped, gyp'ping
  or gip'ping
gyp'sum
Gyp'sy *also* Gip'sy
gy'rate', -rat'ed,
  -rat'ing
gy•ra'tion
gyr'fal'con *also*
  ger'fal'con
gy'ro *pl.*-ros
gy'ro•com'pass
gy'ro•scope'
gy'ro•scop'ic

H

ha *also* hah
ha'be•as cor'pus
hab'er•dash'er
hab'er•dash'er•y
ha•bil'i•ment
hab'it
hab'it•a•bil'i•ty
hab'it•a•ble
hab'i•tat'
hab'i•ta'tion

hab'it-form'ing
ha•bit'u•al
ha•bit'u•ate',
  -at'ed, -at'ing
ha•bit'u•a'tion
hab'i•tude'
ha•bit'u•é'
ha'ci•en'da
hack
hack'er
hack'le
hack'ney *pl.* -neys
hack'neyed
hack'saw'
had'dock *pl.* -dock
  or -docks
haf'ni•um
haft
hag
hag'gard
hag'gle, -gled,
  -gling
hag'gler
hag•i•og'ra•pher
hag'i•o•graph'ic *or*
  hag'i•o•graph'i•cal
hag'i•og'ra•phy
hah'ni•um
Hai'da *pl.* -da *or* -das
Hai'dan
hai'ku *pl.* -ku *also*
  -kus
hail *(ice pellets, to*
  greet)
  ✔ *hale*
hail'er
hail'stone'

hail′storm′

hair *(threadlike growth)*
  ✔ hare

hair′brush′

hair′cloth′

hair′cut′

hair′do′ *pl.* -dos′

hair′dress′er

hair′i•ness

hair′line′

hair′piece′

hair′pin′

hair′-rais′ing

hairs′breadth′ *or* hair′s′-breadth′ *also* hair′breadth′

hair′split′ter

hair′split′ting

hair′ spray′

hair′spring′

hair′style′

hair′-trig′ger *adj.*

hair′y

Hai′tian

hake *pl.* hake *or* hakes

hal′berd

hal′cy•on

hale *(healthy),* hal′er, hal′est
  ✔ hail

hale *(to force),* haled, hal′ing
  ✔ hail

half *pl.* halves

half′-and-half′

half′back′

half′-baked′

half′-cocked′

half′-dol′lar

half′heart′ed

half′-hour′

half′-life′

half′-mast′

half′-moon′

half′pen•ny *pl.* -pence *or* -pen•nies

half′-slip′

half′-staff′

half′-tim′bered *also* half′-tim′ber

half′time′

half′tone′ *(value between light and dark)*

half′ tone′ *(semitone)*

half′-track′

half′-truth′

half′way′

half′-wit′ted

hal′i•but *pl.* -but *or* -buts

hal′ite

hal′i•to′sis

hall *(corridor)*
  ✔ haul

hal′le•lu′jah

hall′mark′

hal•loo′, -looed′, -loo′ing

hal′low

hal′lowed

Hal′low•een′ *also* Hal′low•e′en′

hal•lu′ci•nate′, -nat′ed, -nat′ing

hal•lu′ci•na′tion

hal•lu′ci•na•to′ry

hal•lu′cin•o•gen

hal•lu′cin•o•gen′ic

hall′way′

ha′lo *pl.* -los *or* -loes

hal′o•gen

halt

hal′ter

halt′ing

halve *(to divide),* halved, halv′ing
  ✔ have

hal′yard

ham, hammed, ham′ming

ham′burg′er *also* ham′burg′

ham′let

ham′mer

ham′mer•head′

ham′mer•lock′

ham′mock

ham′per

ham′ster

ham′string′, -strung′, -string′ing

hand′bag′

hand′ball′

hand′bill′

hand′book′

hand′cart′

hand′craft′

hand'cuff'
hand'ful'
hand'gun'
hand'i·cap',
    -capped', -cap'ping
hand'i·craft' *also*
    hand'craft'
hand'i·ly
hand'i·work'
hand'ker·chief *pl.*
    -chiefs *also* -chieves
han'dle, -dled,
    -dling
han'dle·bar'
han'dler
hand'made'
hand'maid' *also*
    hand'maid'en
hand'-me-down'
hand'-off' *n.*
hand'out' *n.*
hand'pick'
hand'rail'
hand'saw'
hand'shake'
hand'some (*good-
    looking*), -som·er,
    -som·est
    ✔ hansom
hands'-on'
hand'spike'
hand'spring'
hand'stand'
hand'-to-hand'
    adj.
hand'-to-mouth'
    adj.

hand'work'
hand'writ'ing
hand'y
hand'y·man' *also*
    hand'y man'
hang (*to fasten from
    above*), hung,
    hang'ing
hang (*to execute*),
    hanged, hang'ing
han'gar (*building*)
    ✔ hanger
hang'dog'
hang'er (*one that
    hangs something*)
    ✔ hangar
hang'er-on' *pl.*
    hang'ers-on'
hang' glid'er
hang' glid'ing
hang'man'
hang'nail'
hang'out' *n.*
hang'o'ver
hang'-up' *n.*
hank
han'ker
han'som (*carriage*)
    ✔ handsome
Ha'nuk·kah *or*
    Ha'nu·kah *also*
    Cha'nu·kah
hap, happed,
    hap'ping
hap·haz'ard
hap'less
hap'loid'

hap'ly (*by chance*)
    ✔ happily
hap'pen
hap'pen·ing
hap'pen·stance'
hap'pi·ly (*in a
    happy way*)
    ✔ haply
hap'pi·ness
hap'py
hap'py-go-luck'y
ha'ra-ki'ri *pl.* -ris
ha·rangue',
    -rangued',
    -rangu'ing
ha·rass'
ha·rass'ment
har'bin·ger
har'bor
hard'back'
hard'ball'
hard'-bit'ten
hard'-boiled'
hard'bound'
hard'-core' *also*
    hard'core' *adj.*
hard'cov'er
hard' disk'
hard'en
hard'hat' *or*
    hard'-hat'
hard'head'ed
hard'heart'ed
har'di·hood'
hard'-line' *also*
    hard'line' *adj.*
hard'lin'er

hard′ly
hard′pan′
hard′-shell′ *also*
    hard′-shelled′ *adj.*
hard′ship′
hard′tack′
hard′top′
hard′ware′
hard′wood′
har′dy
hare *(animal)*
    ✓ *hair*
hare′bell′
hare′brained′
hare′lip′
hare′lipped′
har′em
hark
har′le·quin
har′lot
harm′ful
harm′less
har·mon′ic
har·mon′i·ca
har·mo′ni·ous
har·mo′ni·um
har′mo·ni·za′tion
har′mo·nize′,
    -nized′, -niz′ing
har′mo·ny
har′ness
harp
harp′ist
har·poon′
harp′si·chord′
Har′py *also* har′py
har′que·bus *also*

ar′que·bus
har′ri·dan
har′ri·er
har′row
har′row·er
har′row·ing
har′ry, -ried, -ry·ing
harsh
hart *(male deer),* pl.
    harts *or* hart
    ✓ *heart*
har′te·beest′ pl.
    -beests′ *or* -beest′
har′um-scar′um
har′vest
har′vest·er
has′-been′ *n.*
hash
hash′ish′ *also*
    hash′eesh′
Ha′sid *or* Has′sid
    also Chas′sid pl.
    Ha·si′dim *or*
    Has·si′dim *also*
    Chas·si′dim
has′n′t
hasp
has′sle, -sled, -sling
has′sock
haste
has′ten
hast′i·ly
hast′y
hat′band′
hat′box′
hatch
hatch′back′

hatch′er·y
hatch′et
hatch′way′
hate, hat′ed, hat′ing
hate′ful
hat′er
hat′pin′
ha′tred
hat′ter
hau′berk
haugh′ti·ly
haugh′ty
haul *(to tug)*
    ✓ *hall*
haul′er
haunch
haunt
haunt′ed
haunt′ing
Hau′sa pl. -sa *or* -sas
haut′boy′ pl. -boys′
hau·teur′
have *(to own),* had,
    hav′ing, has
    ✓ *halve*
ha′ven
have′-not′ *n.*
have′n′t
hav′er·sack′
hav′oc
haw
Ha·wai′ian
hawk
hawk′er
hawk′-eyed′
haw′ser
haw′thorn′

hay *(grass)*
  ✔ hey
hay'cock'
hay' fe'ver
hay'fork'
hay'loft'
hay'mow'
hay'rack'
hay'rick'
hay'ride'
hay'seed'
hay'stack'
hay'wire'
haz'ard
haz'ard•ous
haze *(air)*
haze *(to humiliate)*,
  hazed, haz'ing
ha'zel
ha'zel•nut'
haz'i•ly
haz'y
H'-bomb'
he
head
head'ache'
head'band'
head'board'
head'cheese'
head'dress'
head'ed
head'first'
head'gear'
head'hunt'er
head'hunt'ing
head'ing
head'land

head'light'
head'line', -lined',
  -lin'ing
head'lin'er
head'lock'
head'long'
head'man
head'mas'ter
head'mis'tress
head'-on'
head'phone'
head'piece'
head'quar'ters
head'rest'
head'room'
head'set'
head'stand'
head'stone'
head'strong'
head'wait'er
head'wa'ters
head'way'
head'wind'
head'word'
head'work'
head'y
heal *(to cure)*
  ✔ heel
heal'er
health
health'i•ly
health'y
heap
hear *(to perceive
  sound)*, heard,
  hear'ing
  ✔ here

hear'er
hear'ing-
  im•paired'
hear'ken *also*
  har'ken
hear'say'
hearse
heart *(organ)*
  ✔ hart
heart'ache'
heart'beat'
heart'break'
heart'break'ing
heart'bro'ken
heart'burn'
heart'en
heart'felt'
hearth
hearth'stone'
heart'i•ly
heart'land'
heart'less
heart'-rend'ing *or*
  heart'rend'ing
hearts'ease' *also*
  heart's'-ease'
heart'sick'
heart'strings'
heart'-to-heart'
heart'wood'
heart'y
heat
heat'ed
heat'er
heath
hea'then *pl.* -thens
  or -then

heath′er
heave, heaved *or*
  hove, heav′ing
heave′-ho′
heav′en
heav′en·li·ness
heav′en·ly
heav′en·ward
heav′i·ly
heav′y
heav′y-dut′y
heav′y-hand′ed
heav′y-heart′ed
heav′y·set′
heav′y·weight′
He·bra′ic
He′brew
heck′le, -led, -ling
heck′ler
hec′tare′
hec′tic
hec′to·me′ter
hec′tor
hedge, hedged,
  hedg′ing
hedge′hog′
hedge′row′
he′don·ism
he′don·ist
he′don·is′tic
heed
heed′less
hee′haw′
heel *(part of a foot, to
  tilt)*
  ✔ *heal*
heft

heft′y
he·gem′o·ny
he·gi′ra *also* he·ji′ra
heif′er
heigh′-ho′
height
height′en
Heim′lich′
  ma·neu′ver
hei′nous
heir *(person who in-
  herits)*
  ✔ *air, are, e′er, ere*
heir′ ap·par′ent *pl.*
  heirs′ ap·par′ent
heir′ess
heir′loom′
heir′ pre·sump′-
  tive *pl.* heirs′
  pre·sump′tive
heist
hel′i·cal
hel′i·con′
hel′i·cop′ter
he′li·o·cen′tric
he′li·o·trope′
he′li·ot′ro·pism
hel′i·pad′
hel′i·port′
he′li·um
he′lix *pl.* -lix·es *or*
  hel′i·ces′
hell
hell′-bent′ *or*
  hell′bent′
hell′cat′
hel′le·bore′

Hel′ene′
Hel·len′ic
Hel′le·nism
Hel′le·nis′tic
hell′-for-leath′er
hell′hole′
hel′lion
hell′ish
hel·lo′ *also* hul·lo′
  pl. -los′
helm
hel′met
helms′man
hel′ot
help′er
help′ful
help′ing
help′less
help′mate′
hel′ter-skel′ter
helve
hem, hemmed,
  hem′ming
he′ma·tite′
he′ma·to·log′ic *or*
  he′ma·to·log′i·cal
he′ma·tol′o·gist
he′ma·tol′o·gy
hem′i·sphere′
hem′i·spher′ic *or*
  hem′i·spher′i·cal
hem′lock′
he′mo·di·al′y·sis
  pl. -ses′
he′mo·glo′bin
he′mo·phil′i·a
he′mo·phil′i·ac′

hem′or·rhage,
  -rhaged, -rhag′ing
hem′or·rhag′ic
hem′or·rhoid′
hemp
hemp′en
hem′stitch′
hen
hen′bane′
hence
hence′forth′
hence·for′ward
hench′man
hen′na, -naed,
  -na·ing
hen′ry *pl.* -ries *or*
  -rys
hep′a·rin
he·pat′i·ca
hep′a·ti′tis *pl.*
  -tit′i·des′
hep′ta·gon′
hep·tag′o·nal
hep·tath′lon
her
her′ald
he·ral′dic
her′ald·ry
herb
her·ba′ceous
herb′age
herb′al
herb′al·ist
her·bar′i·um *pl.*
  -i·ums *or* -i·a
her′bi·cid′al
her′bi·cide′

her′bi·vore′
her·biv′o·rous
Her·cu′le·an
herd *(group)*
  ✔ *heard*
herd′er
herds′man
here *(at this place)*
  ✔ *hear*
here′a·bout′ *also*
  here′a·bouts′
here·af′ter
here·by′
he·red′i·tar′y
he·red′i·ty
Here′ford
here·in′
here·of′
here·on′
her′e·sy
her′e·tic
he·ret′i·cal
here·to′
here·to·fore′
here·un′to
here·up·on′
here·with′
her′i·ta·bil′i·ty
her′i·ta·ble
her′i·tage
her·maph′ro·dite′
her·maph′ro·dit′ic
her·met′ic *also*
  her·met′i·cal
her′mit
her′mit·age
her′ni·a *pl.* -ni·as *or*

-ni·ae′
he′ro *pl.* -roes
he·ro′ic *also*
  he·ro′i·cal
her′o·in *(narcotic)*
her′o·ine *(female
  character)*
her′o·ism
her′on
her′pes
her′pe·tol′o·gist
her′pe·tol′o·gy
her′ring *pl.* -ring *or*
  -rings
her′ring·bone′
hers
her·self′
hertz *pl.* hertz
hes′i·tan·cy
hes′i·tant
hes′i·tate′, -tat′ed,
  -tat′ing
hes′i·tat′er
hes′i·ta′tion
Hes′sian
het′er·o·dox′
het′er·o·dox′y
het′er·o·ge·ne′i·ty
het′er·o·ge′ne·ous
  also het′er·og′e·
  nous
het′er·ol′o·gous
het′er·o·sex′ism
het′er·o·sex′u·al
het′er·o·sex′u·al′-
  i·ty
het′er·o·zy′gous

heu•ris'tic

hew (*to cut*), hewed,
  hewn *or* hewed,
  hew'ing
  ✔ hue

hex

hex'a•dec'i•mal

hex'a•gon'

hex•ag'o•nal

hex'a•he'dron *pl.*
  -drons *or* -dra

hex•am'e•ter

hey *interj.*
  ✔ hay

hey'day'

hi *interj.*
  ✔ hie, high

hi•a'tus *pl.* -tus•es *or*
  -tus

hi•ba'chi *pl.* -chis

hi'ber•nate',
  -nat'ed, -nat'ing

hi'ber•na'tion

hi•bis'cus

hic'cup *also*
  hic'cough, -cupped
  also -coughed,
  -cup'ping *also*
  -cough•ing

hick

hick'o•ry

hide, hid, hid'den *or*
  hid, hid'ing

hide'-and-seek'

hide'a•way'

hide'bound'

hid'e•ous

hide'out' *n.*

hie (*hurry*), hied,
  hie'ing *or* hy'ing
  ✔ hi, high

hi'er•ar'chi•cal *or*
  hi'er•ar'chic

hi'er•ar'chy

hi'er•o•glyph' *also*
  hi'er•o•glyph'ic *n.*

hi'er•o•glyph'ic
  also hi'er•o•glyph'-
  i•cal *adj.*

hi'-fi' *pl.* -fis'

hig'gle•dy-
  pig'gle•dy

high (*tall*)
  ✔ hi, hie

high'ball'

high'born'

high'boy'

high'bred'

high'brow'

high'chair'

high'-class' *adj.*

high'-den'si•ty *adj.*

high'-end' *adj.*

high'er-up' *n.*

high'fa•lu'tin *or*
  hi'fa•lu'tin

high'-five' *n.*

high'fli'er *also*
  high'-fli'er

high'-flown'

high'-fly'ing *adj.*

high'-grade'

high'hand'ed

high'-hat',

-hat'ted, -hat'ting

high' jinks' *or*
  hi'jinks'

high'land

high'land•er

high'light',
  -light'ed, -light'ing

high'ly

high'-mind'ed

high'-pitched'

high'-pres'sure

high'-rise'

high' school' *n.*

high'-school' *adj.*

high'-speed' *adj.*

high'-spir'it•ed

high'-strung'

high'-tail' *v.*

high'-ten'sion

high'-wa'ter
  mark'

high'way'

high'way'man

hi'jack'

hi'jack'er

hike, hiked, hik'ing

hik'er

hi•lar'i•ous

hi•lar'i•ty

hill'bil'ly

hill'i•ness

hill'ock

hill'side'

hill'top'

hill'y

hilt

hi'lum *pl.* -la

him *pron.*
  ✔ hymn
him·self′
hind
hin′der
Hin′di
hind′most′
hind′quar′ter
hin′drance
hind′sight′
Hin′du
Hin′du·ism
Hin′du·sta′ni
hinge, hinged,
  hing′ing
hint
hint′er
hin′ter·land′
hip, hip′per,
  hip′pest
hip′bone′
hip′ joint′
hip′pie *also* hip′py
  pl. -pies
hip′po *pl.* -pos
Hip′po·crat′ic
  oath′
hip′po·drome′
hip′po·pot′a·mus
  pl. -mus·es *or* -mi′
hire, hired, hir′ing
hire′ling
hir′sute′
his
His·pan′ic
hiss
his′ta·mine′

his′ta·min′ic
his′to·log′i·cal *or*
  his′to·log′ic
his·tol′o·gy
his·to′ri·an
his·tor′ic *(important
  in history)*
his·tor′i·cal *(relat-
  ing to history)*
his·tor′i·cize′,
  -cized′, -ciz′ing
his′to·ried′
his·to′ri·og′ra·
  pher
his·to′ri·og′ra·phy
his′to·ry
his′tri·on′ic *also*
  his′tri·on′i·cal
hit, hit, hit′ting
hit′-and-run′
hitch
hitch′hike′,
  -hiked′, -hik′ing
hitch′hik′er
hith′er
hith′er·to′
hit′-or-miss′ *adj.*
hit′ter
Hit′tite′
hive, hived, hiv′ing
hives
ho *interj.*
  ✔ hoe
hoar *(white or gray)*
  ✔ whore
hoard *(cache)*
  ✔ horde

hoard′er
hoar′frost′
hoar′i·ness
hoarse *(grating)*,
  hoars′er, hoars′est
  ✔ horse
hoar′y
hoax
hoax′er
hob
hob′ble, -bled,
  -bling
hob′by
hob′by·horse′
hob′by·ist
hob′gob′lin
hob′nail′
hob′nob′,
  -nobbed′,
  -nob′bing
ho′bo *pl.* -boes *or*
  -bos
hock
hock′ey
ho′cus-po′cus
hod
hodge′podge′
hoe *(to weed)*, hoed,
  hoe′ing
  ✔ ho
hoe′cake′
hoe′down′
hog, hogged,
  hog′ging
ho′gan′
hog′gish
hogs′head′

hog'-tie' *also*
   hog'tie', -tied',
   -tie'ing *or* -ty'ing
hog'wash'
hog'-wild'
hoi' pol•loi'
hoist
hold, held, hold'ing
hold'er
hold'out' *n.*
hold'o'ver *n.*
hold'up' *n.*
hole *(opening)*,
   holed, hol'ing
   ✔ *whole*
hol'ey *(having holes)*
   ✔ *holy, wholly*
hol'i•day'
ho'li•er-than-
   thou' *adj.*
ho'li•ness
ho•lis'tic
hol'lan•daise'
   sauce'
hol'ler
hol'low
hol'ly
hol'ly•hock'
hol'mi•um
hol'o•caust' *also*
   Hol'o•caust'
Hol'o•cene'
hol'o•gram'
hol'o•graph'
hol'o•graph'ic *also*
   hol'o•graph'i•cal
ho•log'raph•y

Hol'stein'
hol'ster
ho'ly *(sacred)*
   ✔ *holey, wholly*
hom'age
hom'bre
home, homed,
   hom'ing
home' base'
home'bod'y
home'-brew'
home'-brewed'
home'buy'er
home'com'ing
home'grown'
home'land'
home'less
home'li•ness
home'ly
home'made'
home'mak'er
home'mak'ing
ho'me•o•path' *or*
   ho'me•op'a•thist
ho'me•o•path'ic
ho'me•op'a•thy
ho'me•o•sta'sis
home'own'er
home' plate'
hom'er
Ho•mer'ic
home'room'
home'sick'
home'spun'
home'stead'
home'stead'er
home'stretch'

home'ward
home'wards
home'work'
hom'ey *also* hom'y,
   -i•er, -i•est
hom'i•cid'al
hom'i•cide'
hom'i•let'ic *also*
   hom'i•let'i•cal
hom'i•ly
hom'i•nid
hom'i•noid'
hom'i•ny
ho'mo•ge•ne'i•ty
ho'mo•ge'ne•ous
ho'mog'e•ni•za'-
   tion
ho•mog'e•nize',
   -nized', -niz'ing
hom'o•graph'
ho•mol'o•gous
hom'o•nym'
ho•mon'y•mous
hom'o•phone'
hom'o•phon'ic
ho•moph'o•nous
ho•moph'o•ny
ho•mop'ter•ous
Ho'mo sa'pi•ens
ho'mo•sex'u•al
ho'mo•sex'u•al'i•ty
ho'mo•zy'gous
hon'cho *pl.* -chos
Hon•du'ran
hone, honed,
   hon'ing
hon'est

hon'es·ty
hon'ey pl. -eys
hon'ey, -eyed or
 -ied, -ey·ing
hon'ey·bee'
hon'ey·comb'
hon'ey·dew'
hon'ey·moon'
hon'ey·moon'er
hon'ey·suck'le
honk
honk'er
hon'or
hon'or·a·ble
hon'or·a·bly
hon'o·rar'i·um pl.
 -i·ums or -i·a
hon'or·ar'y
hon'or·if'ic
hood
hood'ed
hood'lum
hood'wink'
hoo'ey
hoof pl. hoofs or
 hooves
hook
hook'ah
hook'up' n.
hook'worm'
hook'y
hoo'li·gan
hoop (circle)
 ✔ whoop
hoop'la
hoo·ray'
hoot

hoot'en·an'ny
hop, hopped,
 hop'ping
hope, hoped,
 hop'ing
hope'ful
hope'less
Ho'pi pl. -pi or -pis
hop'per
hop'scotch'
ho'ra
horde (group)
 ✔ hoard
hore'hound'
ho·ri'zon
hor'i·zon'tal
hor·mon'al
hor'mone'
horn'bill'
horn'book'
horned
hor'net
horn'pipe'
horn'y
hor'o·scope'
hor·ren'dous
hor'ri·ble
hor'ri·bly
hor'rid
hor·rif'ic
hor'ri·fy', -fied',
 -fy'ing
hor'ror
hors d'oeuvre' pl.
 hors d'oeuvres' or
 hors d'oeuvre'
horse (animal)

 ✔ hoarse
horse'back'
horse'fly'
horse'hair'
horse'hide'
horse'man
horse'man·ship'
horse'play'
horse'pow'er
horse'rad'ish
horse'shoe'
horse'whip',
 -whipped',
 -whip'ping
horse'wom'an
hors'y also hors'ey,
 -i·er, -i·est
hor'ta·tive
hor'ta·to'ry
hor'ti·cul'tur·al
hor'ti·cul'ture
hor'ti·cul'tur·ist
ho·san'na
hose pl. hose or
 hos'es
hose, hosed, hos'ing
ho'sier·y
hos'pice
hos'pi·ta·ble
hos'pi·ta·bly
hos'pi·tal
hos'pi·tal'i·ty
hos'pi·tal·i·za'tion
hos'pi·tal·ize',
 -ized', -iz'ing
host
hos'tage

hos'tel (lodging)
  ✔ hostile
hos'tel•ry
host'ess
hos'tile (showing enmity)
  ✔ hostel
hos•til'i•ty
hos'tler also os'tler
hot, hot'ter, hot'test
hot'bed'
hot'-blood'ed
hot'cake'
hot' dog' or
  hot'dog'
ho•tel'
hot'foot' v.
hot'head'ed
hot'house'
hot' line' or
  hot'line'
hot' plate'
hot'shot'
hound
hour (time)
  ✔ our
hour'glass'
hour'long' or
  hour'-long' adj.
house, housed,
  hous'ing
house'boat'
house'break',
  -broke', -bro'ken,
  -break'ing
house'clean'ing

house'fly'
house'guest'
house'hold'
house'hold'er
house'hus'band
house'keep'er
house'keep'ing
house'maid'
house'moth'er
house'plant'
house'top'
house'wares'
house'warm'ing
house'wife'
house'work'
hous'ing
hov'el
hov'er
hov'er•craft'
how
how'dah
how'dy
how•ev'er
how'it•zer
howl'er
how'so•ev'er
hoy'den
hub'bub'
hub'cap'
hu'bris
huck'le•ber'ry
huck'ster
hud'dle, -dled,
  -dling
hue (color, clamor)
  ✔ hew

huff'i•ly
huff'y
hug, hugged,
  hug'ging
huge, hug'er,
  hug'est
Hu'gue•not'
hu'la
hulk'ing
hull
hul'la•ba•loo' pl.
  -loos'
hum, hummed,
  hum'ming
hu'man
hu•mane'
hu'man•ism
hu'man•ist
hu•man'i•tar'i•an
hu•man'i•tar'i•an•
  ism
hu•man'i•ty
hu'man•i•za'tion
hu'man•ize', -ized',
  -iz'ing
hu'man•kind'
hu'man•oid'
hum'ble, -bled,
  -bling
hum'bly
hum'bug',
  -bugged', -bug'ging
hum'drum'
hu'mer•us (bone),
  pl. -mer•i'
  ✔ humorous

hu′mid
hu·mid′i·fi′er
hu·mid′i·fy′, -fied′,
 -fy′ing
hu·mid′i·ty
hu·mil′i·ate′,
 -at′ed, -at′ing
hu·mil′i·a′tion
hu·mil′i·ty
hum′ming·bird′
hum′mock
hum′mus *also*
 hum′us *or* hom′-
 mos *(mashed chick-*
 peas)
 ✔ *humus*
hu′mor
hu′mor·ist
hu′mor·ous *(funny)*
 ✔ *humerus*
hump′back′
hump′backed′
humph
hu′mus *(decayed*
 matter)
 ✔ *hummus*
Hun
hunch′back′
hunch′backed′
hun′dred *pl.* -dred
 or -dreds
hun′dredth
hun′dred·weight′
 pl. -weight′ *or*
 -weights′
Hun·gar′i·an

hun′ger
hun′gri·ly
hun′gri·ness
hun′gry
hunk
Hunk′pa′pa *pl.* -pa
 or -pas
Hun′nish
hunt
hunt′er
hunt′ing
hunts′man
hur′dle *(to leap*
 over), -dled, -dling
 ✔ *hurtle*
hur′dler
hur′dy-gur′dy
hurl
hurl′er
hur′ly-bur′ly
Hu′ron *pl.* -ron *or*
 -rons
hur·rah′ *also*
 hoo·ray′ *or*
 hur·ray′
hur′ri·cane′
hur′ry, -ried, -ry·ing
hurt, hurt, hurt′ing
hurt′ful
hur′tle *(to hurl)*,
 -tled,-tling
 ✔ *hurdle*
hus′band
hus′band·ry
husk′y *(hoarse,*
 burly)

hus′ky *also* hus′kie
 (dog)
hus·sar′
hus′sy
hus′tle, -tled,
 -tling
hut
hutch
hy′a·cinth′
hy′brid
hy′brid·i·za′tion
hy′brid·ize′, -ized,
 -iz′ing
hy′dra
hy′dran′gea
hy′drant
hy′drate′, -drat′ed,
 -drat′ing
hy·dra′tion
hy·drau′lic
hy′dra·zine′
hy′dride′
hy′dro·car′bon
hy′dro·ce·phal′ic
 or hy′dro·ceph′-
 a·loid′ *or* hy′dro·
 ceph′a·lous
hy′dro·ceph′a·lus
hy′dro·ceph′a·ly
hy′dro·chlo′ric
 ac′id
hy′dro·cor′ti·sone′
hy′dro·cy·an′ic
 ac′id
hy′dro·dy·nam′ic
hy′dro·e·lec′tric

hy'dro•e•lec•tric'-
  i•ty
hy'dro•fluor'ic
  ac'id
hy'dro•foil'
hy'dro•gen
hy'dro•gen•ate',
  -at'ed, -at'ing
hy'dro•gen•a'tion
hy•drog'e•nous
hy'dro•graph'ic
hy•drog'ra•phy
hy•drol'o•gy
hy•drol'y•sis
hy'dro•lyze',
  -lyzed', -lyz'ing
hy•drom'e•ter
hy'dro•pho'bi•a
hy'dro•plane'
hy'dro•pon'ics
hy'dro•pow'er
hy'dro•sphere'
hy'dro•stat'ic *also*
  hy'dro•stat'i•cal
hy'dro•ther'a•py
hy'drot'ro•pism
hy'drous
hy•drox'ide
hy•drox'yl
hy'dro•zo'an
hy•e'na *also*
  hy•ae'na
hy'giene'
hy•gi•en'ic
hy•gien'ist
hy•grom'e•ter
hy'gro•met'ric

hy'grom'e•try
hy'gro•scope'
hy'gro•scop'ic
hy'men
hy'me•ne'al
hymn *(song)*
  ✔ *him*
hym'nal
hype, hyped,
  hyp'ing
hy•per•ac'id
hy'per•a•cid'i•ty
hy'per•ac'tive
hy•per'bo•la *pl.* -las
  or -lae
hy•per'bo•le
hy'per•bol'ic
hy'per•crit'i•cal
  (overcritical)
  ✔ *hypocritical*
hy'per•gly•ce'mi•a
hy'per•sen'si•tive
hy'per•sen'si•tiv'i•
  ty
hy'per•son'ic
hy'per•ten'sion
hy'per•text'
hy'per•thy'roid'
hy'per•thy'roid•
  ism
hy•per'tro•phy
hy'per•ven'ti•late',
  -lat'ed, -lat'ing
hy'per•ven'ti•la'-
  tion
hy'pha *pl.* -phae
hy'phen

hy'phen•ate',
  -at'ed, -at'ing
hy'phen•a'tion
hyp•no'sis *pl.* -ses
hyp'no•ther'a•py
hyp•not'ic
hyp'no•tism
hyp'no•tist
hyp'no•tize',
  -tized', -tiz'ing
hyp'no•tiz'er
hy'po *pl.* -pos
hy'po•chon'dri•a
hy'po•chon'dri•
  ac'
hy•poc'ri•sy
hyp'o•crite'
hyp'o•crit'i•cal
  (insincere)
  ✔ *hypercritical*
hy'po•der'mic
hy'po•gly•ce'mi•a
hy'po•sul'fite'
hy'po•sul•fu'rous
  ac'id
hy•pot'e•nuse'
hy'po•thal'a•mus
hy•poth'e•sis *pl.*
  -ses'
hy•poth'e•size',
  -sized', -siz'ing
hy'po•thet'i•cal
  also hy'po•thet'ic
hy'po•thy'roid•ism
hy'rax' *pl.* -rax'es *or*
  -ra'ces'
hys'sop

hys'ter•ec'to•my
hys•ter'i•a
hys•ter'ic
hys•ter'i•cal

I

I pron.
   ✔ *aye, eye*
i'amb'
i•am'bic
I•be'ri•an
i'bex' *pl.* i'bex' *or*
   i'bex•es
i'bi•dem
i'bis *pl.* i'bis *or*
   i'bis•es
ice, iced, ic'ing
ice'berg'
ice'boat'
ice'bound'
ice'box'
ice'break'er
ice'cap' *or* ice' cap'
ice'-cold'
ice' cream'
ice'-cream' cone'
Ice'land•er
Ice•land'ic
ice'man
ice' skate' *n.*
ice'-skate', -skat'ed,
   -skat'ing
ice' skat'er
ich•neu'mon
ich'thy•ol'o•gist

ich'thy•ol'o•gy
ich'thy•o•saur'
i'ci•cle
i'ci•ly
i'ci•ness
ic'ing
i'con'
i•con'o•clast'
i•con'o•clas'tic
ic'y
i•de'a
i•de'al
i•de'al•ism
i•de'al•ist
i•de'al•is'tic
i•de'al•i•za'tion
i•de'al•ize', -ized',
   -iz'ing
i•den'ti•cal
i•den'ti•fi'a•ble
i•den'ti•fi•ca'tion
i•den'ti•fy', -fied',
   -fy'ing
i•den'ti•ty
id'e•o•gram'
id'e•o•graph'
i'de•o•log'i•cal
i'de•ol'o•gy
ides
id'i•o•cy
id'i•om
id'i•o•mat'ic
id'i•o•syn'cra•sy
id'i•o•syn•crat'ic
id'i•ot
id'i•ot'ic
id'i•ot'i•cal•ly

i'dle *(to pass time
   lazily),* i'dled,
   i'dling
   ✔ *idol, idyll*
i'dly
i'dler
i'dol *(image)*
   ✔ *idle, idyll*
i•dol'a•ter *or*
   i•dol'a•tor
i•dol'a•trous
i•dol'a•try
i'dol•ize', -ized',
   -iz'ing
i'dyll *also* i'dyl
   (poem)
   ✔ *idle, idol*
i•dyl'lic
i•dyl'li•cal•ly
if
if'fy
ig'loo *pl.* -loos
ig'ne•ous
ig•nite', -nit'ed,
   -nit'ing
ig•ni'tion
ig•no'ble
ig•no'bly
ig'no•min'i•ous
ig'no•min'y
ig•no•ra'mus *pl.*
   -mus•es
ig'no•rance
ig'no•rant
ig•nore', -nored',
   -nor'ing
i•gua'na

il'e•ac'
il'e•i'tis
il'e•um (*intestine*),
  pl. -e•a
il'i•um (*bone*), pl.
  -i•a
ilk
ill, worse, worst
ill'-ad•vised'
ill'-bred'
il•le'gal
il'le•gal'i•ty
il•leg'i•ble
il'le•git'i•ma•cy
il'le•git'i•mate
ill'-fat'ed
ill'-fa'vored
ill'-got'ten
ill'-hu'mored
il•lib'er•al
il•lic'it (*unlawful*)
  ✔ elicit
il•lim'it•a•ble
il•lit'er•a•cy
il•lit'er•ate
ill'-man'nered
ill'-na'tured
ill'ness
il•log'i•cal
ill'-starred'
ill'-tem'pered
ill'-timed'
ill'-treat'
ill'-treat'ment
il•lu'mi•nate',
  -nat'ed, -nat'ing
il•lu'mi•na'tion

il•lu'mine, -mined,
  -min•ing
ill•us'age
ill-use', -used',
  -us'ing
ill-use' *n.*
il•lu'sion (*miscon-
  ception*)
  ✔ allusion
il•lu'sive (*deceptive*)
  ✔ allusive, elusive
il•lu'so•ry
il'lus•trate',
  -trat'ed, -trat'ing
il'lus•tra'tion
il'lus•tra'tive
il'lus•tra'tor
il•lus'tri•ous
im'age
im'age•ry
i•mag'i•na•ble
i•mag'i•nar'y
i•mag'i•na'tion
i•mag'i•na•tive
i•mag'ine, -ined,
  -in•ing
i•ma'go pl. -goes *or*
  -gi•nes'
i•mam'
im•bal'ance
im'be•cile
im•bibe', -bibed',
  -bib'ing
im•bro'glio *pl.*
  -glios
im•bue', -bued',
  -bu'ing

im'i•ta•ble
im'i•tate', -tat'ed,
  -tat'ing
im'i•ta'tion
im'i•ta'tive
im'i•ta'tor
im•mac'u•late
im•ma'nent
  (*inherent*)
  ✔ eminent, immi-
  nent
im•ma•te'ri•al
im•ma•ture'
im•ma•tur'i•ty
im•meas'ur•a•ble
im•me'di•a•cy
im•me'di•ate
im•me•mo'ri•al
im•mense'
im•men'si•ty
im•merse',
  -mersed', -mers'ing
im•mer'sion
im'mi•grant (*one
  who settles in a for-
  eign country*)
  ✔ emigrant
im'mi•grate' (*to set-
  tle in a foreign coun-
  try*), -grat'ed,
  -grat'ing
  ✔ emigrate
im'mi•gra'tion
  (*settling in a foreign
  country*)
  ✔ emigration
im'mi•nence

im'mi·nent (*about to happen*)
✔ eminent, immanent
im·mo'bile
im·mo·bil'i·ty
im·mo'bi·li·za'tion
im·mo'bi·lize',
-lized', -liz'ing
im·mod'er·ate
im·mod'est
im·mod'es·ty
im'mo·late',
-lat'ed, -lat'ing
im'mo·la'tion
im·mor'al
im'mor·al'i·ty
im·mor'tal
im·mor·tal'i·ty
im·mor'tal·ize',
-ized', -iz'ing
im·mov'a·ble
im·mune'
im·mu'ni·ty
im'mu·ni·za'tion
im'mu·nize',
-nized', -niz'ing
im'mu·nol'o·gy
im·mure', -mured',
-mur'ing
im·mu'ta·bil'i·ty
or im·mu'ta·ble·
ness
im·mu'ta·bly
imp
im'pact' n.
im·pact' v.

im·pair'
im·pair'ment
im·pa'la
im·pale', -paled',
-pal'ing
im·pal'pa·ble
im·pal'pa·bly
im·pan'el, -eled or
-elled, -el'ing or
-el'ling
im·part'
im·par'tial
im'par·ti·al'i·ty
im·pass'a·bil'i·ty
im·pass'a·ble (*impossible to cross*)
✔ impassible
im·pass'a·bly
im'passe'
im·pass'i·ble
(*unfeeling*)
✔ impassable
im·pas'sioned
im·pas'sive
im'pas·siv'i·ty
im·pa'tience
im·pa'tient
im·peach'
im·pec'ca·ble
im·pec'ca·bly
im'pe·cu'ni·ous
im·pede', -ped'ed,
-ped'ing
im·ped'i·ment
im·pel', -pelled',
-pel'ling
im·pend'

im·pen'e·tra·bil'-
i·ty
im·pen'e·tra·ble
im·pen'e·tra·bly
im·pen'i·tent
im·per'a·tive
im'per·cep'ti·bil'-
i·ty
im'per·cep'ti·ble
im'per·cep'ti·bly
im·per'fect
im'per·fec'tion
im·per'fo·rate
im·pe'ri·al
im·pe'ri·al·ism
im·pe'ri·al·ist
im·pe'ri·al·is'tic
im·per'il, -iled or
-illed, -il'ing or
-il·ling
im·pe'ri·ous
im·per'ish·a·ble
im·per'ma·nence
im·per'ma·nent
im·per'me·a·ble
im·per'son·al
im·per'son·al'i·ty
im·per'son·ate',
-at'ed, -at'ing
im·per'son·a'tion
im·per'son·a'tor
im·per'ti·nence
im·per'ti·nent
im'per·turb'a·bil'-
i·ty
im'per·turb'a·ble
im'per·turb'a·bly

im·per'vi·ous
im·pe·ti'go *pl.* -gos
im·pet'u·os'i·ty
im·pet'u·ous
im·pe'tus *pl.* -tus·es
im·pi'e·ty
im·pinge',
 -pinged', -ping'ing
im·pi'ous
imp'ish
im·plac'a·bil'i·ty
im·plac'a·ble
im·plac'a·bly
im·plant' *v.*
im'plant' *n.*
im·plan·ta'tion
im·plau'si·bil'i·ty
im·plau'si·ble
im·plau'si·bly
im'ple·ment
im'ple·men·ta'tion
im'pli·cate',
 -cat'ed, -cat'ing
im'pli·ca'tion
im·plic'it
im·plode',
 -plod'ed, -plod'ing
im·plore', -plored',
 -plor'ing
im·plo'sion
im·plo'sive
im·ply', -plied',
 -ply'ing
im'po·lite'
im·pol'i·tic
im·pon'der·a·ble
im·port' *v.*

im'port' *n.*
im·por'tance
im·por'tant
im·por·ta'tion
im·port'er
im·por'tu·nate
im·por·tune',
 -tuned', -tun'ing
im·por·tu'ni·ty
im·pose', -posed',
 -pos'ing
im'po·si'tion
im·pos'si·bil'i·ty
im·pos'si·ble
im·pos'si·bly
im'post'
im·pos'tor
im·pos'ture
im'po·tence
im'po·tent
im·pound'
im·pov'er·ish
im·prac'ti·ca·ble
im·prac'ti·ca·bly
im·prac'ti·cal
im·prac'ti·cal'i·ty
im'pre·cate',
 -cat'ed, -cat'ing
im'pre·ca'tion
im'pre·ca·to'ry
im'pre·cise'
im'pre·ci'sion
im·preg'na·ble
im·preg'na·bly
im·preg'nate',
 -nat'ed, -nat'ing
im'preg·na'tion

im'pre·sa'ri·o' *pl.*
 -os'
im·press' *v.*
im'press' *n.*
im·pres'sion
im·pres'sion·a·bil'-
 i·ty
im·pres'sion·a·ble
im·pres'sion·ism
im·pres'sion·ist
im·pres'sion·is'tic
im·pres'sive
im·print' *v.*
im'print' *n.*
im·pris'on
im·pris'on·ment
im·prob'a·bil'i·ty
im·prob'a·ble
im·prob'a·bly
im·promp'tu
im·prop'er
im'pro·pri'e·ty
im·prove',
 -proved', -prov'ing
im·prove'ment
im·prov'i·dence
im·prov'i·dent
im·prov'i·sa'tion
im'pro·vise',
 -vised', -vis'ing
im'pro·vis'er
im·pru'dence
im·pru'dent
im'pu·dence
im'pu·dent
im·pugn'
im'pulse

im·pul'sion
im·pul'sive
im·pu'ni·ty
im·pure', -pur'er,
-pur'est
im·pu'ri·ty
im·put'a·ble
im'pu·ta'tion
im·pute', -put'ed,
-put'ing
in (within)
✔ inn
in'a·bil'i·ty
in'ac·ces'si·ble
in'ac·ces'si·bly
in·ac'cu·ra·cy
in·ac'cu·rate
in·ac'tion
in·ac'tive
in'ac·tiv'i·ty
in·ad'e·qua·cy
in·ad'e·quate
in'ad·mis'si·bil'i·ty
in'ad·mis'si·ble
in'ad·ver'tence
in'ad·ver'tent
in'ad·vis'a·bil'i·ty
in'ad·vis'a·ble
in·al'ien·a·ble
in·ane'
in·an'i·mate
in·an'i·ty
in·ap'pli·ca·bil'i·ty
in·ap'pli·ca·ble
in'ap·pre'cia·ble
in'ap·pre'cia·bly
in'ap·pro'pri·ate

in·apt'
in·ap'ti·tude'
in'ar·tic'u·late
in'ar·tis'tic
in'as·much' as'
in'at·ten'tion
in'at·ten'tive
in·au'di·ble
in·au'di·bly
in·au'gu·ral
in·au'gu·rate',
-rat'ed, -rat'ing
in·au'gu·ra'tion
in'aus·pi'cious
in'board'
in'born'
in'bound'
in'bred'
in'breed', -bred',
-breed'ing
in'breed'ing
In'ca pl. -ca or -cas
in·cal'cu·la·bil'i·ty
in·cal'cu·la·ble
In'can
in'can·des'cence
in'can·des'cent
in'can·ta'tion
in'ca·pa·bil'i·ty
in·ca'pa·ble
in'ca·pac'i·tate',
-tat'ed, -tat'ing
in'ca·pac'i·ta'tion
in'ca·pac'i·ty
in·car'cer·ate',
-at'ed, -at'ing
in·car'cer·a'tion

in·car'nate',
-nat'ed, -nat'ing
in'car·na'tion
in·cau'tious
in·cen'di·ar'y
in·cense' (to infuri-
ate), -censed',
-cens'ing
in'cense' (aromatic
substance)
in·cen'tive
in·cep'tion
in·cer'ti·tude'
in·ces'sant
in'cest'
in·ces'tu·ous
in·cho'ate
inch'worm'
in'ci·dence
in'ci·dent
in'ci·den'tal
in·cin'er·ate',
-at'ed, -at'ing
in·cin'er·a'tion
in·cin'er·a'tor
in·cip'i·en·cy or
in·cip'i·ence
in·cip'i·ent
in·cise', -cised',
-cis'ing
in·ci'sion
in·ci'sive
in·ci'sor
in·cite' (to provoke),
-cit'ed, -cit'ing
✔ insight
in·cite'ment

in·clem'en·cy
in·clem'ent
in·cli·na'tion
in·cline', -clined',
  -clin'ing
in·clude', -clud'ed,
  -clud'ing
in·clu'sion
in·clu'sive
in'cog·ni'to
in·co·her'ence *also*
  in'co·her'en·cy
in'co·her'ent
in'com·bus'ti·ble
in'come'
in'com'ing
in·com·men'su·
  rate
in'com·mode',
  -mod'ed, -mod'ing
in'com·mo'di·ous
in'com·mu'ni·ca·
  ble
in'com·mu'ni·
  ca'do
in'com·mu'ni·ca·
  tive
in·com'pa·ra·ble
in·com'pa·ra·bly
in'com·pat'i·bil'-
  i·ty
in'com·pat'i·ble
in'com·pat'i·bly
in·com'pe·tence *or*
  in'com'pe·ten·cy
in·com'pe·tent
in'com·plete'

in'com·pre·hen'-
  si·bil'i·ty
in'com·pre·hen'-
  si·ble
in'com·pre·hen'-
  si·bly
in'com·pre·hen'-
  sion
in'com·press'i·ble
in'con·ceiv'a·bil'-
  i·ty
in'con·ceiv'a·ble
in'con·ceiv'a·bly
in'con·clu'sive
in·con'gru·ent
in'con·gru'i·ty
in·con'gru·ous
in·con'se·quen'-
  tial
in'con·sid'er·a·ble
in'con·sid'er·a·bly
in'con·sid'er·ate
in'con·sis'ten·cy
in'con·sis'tent
in'con·sol'a·ble
in'con·sol'a·bly
in'con·spic'u·ous
in·con'stan·cy
in·con'stant
in'con·test'a·ble
in·con'ti·nence
in·con'ti·nent
in'con·tro·vert'i·
  ble
in'con·tro·vert'i·
  bly
in'con·ven'ience,

-ienced, -ienc'ing
in'con·ven'ient
in·cor'po·rate',
  -rat'ed, -rat'ing
in·cor'po're·al
in'cor·rect'
in·cor'ri·gi·bil'i·ty
in·cor'ri·gi·ble
in·cor'ri·gi·bly
in'cor·rupt'i·bil'-
  i·ty
in'cor·rupt'i·ble
in·crease',
  -creased',
  -creas'ing
in'crease' *n.*
in·cred'i·ble *(unbe-
  lievable)*
  ✔ incredulous
in·cred'i·bly
in·cre·du'li·ty
in·cred'u·lous
  (skeptical)
  ✔ incredible
in'cre·ment
in·crim'i·nate',
  -nat'ed, -nat'ing
in·crim'i·na'tion
in·crim'i·na'tor
in·crim'i·na·to'ry
in·crust'
in'cu·bate', -bat'ed,
  -bat'ing
in'cu·ba'tion
in'cu·ba'tor
in'cul'cate',
  -cat'ed, -cat'ing

in·cul·ca′tion
in·cum′ben·cy
in·cum′bent
in·cur′, -curred′,
  -cur′ring
in·cur′a·ble
in·cur′a·bly
in·cu′ri·ous
in·cur′sion
in′cus *pl.* in·cu′des
in·debt′ed
in·de·cen′cy
in·de′cent
in′de·ci′pher·
  a·ble
in·de·ci′sion
in·de·ci′sive
in·dec′o·rous
in·deed′
in′de·fat′i·ga·ble
in′de·fat′i·ga·bly
in′de·fen′si·ble
in′de·fen′si·bly
in′de·fin′a·ble
in′de·fin′a·bly
in·def′i·nite
in·del′i·bil′i·ty *or*
  in·del′i·ble·ness
in·del′i·ble
in·del′i·bly
in·del′i·ca·cy
in·del′i·cate
in·dem′ni·fi·ca′-
  tion
in·dem′ni·fy′,
  -fied′, -fy′ing
in·dem′ni·ty

in·dent′
in′den·ta′tion
in·den′ture, -tured,
  -tur·ing
in′de·pend′ence
in′de·pend′ent
in′-depth′
in′de·scrib′a·ble
in′de·scrib′a·bly
in′de·struc′ti·ble
in′de·struc′ti·bly
in·de·ter′mi·nate
in′dex′ *pl.* -dex′es *or*
  -di·ces′
In′di·an
In′di·an′an *or*
  In′di·an′i·an
In′dic
in′di·cate′, -cat′ed,
  -cat′ing
in′di·ca′tion
in·dic′a·tive
in′di·ca′tor
in·dict′ *(to accuse)*
  ✔ indite
in·dict′a·ble
in·dict′er *or*
  in·dic′tor
in·dict′ment
in·dif′fer·ence
in·dif′fer·ent
in′di·gence
in·dig′e·nous
in′di·gent
in′di·gest′i·ble
in′di·ges′tion
in·dig′nant

in′dig·na′tion
in·dig′ni·ty
in′di·go′ *pl.* -gos′ *or*
  -goes′
in′di·rect′
in′di·rec′tion
in′dis·creet′ *(lack-
  ing discretion)*
in′dis·crete′ *(not
  divided)*
in′dis·cre′tion
in′dis·crim′i·nate
in′dis·pen′sa·ble
in′dis·pen′sa·bly
in′dis·posed′
in·dis′po·si′tion
in′dis·put′a·ble
in′dis·put′a·bly
in′dis·sol′u·ble
in′dis·sol′u·bly
in′dis·tinct′
in′dis·tin′guish·
  a·ble
in·dite′ *(to write)*
  ✔ indict
in′di·um
in′di·vid′u·al
in′di·vid′u·al·ism
in′di·vid′u·al·ist
in′di·vid′u·al·is′tic
in′di·vid′u·al′i·ty
in′di·vid′u·al·ize′,
  -ized′, -iz′ing
in′di·vis′i·bil′i·ty
in′di·vis′i·ble
in′di·vis′i·bly
In′do·chi′nese′

in·doc'tri·nate',
  -nat'ed, -nat'ing
in·doc'tri·na'tion
In'do-Eu'ro·pe'an
In'do-I·ra'ni·an
in'do·lence
in'do·lent
in·dom'i·ta·ble
in·dom'i·ta·bly
In'do·ne'sian
in'door' *adj.*
in'doors' *adv.*
in·du'bi·ta·ble
in·du'bi·ta·bly
in·duce', -duced',
  -duc'ing
in·duce'ment
in·duct'
in·duc'tance
in'duct·ee'
in·duc'tion
in·duc'tive
in·duc'tor
in·dulge', -dulged',
  -dulg'ing
in·dul'gence
in·dul'gent
in·dus'tri·al
in·dus'tri·al·ist
in·dus'tri·al·i·za'-
  tion
in·dus'tri·al·ize',
  -ized', -iz'ing
in·dus'tri·ous
in'dus·try
in·e'bri·ate', -at'ed,
  -at'ing

in·e'bri·a'tion
in·ed'i·ble
in·ef'fa·ble
in·ef'fa·bly
in'ef·fec'tive
in'ef·fec'tu·al
in'ef·fi'cien·cy
in'ef·fi'cient
in'e·las'tic
in'e·las·tic'i·ty
in·el'e·gance
in·el'e·gant
in·el'i·gi·bil'i·ty
in·el'i·gi·ble
in·el'i·gi·bly
in·ept'
in·ep'ti·tude'
in·e'qual'i·ty
in·eq'ui·ta·ble
in·eq'ui·ta·bly
in·eq'ui·ty *(unfair-
  ness)*
  ✔ iniquity
in·ert'
in·er'tia
in'es·cap'a·ble
in'es·cap'a·bly
in·es'ti·ma·ble
in·es'ti·ma·bly
in·ev'i·ta·bil'i·ty
in·ev'i·ta·ble
in·ev'i·ta·bly
in·ex·act'
in'ex·cus'a·ble
in'ex·cus'a·bly
in'ex·haust'i·ble
in'ex·haust'i·bly

in·ex'o·ra·ble
in·ex'o·ra·bly
in'ex·pe'di·ent
in'ex·pen'sive
in'ex·pe'ri·ence
in'ex·pe'ri·enced
in·ex'pert'
in'ex·pli·ca·ble
in'ex·pli·ca·bly
in'ex·press'i·ble
in'ex·press'i·bly
in'ex·tin'guish·
  a·ble
in·ex'tri·ca·ble
in·fal'li·bil'i·ty
in·fal'li·ble
in'fa·mous
in'fa·my
in'fan·cy
in'fant
in·fan'ti·cide'
in'fan·tile'
in'fan·try
in'fan·try·man
in·fat'u·ate', -at'ed,
  -at'ing
in·fat'u·a'tion
in·fect'
in·fec'tion
in·fec'tious
in·fe·lic'i·tous
in·fe·lic'i·ty
in·fer', -ferred',
  -fer'ring
in·fer'a·ble
in'fer·ence
in'fer·en'tial

in•fe′ri•or
in•fe′ri•or′i•ty
in•fer′nal
in•fer′no *pl.* -nos
in•fer′tile
in′fer•til′i•ty
in•fest′
in′fes•ta′tion
in′fi•del
in•fi•del′i•ty
in′field′
in′field′er
in′fight′ing
in′fil•trate′,
　-trat′ed, -trat′ing
in′fil•tra′tion
in′fi•nite
in′fin•i•tes′i•mal
in•fin′i•tive
in•fin′i•ty
in•firm′
in•fir′ma•ry
in•fir′mi•ty
in•flame′, -flamed′,
　-flam′ing
in•flam′ma•ble
　(*easily ignited*)
　✔ flammable,
　nonflammable
in′flam•ma′tion
in•flam′ma•to′ry
in•flat′a•ble
in•flate′, -flat′ed,
　-flat′ing
in•flat′er *or* in•fla′tor
in•fla′tion
in•fla′tion•ar′y

in•flect′
in•flec′tion
in•flex′i•bil′i•ty
in•flex′i•ble
in•flict′
in•flic′tion
in′flo•res′cence
in′flow′
in′flu•ence, -enced,
　-enc•ing
in′flu•en′tial
in′flu•en′za
in′flux′
in′fo
in•form′
in•for′mal
in′for•mal′i•ty
in•form′ant
in′for•ma′tion
in•form′a•tive
in•formed′
in•form′er
in•frac′tion
in′fra•red′
in′fra•son′ic
in′fra•struc′ture
in•fre′quen•cy *or*
　in•fre′quence
in•fre′quent
in•fringe′,
　-fringed′, -fring′ing
in•fringe′ment
in•fu′ri•ate′, -at′ed,
　-at′ing
in•fuse′, -fused′,
　-fus′ing
in•fus′i•ble

in•fu′sion
in•gen′ious (*clever*)
　✔ ingenuous
in′gé•nue′
in′ge•nu′i•ty
in•gen′u•ous
　(*candid*)
　✔ ingenious
in•gest′
in•ges′tion
in•glo′ri•ous
in′got
in•grain′
in•grained′
in′grate′
in•gra′ti•ate′,
　-at′ed, -at′ing
in•gra′ti•a′tion
in•grat′i•tude′
in•gre′di•ent
in′gress′
in′grown′
in•hab′it
in•hab′it•a•ble
in•hab′i•tant
in•ha′lant
in′ha•la′tion
in•ha′la•tor
in•hale′, -haled′,
　-hal′ing
in•hal′er
in′har•mo′ni•ous
in•her′ent
in•her′it
in•her′it•a•ble
in•her′i•tance
in•her′i•tor

in•hib'it
in'hi•bi'tion
in•hib'i•tor
in•hib'i•to'ry
in•hos'pi•ta•ble
in•hos'pi•ta•bly
in'-house' *adj. &*
adv.
in•hu'man
in'hu•mane'
in'hu•man'i•ty
in•im'i•cal
in•im'i•ta•bil'i•ty
in•im'i•ta•ble
in•im'i•ta•bly
in•iq'ui•tous
in•iq'ui•ty *(sin)*
✔ *inequity*
in•i'tial, -tialed *also*
-tialled, -tial•ing
also -tial•ling
in•i'ti•ate', -at'ed,
-at'ing
in•i'ti•a'tion
in•i'ti•a•tive
in•i'ti•a'tor
in•ject'
in•jec'tion
in•jec'tor
in'ju•di'cious
in•junc'tion
in'jure, -jured,
-jur'ing
in•ju'ri•ous
in'ju•ry
in•jus'tice
ink'blot'

ink'horn'
in'kling
ink'stand'
ink'well'
ink'y
in'laid'
in'land
in'-law'
in'lay', -laid',
-lay'ing
in'let'
in'mate'
in'most'
inn *(hotel)*
✔ *in*
in'nards
in•nate'
in'ner
in'ner-cit'y *adj.*
in'ner•most'
in'ner•vate',
-vat'ed, -vat'ing
in'ning
inn'keep'er
in'no•cence
in'no•cent
in•noc'u•ous
in'no•vate', -vat'ed,
-vat'ing
in'no•va'tion
in'no•va'tive
in'no•va'tor
in'nu•en'do *pl.*
-does
in•nu'mer•a•ble
in•nu'mer•a•bly
in•nu'mer•ate

in•oc'u•late',
-lat'ed, -lat'ing
in•oc'u•la'tion
in'of•fen'sive
in•op'er•a•ble
in•op'er•a•tive
in•op'por•tune'
in•or'di•nate
in'or•gan'ic
in'pa'tient
in'put', -put'ted *or*
-put', -put'ting
in'quest'
in•qui'e•tude'
in•quire' *also*
en•quire', -quired',
-quir'ing
in•quir'y *also*
en•quir'y
in'qui•si'tion
in•quis'i•tive
in•quis'i•tor
in•quis'i•to'ri•al
in'road'
in'rush'
in'sa•lu'bri•ous
in•sane'
in•san'i•tar'y
in•san'i•ty
in•sa'tia•ble
in•sa'tia•bly
in•sa'ti•ate
in•scribe', -scribed',
-scrib'ing
in•scrip'tion
in•scru'ta•bil'i•ty
in•scru'ta•ble

in·scru′ta·bly
in′seam′
in′sect′
in·sec′ti·cide′
in·sec′ti·vore′
in·sec·tiv′o·rous
in·se·cure′
in·se·cu′ri·ty
in·sem′i·nate′,
  -nat′ed, -nat′ing
in·sem′i·na′tion
in·sen′sate′
in·sen′si·bil′i·ty
in·sen′si·ble
in·sen′si·bly
in·sen′si·tive
in·sen′si·tiv′i·ty
in·sep′a·ra·bil′i·ty
in·sep′a·ra·ble
in·sep′a·ra·bly
in·sert′ *v.*
in′sert′ *n.*
in·ser′tion
in·set′, -set′,
  -set′ting
in′shore′
in·side′
in·sid′er
in·sid′i·ous
in′sight′ *(under-*
  standing)
  ✓ *incite*
in′sight′ful
in·sig′ni·a *pl.* -ni·a
  or -ni·as
in′sig·nif′i·cance
in′sig·nif′i·cant

in′sin·cere′
in′sin·cer′i·ty
in·sin′u·ate′,
  -at′ed, -at′ing
in·sin′u·a′tion
in·sip′id
in·sist′
in·sis′tence *or*
  in·sis′ten·cy
in·sis′tent
in′so·far′ as
in′sole′
in′so·lence
in′so·lent
in·sol′u·bil′i·ty
in·sol′u·ble
in·sol′u·bly
in·sol′ven·cy
in·sol′vent
in·som′ni·a
in·som′ni·ac′
in′so·much′ as
in·sou′ci·ance
in·sou′ci·ant
in·spect′
in·spec′tion
in·spec′tor
in′spi·ra′tion
in′spi·ra′tion·al
in·spire′, -spired′,
  -spir′ing
in·spir′it
in′sta·bil′i·ty
in·stall′ *also*
  in·stal′, -stalled′,
  -stall′ing
in′stal·la′tion

in·stall′ment
in′stance
in′stant
in′stan·ta′ne·ous
in·stead′
in′step′
in′sti·gate′, -gat′ed,
  -gat′ing
in′sti·ga′tion
in′sti·ga′tor
in·still′
in′stinct′
in·stinc′tive
in·stinc′tu·al
in′sti·tute′, -tut′ed,
  -tut′ing
in′sti·tu′tion
in′sti·tu′tion·al
in′sti·tu′tion·al·
  ize′, -ized′, -iz′ing
in·struct′
in·struc′tion
in·struc′tive
in·struc′tor
in′stru·ment
in′stru·men′tal
in′stru·men′tal·ist
in′stru·men·tal′i·ty
in′stru·men·ta′-
  tion
in′sub·or′di·nate
in′sub·or′di·na′-
  tion
in′sub·stan′tial
in′sub·stan′ti·al′-
  i·ty
in·suf′fer·a·ble

in•suf′fer•a•bly
in′suf•fi′cien•cy
in′suf•fi′cient
in′su•lar
in′su•lar′i•ty
in′su•late′, -lat′ed,
　-lat′ing
in′su•la′tion
in′su•la′tor
in′su•lin
in•sult′ *v.*
in′sult′ *n.*
in•su′per•a•ble
in•su′per•a•bly
in•sup•port′a•ble
in•sur′a•ble
in•sur′ance
in•sure′ *(to cover*
　with insurance, to
　make sure), -sured′,
　-sur′ing
　✔ *assure, ensure*
in•sur′er
in•sur′gence
in•sur′gen•cy
in•sur′gent
in′sur•mount′a•ble
in′sur•rec′tion
in•tact′
in′take′
in•tan′gi•ble
in•tan′gi•bly
in′te•ger
in′te•gral
in′te•grate′,
　-grat′ed, -grat′ing
in′te•gra′tion

in•teg′ri•ty
in•teg′u•ment
in′tel•lect′
in′tel•lec′tu•al
in•tel′li•gence
in•tel′li•gent
in•tel′li•gent′si•a
in•tel′li•gi•bil′i•ty
in•tel′li•gi•ble
in•tel′li•gi•bly
in•tem′per•ance
in•tem′per•ate
in•tend′
in•tend′ed
in•tense′
in•ten′si•fi•ca′tion
in•ten′si•fi•er
in•ten′si•fy′, -fied′,
　-fy′ing
in•ten′si•ty
in•ten′sive
in•tent′
in•ten′tion
in•ten′tion•al
in•ter′, -terred′,
　-ter′ring
in′ter•act′
in′ter•ac′tion
in′ter•ac′tive
in′ter•breed′,
　-bred′, -breed′ing
in′ter•cede′,
　-ced′ed, -ced′ing
in′ter•cel′lu•lar
in′ter•cept′
in′ter•cep′tion
in′ter•cep′tor *also*

in′ter•cept′er
in′ter•ces′sion
in′ter•ces′sor
in′ter•change′,
　-changed′,
　-chang′ing
in′ter•change′ *n.*
in′ter•change′a•ble
in′ter•change′-
　a•bly
in′ter•col•le′giate
in′ter•com′
in′ter•com•mu′ni•
　cate′, -cat′ed,
　-cat′ing
in′ter•com•mu′ni•
　ca′tion
in′ter•con•nect′
in′ter•con•nec′tion
in′ter•con′ti•nen′-
　tal
in′ter•course′
in′ter•de•nom′i•
　na′tion•al
in′ter•de•part′•
　men′tal
in′ter•de•pend′-
　ence
in′ter•de•pend′ent
in′ter•dict′
in′ter•dic′tion
in′ter•dis′ci•pli•
　nar′y
in′ter•est
in′ter•face′, -faced′,
　-fac′ing
in′ter•faith′

in'ter•fere', -fered',
-fer'ing
in'ter•fer'ence
in'ter•fer'on'
in'ter•ga•lac'tic
in'ter•im
in•te'ri•or
in'ter•ject'
in'ter•jec'tion
in'ter•lace', -laced',
-lac'ing
in'ter•lard'
in'ter•lock'
in'ter•loc'u•tor
in'ter•lop'er
in'ter•lude'
in'ter•mar'riage
in'ter•mar'ry, -ried,
-ry•ing
in'ter•me'di•ar'y
in'ter•me'di•ate
in•ter'ment
in'ter•mez'zo *pl.*
-zos *or* -zi
in•ter'mi•na•ble
in•ter'mi•na•bly
in'ter•min'gle,
-gled, -gling
in'ter•mis'sion
in'ter•mit'tent
in'ter•mix'
in•tern' *also*
in'terne'
in•ter'nal
in•ter'nal•ize',
-ized', -iz'ing
in'ter•na'tion•al

in'ter•na'tion•al•
ism
in'ter•na'tion•al•
ize', -ized', -iz'ing
in'ter•nec'ine'
in'tern•ee'
In'ter•net'
in•ter'nist
in•tern'ment
in'tern•ship'
in'ter•per'son•al
in'ter•phase'
in'ter•plan'e•tar'y
in'ter•play'
in•ter'po•late',
-lat'ed, -lat'ing
in•ter'po•la'tion
in•ter'po•la'tor
in'ter•pose',
-posed', -pos'ing
in'ter•po•si'tion
in•ter'pret
in•ter'pret•a•ble
in•ter'pre•ta'tion
in•ter'pret•er
in•ter'pre•tive *also*
in•ter'pre•ta'tive
in'ter•ra'cial
in'ter•reg'num *pl.*
-nums *or* -na
in'ter•re•late',
-lat'ed, -lat'ing
in'ter•re•la'tion
in'ter•re•la'tion•
ship'
in•ter'ro•gate',
-gat'ed, -gat'ing

in•ter'ro•ga'tion
in'ter•rog'a•tive
in•ter'ro•ga'tor
in•ter'rog'a•to'ry
in'ter•rupt'
in'ter•rup'tion
in'ter•scho•las'tic
in'ter•sect'
in'ter•sec'tion
in'ter•sperse',
-spersed',
-spers'ing
in'ter•sper'sion
in'ter•state' *(be-
tween states)*
✔ intrastate
in'ter•stel'lar
in•ter'stice *pl.*
-sti•ces'
in'ter•sti'tial
in'ter•twine',
-twined',
-twin'ing
in'ter•val
in'ter•vene',
-vened', -ven'ing
in'ter•ven'tion
in'ter•view'
in'ter•view'er
in'ter•weave',
-wove', -wo'ven,
-weav'ing
in•tes'tate'
in•tes'ti•nal
in•tes'tine
in'ti•ma•cy
in'ti•mate *adj. & n.*

in'ti•mate',
-mat'ed, -mat'ing
in'ti•ma'tion
in•tim'i•date',
-dat'ed, -dat'ing
in•tim'i•da'tion
in•tim'i•da'tor
in'to
in•tol'er•a•ble
in•tol'er•a•bly
in•tol'er•ance
in•tol'er•ant
in'to•na'tion
in•tone', -toned',
-ton'ing
in•tox'i•cant
in•tox'i•cate',
-cat'ed, -cat'ing
in•tox'i•ca'tion
in•tox'i•ca'tor
in'tra•cel'lu•lar
in•trac'ta•bil'i•ty
in•trac'ta•ble
in•trac'ta•bly
in'tra•mu'ral
in•tran'si•gence
in•tran'si•gent
in•tran'si•tive
in'tra•state' (within
a state)
  ✔ interstate
in'tra•u'ter•ine
in'tra•ve'nous
in•trep'id
in'tre•pid'i•ty
in'tri•ca•cy
in'tri•cate

in'trigue' n.
in•trigue', -trigued',
-trigu'ing
in•trin'sic
in•tro' pl. -tros'
in'tro•duce',
-duced', -duc'ing
in'tro•duc'tion
in'tro•duc'to•ry
in'tro•spec'tion
in'tro•spec'tive
in'tro•ver'sion
in'tro•vert'
in•trude', -trud'ed,
-trud'ing
in•trud'er
in•tru'sion
in•tru'sive
in•tu•i'tion
in•tu'i•tive
In'u•it pl. -it or -its
in'un•date',
-dat'ed, -dat'ing
in'un•da'tion
in•ure', -ured',
-ur'ing
in•vade', -vad'ed,
-vad'ing
in•vad'er
in•va'lid (ill)
in•val'id (without
authority)
in•val'i•date',
-dat'ed, -dat'ing
in•val'i•da'tion
in•val'u•a•ble
in•var'i•a•bil'i•ty

in•var'i•a•ble
in•var'i•a•bly
in•var'i•ance
in•var'i•ant
in•va'sion
in•va'sive
in•vec'tive
in•veigh'
in•vei'gle, -gled,
-gling
in•vent'
in•ven'tion
in•ven'tive
in•ven'tor
in'ven•to'ry, -ried,
-ry'ing
in•verse' adj.
in'verse' n.
in•ver'sion
in•vert'
in•ver'te•brate
in•vest'
in•ves'ti•gate',
-gat'ed, -gat'ing
in•ves'ti•ga'tion
in•ves'ti•ga'tive
  also in•ves'ti•ga•
  to'ry
in•ves'ti•ga'tor
in•ves'ti•ture'
in•vest'ment
in•ves'tor
in•vet'er•ate
in•vid'i•ous
in•vig'or•ate',
-at'ed, -at'ing
in•vig'or•a'tion

in•vin'ci•bil'i•ty
in•vin'ci•ble
in•vin'ci•bly
in•vi'o•la•ble
in•vi'o•late
in•vis'i•bil'i•ty
in•vis'i•ble
in•vis'i•bly
in'vi•ta'tion
in•vite', -vit'ed,
  -vit'ing
in vi'tro
in vi'vo
in'vo•ca'tion
in'voice', -voiced',
  -voic'ing
in•voke', -voked',
  -vok'ing
in•vol'un•tar'i•ly
in•vol'un•tar'y
in'vo•lu'tion
in•volve', -volved',
  -volv'ing
in•volve'ment
in•vul'ner•a•bil'i•ty
in•vul'ner•a•ble
in•vul'ner•a•bly
in'ward *adj. & adv.*
in'wards *adv.*
i'o•dide'
i'o•dine'
i'o•dize', -dized',
  -diz'ing
i'on
I•o'ni•an
i•on'ic *(relating to*
  ions)

I•on'ic *(relating to*
  Ionia)
i'on•i•za'tion
i'on•ize', -ized',
  -iz'ing
i•on'o•sphere'
i•o'ta
IOU *pl.* IOU's *or*
  IOUs
I'o•wa *pl.* -wa *or*
  -was
I'o•wan
ip'e•cac'
I•ra'ni•an
I•ra'qi *pl.* -quis
i•ras'ci•bil'i•ty
i•ras'ci•ble
i•ras'ci•bly
i•rate'
ire
ir'i•des'cence
ir'i•des'cent
ir•rid'i•um
i'ris *pl.* i'ris•es *or*
  i'ri•des'
I'rish
I'rish•man
I'rish•wom'an
irk
irk'some
i'ron
i'ron•clad'
i•ron'ic *also*
  i•ron'i•cal
i'ron•wood'
i'ron•work'
i'ron•work'er

i'ron•works'
i'ro•ny
Ir'o•quoi'an
Ir'o•quois' *pl.*
  -quois'
ir•ra'di•ate', -at'ed,
  -at'ing
ir•ra'di•a'tion
ir•ra'di•a'tor
ir•ra'tion•al
ir•ra'tion•al'i•ty
ir're•claim'a•ble
ir'rec•on•cil'a•ble
ir're•cov'er•a•ble
ir're•deem'a•ble
ir're•duc'i•ble
ir're•duc'i•bly
ir•ref'u•ta•ble
ir•ref'u•ta•bly
ir•reg'u•lar
ir•reg'u•lar'i•ty
ir•rel'e•vance
ir•rel'e•vant
ir're•lig'ious
ir're•me'di•a•ble
ir're•me'di•a•bly
ir•rep'a•ra•ble
ir•rep'a•ra•bly
ir're•place'a•ble
ir're•press'i•ble
ir're•press'i•bly
ir're•proach'a•ble
ir're•proach'a•bly
ir're•sist'i•bil'i•ty
ir're•sis'ti•ble
ir're•sis'ti•bly
ir•res'o•lute'

ir·res′o·lute′ness *or*
  ir·res′o·lu′tion
ir′re·spec′tive of
ir′re·spon′si·bil′i·ty
ir′re·spon′si·ble
ir′re·spon′si·bly
ir′re·triev′a·ble
ir′re·triev′a·bly
ir·rev′er·ence
ir·rev′er·ent
ir′re·vers′i·bil′i·ty
ir′re·vers′i·ble
ir′re·vers′i·bly
ir·rev′o·ca·bil′i·ty
ir·rev′o·ca·ble
ir·rev′o·ca·bly
ir′ri·gate′, -gat′ed,
  -gat′ing
ir′ri·ga′tion
ir′ri·ta·bil′i·ty
ir′ri·ta·ble
ir′ri·ta·bly
ir′ri·tant
ir′ri·tate′, -tat′ed,
  -tat′ing
ir′ri·ta′tion
ir′ri·ta′tor
ir·rupt′ *(to burst in,*
  to increase)
  ✔ *erupt*
ir·rup′tion
ir·rup′tive
is
is′chi·um *pl.* -chi·a
i′sin·glass′
Is·lam
Is·lam′ic

is′land
is′land·er
isle *(island)*
  ✔ *aisle*
is′let *(small island)*
  ✔ *eyelet*
is′n′t
i′so·bar′
i′so·bar′ic
i′so·late′, -lat′ed,
  -lat′ing
i′so·la′tion
i′so·la′tion·ism
i′so·la′tion·ist
i′so·mer
i′so·mer′ic
i·som′er·ism
i′so·met′ric *also*
  i′so·met′ri·cal
i′so·pro′pyl
  al′co·hol′
i·sos′ce·les′
i′so·therm′
i′so·ther′mal
i′so·tope′
i′so·top′ic
i′so·trop′ic
i·sot′ro·py *or*
  i·sot′ro·pism
Is·rae′li *pl.* -lis
Is′ra·el·ite′
is′su·ance
is′sue, -sued, -su·ing
is′su·er
isth′mus *pl.* -mus·es
  or -mi′
I·tal′ian

i·tal′ic
i·tal′i·cize′, -cized′,
  -ciz′ing
itch′y
i′tem
i′tem·i·za′tion
i′tem·ize′, -ized′,
  -iz′ing
it′er·ate′, -at′ed,
  -at′ing
it′er·a′tion
it′er·a′tive
i·tin′er·ant
i·tin′er·ar′y
its *pron.*
it's *contraction*
it·self′
i′vo·ry
i′vy

J

jab, jabbed, jab′bing
jab′ber
ja·bot′
jac′a·ran′da
jack′al
jack′a·napes′
jack′ass′
jack′boot′
jack′daw′
jack′et
jack′ham′mer
jack′-in-the-box′
  pl. jack′-in-the-
  box′es *or* jacks′-in-

the-box'
jack'-in-the-
  pul'pit *pl.* jack'-
  in-the-pul'pits
jack'knife',
  -knifed', -knif'ing
jack'-of-all'-
  trades' *pl.* jacks'-
  of-all'-trades'
jack'-o'-lan'tern *pl.*
  jack'-o'-lan'terns
jack'pot'
jack'rab'bit *or* jack'
  rab'bit
jack'stone'
jack'straw'
jade
jad'ed
jag, jagged, jag'ging
jag'ged *adj.*
jag'uar
jai' a•lai'
jail
jail'bird'
jail'break'
jail'er *also* jail'or
jal'a•pe'ño *pl.* -ños
ja•lop'y
jal'ou•sie
jam (*to wedge in*),
  jammed, jam'ming
  ✔ *jamb*
jam (*fruit preserve*)
  ✔ *jamb*
Ja•mai'can
jamb (*door post*)
  ✔ *jam*

jam'bo•ree'
jan'gle, -gled, -gling
jan'i•tor
Jan'u•ar'y
Jap'a•nese' *pl.* -nese'
jar, jarred, jar'ring
jar'gon
jas'mine *also*
  jes'sa•mine
jas'per
jaun'dice, -diced,
  -dic•ing
jaunt
jaun'ty
ja'va
Jav'a•nese' *pl.* -nese'
jave'lin
jaw'bone'
jay'walk'
jazz'y
jeal'ous
jeal'ous•y
jeans
jeep
jeer
Je•ho'vah's
  Wit'ness
je•june'
je•ju'num *pl.* -na
jell (*to congeal*)
  ✔ *gel*
jel'ly, -lied, -ly•ing
jel'ly•bean'
jel'ly•fish' *pl.* -fish'
  or -fish'es
jel'ly•roll'
jen'net

jen'ny
jeop'ard•ize',
  -ized', -iz'ing
jeop'ard•y
jer•bo'a
jer'e•mi'ad
jerk
jerk'i•ly
jer'kin
jerk'y
jer'ry•build',
  -built', -build'ing
jer'sey *pl.* -seys
jest
jest'er
Jes'u•it
jet, jet'ted, jet'ting
jet'-pro•pelled'
jet'sam
jet'ti•son
jet'ty
Jew
jew'el, -eled *or*
  -elled, -el•ing *or*
  -el•ling
jew'el•er
jew'el•ry
Jew'ish
Jew'ry
jew's'-harp'
jib
jibe (*to shift a sail, to*
  agree), jibed, jib'ing
  ✔ *gibe*
jif'fy
jig, jigged, jig'ging
jig'ger

jig'gle, -gled, -gling

jig'saw'

ji•had'

jilt

Jim' Crow' *or* jim'
 crow'

jim'my, -mied,
 -my'ing

jim'son•weed'

jin'gle, -gled, -gling

jin'go *pl.* -goes

jin'go•ism

jin'go•is'tic

jin'ni *pl.* jinn

jin•rik'sha' *or*
 jin•rick'sha *also*
 jin•riki'sha

jinx

jit'ney *pl.* -neys

jit'ter•bug',
 -bugged', -bug'ging

jit'ters

jit'ter•y

jive

job

job'ber

jock

jock'ey *pl.* -eys

jock'strap'

jo•cose'

jo•cose'ness *or*
 jo•cos'i•ty

joc'u•lar

joc'u•lar'i•ty

joc'und

jo•cun'di•ty

jodh'purs

jog, jogged, jog'ging

jog'ger

jog'gle, -gled, -gling

john'ny•cake'

John'ny-come-
 late'ly *pl.* John'ny-
 come-late'lies *or*
 John'nies-come-
 late'ly

joie' de vi'vre

join

join'er

join'er•y

joint

join'ture

joist

joke, joked, jok'ing

jok'er

joke'ster

jol'li•ty

jol'ly

jolt

jon'quil

Jor•da'ni•an

josh

jos'tle, -tled, -tling

jos'tler

jot, jot'ted, jot'ting

joule

jounce, jounced,
 jounc'ing

jour'nal

jour'nal•ism

jour'nal•ist

jour'nal•is'tic

jour'ney *pl.* -neys

jour'ney•man

joust

jo'vi•al

jo'vi•al'i•ty

jowl

joy'ful

joy'ous

ju'bi•lance

ju'bi•lant

ju'bi•la'tion

ju'bi•lee'

Ju•da'ic *also*
 Ju•da'i•cal

Ju'da•ism

Ju'das

judge, judged,
 judg'ing

judge'ship'

judg'ment *also*
 judge'ment

judg•men'tal

ju'di•ca•ble

ju'di•ca•to'ry

ju•di'cial *(relating to
 the law)*
 ✔ judicious

ju•di'ci•ar'y

ju•di'cious *(prudent)*
 ✔ judicial

ju'do

jug

jug'ger•naut'

jug'gle, -gled,
 -gling

jug'gler

jug'u•lar

juice

juic'er

juic′i•ness
juic′y
ju•jit′su *also*
  ju•jut′su
juke′box′
ju′lep
Jul′ian cal′en•dar
ju′li•enne′
Ju•ly′
jum′ble, -bled,
  -bling
jum′bo *pl.* -bos
jump
jump′er
jump′-start′
jump′ suit′ *also*
  jump′suit′
jump′y
jun′co *pl.* -cos *or*
  -coes
junc′tion
junc′ture
June
June′ bug′
jun′gle
jun′ior
ju′ni•per
junk
jun′ket
junk′ie *also* junk′y
junk′yard′
jun′ta
Ju•ras′sic
ju•rid′i•cal
ju′ris•dic′tion
ju′ris•pru′dence
ju′rist

ju′ror
ju′ry
just
jus′tice
jus′ti•fi′a•bil′i•ty
jus′ti•fi′a•ble
jus′ti•fi′a•bly
jus′ti•fi•ca′tion
jus′ti•fy′, -fied′,
  -fy′ing
jut, jut′ted, jut′ting
jute *(fiber)*
Jute *(Germanic people)*
ju′ve•nile′
jux′ta•pose′,
  -posed′, -pos′ing
jux′ta•po•si′tion

K

ka•bu′ki
Kai′ser
kale
ka•lei′do•scope′
ka•lei′do•scop′ic
ka′mi•ka′ze
kan′ga•roo′ *pl.*
  -roo′ *or* -roos′
Kan′san
ka′o•lin *also*
  ka′o•line
ka′pok
kap′pa
ka•put′
kar′a•kul
kar′a•o•ke

kar′at *also* car′at
  (unit of measure)
  ✔ carat, caret, carrot
ka•ra′te
kar′ma
ka′ty•did′
kay′ak′
kay•o′, -oed′,
  -o′ing
ka•zoo′ *pl.* -zoos′
ke•bab′ *or* ke•bob′
  also ka•bob′
keel
keel′haul′
keen
keep, kept, keep′ing
keep′er
keep′sake′
keg
kelp
kel′vin
ken, kenned *or* kent,
  ken′ning
ken′nel, -neled *or*
  -nelled, -nel•ing *or*
  -nel•ling
ke′no
Ken•tuck′i•an
ke′pi *pl.* -pis
ker′a•tin
ker′chief *pl.* -chiefs
  also -chieves
ker′nel *(grain)*
  ✔ colonel
ker′o•sene′
kes′trel
ketch

ketch'up *also*
  cat'sup
ket'tle
ket'tle·drum'
key *(implement, island)*, pl. keys
  ✔ cay, quay
key'board'
key'board·er
key'hole'
key'note'
key'pad'
key'punch'
key'stone'
key'stroke'
khak'i
khan
Khmer pl. Khmer *or* Khmers
kib'ble, -bled, -bling
kib·butz' pl. kib·but·zim'
kib'itz
kib'itz·er
ki'bosh'
kick
Kick'a·poo' pl. -poo' *or* -poos'
kick'back' *n.*
kick'ball'
kick'box'ing
kick'er
kick'off'
kick'stand'
kid, kid'ded, kid'ding
kid'der

kid'nap', -napped' *or* -naped', -nap'ping *or* -nap'ing
kid'nap'per *or* kid'nap'er
kid'ney pl. -neys
kid'skin'
kill
kill'deer' pl. -deer' *or* -deers'
kill'er
kill'joy'
kiln
ki'lo pl. -los
kil'o·byte'
kil'o·cal'o·rie
kil'o·cy'cle
kil'o·gram'
kil'o·hertz'
kil'o·me'ter
kil'o·met'ric
kil'o·ton'
kil'o·watt'
kil'o·watt-hour'
kilt
kil'ter
ki·mo'no pl. -nos
kin
kind
kin'der·gar'ten
kind'heart'ed
kin'dle, -dled, -dling
kind'li·ness
kin'dling
kind'ly

kind'ness
kin'dred
kin'e·mat'ics
kin'e·scope'
ki·ne'sics
ki·net'ic
kin'folk' *also* kins'folk' *or* kin'folks'
king
king'bird'
king'bolt'
king'dom
king'fish'er
king'li·ness
king'ly
king'pin'
king'-size' *or* king'-sized'
kink
kink'a·jou'
kink'i·ness
kink'y
kin'ship'
kins'man
kins'wom'an
ki'osk'
Ki'o·wa' pl. -wa' *or* -was'
kip'per
kis'met
kiss
kiss'er
kit
kitch'en
kitch'en·ette'
kite

kith' and kin'
kitsch
kit'ten
kit'ty
kit'ty-cor'nered *or* kit'ty-cor'ner
ki'wi *pl.* -wis
Klans'man
klep'to•ma'ni•a
klep'to•ma'ni•ac'
klieg' light'
klutz
knack
knack'wurst' *or* knock'wurst'
knap'sack'
knave *(scoundrel)*
✔ nave
knav'er•y
knav'ish
knead *(to press with the hands)*
✔ need
knee, kneed, knee'ing
knee'cap'
knee'-deep'
knee'-high'
kneel, knelt *or* kneeled, kneel'ing
knee'pad'
knell
knew *past tense of* know
✔ gnu, new
knick'er•bock'ers
knick'ers

knick'knack' *also* nick'nack'
knife *pl.* knives
knife, knifed, knif'ing
knife'-edge'
knight *(soldier)*
✔ night
knight'-er'rant *pl.* knights'-er'rant
knight'hood'
knish
knit *(to loop yarn)*, knit *or* knit'ted, knit'ting
✔ nit
knit'ter
knit'wear'
knob
knob'by
knock
knock'a•bout'
knock'down' *n. & adj.*
knock'er
knock'-knee'
knock'-kneed'
knock'out' *n.*
knoll
knot *(to tie)*, knot'ted, knot'ting
✔ not
knot'hole'
knot'ty
know *(to have knowledge)*, knew, known, know'ing

✔ no
know'-how'
know'-it-all'
knowl'edge
knowl'edge•a•ble
knuck'le, -led, -ling
knuck'le•bone'
knuck'le•head'
KO, KO'd, KO'ing, KO's
KO *pl.* KO's
ko•a'la
kohl *(cosmetic)*
✔ coal
kohl'ra•bi *pl.* -bies
Ko•mo'do drag'on
kook
kook'a•bur'ra
kook'i•ness
kook'y
ko'peck
Ko•ran' *or* Qur•'an'
Ko•re'an
ko'sher
kow•tow'
krill *pl.* krill
Krish'na
kro'na *(monetary unit of Iceland)*, *pl.* -nur
kro'na *(monetary unit of Sweden)*, *pl.* -nor
kro'ne *(monetary unit of Norway and Denmark)*, *pl.* -ner
kryp'ton

ku'dos'
kud'zu
Ku' Klux Klan'
kum'quat'
kung' fu'
kur'cha•tov'i•um
Kwan'zaa

L

la'bel, -beled or
 -belled, -bel•ing or
 -bel•ling
la'bi•al
la'bi•um pl. -bi•a
la'bor
lab'o•ra•to'ry
la'bored
la'bor•er
la'bor-in•ten'sive
la'bo'ri•ous
la'bor•sav'ing
Lab'ra•dor
 re•triev'er
la•bur'num
lab'y•rinth'
lab'y•rin'thine
lac (resin)
 ✓ lack
lace, laced, lac'ing
lac'er•ate, -at'ed,
 -at'ing
lac'er•a'tion
lace'wing'
lach'ry•mal
lach'ry•mose'

lack (shortage)
 ✓ lac
lack'a•dai'si•cal
lack'ey pl. -eys
lack'lus'ter
la•con'ic
lac'quer
la•crosse'
lac'tase'
lac'tate', -tat'ed,
 -tat'ing
lac•ta'tion
lac'te•al
lac'tic
lac'tose'
la•cu'na pl. -nae or
 -nas
lac'y
lad
lad'der
lad'die
lade, lad'ed, lad'en
 or lad'ed, lad'ing
la'dle, -dled, -dling
la'dy
la'dy•bird'
la'dy•bug'
la'dy•fin'ger also
 la'dys•fin'ger
la'dy in wait'ing
 pl. la'dies in
 wait'ing
la'dy•like'
la'dy•ship'
la'dy's slip'per pl.
 la'dy's slip'pers
lag, lagged, lag'ging

la'ger
lag'gard
la•goon'
laid'-back'
lair
lais'sez faire'
la'i•ty
lake
La•ko'ta pl. -ta
lam (to thrash, to
 escape), lammed,
 lam'ming
 ✓ lamb
la'ma (monk)
 ✓ llama
lamb (young sheep)
 ✓ lam
lam•baste',
 -bast'ed, -bast'ing
lamb'da
lam'bent
lamb'skin'
lame, lam'er,
 lam'est
lame, lamed,
 lam'ing
la•mé'
la•ment'
la•men'ta•ble
lam'en•ta•bly
lam'en•ta'tion
lam'i•na pl. -nae' or
 -nas
lam'i•nate',
 -nat'ed, -nat'ing
lam'i•na'tion
lam'i•na'tor

lamp'black'
lamp'light'
lam·poon'
lamp'post'
lam'prey' *pl.* -preys'
lamp'shade'
la·nai'
lance, lanced,
    lanc'ing
lanc'er
lan'cet
lan'dau'
land'ed
land'fall'
land'fill'
land'form'
land'hold'er
land'ing
land'la'dy
land'locked'
land'lord'
land'lub'ber
land'mark'
land'mass'
land' mine'
land'own'er
land'scape',
    -scaped', -scap'ing
land'slide'
land'ward *adv. &*
    adj.
land'wards *adv.*
lane
lan'guage
lan'guid
lan'guish
lan'guor

lan'guor·ous
lank'i·ness
lank'ly
lank'y
lan'o·lin
lan'tern
lan'tha·nide'
lan'tha·num
lan'yard
Lao *pl.* Lao *or* Laos
La·o'tian
lap *(to fold over),*
    lapped, lap'ping
    ✔ Lapp
la·pel'
lap'i·dar'y
lap'is laz'u·li
Lapp *(native of*
    Lapland)
    ✔ lap
lapse, lapsed,
    laps'ing
lap'top'
lap'wing'
lar'board'
lar'ce·nous
lar'ce·ny
larch
lard
lar'der
large, larg'er,
    larg'est
large'-heart'ed
large'ly
large'-scale'
lar·gess' *also*
    lar·gesse'

lar'go
lar'i·at
lark
lark'spur'
lar'va *pl.* -vae *or* -vas
lar'val
la·ryn'ge·al *also*
    la·ryn'gal
lar'yn·gi'tis
lar'ynx *pl.*
    la·ryn'ges *or*
    lar'ynx·es
la·sa'gna
las·civ'i·ous
la'ser
lash
lass
las'sie
las'si·tude'
las'so *pl.* -sos *or*
    -soes
last'ing
last'-min'ute *adj.*
latch
latch'key'
late, lat'er, lat'est
late'com'er
la·teen'
late'ly
la'ten·cy
late'ness
la'tent
lat'er·al
la'tex' *pl.* la'ti·ces'
    or la'tex'es
lath *(narrow strip)*
lathe *(machine)*

lathe (*to cut on a lathe*), lathed, lath'ing
lath'er
Lat'in
La·ti'na *pl.* -nas
Lat'in A·mer'i·can *or* Lat'in-A·mer'i·can
La·ti'no *pl.* -nos
lat'i·tude'
lat'i·tu'di·nal
la·trine'
lat'te
lat'ter
Lat'ter-day' Saint'
lat'ter·ly
lat'tice, -ticed, -tic·ing
lat'tice·work'
Lat'vi·an
laud
laud'a·ble
laud'a·bly
lau'da·num
laud'a·to'ry
laugh
laugh'a·ble
laugh'a·bly
laugh'ing·stock'
laugh'ter
launch
launch'er
laun'der
laun'dress
laun'dry
lau're·ate

lau'rel
la'va
lav'a·to'ry
lave, laved, lav'ing
lav'en·der
lav'ish
law'-a·bid'ing
law'break'er
law'ful
law'giv'er
law'less
law'mak'er
law'mak'ing
lawn
lawn' mow'er *also* lawn'mow'er
law·ren'ci·um
law'suit'
law'yer
lax
lax'a·tive
lax'i·ty
lay (*put*), laid, lay'ing
  ✔ lei
lay (*relating to lay-people*)
  ✔ lei
lay (*ballad*)
  ✔ lei
lay'a·way'
lay'er
lay·ette'
lay'man
lay'off' *n.*
lay'out' *n.*
lay'o·ver *n.*

lay'peo'ple *or* lay'peo'ple
lay'per'son
lay'-up' *n.*
lay'wom'an
laze, lazed, laz'ing
la'zi·ly
la'zi·ness
la'zy
lea (*meadow*)
  ✔ lee
leach (*to dissolve*)
  ✔ leech
lead (*to guide*), led, lead'ing
  ✔ lied
lead (*element*)
  ✔ led
lead'en
lead'er
lead'er·ship'
lead'-in' *n.*
lead'ing
lead'off' *n. & adj.*
leaf (*plant part*), *pl.* leaves
  ✔ lief
leaf'let
leaf'stalk'
leaf'y
league, leagued, leagu'ing
leagu'er
leak (*escape*)
  ✔ leek
leak'age
leak'i·ness

leak′y
lean *(to bend)*
  ✔ lien
lean *(thin)*
  ✔ lien
lean′ing
lean′-to′ pl. -tos′
leap, leaped or leapt,
  leap′ing
leap′frog′,
  -frogged′,
  -frog′ging
learn, learned *also*
  learnt, learn′ing
learn′ed adj.
lease, leased,
  leas′ing
leash
least
least′wise′
leath′er
leath′er•ette′
leath′ern
leath′er•y
leave, left, leav′ing
leav′en
leav′en•ing
leave′-tak′ing
leav′ings
Leb′a•nese′ pl.
  -nese′
lech′er•ous
lech′er•y
lec′i•thin
lec′tern
lec′tor
lec′ture, -tured,

-tur•ing
lec′tur•er
ledge
ledg′er
lee *(shelter)*
  ✔ lea
leech *(worm)*
  ✔ leach
leek *(plant)*
  ✔ leak
leer
leer′y
lees
lee′ward
lee′way′
left′-hand′ adj.
left′-hand′ed
left′-hand′er
left′ist
left′o′ver adj.
left′-wing′ adj.
left′wing′er
left′y
leg
leg′a•cy
le′gal
le•gal′i•ty
le′gal•i•za′tion
le′gal•ize′, -ized′,
  -iz′ing
leg′ate
leg′a•tee′
le•ga′tion
le•ga′to
leg′end
leg′en•dar′y
leg′er•de•main′

leg′ged
leg′ging
leg′gy
leg′horn′
leg′i•bil′i•ty or
  leg′i•ble•ness
leg′i•ble
leg′i•bly
le′gion
le′gion•ar′y
le′gion•naire′
leg′is•late′, -lat′ed,
  -lat′ing
leg′is•la′tion
leg′is•la′tive
leg′is•la′tor
leg′is•la′ture
le•git′i•ma•cy
le•git′i•mate
le•git′i•mize′,
  -mized′, -miz′ing
leg•ume′
le•gu′mi•nous
leg′work′
lei *(garland)*, pl. leis
  ✔ lay
lei′sure
lem′ma pl. -mas or
  lem′a•ta
lem′ming
lem′on
lem′on•ade′
le′mur
Len′a•pe pl. -pe or
  -pes
lend, lent, lend′ing
lend′er

length
length'en
length'wise'
length'y
le'ni·ence *or*
  le'ni·en·cy
le'ni·ent
Len'ni Len'a·pe
lens *pl.* lens'es
Lent
Lent'en
len'til
le'o·nine'
leop'ard
le'o·tard'
lep'er
lep're·chaun'
lep'ro·sy
lep'rous
les'bi·an
le'sion
less
les·see'
less'en *(to make less)*
  ✔ *lesson*
less'er *a comparative*
  of little
  ✔ *lessor*
les'son *(instruction)*
  ✔ *lessen*
les'sor *(landlord)*
  ✔ *lesser*
lest
let *(to permit, to*
  lease), let, let'ting
  ✔ *Lett*
let'down' *n.*

le'thal
le·thar'gic
leth'ar·gy
le'the
Lett *(Baltic people)*
  ✔ *let*
let'ter
let'ter·head'
let'ter·ing
let'ter-per'fect
Let'tish
let'tuce
let'up' *n.*
leu·ke'mi·a
leu'ko·cyte' *also*
  leu'co·cyte'
lev'ee *(embankment)*
  ✔ *levy*
lev'el, -eled *or*
  -elled, -el·ing *or*
  -el·ling
lev'el·er *or* lev'el·ler
lev'el·head'ed
lev'er
lev'er·age
le·vi'a·than
lev'i·tate', -tat'ed,
  -tat'ing
lev'i·ta'tion
lev'i·ta'tor
Le'vite'
lev'i·ty
lev'y *(collect)*, -ied,
  -y·ing
  ✔ *levee*
lewd
lex'i·cog'ra·pher

lex'i·co·graph'ic *or*
  lex'i·co·graph'i·cal
lex'i·cog'ra·phy
lex'i·con'
Lha'sa ap'so
li'a·bil'i·ty
li'a·ble *(likely)*
  ✔ *libel*
li·ai'son
li'ar *(one who lies)*
  ✔ *lyre*
li·ba'tion
li'bel *(to defame)*,
  -beled *or* -belled,
  -bel·ing *or* -bel·ling
  ✔ *liable*
li'bel·er
li'bel·ous *also*
  li'bel·lous
lib'er·al
lib'er·al·ism
lib'er·al'i·ty
lib'er·al·i·za'tion
lib'er·al·ize', -ized',
  -iz'ing
lib'er·ate', -at'ed,
  -at'ing
lib'er·a'tion
lib'er·a'tor
Li·be'ri·an
lib'er·tar'i·an
lib'er·tine'
lib'er·ty
li·bid'i·nal
li·bid'i·nous
li·bi'do *pl.* -dos
li·brar'i·an

li'brar·'y
li·bret'tist
li·bret'to *pl.* -tos *or*
    -ti
Lib'y·an
lice *sing.* louse
li'cens·a·ble
li'cense, -censed,
    -cens·ing
li'cens·ee'
li'cens·er *or*
    li'cen·sor
li'cen·sure
li·cen'ti·ate
li·cen'tious
li'chen *(plant)*
    ✔ liken
lic'it
lick
lic'o·rice
lid
lie *(to recline)*, lay,
    lain, ly'ing
    ✔ lye
lie *(to deceive)*, lied,
    ly'ing
    ✔ lye
lied *(song)*, *pl.* lie'der
    ✔ lead
lief *(willingly)*
    ✔ leaf
liege
liege'man
lien *(claim)*
    ✔ lean
lieu
lieu·ten'an·cy

lieu·ten'ant
life *pl.* lives
life'blood'
life'boat'
life'guard'
life'less
life'like'
life'line'
life'long'
life'sav'er
life'sav'ing
life'size' *also*
    life'-sized'
life'style' *also*
    life'-style' *or*
    life' style'
life'-sup·port'
life'time'
life'work'
lift
lift'off' *n.*
lig'a·ment
lig'a·ture
light, light'ed *or* lit,
    light'ing
light'en
light'er
light'face'
light'-faced'
light'-fin'gered
light'-foot'ed
light'head'ed
light'heart'ed
light'house'
light'ing
light'ning
light'ship'

light'weight'
light'-year'
lig'nite'
lik'a·ble *also*
    like'a·ble
like, liked, lik'ing
like'li·hood'
like'ly
like'-mind'ed
lik'en *(to compare)*
    ✔ lichen
like'ness
like'wise'
li'lac
Lil'li·pu'tian *also*
    lil'li·pu'tian
lilt
lil'y
lil'y of the val'ley
    pl. lil'ies of the
    val'ley
lily'-white'
li'ma bean'
limb *(body part)*
    ✔ limn
lim'ber
lim'bo *pl.* -bos
Lim'burg'er
lime
lime·ade'
lime'light'
lim'er·ick
lime'stone'
lime'wa'ter
lim'it
lim'i·ta'tion
lim'it·ed

limn *(to draw)*
✔ *limb*
lim'ou·sine'
limp
lim'pet
lim'pid
lim'y
lin'age *also* line'age
(*number of lines*)
✔ *lineage*
linch'pin'
lin'den
line, lined, lin'ing
lin'e·age *(ancestry)*
✔ *linage*
lin'e·al
lin'e·a·ment
lin'e·ar
line'back'er
line'man
lin'en
lin'er
lines'man
line'up' *also*
line'-up' *n.*
lin'ger
lin'ge·rie'
lin'go *pl.* -goes
lin'gua fran'ca *pl.*
lin'gua fran'cas
lin'gual
lin·gui'ça
lin·gui'ne *also*
lin·gui'ni
lin'guist
lin·guis'tic
lin'i·ment

lin'ing
link
link'age
links *(golf course)*
✔ *lynx*
lin'net
li·no'le·um
lin'seed'
lin'sey-wool'sey
pl. -seys
lint
lin'tel
li'on
li'on·ess
li'on·heart'ed
li'on·i·za'tion
li'on·ize', -ized',
-iz'ing
lip
lip'ase'
lip'id *also* lip'ide'
lip'oid'
lip'-read', -read',
-read'ing
lip' read'ing *n.*
lip'stick'
liq'ue·fac'tion
liq'ue·fi'er
liq'ue·fy', -fied',
-fy'ing
li·queur'
liq'uid
liq'ui·date',
-dat'ed, -dat'ing
liq'ui·da'tion
li·quid'i·ty
liq'uor

li'ra *pl.* -re *or* -ras
lisle
lisp
lis'some *also*
lis'som
list
lis'ten
lis'ten·er
list'ing
list'less
lit'a·ny
li'tchi *also* li'chee *or*
ly'chee
li'ter
lit'er·a·cy
lit'er·al *(verbatim)*
✔ *littoral*
lit'er·ar'y
lit'er·ate
lit'er·a·ture
lithe, lith'er, lith'est
lith'i·um
lith'o·graph'
li·thog'ra·pher
lith'o·graph'ic *or*
lith'o·graph'i·cal
li·thog'ra·phy
lith'o·sphere'
Lith'u·a'ni·an
lit'i·gant
lit'i·gate', -gat'ed,
-gat'ing
lit'i·ga'tion
lit'i·ga'tor
li·ti'gious
lit'mus
lit'ter

lit′ter•bug′
lit′ter•mate′
lit′tle, lit′tler *or* less,
  lit′tlest *or* least
lit′tle•neck′
littoral *(coastal region)*
  ✔ literal
li•tur′gi•cal
lit′ur•gy
liv′a•ble *also*
  live′a•ble
live, lived, liv′ing
live *adj.*
live′-in′ *adj.*
live′li•hood′
live′li•ness
live′long′
live′ly
li′ven
liv′er
liv′er•ied
liv′er•wort′
liv′er•wurst′
liv′er•y
live′stock′
liv′id
liv′ing room′
liz′ard
lla′ma *(animal)*
  ✔ lama
lla′no *pl.* -nos
lo *interj.*
  ✔ low
load *(weight)*
  ✔ lode
load′ed

load′er
loaf *pl.* loaves
loaf *v.*
loaf′er
loam
loam′y
loan *(something lent)*
  ✔ lone
loan′ word′ *or*
  loan′word′
loath *(not willing)*
loathe *(to detest)*,
  loathed, loath′ing
loath′some
lob, lobbed,
  lob′bing
lo′bar
lob′by, -bied,
  -by•ing
lob′by•ist
lobe
lobed
lo•be′li•a
lob′lol′ly pine′
lob′ster
lo′cal
lo•cale′
lo•cal′i•ty
lo′cal•i•za′tion
lo′cal•ize′, -ized′,
  -iz′ing
lo′cate′, -cat′ed,
  -cat′ing
lo•ca′tion
lo′ca•tor
loch *(lake)*
lock *(security device,*

  hair)
lock′er
lock′et
lock′jaw′
lock′out′ *n.*
lock′smith′
lock′up′ *n.*
lo′co•mo′tion
lo′co•mo′tive
lo′co•weed′
lo′cus *pl.* -ci′
lo′cust
lo•cu′tion
lode *(ore deposit)*
  ✔ load
lode′star′ *also*
  load′star′
lode′stone′ *also*
  load′stone′
lodge, lodged,
  lodg′ing
lodg′er
lodg′ment *also*
  lodge′ment
lo′ess
loft
loft′y
log, logged, log′ging
lo′gan•ber′ry
log′a•rithm
log′a•rith′mic *or*
  log′a•rith′mi•cal
log′book′
log′ger
log′ger•head′
log′gi•a
log′ic

log'i•cal
lo•gi'cian
lo•gis'tic *also*
  lo•gis'ti•cal
lo•gis'tics
log'jam'
lo'go (symbol), pl.
  -gos
LO'GO (computer
  language)
log'roll'ing
lo'gy
loin
loin'cloth'
loi'ter
loi'ter•er
loll
lol'la•pa•loo'za
  also lal'a•pa•loo'za
  or lal'la•pa•loo'za
lol'li•pop' *also*
  lol'ly•pop'
lone (solitary)
  ✔ loan
lone'li•ness
lone'ly
lon'er
lone'some
long
long'boat'
long'bow'
long'-dis'tance
  adj.
lon•gev'i•ty
long'hair' *or*
  long'haired'

long'hand'
long'horn'
long'house' *or*
  long' house'
long'ing
lon'gi•tude'
lon'gi•tu'di•nal
long'-lived'
long'-play'ing
long'-range'
long'shore'man
long'-stand'ing
long'-suf'fer•ing
long'-term'
long'-time' *also*
  long'time'
long'-wind'ed
loo'fa *or* loo'fah *also*
  luf'fa
look
look'er
look'ing glass'
look'out' *n.*
look'-up' *n.*
loom
loon'y
loop (circular path)
  ✔ loupe
loop'hole'
loose, loos'er,
  loos'est
loose, loosed,
  loos'ing
loose'-leaf'
loos'en
loot (stolen goods)

  ✔ lute
loot'er
lop, lopped,
  lop'ping
lope, loped, lop'ing
lop'-eared'
lop'sid'ed
lo•qua'cious
lo•quac'i•ty
lord
lord'li•ness
lord'ly
lord'ship'
lore
lor•gnette'
lor'ry
lose, lost, los'ing
los'er
loss
lot
lo'tion
lot'ter•y
lot'to
lo'tus
loud
loud'mouth'
loud'mouthed'
loud'speak'er
lounge, lounged,
  loung'ing
loupe (magnifying
  glass)
  ✔ loop
lour
louse (insect), pl. lice
louse (contemptible

person), pl. lous'es
lous'y
lout
lou'ver
lou'vered
lov'a·ble *also*
  love'a·ble
lov'a·bly
love, loved, lov'ing
love'bird'
love'less
love'li·ness
love'lorn'
love'ly
lov'er
love' seat' *or*
  love'seat'
love'sick'
low *(not high)*
  ✔ lo
low *(to bellow)*
  ✔ lo
low'boy'
low'brow'
low'down' *n.*
low'-down' *adj.*
low'er *(to scowl)*
low'er *(below)*
low'er·case' *or*
  low'er-case'
low'er-class' *adj.*
low'er·most'
low'-key' *also*
  low-keyed
low'land
low'li·ness

low'ly
low'-pitched'
low'-pres'sure *adj.*
low'-rise'
low'-spir'it·ed
lox *pl.* lox *or* lox'es
loy'al
loy'al·ist
loy'al·ty
loz'enge
LP *pl.* LP's *or* LPs
lu'au'
lub'ber
lu'bri·cant
lu'bri·cate', -cat'ed,
  -cat'ing
lu'bri·ca'tion
lu'bri·ca'tor
lu'cent
lu'cid
lu·cid'i·ty
luck'i·ly
luck'y
lu'cra·tive
lu'cre
lu'di·crous
luff
lug, lugged, lug'ging
lug'gage
lug'sail
lu·gu'bri·ous
lug'worm'
luke'warm'
lull
lull'a·by'
lum·ba'go

lum'bar *(relating to*
  the lower back)
lum'ber *(wood)*
lum'ber *(to move*
  clumsily)
lum'ber·jack'
lum'ber·yard'
lu'men *pl.*
  -mens *or* -mi·na
lu'mi·nar'y
lu'mi·nes'cence
lu'mi·nes'cent
lu'mi·nos'i·ty
lu'mi·nous
lump'i·ness
lump'y
lu'na·cy
lu'nar
lu'na·tic
lunch
lunch'eon
lunch'eon·ette'
lunch'room'
lung
lunge, lunged,
  lung'ing
lung'fish' *pl.* -fish'
  or -fish'es
lu'pine *also* lu'pin
lu'pus
lurch
lure, lured, lur'ing
lu'rid
lurk
lurk'er
lus'cious

lush

lust

lust'er *(person who lusts)*

lus'ter *(sheen)*

lust'ful

lus'trous

lust'y

lute *(musical instrument)*
　✔ loot

lu•te'ti•um *also* lu•te'ci•um

Lu'ther•an

lux•u'ri•ance

lux•u'ri•ant

lux•u'ri•ate', -at'ed, -at'ing

lux•u'ri•ous

lux'u•ry

ly•ce'um

lye *(alkaline solution)*
　✔ lie

Lyme' dis•ease'

lymph

lym•phat'ic

lym'pho•cyte'

lym'phoid'

lynch

lynch'er

lynx *(animal)*, pl. lynx *or* lynx'es
　✔ links

lyre *(musical instrument)*
　✔ liar

lyr'ic

lyr'i•cal

lyr'i•cism

lyr'i•cist

ly'sin

ly'sine'

ly'sis pl. -ses

M

ma'am

ma•ca'bre

mac•ad'am

mac•ad'am•ize', -ized', -iz'ing

ma•caque'

mac'a•ro'ni pl. -ni

mac'a•roon'

ma•caw'

mace

Mac'e•do'ni•an

mac'er•ate', -at'ed, -at'ing

mac'er•a'tion

mac'er•a'tor *also* mac'er•a'ter

ma•chet'e

Mach'i•a•vel'li•an

mach'i•na'tion

ma•chine', -chined', -chin'ing

ma•chine' gun' *n.*

ma•chine'-gun', -gunned', -gun'ning

ma•chine'-read'a•ble

ma•chin'er•y

ma•chin'ist

ma•chis'mo

ma'cho pl. -chos

mack'er•el pl. -el or -els

mack'i•naw'

mack'in•tosh' *also* mac'in•tosh' *(raincoat)*
　✔ McIntosh

mac'ra•mé'

mac'ro' pl. -ros'

mac'ro•bi•ot'ics

mac'ro•cosm

mac'ro•cos'mic

mac'ro•ec'o•nom'-ics

ma•crog'ra•phy

mac'ro•mol'e•cule

ma'cron'

mac'ro•nu'cle•us pl. -cle•i'

mac'ro•scop'ic *also* mac'ro•scop'i•cal

mac'u•la pl. -lae'

mac'u•lar

mac'u•late', -lat'ed, -lat'ing

mac'u•la'tion

mad, mad'der, mad'dest

Mad'am pl. Mad'ams or Mes•dames'

Ma•dame' pl. Mes•dames'

mad'cap'
mad'den
mad'den·ing
made (created)
  ✔ maid
Mad'e·moi·selle'
  pl. Mad'e·moi·
  selles' or Mes'de·
  moi·selles'
made'-to-or'der
made'-up' adj.
mad'house'
mad'man'
Ma·don'na
mad'ras
mad'ri·gal
mael'strom
mae'nad'
maes'tro pl. -tros or
  -tri
Ma'fi·a
Ma'fi·o'so' pl. -si'
mag'a·zine'
ma·gen'ta
mag'got
Ma'gi'
mag'ic
mag'i·cal
ma·gi'cian
mag·is·te'ri·al
mag·is·tra·cy
mag'is·trate'
mag'ma pl.
  mag'ma·ta or
  mag'mas
Mag'na Car'ta or
  Mag'na Char'ta

mag'na cum
  lau'de
mag'na·nim'i·ty
mag·nan'i·mous
mag'nate'
mag·ne'sia
mag·ne'si·um
mag'net
mag·net'ic
mag'net·ism
mag'net·ite'
mag'net·i·za'tion
mag'net·ize', -ized',
  -iz'ing
mag'net·iz'er
mag·ne'to pl. -tos
mag·ne·tom'e·ter
mag·ne'to·sphere'
mag'ne·tron'
mag'ni·fi·ca'tion
mag·nif'i·cence
mag·nif'i·cent
  (splendid)
  ✔ munificent
mag'ni·fi'er
mag'ni·fy', -fied',
  -fy'ing
mag·nil'o·quence
mag·nil'o·quent
mag'ni·tude'
mag·no'lia
mag'num
mag'pie
ma·guey' pl.
  -gueys'
Mag'yar'
ma'ha·ra'jah or

ma'ha·ra'ja
ma'ha·ra'ni or
  ma'ha·ra'nee
ma·hat'ma
Ma·hi'can also
  Mo·hi'can pl. -can
  or -cans
mah'jong also
  mah'jongg'
ma·hog'a·ny
maid (girl, servant)
  ✔ made
maid'en
maid'en·hair'
maid'en·hood'
maid' of hon'or
  pl. maids' of
  hon'or
maid'ser'vant
mail (postal material,
  armor)
  ✔ male
mail'bag'
mail'boat'
mail'box'
mail'man'
mail'-or'der
  house'
mail'room'
maim
main (principal)
  ✔ mane
main'frame'
main'land'
main'line', -lined',
  -lin'ing
main'mast'

main'sail'
main'sheet'
main'spring'
main'stay'
main'stream'
main·tain'
main'te·nance
main'top'
maî'tre d'hô·tel'
  pl. maî'tres
  d'hô·tel'
maize *(grain)*
  ✔ *maze*
ma·jes'tic
ma·jes'ti·cal
maj'es·ty
ma·jol'i·ca
ma'jor
ma'jor-do'mo *pl.*
  -mos
ma'jor·ette'
ma·jor'i·ty
ma'jor-league' *adj.*
ma'jor-lea'guer
ma'jor-med'i·cal
  adj.
ma·jus'cule
make, made,
  mak'ing
make'-be·lieve' *n.*
  & *adj.*
make'-do' *adj.* & *n.*
make'-or-break'
  adj.
make'o'ver *n.*
mak'er
make'-read'y *n.*

make'shift'
make'up *or*
  make'-up *n.*
mal'a·chite'
mal'ad·just'ed
mal'a·droit'
mal'a·dy
Mal'a·gas'y *pl.*
  -gas'y *or* -gas'ies
mal·aise'
mal'a·mute' *or*
  mal'e·mute'
mal'a·prop'
mal'a·prop·ism'
mal'a·pro·pos'
ma·lar'i·a
ma·lar'i·al *or*
  ma·lar'i·an *or*
  ma·lar'i·ous
ma·lar'key *also*
  ma·lar'ky
Ma·lay'
Ma·lay'an
Mal'a·ya'lam
mal'con·tent' *adj.*
  & *n.*
male *(masculine)*
  ✔ *mail*
mal'e·dic'tion
mal'e·fac'tion
mal'e·fac'tor
ma·lef'ic
ma·lef'i·cent
ma·lev'o·lence
ma·lev'o·lent
mal·fea'sance
mal·fea'sant

mal'for·ma'tion
mal·formed'
mal·func'tion
mal'ice
ma·li'cious
ma·lign'
ma·lig'nan·cy
ma·lig'nant
ma·lig'ni·ty
ma·lin'ger
ma·lin'ger·er
mall *(promenade)*
  ✔ *maul*
mal'lard *pl.* -lard *or*
  -lards
mal'le·a·bil'i·ty
mal'le·a·ble
mal'let
mal'le·us *pl.* -le·i'
mal'low
malm'sey *pl.* -seys
mal·nour'ished
mal'nu·tri'tion
mal'oc·clu'sion
mal·o'dor
mal·o'dor·ous
mal·prac'tice
mal·prac'ti'tion·er
mal'tase'
Mal·tese' *pl.* -tese'
mal'tose'
mal·treat'
ma'ma *or* mam'ma
mam'ba *(snake)*
mam'bo *(dance), pl.*
  -bos
mam'mal

mam·ma′li·an
mam′ma·ry
mam′mo·gram′
mam·mog′ra·phy
mam′moth
man *pl.* men
man, manned,
 man′ning
man′a·cle, -cled,
 -cling
man′age, -aged,
 -ag′ing
man′age·a·bil′i·ty
man′age·a·ble
man′age·ment
man′ag·er
man′a·ge′ri·al
ma·ña′na
man′-at-arms′ *pl.*
 men′-at-arms′
man′a·tee′
Man′chu *pl.* -chu *or*
 -chus
Man·chur′i·an
man′da·la
Man′dan′ *pl.* -dan
 or -dans
man′da·rin
man′date′, -dat′ed,
 -dat′ing
man′da·to′ry
man′di·ble
man′do·lin′
man′drake′
man′drel *or* man′-
 dril *(spindle)*
man′drill *(baboon)*

mane *(hair)*
 ✔ main
man′-eat′er
man′-eat′ing
ma·neu′ver
ma·neu′ver·a·bil′i·
 ty
ma·neu′ver·a·ble
man′ga·nese′
mange
man′ger
man′gi·ness
man′gle, -gled,
 -gling
man′go *pl.* -goes *or*
 -gos
man′grove′
mang′y
man′han′dle,
 -dled, -dling
Man·hat′tan *also*
 man·hat′tan
 (cocktail)
Man·hat′tan
 (people)
man′hole′
man′hood′
man′-hour′
man′hunt′
ma′ni·a
ma′ni·ac′
ma·ni′a·cal
man′ic
man′ic-
 de·pres′sive
man′i·cot′ti
man′i·cure′,

-cured′, -cur′ing
man′i·cur′ist
man′i·fest′
man′i·fes·ta′tion
man′i·fes′to *pl.*
 -toes *or* -tos
man′i·fold
man′i·kin *or*
 man′ni·kin *(dwarf)*
 ✔ mannequin
ma·nil′a *or*
 ma·nil′la
man′i·oc′ *also*
 man′i·o′ca
man′i·ple
ma·nip′u·la·ble
ma·nip′u·late′,
 -lat′ed, -lat′ing
ma·nip′u·la′tion
ma·nip′u·la′tive
ma·nip′u·la′tor
man′i·tou′ *pl.*
 -tous′
man′kind′
man′li·ness
man′ly
man′-made′
man′na
manned
man′ne·quin
 (model)
 ✔ manikin
man′ner *(behavior)*
 ✔ manor
man′nered
man′ner·ism
man′nish

man'-of-war' pl.
  men'-of-war'
ma·nom'e·ter
man'or (estate)
  ✔ manner
ma·no'ri·al
man'pow'er
man·qué'
man'sard
manse
man'ser'vant pl.
  men'ser'vants
man'sion
man'-sized' also
  man'-size'
man'slaugh'ter
man'ta
man'-tai'lored
man'tel also
  man'tle (shelf)
  ✔ mantle
man'tel·piece' also
  man'tle·piece'
man'tic
man·til'la
man'tis pl. -tis·es or
  -tes
man·tis'sa
man'tle (to cloak),
  -tled, -tling
  ✔ mantel
man'tra
man'trap'
man'u·al
man'u·fac'to·ry
man'u·fac'ture,
  -tured, -tur·ing

man'u·fac'tur·er
man'u·mis'sion
man'u·mit',
  -mit'ted, -mit'ting
ma·nure', -nured',
  -nur'ing
man'u·script'
Manx pl. Manx
man'y, more, most
Mao'ism
Mao'ist
Mao'ri pl. -ri or -ris
map, mapped,
  map'ping
ma'ple
mar, marred,
  mar'ring
mar'a·bou'
ma·ra'ca
mar'a·schi'no
mar'a·thon'
mar'a·thon'er
ma·raud'
mar'ble, -bled,
  -bling
march (journey)
March (month)
mar'chio·ness
Mar'di gras'
mare (female horse)
ma're (region of the
  moon), pl. -ri·a
mar'ga·rine
mar'ga·ri'ta
mar'gin
mar'gin·al
mar'gue·rite'

mar'i·gold'
mar'i·jua'na or
  mar'i·hua'na
ma·rim'ba
ma·ri'na
mar'i·nade'
mar'i·nate',
  -nat'ed, -nat'ing
ma·rine'
mar'i·ner
mar'i·o·nette'
mar'i·po'sa
mar'i·tal
mar'i·time'
mar'jo·ram
mark'down'
marked
mark'ed·ly
mark'er
mar'ket
mar'ket·a·bil'i·ty
mar'ket·a·ble
mar'ket·er
mar'ket·ing
mar'ket·place'
mark'ing
marks'man
marks'man·ship'
marks'wom'an
mark'up'
marl
mar'lin (fish)
mar'line (rope)
mar'line·spike'
mar'ma·lade'
mar·mo're·al
mar'mo·set'

mar'mot
ma·roon'
mar·quee' *(tent, entrance)*
mar'quis *or* mar'quess *(nobleman)*, *pl.* -quis·es *or* mar·quis' *or* -quess·es
mar·quise' *(marchioness)*
mar'qui·sette'
mar'riage
mar'riage·a·ble
mar'ried
mar'row
mar'ry, -ried, -ry·ing
mar·sa'la
marsh
mar'shal *(to organize)*, -shaled *or* -shalled, -shal·ing *or* -shal·ling
 ✔ martial
marsh'i·ness
marsh'land'
marsh'mal'low
marsh'y
mar·su'pi·al
mar'ten *(animal)*, *pl.* -ten *or* -tens
 ✔ martin
mar'tial *(warlike)*
 ✔ marshal
Mar'tian
mar'tin *(bird)*

 ✔ marten
mar'ti·net'
mar'tin·gale'
mar·ti'ni *pl.* -nis
mar'tyr
mar'tyr·dom
mar'vel -veled *or* -velled, -vel·ing *or* -vel·ling
mar'vel·ous *also* mar'vel·lous
Marx'i·an
Marx'ism
Marx'ist
mar'zi·pan'
mas·car'a
mas'cot
mas'cu·line
mas'cu·lin'i·ty
ma'ser
mash'er
mask *(covering)*
 ✔ masque
masked
mask'ing tape'
mas'och·ism
mas'o·chist
mas'o·chis'tic
ma'son
Ma·son'ic
Ma'son jar'
ma'son·ry
masque *(drama)*
 ✔ mask
mas'quer·ade', -ad'ed, -ad'ing
mas'quer·ad'er

mass *(matter)*
Mass *also* mass *(Eucharist ceremony)*
Mas'sa·chu'sett *also* Mas'sa·chu'set *pl.* -sett *or* -setts *also* -set *or* -sets
mas'sa·cre, -cred, -cring
mas·sage', -saged', -sag'ing
mas·seur'
mas·seuse'
mas'sif' *(mountain)*
mas'sive *(large)*
mass'-pro·duce', -duced', -duc'ing
mas·tec'to·my
mas'ter
mas'ter-at-arms' *pl.* mas'ters-at-arms'
mas'ter·ful
mas'ter·li·ness
mas'ter·ly
mas'ter·mind'
mas'ter·piece'
mas'ter·stroke'
mas'ter·work'
mas'ter·y
mast'head'
mas'ti·cate', -cat'ed, -cat'ing
mas'ti·ca'tion
mas'ti·ca'tor
mas'tiff
mas'to·don

mas'toid'
mas'tur·bate',
 -bat'ed, -bat'ing
mas'tur·ba'tion
mat, mat'ted,
 mat'ting
mat'a·dor'
match'book'
match'box'
match'mak'er
match'mak'ing
match'stick
match'up' *n.*
mate, mat'ed,
 mat'ing
ma'té *or* ma'te
ma·te'ri·al *(sub-*
 stance)
 ✔ *materiel*
ma·te'ri·al·ism
ma·te'ri·al·ist
ma·te'ri·al·is'tic
ma·te'ri·al·i·za'-
 tion
ma·te'ri·al·ize',
 -ized', -iz'ing
ma·te'ri·el' *or*
 ma·té'ri·el' *(equip-*
 ment)
 ✔ *material*
ma·ter'nal
ma·ter'ni·ty
math'e·mat'i·cal
math'e·ma·ti'cian
math'e·mat'ics
mat'i·nee' *or*
 mat'i·née'

mat'ins
ma'tri·arch'
ma'tri·ar'chal
ma'tri·ar'chy
mat'ri·cid'al
mat'ri·cide'
ma·tric'u·late',
 -lat'ed, -lat'ing
ma·tric'u·la'tion
mat'ri·lin'e·age
mat'ri·lin'e·al
mat'ri·mo'ni·al
mat'ri·mo'ny
ma'trix *pl.* -tri·ces'
 or -trix·es'
ma'tron
ma'tron of hon'or
 pl. ma'trons of
 hon'or
mat'ted
mat'ter
mat'ter-of-fact'
mat'ting
mat'tock
mat'tress
mat·u'rate', -rat'ed,
 -rat'ing
mat'u·ra'tion
mat'u·ra'tive
ma·ture', -tured',
 -tur'ing
ma·ture', -tur'er,
 -tur'est
ma·tur'i·ty
mat'zo *pl.* -zos *or*
 -zot' *or* -zoth'
maud'lin

maul *(hammer)*
 ✔ *mall*
maun'der
Mau'ri·ta'ni·an
Mau·ri'ti·an
mau·so·le'um *pl.*
 -le'ums *or* -le'a
mauve
mav'er·ick
maw
mawk'ish
max·il'la *pl.* -lae *or*
 -las
max'il·lar
max'il·lar'y
max'im
max'i·mize',
 -mized', -miz'ing
max'i·mum *pl.*
 -mums *or* -ma
may, *aux. v., past*
 tense might
May *(month)*
Ma'ya *pl.* -ya *or* -yas
Ma'yan
may'be
may'day' *(signal)*
may'flow·'er
may'fly'
may'hem'
may'on·naise'
may'or
may'or·al
may'or·al·ty
May'pole' *also*
 may'pole'
maze *(labyrinth)*

✓ maize
ma•zur′ka *also*
  ma•zour′ka
Mc′In•tosh′ *(apple)*
  ✓ mackintosh
me *pron.*
  ✓ mi
mead *(beverage,*
  meadow)
  ✓ meed
mead′ow
mead′ow•lark′
mea′ger *also*
  mea′gre
meal
meal′i•ness
meal′time′
meal′y
meal′y-mouthed′
mean *(to signify),*
  meant, mean′ing
  ✓ mien
mean *(unkind)*
  ✓ mien
mean *(midpoint)*
  ✓ mien
me•an′der
mean′ing
mean′time′
mean′while′
mea′sles
mea′sly
meas′ur•a•ble
meas′ur•a•bly
meas′ure, -ured,
  -ur•ing
meas′ured *adj.*

meas′ure•ment
meat *(food)*
  ✓ meet, mete
meat′ball′
meat′i•ness
meat′pack′ing
meat′y
mec′ca
me•chan′ic
me•chan′i•cal
me•chan′ics
mech′a•nism
mech′a•nis′tic
mech′a•ni•za′tion
mech′a•nize′,
  -nized′, -niz′ing
med′al *(award)*
  ✓ meddle
med′al•ist
me•dal′lion
med′dle *(to interfere),*
  -dled, -dling
  ✓ medal
med′dler
med′dle•some
me′di•a
me′di•al
me′di•an
me′di•ate′, -at′ed,
  -at′ing
me′di•a′tion
me′di•a′tor
med′ic
Med′i•caid′ *also*
  med′i•caid′
med′i•cal
me•dic′a•ment

Med′i•care′ *also*
  med′i•care′
med′i•cate′, -cat′ed,
  -cat′ing
med′i•ca′tion
me•dic′i•nal
med′i•cine
med′i•co′ *pl.* -cos′
me′di•e′val *also*
  me′di•ae′val
me′di•o′cre
me′di•oc′ri•ty
med′i•tate′, -tat′ed,
  -tat′ing
med′i•ta′tion
med′i•ta′tive
med′i•ta′tor
me′di•um *pl.* -di•a
  or -di•ums
med′ley *pl.* -leys
me•dul′la *pl.*
  -dul′las *or* -dul′lae
me•dul′la
  ob′lon•ga′ta *pl.*
  me•dul′la
  ob′lon•ga′tas *or*
  me•dul′lae
  ob′lon•ga′tae
meed *(reward)*
  ✓ mead
meek′ly
meer′schaum
meet *(to come upon),*
  met, meet′ing
  ✓ meat, mete
meet *(fitting)*
  ✓ meat, mete

meet′ing

meet′ing·house′

meg′a·bit′

meg′a·buck′

meg′a·byte′

meg′a·cy′cle

meg′a·hertz′ *pl.*
-hertz′

meg′a·lith′

meg′a·lith′ic

meg′a·lo·ma′ni·a

meg′a·lo·ma′ni·ac′

meg′a·lop′o·lis

meg′a·phone′

meg′a·ton′

meg′a·watt′

mei·o′sis *pl.* -ses′

mei·ot′ic

mel′a·mine′

mel′an·cho′li·a

mel′an·chol′ic

mel′an·chol′y

Mel·a·ne′sian

mé·lange′ *also*
me·lange′

mel′a·nin

mel′a·no′ma *pl.*
-mas *or* -ma·ta

Mel′ba toast′

meld

me′lee′ *also* mê·lée′

mel′io·rate′, -rat′ed,
-rat′ing

mel′io·ra′tion

mel·lif′lu·ous

mel′low

mel·lo′de·on

me·lod′ic

me·lo′di·ous

mel′o·dra′ma

mel′o·dra·mat′ic

mel′o·dy

mel′on

melt′down′

melt′er

melt′ing point′

mem′ber

mem′ber·ship′

mem′brane′

mem′bra·nous

me·men′to *pl.* -tos
or -toes

mem′o *pl.* -os

mem′oir′

mem′o·ra·bil′i·a

mem′o·ra·ble

mem′o·ra·bly

mem′o·ran′dum
pl. -dums *or* -da

me·mo′ri·al

me·mo′ri·al·i·za′-
tion

me·mo′ri·al·ize′,
-ized′, -iz′ing

mem′o·ri·za′tion

mem′o·rize′,
-rized′, -riz′ing

mem′o·riz′er

mem′o·ry

men′ace, -aced,
-ac·ing

mé·nage′

me·nag′er·ie

men·da′cious

men·dac′i·ty

men′de·le′vi·um

mend′er

men′di·can·cy

men′di·cant

men′folk′ *or*
men′folks′

men·ha′den *pl.*
-den *or* -dens

me′ni·al

men′in·gi′tis

me·ninx *pl.*
me·nin′ges

me·nis′cal *also*
me·nis′cate′ *also*
me·nis′coid′ *also*
men·is·coi′dal

me·nis′cus *pl.* -ci′
or -cus·es

Men′non·ite′

Me·nom′i·nee *pl.*
-nee *or* -nees

men′o·paus′al

men′o·pause′

me·no′rah

men′sal

men′ses

men′stru·al

men′stru·ate′,
-at′ed, -at′ing

men′stru·a′tion

men′su·ra·bil′i·ty

men′su·ra·ble

men′su·ra′tion

men′su·ra′tive

men′tal

men·tal′i·ty

men'thol'
men'tho•lat'ed
men'tion
men'tor
men'u
me•ow'
me•phit'ic *also*
  me•phit'i•cal
me•phi'tis
mer'can•tile'
mer'can•til•ism
mer'can•til•ist
mer'ce•nar'y
mer'cer•ize', -ized',
  -iz'ing
mer'chan•dise',
  -dised', -dis'ing
mer'chan•dis'er
mer'chant
mer'ci•ful
mer'ci•less
mer•cu'ri•al
mer•cu'ri•al•ism
mer•cu'ric
mer•cu'rous
mer'cu•ry
mer'cy
mere *superl.* mer'est
mer•e•tri'cious
mer•gan'ser
merge, merged,
  merg'ing
merg'er
me•rid'i•an
me•ringue'
me•ri'no *pl.* -nos
mer'it

mer'i•toc'ra•cy
mer'it•o•crat'
mer'i•to'ri•ous
merle *also* merl
mer•lot'
mer'maid'
mer'man'
mer'ri•ly
mer'ri•ment
mer'ry
mer'ry-go-round'
mer'ry•mak'er
mer'ry•mak'ing
me'sa
mes•cal'
mes•ca•line'
mes'en•ter'ic
mes'en•ter'y *also*
  mes'en•ter'i•um *pl.*
  -i•a
mes'mer•ism
mes'mer•ize', -ized',
  -iz'ing
mes'o•derm'
Mes'o•lith'ic
mes'on'
Mes'o•po•ta'mi•an
mes'o•sphere'
Mes'o•zo'ic
mes•quite'
mess
mes'sage
mes'sen•ger
Mes•si'ah
mes'si•an'ic
mess'i•ly
mess'i•ness

mess'mate'
mess'y
mes•ti'za
mes•ti'zo *pl.* -zos *or*
  -zoes
met'a•bol'ic
me•tab'o•lism
me•tab'o•lize'
  -lized', -liz'ing
met'a•car'pal
met'a•car'pus *pl.*
  -pi
met'al *(element)*
  ✔ mettle
me•tal'lic
met'al•loid'
met'al•lur'gi•cal
met'al•lur'gist
met'al•lur'gy
met'al•work'
met'al•work'ing
met'a•mor'phic
met'a•mor'phism
met'a•mor'phose',
  -phosed', -phos'ing
met'a•mor'pho•sis
  pl. -ses'
met'a•phase'
met'a•phor'
met'a•phor'i•cal *or*
  met'a•phor'ic
met'a•phor'i•cal•ly
met'a•phys'i•cal
met'a•phy•si'cian
met'a•phys'ics
me•tas'ta•sis *pl.*
  -ses'

me·tas′ta·size′,
-sized′, -siz′ing

met′a·tar′sal

met′a·tar′sus *pl.* -si

met′a·zo′an

mete *(to distribute),*
met′ed, met′ing
✔ *meat, meet*

me′te·or

me′te·or′ic

me′te·or·ite′

me′te·or·oid′

me′te·or·o·log′-
i·cal

me′te·or·ol′o·gist

me′te·or·ol′o·gy

me′ter

meth′ane′

meth′a·no′

me·thinks′ *past
tense* me·thought′

meth′od

me·thod′i·cal *also*
me·thod′ic

Meth′od·ist

meth′od·o·log′i·cal

meth′od·ol′o·gy

meth′yl

me·tic′u·lous

mé·tier′

met′o·nym′

me·ton′y·my

met′ric

met′ri·cal

met′ri·ca′tion

met′ro *pl.* -ros

me·trol′o·gy

met′ro·nome′

met′ro·nom′ic

me·trop′o·lis

met′ro·pol′i·tan

met′tle *(spirit)*
✔ *metal*

met′tle·some

mew

mewl *(to cry)*
✔ *mule*

mews *(street)*
✔ *muse*

Mex′i·can

me·zu′zah *also*
me·zu′za *pl.* -zahs
also -zas *or*
me·zu′zot′

mez′za·nine′

mez′zo for′te′

mez′zo-so·pran′o
pl. -os

mez′zo-tint′

mho *(electrical unit),*
pl. mhos
✔ *mow*

mi *(musical tone)*
✔ *me*

Mi·am′i *pl.* -am′i *or*
-am′is

mi·as′ma *pl.* -mas *or*
-ma·ta

mi·as′mal *also*
mi′as·mat′ic *also*
mi·as′mic

mi′ca

mice

Mic′mac′ *pl.* -mac′

or -macs′

mi′crobe′

mi′cro·bi·o·log′i·
cal

mi′cro·bi·ol′o·gist

mi′cro·bi·ol′o·gy

mi′cro·chip′

mi′cro·cir′cuit

mi′cro·coc′cus *pl.*
-coc′ci′

mi′cro·com·put′er

mi′cro·cosm′

mi′cro·cos′mic
also mi′cro·cos′-
mi·cal

mi′cro·ec′o·nom′-
ics

mi′cro·fiche′

mi′cro·film′

mi·crom′e·ter
(measuring device)

mi′cro·me′ter *(unit
of measurement)*

mi·crom′e·try

mi′cron′ *also*
mi′kron′ *pl.* -crons′
or -cra *also* -krons′
or -kra

Mi′cro·ne′sian

mi′cro·nu′cle·us
pl. -cle·i′ *or*
-cle·us·es

mi′cro·or′gan·ism

mi′cro·phone′

mi′cro·proc′es·sor

mi′cro·scope′

mi′cro·scop′ic *also*

mi′cro•scop′i•cal
mi•cros′co•pist
mi•cros′co•py
mi′cro•sec′ond
mi′cro•sur′ger•y
mi′cro•wave′,
-waved′, -wav′ing
mid′air′
mid′brain′
mid′course′
mid′day′
mid′dle
mid′dle-aged′
mid′dle-class′
mid′dle•man′
mid′dle•weight′
mid′dling
mid′dy *(blouse)*
✔ *midi*
midge
midg′et
mid′i *(skirt)*
✔ *middy*
mid′land
mid′lev′el
mid′life′
mid′morn′ing
mid′most′
mid′night′
mid′point′
mid′range′
mid′rib′
mid′riff′
mid′sec′tion
mid′ship′
mid′ship′man
midst

mid′stream′
mid′sum′mer
mid′term′
mid′town′
mid′way′
mid′week′
mid′wife′ *pl.*
-wives′
mid′wife′ry
mid′win′ter
mid′year′
mien *(bearing)*
✔ *mean*
miff
might *past tense of*
may
✔ *mite*
might′y
mi′gnon•ette′
mi′graine′
mi′grant
mi′grate′, -grat′ed,
-grat′ing
mi•gra′tion
mi′gra•to′ry
mi•ka′do *pl.* -dos
mike
mil *(unit of length)*
✔ *mill*
mi•la′dy
milch
mild
mil′dew′
mild′ly
mile′age
mile′post′
mile′stone′

mi•lieu′ *pl.* -lieus′ *or*
-lieux′
mil′i•tan•cy
mil′i•tant
mil′i•tar′i•ly
mil′i•ta•rism
mil′i•ta•rist
mil′i•ta•ris′tic
mil′i•ta•ri•za′tion
mil′i•ta•rize′,
-rized′, -riz′ing
mil′i•tar′y
mil′i•tate′, -tat′ed,
-tat′ing
mi•li′tia
mi•li′tia•man
milk′er
milk′i•ness
milk′maid′
milk′man′
milk′ shake′
milk′ snake′
milk′sop′
milk′ tooth′
milk′weed′
milk′y
mill *(grinder)*
✔ *mil*
mill *(money)*
✔ *mil*
mill′age
mill′dam′
mil′le•nar′i•an
mil′le•nar′y
(thousand)
✔ *millinery*
mil•len′ni•al

mil·len′ni·um pl.
 -ni•ums or -ni•a
mill′er
mil′let
mil′li•bar′
mil′li•gram′
mil′li•li′ter
mil′li•me•ter
mil′li•ner
mil′li•ner′y (hats)
 ✔ millenary
mill′ing
mil′lion pl. -lion or
 -lions
mil′lion•aire′
mil′lionth
mil′li•pede′ or
 mil′le•pede′
mill′pond′
mill′race′
mill′stone′
mill′stream′
mill′ wheel′
mi•lord′
milque′toast′
mime, mimed,
 mim′ing
mim′e•o•graph′
mim′er
mi•me′sis
mi•met′ic
mim′ic, -icked,
 -ick•ing
mim′ick•er
mim′ic•ry
mi•mo′sa
min′a•ret′

min′a•to′ry
mince, minced,
 minc′ing
mince′meat′
mind
mind′-al′ter•ing
mind′-bog′gling
mind′ed
mind′ful
mind′less
mind′ read′er
mind′set′ or
 mind′-set′
mine, mined,
 min′ing
mine pron.
min′er (one that
 mines)
 ✔ minor
min′er•al
min′er•a•log′i•cal
min′er•al′o•gist
min′er•al′o•gy
min′e•stro′ne
min′gle, -gled,
 -gling
min′i pl. -is
min′i•a•ture
min′i•a•tur•ize′,
 -ized′, -iz′ing
min′i•bar′
min′i•bike′
min′i•bus′
min′i•com•put′er
min′im
min′i•mal′
min′i•mal•ism

min′i•mal•ist
min′i•mal•ize′,
 -ized′, -iz′ing
min′i•mi•za′tion
min′i•mize′,
 -mized′, -miz′ing
min′i•miz′er
min′i•mum pl.
 -mums or -ma
min′ing
min′ion
min′i•se′ries
min′i•skirt′
min′is•ter
min′is•te′ri•al
min′is•tra′tion
min′is•try
min′i•van′
mink pl. mink or
 minks
Min′ne•so′tan
min′now pl. -now
 or -nows
Mi•no′an
mi′nor (lesser or
 smaller)
 ✔ miner
mi•nor′i•ty
mi′nor-league′ adj.
min′strel
mint′age
min′u•end′
min′u•et′
mi′nus
min•us•cule′ also
 min′is•cule′
min′ute (unit of

mi·nute' *(small)*
min'ute·ly *(once a minute)*
mi·nute'ly *(on a small scale)*
min'ute·man'
mi·nu'ti·a *pl.* -ti·ae'
minx
Mi'o·cene'
mir'a·cle
mi·rac'u·lous
mi·rage'
mire, mired, mir'ing
mir'ror
mirth
mir'y
mis'ad·ven'ture
mis'al·li'ance
mis·al'lo·cate',
-cat'ed, -cat'ing
mis'an·thrope' *also* mis'an·throp·pist
mis'an·throp'ic
also mis'an·throp'-
i·cal
mis·an'thro·py
mis'ap·pli·ca'tion
mis'ap·ply', -plied',
-ply'ing
mis'ap·pre·hend'
mis'ap·re·hen'sion
mis'ap·pro'pri·ate',
-at'ed, -at'ing
mis'ap·pro'pri·a'-
tion
mis'be·got'ten

mis·be·have',
-haved', -hav'ing
mis·be·hav'ior
mis·cal'cu·late',
-lat'ed, -lat'ing
mis·cal'cu·la'tion
mis·call'
mis·car'riage
mis·car'ry, -ried,
-ry·ing
mis·cast', -cast',
-cast'ing
mis·ceg'e·na'tion
mis'cel·la'ne·ous
mis'cel·la'ny
mis·chance'
mis'chief
mis'chie·vous
mis'ci·bil'i·ty
mis'ci·ble
mis'con·ceive',
-ceived', -ceiv'ing
mis'con·cep'tion
mis·con'duct
mis'con·strue',
-strued', -stru'ing
mis'count' *n.*
mis·count' *v.*
mis'cre·ant
mis·deal', -dealt',
-deal'ing
mis·deal' *n.*
mis·deed'
mis·de·mean'or
mis'di·rect'
mis'di·rec'tion
mis·do'ing

mi'ser
mis'er·a·ble
mis'er·a·bly
mi'ser·li·ness
mi'ser·ly
mis'er·y
mis·fire', -fired',
-fir'ing
mis'fire' *n.*
mis'fit'
mis·for'tune
mis·giv'ing
mis·gov'ern
mis·gov'ern·ment
mis·guid'ance
mis·guide',
-guid'ed, -guid'ing
mis·han'dle, -dled,
-dling
mis'hap'
mis·hear', -heard',
-hear'ing
mish'mash'
mis'in·form'
mis'in·for·ma'tion
mis'in·ter'pret
mis'in·ter'pre·ta'-
tion
mis·judge',
-judged', -judg'ing
mis·judg'ment
mis·lay', -laid',
-lay'ing
mis·lead', -led',
-lead'ing
mis·man'age,
-aged, -ag·ing

mis·man'age·ment
mis·match'
mis·name',
  -named', -nam'ing
mis·no'mer
mi·sog'a·my
mi·sog'y·nist
mi·sog'y·nous
mi·sog'y·ny
mis·place', -placed',
  -plac'ing
mis·play'
mis·print' *v.*
mis'print' *n.*
mis'pro·nounce',
  -nounced',
  -nounc'ing
mis'pro·nun'ci·a'-
  tion
mis'quo·ta'tion
mis·quote',
  -quot'ed, -quot'ing
mis·read', -read',
  -read'ing
mis·rep're·sent'
mis·rep're·sen·ta'-
  tion
mis·rule', -ruled',
  -rul'ing
miss
mis'sal *(prayer book)*
  ✔ missile
mis·shape',
  -shaped, -shaped' or
  -shap'en, -shap'ing
mis'sile *(weapon)*
  ✔ missal

miss'ing
mis'sion
mis'sion·ar'y
Mis·sis·sip'pi·an
mis'sive
Mis·sou'ri *pl.* -ri or
  -ris
mis·speak', -spoke',
  -spo'ken,
  -speak'ing
mis·spell', -spelled'
  or -spelt', -spell'ing
mis·spend', -spent',
  -spend'ing
mis·state', -stat'ed,
  -stat'ing
mis·state'ment
mis·step'
miss'y
mist
mis·tak'a·ble
mis·take', -took',
  -tak'en, -tak'ing
Mis'ter
mist'i·ness
mis'tle·toe'
mis'tral
mis·treat'
mis·treat'ment
mis'tress
mis·tri'al
mis·trust'
mist'y
mis·un·der·stand',
  -stood', -stand'ing
mis·use', -used',
  -us'ing

mite *(organism,*
  small amount)
  ✔ might
mi'ter
mit'i·gate', -gat'ed,
  -gat'ing
mit'i·ga'tion
mi·to·chon'dri·on
  pl. -dri·a
mi·to'sis *pl.* -ses
mi·tot'ic
mitt
mit'ten
mix
mixed
mix'er
mix'ture
mix'-up' *also*
  mix'up'
miz'zen *or* miz'en
miz'zen·mast *or*
  miz'en·mast
mne·mon'ic
mo'a
moan
moat *(ditch)*
  ✔ mote
mob, mobbed,
  mob'bing
mo'bile
mo·bil'i·ty
mo'bi·li·za'tion
mo'bi·lize', -lized',
  -liz'ing
Mö'bi·us strip'
mob'ster
moc'ca·sin

mo'cha
mock
mock'er
mock'er•y
mock'-he•ro'ic
mock'ing•bird'
mock'up' *also*
  mock'-up' *n.*
mod
mod'al
mo•dal'i•ty
mode
mod'el, -eled *also*
  -elled, -el•ing *or*
  -el•ling
mo'dem'
mod'er•ate', -at'ed,
  -at'ing
mod'er•a'tion
mod'e•ra'to *pl.* -tos
mod'er•a'tor
mod'ern
mod'ern•ism
mod'ern•ist
mod'ern•is'tic
mo•der'ni•ty
mod'ern•i•za'tion
mod'ern•ize', -ized',
  -iz'ing
mod'est
mod'es•ty
mod'i•cum *pl.*
  -cums *or* -ca
mod'i•fi•ca'tion
mod'i•fi'er
mod'i•fy', -fied',
  -fy'ing

mod'ish
mod'u•lar
mod'u•late', -lat'ed,
  -lat'ing
mod'u•la'tion
mod'u•la'tor
mod'ule
mo'gul *(magnate)*
Mo'gul *(Indian
  Moslem)*
mo'hair'
Mo•ha've *also*
  Mo•ja've *pl.* -ve *or*
  -ves
Mo'hawk' *pl.*
  -hawk' *or* -hawks'
Mo•he'gan *pl.*
  -gan *or* -gans
Mohs' scale'
moi'e•ty
moi•ré'
moist
mois'ten
mois'ture
mo'lar
mo•las'ses
mold'a•ble
mold'i•ness
mold'ing
mold'y
mole
mo•lec'u•lar
mol'e•cule'
mole'hill'
mole'skin'
mo•lest'
mo•les•ta'tion

mo•lest'er
moll
mol'li•fi'a•ble
mol'li•fi•ca'tion
mol'li•fy', -fied',
  -fy'ing
mol'lusk *also*
  mol'lusc
mol'ly•cod'dle,
  -dled, -dling
molt
mol'ten
mol'to
mo•lyb'de•num
mom
mom'-and-pop'
  adj.
mo'ment
mo'men•tar'i•ly
mo'men•tar'y
mo•men'tous
mo•men'tum *pl.*
  -ta *or* -tums
mom'my
mo'nad
mon'arch
mo•nar'chic
mo•nar'chi•cal
mon'ar•chism
mon'ar•chist
mon'ar•chy
mon'as•te'ri•al
mon'as•ter'y
mo•nas'tic
mon'a•tom'ic
mon•au'ral
Mon'day

mo·ne′ran
mon′e·tar′i·ly
mon′e·tar·ism
mon′e·tar′y
mon′ey *pl.* -eys or
  -ies
mon′ey·bag′
mon′ey·chang′er
mon′eyed *also*
  mon′ied
mon′ey·lend′er
mon′ey·mak′er
mon′ey·mak′ing
mon′ger
Mon′gol
Mon·go′li·an
mon′goose′ *pl.*
  -goos′es
mon′grel
mon′i·ker *or*
  mon′ick·er
mo′nism
mo·ni′tion
mon′i·tor
mon′i·to′ry
monk
mon′key *pl.* -keys
mon′key·shine′
monk′ish
monks′hood
mon′o
mon′o·chro·mat′ic
mon′o·chro′ma·
  tism
mon′o·chrome′
mon′o·cle
mon′o·cot

mon′o·cot′y·le′-
  don
mon′o·cot′y·le′-
  don·ous
mo·noc′u·lar
mon′o·cul′ture
mon′o·dy
mo·nog′a·mist
mo·nog′a·mous
mo·nog′a·my
mon′o·gram′,
  -grammed′ *also*
  -gramed′,
  -gram′ming *or*
  -gram′ing
mon′o·graph′
mon′o·lith′
mon′o·lith′ic
mon′o·logue′
mon′o·ma′ni·a
mon′o·ma′ni·ac′
mon′o·ma′ni′a·cal
mon′o·no′mer
mo·no′mi·al
mon′o·nu′cle·
  o′sis
mon′o·phon′ic
mon′o·plane′
mo·nop′o·lis′tic
mo·nop′o·li·za′-
  tion
mo·nop′o·lize′,
  -lized′, -liz′ing
mo·nop′o·liz′er
mo·nop′o·ly
mon′o·rail′
mon′o·so′di·um

glu′ta·mate′
mon′o·syl·lab′ic
mon′o·syl′la·ble
mon′o·the′ism
mon′o·the′ist
mon′o·the·is′tic
mon′o·tone′
mo·not′o·nous
mo·not′o·ny
mon·ox′ide′
Mon·sei·gneur′ *pl.*
  Mes·sei·gneurs′
Mon·sieur′ *pl.*
  Mes·sieurs′
Mon·si′gnor *also*
  mon·si′gnor
mon·soon′
mon′ster
mon·stros′i·ty
mon′strous
mon·tage′
Mon·tan′an
month
mon′u·ment
mon′u·men′tal
moo *pl.* moos
moo, mooed,
  moo′ing
mooch′er
mood′i·ly
mood′i·ness
mood′y
moon′beam′
moon′calf′
moon′light′
moon′light′er
moon′lit′

moon'scape'
moon'shine'
moon'stone'
moon'struck'
moon'walk'
moor (to secure)
moor (open land)
Moor (North African)
moor'ing
Moor'ish
moose (animal), pl.
moose
  ✔ mousse
moot
mop, mopped,
  mop'ping
mope, moped,
  mop'ing
mo'ped'
mop'pet
mo•raine'
mor'al
mo•rale'
mor'al•ist
mor'al•is'tic
mo•ral'i•ty
mor'al•i•za'tion
mor'al•ize', -ized',
  -iz'ing
mo•rass'
mor'a•to'ri•um pl.
  -ri•ums or -ri•a
Mo•ra'vi•an
mo'ray
mor'bid
mor•bid'i•ty
mor•da'cious

mor•dac'i•ty
mor'dan•cy
mor'dant (caustic)
mor'dent (melodic
  ornament)
mo•rel'
more•o'ver
mo'res'
mor'ga•nat'ic
morgue
mor'i•bund'
Mor'mon
morn (morning)
  ✔ mourn
morn'ing (dawn)
  ✔ mourning
Mo'ro pl. -ro or
  -ros
Mo•roc'can
mo•roc'co pl. -cos
mo'ron'
mo•ron'ic
mo•rose'
mor'pheme'
mor'phine'
mor•pho•log'i•cal
  or mor'pho•log'ic
mor•phol'o•gy
mor'row
Morse' code'
mor'sel
mor'tal
mor•tal'i•ty
mor'tar
mor'tar•board'
mort'gage, -gaged,
  -gag'ing

mort'ga•gee'
mort'ga•gor' also
  mort'gag•er
mor•ti'cian
mor'ti•fi•ca'tion
mor'ti•fi'er
mor'ti•fy', -fied',
  -fy'ing
mor'tise also
  mor'tice, -tised also
  -ticed, -tis'ing or
  -tic'ing
mor'tu•ar'y
mo•sa'ic
mo'sey, -seyed,
  -sey•ing
mosque
mos•qui'to pl. -toes
  or -tos
moss
moss'back'
moss'y
most'ly
mote (speck)
  ✔ moat
mo•tel'
moth
moth'ball'
moth'-eat'en
moth'er
moth'er•hood'
moth'er-in-law' pl.
  moth'ers-in-law'
moth'er•land'
moth'er•li•ness
moth'er•ly
moth'er-of-pearl'

moth′er su•pe′ri•or
  pl. moth′ers
  su•pe′ri•or *or*
  moth′er su•pe′ri•ors
mo•tif′ *(design)*
  ✔ motive
mo′tile
mo•til′i•ty
mo′tion
mo′ti•vate′, -vat′ed,
  -vat′ing
mo′ti•va′tion
mo′tive *(reason, im-
  pulse)*
  ✔ motif
mot′ley *pl.* -leys
mo′tor
mo′tor•bike′
mo′tor•boat′
mo′tor•cade′
mo′tor•car′
mo′tor•cy′cle,
  -cled, -cling
mo′tor•cy′clist
mo′tor•ist
mo′tor•i•za′tion
mo′tor•ize′, -ized′,
  -iz′ing
mot′tle, -tled, -tling
mot′to *pl.* -toes *or*
  -tos
mound
mount
mount′a•ble
moun′tain
moun′tain•eer′
moun′tain•ous

moun′tain•side′
moun′tain•top′
moun′te•bank′
Mount′ie *also*
  Mount′y *pl.* -ies
mount′ing
mourn *(to grieve)*
  ✔ morn
mourn′er
mourn′ing *(grief)*
  ✔ morning
mouse *(animal), pl.*
  mice
mouse *(device), pl.*
  mice *or* mous′es
mouse, moused,
  mous′ing
mous′er
mouse′trap′
mousse *(dessert)*
  ✔ moose
mous′y *also*
  mous′ey
mouth
mouth′ful′
mouth′part′
mouth′piece′
mouth′wash′
mouth′wa′ter•ing
mou•ton′ *(sheep-
  skin)*
  ✔ mutton
mov′a•ble *also*
  move′a•ble
move, moved,
  mov′ing
move′ment

mov′er
mov′ie
mov′ie•mak′er
mov′ing
mow *(to cut down)*,
  mowed, mowed *or*
  mown, mow′ing
  ✔ mho
mow′er
moz′za•rel′la
mu
much, more, most
mu′ci•lage
mu′ci•lag′i•nous
muck
muck′rake′,
  -raked′, -rak′ing
muck′rak′er
mu′cous *(like
  mucus)*
mu′cus *(gland secre-
  tion)*
mud′dle, -dled,
  -dling
mud′dle-head′ed
mud′dy, -died,
  -dy′ing
mud′guard′
mud′sling′er
mud′sling′ing
mu•ez′zin
muff
muf′fin
muf′fle, -fled, -fling
muf′fler
muf′ti
mug, mugged,

mug'ging
mug'ger
mug'gi·ness
mug'gy
mug'wump'
muk'luk'
mu·lat'to *pl.* -tos or
-toes
mul'ber'ry
mulch (covering)
mulct (penalty)
mule (animal,
slipper)
✔ mewl
mul'ish
mull
mul'lein
mul'let *pl.* -let or
-lets
mul'li·gan
mul'li·ga·taw'ny
mul'lion
mul'ti·cel'lu·lar
mul'ti·col'ored
mul'ti·cul'tur·al
mul'ti·cul'tur·al·
ism
mul'ti·di·men'-
sion·al
mul'ti·eth'nic
mul'ti·far'i·ous
mul'ti·form'
mul'ti·gen'er·a'-
tion·al
mul'ti·lat'er·al
mul'ti·me'di·a
mul'ti·mil'lion·

aire'
mul'ti·na'tion·al
mul'ti·pack'
mul'ti·ple
mul'ti·ple-choice'
mul'ti·plex'
mul'ti·pli·cand'
mul'ti·pli·ca'tion
mul'ti·plic'a·tive
mul'ti·plic'i·ty
mul'ti·pli'er
mul'ti·ply', -plied',
-ply'ing
mul'ti·pronged'
mul'ti·pur'pose
mul'ti·ra'cial
mul'ti·stage'
mul'ti·tude'
mul'ti·tu'di·nous
mul'ti·va'lent
mum'ble, -bled,
-bling
mum'bler
mum'ble·ty-peg'
also mum'ble-the-
peg'
mum'bo jum'bo
or mum'bo-jum'bo
mum'mer
mum'mer·y
mum'mi·fi·ca'tion
mum'mi·fy', -fied',
-fy'ing
mum'my
mumps
munch
mun·dane'

mu·nic'i·pal
mu·nic'i·pal'i·ty
mu·nif'i·cence
mu·nif'i·cent
(generous)
✔ magnificent
mu·ni'tions
mu'ral
mu'ral·ist
mur'der
mur'der·er
mur'der·ous
mu'rex *pl.* -ri·ces' or
-rex·es
murk *also* mirk
murk'i·ness
murk'y
mur'mur
mus·ca·tel'
mus'cle (to force),
-cled, -cling
✔ mussel, muzzle
mus'cle·bound'
also mus'cle-
bound'
mus'co·vite' (mica)
Mus'co·vite'
(people)
mus'cu·lar
mus'cu·lar'i·ty
mus'cu·la·ture'
muse (to ponder),
mused, mus'ing
✔ mews
mu·se'um
mu·se'um·go'er
mush'i·ly

mush'i•ness
mush'room'
mush'y
mu'sic
mu'si•cal *(of music)*
mu'si•cale' *(concert)*
mu'si•cal'i•ty
mu•si'cian
mu•si'cian•ship'
musk
mus'kel•lunge' *or*
  mus'ke•lunge' *pl.*
  -lunge' *or* -lung'es
mus'ket
mus'ket•eer'
mus'ket•ry
musk'i•ness
musk'mel'on
Mus•ko'ge•an *also*
  Mus•kho'ge•an
musk'rat' *pl.* -rat' *or*
  -rats'
musk'y
Mus'lim *or*
  Mos'lem
mus'lin
muss
mus'sel *(shellfish)*
  ✔ *muscle, muzzle*
must
mus'tache' *also*
  mous'tache'
mus•ta'chio *pl.*
  -chios
mus'tang'
mus'tard
mus'ter

must'i•ness
must'y
mu•ta•bil'i•ty
mu'ta•ble
mu'tant
mu'tate, -tat•ed,
  -tat•ing
mu•ta'tion
mute, mut'er,
  mut'est
mute, mut'ed
  mut'ing
mu'ti•late', -lat•ed,
  -lat•ing
mu'ti•la'tion
mu'ti•la'tor
mu'ti•neer'
mu'ti•nous
mu'ti•ny, -nied,
  -ny•ing
mutt
mut'ter
mut'ton *(sheep)*
  ✔ *mouton*
mu'tu•al
mu'tu•al'i•ty
muu'muu'
muz'zle *(to restrain)*,
  -zled, -zling
  ✔ *muscle, mussel*
muz'zle•load'er
my
my'as•the'ni•a
my•ce'li•um *pl.* -li•a
my'co•log'i•cal
  also my'co•log'ic
my•col'o•gist

my•col'o•gy
my•co'sis *pl.* -ses'
my'e•lin *also*
  my'e•line
my'na *or* my'nah
  also mi'na
my'o•car'di•al
my'o•car'di•um
my•o'pi•a
my•op'ic
myr'i•ad
myrrh
myr'tle
my•self'
mys•te'ri•ous
mys'ter•y
mys'tic
mys'ti•cal
mys'ti•cism
mys'ti•fi•ca'tion
mys'ti•fy', -fied',
  -fy'ing
mys•tique'
myth
myth'i•cal *also*
  myth'ic
myth'o•log'i•cal
  also myth'o•log'ic
my•thol'o•gist
my•thol'o•gy

N

nab, nabbed,
  nab'bing
na'bob'

na·celle'
na'cho' *pl.* -chos'
na'cre
na'dir
nag, nagged,
  nag'ging
nag'ger
Na'hua'tl *pl.* -tl *or*
  -tls
nai'ad' *pl.* -a·des' *or*
  -ads'
nail
na·ive' *or* na·ïve'
  also na·if' *or* na·ïf'
na'ive·té' *or*
  na'ïve·té'
na'ked
nam'by-pam'by
name, named,
  nam'ing
name'less
name'ly
name'sake'
name'tag'
name'tape'
nan·keen'
nan'ny
nan'o·sec'ond
nan'o·tech·nol'-
  o·gy
nap, napped,
  nap'ping
na'palm'
nape
naph'tha
naph'tha·lene'
nap'kin

na·po'le·on
nap'time'
nar'cis·sism
nar'cis·sist
nar'cis·sis'tic
nar·cis'sus *pl.*
  -cis'sus·es *or* -cis'si'
nar'co·dol'lar
nar·co'sis
nar·cot'ic
Nar'ra·gan'sett *pl.*
  -sett *or* -setts
nar'rate', -rat'ed,
  -rat'ing
nar·ra'tion
nar'ra·tive
nar·ra'tor *also*
  nar'ra'ter
nar'row
nar'row·cast',
  -cast', -cast'ing
nar'row·gauge'
  also nar'row·
  gauged'
nar'row-mind'ed
nar'whal *also*
  nar'wal *or*
  nar'whale'
nar'y
na'sal
na'sal·i·za'tion
na'sal·ize', -ized',
  -iz'ing
nas'cent
nas·tur'tium
nas'ti·ly
nas'ti·ness

nas'ty
na'tal
Natch'ez *pl.* -ez
na'tion
na'tion·al
na'tion·al·ism
na'tion·al·ist
na'tion·al·is'tic
na'tion·al'i·ty
na'tion·al·i·za'tion
na'tion·al·ize',
  -ized', -iz'ing
na'tion·wide'
na'tive
Na'tive
  A·mer'i·can
na'tive-born'
na·tiv'i·ty
nat'ti·ly
nat'ty
nat'u·ral
nat'ur·al·ism
nat'u·ral·ist
nat'u·ral·is'tic
nat'u·ral·i·za'tion
nat'u·ral·ize',
  -ized', -iz'ing
na'ture
na'tured
naught *also* nought
naugh'ti·ly
naugh'ti·ness
naugh'ty
nau'se·a
nau'se·ate', -at'ed,
  -at'ing
nau'seous

nau′ti•cal
nau′ti•lus *pl.* -lus•es
  or -li′
Nav′a•jo′ *also*
  Nav′a•ho′ *pl.* -jo′ or
  -jos′ *also* -ho′ or
  -hos′
na′val *(nautical)*
  ✔ *navel*
nave *(part of a*
  church)
  ✔ *knave*
na′vel *(bellybutton)*
  ✔ *naval*
nav′i•ga•bil′i•ty
nav′i•ga•ble
nav′i•gate′, -gat′ed,
  -gat′ing
nav′i•ga′tion
nav′i•ga′tion•al
nav′i•ga′tor
na′vy
nay *(no)*
  ✔ *née, neigh*
nay′say′, -said′,
  -say′ing
nay′say′er
Naz′a•rene′
Na′zi *pl.* -zis
Na′zism *also*
  Na′zi•ism
Ne•an′der•thal′
Ne′a•pol′i•tan
neap′ tide′
near
near′by′
near′sight′ed

neat
neat′s′-foot′ oil′
neb′bish
neb′u•la *pl.* -lae′ or
  -las
neb′u•lar
neb′u•lous
nec′es•sar′i•ly
nec′es•sar′y
ne•ces′si•tate′,
  -tat′ed, -tat′ing
ne•ces′si•ta′tion
ne•ces′si•ty
neck
neck′band′
neck′er•chief
neck′lace
neck′line′
neck′tie′
neck′wear′
ne•crol′o•gy
nec′ro•man′cer
nec′ro•man′cy
nec′ro•man′tic
ne•crop′o•lis *pl.*
  -lis•es or -leis′
nec′tar
nec′tar•ine′
née *also* nee *(born)*
  ✔ *nay, neigh*
need *(requirement)*
  ✔ *knead*
need′ful
nee′dle, -dled, -dling
nee′dle•fish′ *pl.*
  -fish′ or -fish′es
nee′dle•point′

need′less
nee′dle•work′
need′n′t
need′y
ne′er
ne′er′-do•well′
ne•far′i•ous
ne•gate′, -gat′ed,
  -gat′ing
ne•ga′tion
neg′a•tive
neg′a•tiv•ism
neg′a•tiv•ist
ne•glect′
ne•glect′ful
neg′li•gee′ *also*
  neg′li•gée′ or
  neg′li•gé′
neg′li•gence
neg′li•gent
neg′li•gi•bil′i•ty
neg′li•gi•ble
ne•go′tia•bil′i•ty
ne•go′tia•ble
ne•go′ti•ate′, -at′ed,
  -at′ing
ne•go′ti•a′tion
ne•go′ti•a′tor
Ne•gri′to *pl.* -tos or
  -toes
Ne′gro *pl.* -groes
Ne′groid′
neigh *(horse's cry)*
  ✔ *nay, née*
neigh′bor
neigh′bor•hood′
neigh′bor•li•ness

nei'ther *(not either)*
  ✔ nether
nek'ton
nek'ton'ic
nel'son
nem'a•to•cyst'
nem'a•tode'
nem'e•sis *pl.* -ses'
ne'o•clas'sic *also*
  ne'o•clas'si•cal
ne'o•clas'si•cism
ne'o•clas'si•cist
ne'o•co•lo'ni•al•ist
ne'o•con•ser'va•
  tism
ne'o•dym'i•um
ne•ol'o•gism
ne'on'
ne'o•na'tal
ne'o•nate'
Ne'o-Na'zi
ne'o•phyte'
ne'o•plasm
ne'o•prene'
Nep'al•ese' *pl.* -ese'
neph'ew
neph'rite'
ne•phri'tis *pl.*
  -phrit'i•des' *or*
  -phri'tis•es'
neph'ron
nep'o•tism
nep•tu'ni•um
ner•va'tion
nerve
nerve'-rack'ing *or*
  nerve'-wrack'ing

nerv'i•ness
nerv'ous
nerv'y
nest
nes'tle, -tled, -tling
nest'ling *(young
  bird)*
net, net'ted, net'ting
neth'er *(below)*
  ✔ neither
neth'er•most'
net'su•ke'
net'ting
net'tle, -tled, -tling
net'tle•some
net'work'
net'work'ing
Neuf'châ•tel'
neu'ral
neu•ral'gia
neu•ral'gic
neu•ras•the'ni•a
neu•ri'tis
neu'ro•bi•ol'o•gy
neu'ro•chem'is•try
neu'ro•log'i•cal
neu•rol'o•gist
neu•rol'o•gy
neu'ron'
neu'ro•pa•thol'-
  o•gy
neu•ro'sis *pl.* -ses'
neu•rot'ic
neu'ro•trans•mit•
  ter
neu'ter
neu'tral

neu•tral'i•ty
neu'tral•i•za'tion
neu'tral•ize', -ized',
  -iz'ing
neu'tral•iz'er
neu•tri'no *pl.* -nos
neu'tron'
Ne•vad'an
nev'er
nev'er•more'
nev'er•the•less'
ne'vus
new *(recent)*
  ✔ gnu, knew
new'born'
new'com'er
new'el
New Eng'land•er
new'fan'gled
New'found•land
New Hamp'-
  shir•ite'
New Jer'sey•ite'
new'ly•wed'
New Mex'i•can
news'boy'
news'cast'
news'cast'er
news'gath'er•ing
news'girl'
news'let'ter
news'mak'er
news'man'
news'pa'per
news'pa'per•man'
news'pa'per•
  wom'an

news'print'
news'reel'
news'stand'
news'wom'an
news'wor'thy
news'y
newt
new'ton
New York'er
next
nex'us *pl.* -us *or*
   -us•es
Nez' Perce' *also*
   Nez' Per•cé' *pl.*
   Nez' Perce' *or* Nez'
   Per'ces *also* Nez'
   Per•cé' *or* Nez'
   Per•cés'
ni'a•cin
nib
nib'ble -bled, -bling
Nic'a•ra'guan
nice *(pleasing),*
   nic'er, nic'est
   ✔ gneiss
Ni'cene' Creed'
ni'ce•ty
niche *(recess)*
nick *(notch)*
nick'el
nick'el•o'de•on
nick'name',
   -named', -nam'ing
nic'o•tine'
nic'o•tin'ic
niece
niels•bohr'i•um

nif'ty
Ni•ger'i•an
nig'gard•ly
nig'gling
nigh
night *(darkness)*
   ✔ knight
night'cap'
night'clothes'
night'club'
night'fall'
night'gown'
night'hawk'
night'in•gale'
night'-light'
night'mare'
night'mar'ish
night'ri'der
night'shade'
night'shirt'
night'spot'
night'stick'
night'time'
ni'hil•ism
ni'hil•ist
ni'hil•is'tic
nil
nim'ble, -bler, -blest
nim'bly
nim'bo•stra'tus *pl.*
   -stra'ti
nim'bus *pl.* -bi' *or*
   -bus•es
nin'com•poop'
nine'pin'
nine•teen'
nine•teenth'

nine'ti•eth
nine'ty
nin'ja
nin'ny
ninth
ni•o'bi•um
nip, nipped, nip'ing
nip'per
nip'ple
nip'py
nir•va'na
Ni•sei' *pl.* -sei' *or*
   -seis'
nit *(insect egg)*
   ✔ knit
ni'ter
nit'-pick'
ni'trate', -trat'ed,
   -trat'ing
ni•tra'tion
ni'tric
ni'tride'
ni'tri•fi•ca'tion
ni'tri•fy' -fied',
   -fy'ing
ni'trite'
ni'tro•bac•te'ri•um
   pl. -ri•a
ni'tro•ben'zene'
ni'tro•cel'lu•lose'
ni'tro•gen
ni•trog'e•nous
ni'tro•glyc'er•in
   also ni'tro•glyc'er•
   ine
ni'trous
nit'ty-grit'ty

nit'wit'

nix

no *(refusal), pl.* noes
✔ know

no•bel'i•um

No•bel' Prize'

no•bil'i•ty

no'ble, -bler, -blest

no'ble•man

no•blesse' o•blige'

no'ble•wom'an

no'bly

no'bod'y

noc•tur'nal

noc'turne'

nod, nod'ded,
nod'ding

nod'al

nod'der

node

nod'u•lar

nod'ule

No•ël' *or* No•el'

no'-fault'

nog'gin

no'-good'

no'-hit'ter

noise, noised,
nois'ing

noise'mak'er

nois'i•ly

noi'some

nois'y

no'mad'

no•mad'ic

nom' de plume'
pl. noms' de

plume'

no'men•cla'ture

nom'i•nal

nom'i•nate',
-nat'ed, -nat'ing

nom'i•na'tion

nom'i•na'tive

nom'i•nee'

non'age

non'a•ge•nar'i•an

non'ag•gres'sion

non'a•gon'

non'al•co•hol'ic

non'a•ligned'

nonce

non'cha•lance'

non'cha•lant'

non'com'

non'com•bat'ant

non'com•mis'-
sioned of'ficer

non'com•mit'tal

non'com•pet'i•tive

non'com•pli'ance

non com'pos
men'tis

non'con•duc'tor

non'con•form'ist

non'con•form'i•ty

non'de•nom'i•na'-
tion•al

non'de•script'

none *(not one)*
✔ nun

non•en'ti•ty

non'es•sen'tial

none'such'

none'the•less'

non'-Eu•clid'e•an

non'ex•ist'ence

non'ex•ist'ent

non'fat'

non•fea'sance

non•fer'rous

non•fic'tion

non•fic'tion•al

non•flam'ma•bil'-
i•ty

non•flam'ma•ble
(not easily ignited)
✔ flammable, in-
flammable

non•flow'er•ing

no•nil'lion

no•nil'lionth'

non'in•ter•ven'-
tion

non'judg•men'tal

non•ju'ror

non•mem'ber

non•met'al

non'me•tal'lic

non'ne•go'ti•a•ble

no'-no' *pl.* -noes'

non'ob•jec'tive

no-non'sense'

non'pa•reil'

non•par'ti•san

non•plus', -plused'
or -plussed',
-plus'ing *or*
-plus'sing

non'pre•scrip'tion

non'pro•duc'tive

non·prof'it
non'pro·lif'er·a'-
  tion
non're·cov'er·a·ble
non'rep·re·sen·ta'-
  tion·al
non·res'i·dent
non're·sis'tant
non're·stric'tive
non·sched'uled
non·sec'tar'i·an
non·sense'
non·sen'si·cal
non se'qui·tur
non'skid'
non·smok'er
non·smok'ing
non·stan'dard
non'stop'
non'sup·port'
non·un'ion
non·ver'bal
non·vi'o·lence
non·vi'o·lent
non'white'
noo'dle
nook
noon
noon'day'
no' one'
noon'tide'
noon'time'
noose
Noot'ka *pl.* -ka *or*
  -kas
no'par'
nor

Nor'dic
norm
nor'mal
nor'mal·cy
nor'mal'i·ty
nor'mal·i·za'tion
nor'mal·ize', -ized',
  -iz'ing
nor'ma·tive
Nor'man
Norse
Norse'man
north
North' A·mer'i·
  can
north'bound'
north·east'
North' Car'o·lin'-
  i·an
North' Da·ko'tan
north·east'er
north·east'er·ly
north·east'ern
north·east'ward
  adv. & adj.
north·east'wards
  adv.
north'er
north'er·ly
north'ern
north'ern·er
north'ern·most'
north'ing
north'land'
north'-north·east'
north'-north·
  west'

north'ward *adv. &*
  adj.
north'wards *adv.*
north·west'
north·west'er
north·west'ern
north·west'er·ly
north·west'ward
  adv. & adj.
north·west'wards
  adv.
Nor·we'gian
nose, nosed, nos'ing
nose'bleed'
nose'-dive' -dived'
  or -dove', -div'ing
nose'gay'
nose'piece'
nose' ring'
no'-show'
nos·tal'gi·a
nos·tal'gic
nos'tril
nos'trum
nos'y *or* nos'ey
not *(in no way)*
  ✔ *knot*
no'ta be'ne
no'ta·bil'i·ty
no'ta·ble
no'ta·bly
no'ta·ri·za'tion
no'ta·rize', -rized',
  -riz'ing
no'ta·ry
no'ta·ry pub'lic *pl.*
  no'ta·ries pub'lic

no'tate, -tat•ed,
   -tat•ing
no•ta'tion
notch
note, not'ed, not'ing
note'book'
note'wor'thy
noth'ing
no'tice, -ticed,
   -tic•ing
no'tice•a•ble
no'tice•a•bly
no'ti•fi•ca'tion
no'ti•fi'er
no'ti•fy', -fied',
   -fy'ing
no'tion
no'to•chord'
no•to•ri'e•ty
no•to'ri•ous
no'-trump'
not'with•stand'ing
nou'gat
noun
nour'ish
nour'ish•ment
nou•veau riche' *pl.*
   nou'veaux riches'
no'va *pl.* -vae *or* -vas
No'va Sco'tian
nov'el
nov'el•ette'
nov'el•ist
no•vel'la *pl.* -las *or*
   -le
nov'el•ty
No•vem'ber

no•ve'na *pl.* -nas *or*
   -nae
nov'ice
no•vi'ti•ate
now'a•days'
no'way' *also*
   no'ways'
no'where'
no'-win'
no'wise'
nox'ious
noz'zle
nu
nu'ance'
nub'bin
nub'ble
nub'by
nu'bile
nu'cle•ar
nu'cle•ase'
nu'cle•ate', -at'ed,
   -at'ing
nu'cle•a'tion
nu•cle'ic ac'id
nu•cle'o•lar
nu•cle'o•lus *pl.* -li'
nu'cle•on'
nu'cle•on'ic
nu'cle•o•pro'tein
nu'cle•o•side'
nu'cle•o•tide'
nu'cle•us *pl.* -cle•i'
   or -cle•us•es
nude, nud'er,
   nud'est
nudge, nudged,
   nudg'ing

nud'ism
nud'ist
nu'di•ty
nug'get
nui'sance
nuke, nuked,
   nuk'ing
null
nul'li•fi•ca'tion
nul'li•fi'er
nul'li•fy', -fied',
   -fy'ing
nul'li•ty
numb, numb'er,
   numb'est
num'ber
nu'mer•a•ble
nu'mer•al
nu'mer•ate', -at'ed,
   -at'ing
nu'mer•a'tion
nu'mer•a'tor
nu•mer'i•cal *also*
   nu•mer'ic
nu'mer•o•log'i•cal
nu'mer•ol'o•gist
nu'mer•ol'o•gy
nu'mer•ous
nu•mis•mat'ic
nu•mis'ma•tist
num'skull' *also*
   numb'skull'
nun *(religious sister)*
   ✔ none
nun'ci•o' *pl.* -os'
nun'ner•y
nup'tial

nurse, nursed,
　nurs′ing
nurse′maid′
nurs′er•y
nurs′ling
nur′ture, -tured,
　-tur•ing
nut′crack′er
nut′hatch′
nut′meat′
nut′meg′
nu′tri•ent
nu′tri•ment
nu•tri′tion
nu•tri′tion•al
nu•tri′tion•ist
nu•tri′tious
nu′tri•tive
nut′shell′
nut′ti•ness
nut′ty
nuz′zle -zled, -zling
ny′lon′
nymph
nym•phet′
nym′pho•ma′ni•a
nym′pho•ma′ni•
　ac′

O

oaf
oak′en
oa′kum
oar (paddle)
　✔ o′er, or, ore

oar′lock′
oars′man
oars′wom′an
o•a′sis pl. -ses
oat
oat′en
oath
oat′meal′
ob′bli•ga′to
ob•du′ra•cy
ob′du•rate
o•be′di•ence
o•be′di•ent
o•bei′sance
o•bei′sant
ob′e•lisk
o•bese′
o•be′si•ty
o•bey′
ob•fus′cate′,
　-cat′ed, -cat′ing
ob′fus•ca′tion
ob•fus′ca•to′ry
o′bi
o•bit′u•ar′y
ob′ject′ n.
ob•ject′ v.
ob•jec′tion
ob•jec′tion•a•ble
ob•jec′tion•a•bly
ob•jec′tive
ob′jec•tiv′i•ty
ob•jec′tor
ob′jet d′art′ pl. ob′-
　jets d′art′
ob•la′tion
ob′li•gate′, -gat′ed,

-gat′ing
ob′li•ga′tion
o•blig′a•to′ri•ly
o•blig′a•to′ry
o•blige′, o•bliged′,
　o•blig′ing
o•blique′
o•bliq′ui•ty
o•blit′er•ate′,
　-at′ed, -at′ing
o•blit′er•a′tion
o•blit′er•a′tor
o•bliv′i•on
o•bliv′i•ous
ob•long′
ob′lo•quy pl. -quies
ob•nox′ious
o′boe
o′bo•ist
ob•scene′
ob•scen′i•ty
ob•scure′, -scur′er,
　-scur′est
ob•scure′, -scured′,
　-scur′ing
ob•scu′ri•ty
ob•se′qui•ous
ob′se•quy pl. -quies
ob•serv′a•ble
ob•serv′a•bly
ob•ser′vance
ob•ser′vant
ob′ser•va′tion
ob•ser′va•to′ry
ob•serve′, -served′,
　-serv′ing
ob•serv′er

ob•sess′

ob•ses′sion

ob•ses′sive

ob•sid′i•an

ob′so•les′cence

ob′so•les′cent

ob′so•lete′

ob•sta•cle

ob•stet′ric *also*
 ob•stet′ri•cal

ob•ste•tri′cian

ob′sti•na•cy

ob′sti•nate

ob•strep′er•ous

ob•struct′

ob•struc′tion

ob•struc′tion•ism

ob•struc′tion•ist

ob•struc′tive

ob•struct′er *or*
 ob•struc′tor

ob•tain′

ob•tain′a•ble

ob•trude′, -trud′ed,
 -trud′ing

ob•tru′sion

ob•tru′sive

ob•tuse′, -tus′er,
 -tus′est

ob•verse′ *adj.*

ob•verse′ *n.*

ob•ver′sion

ob•vert′

ob′vi•ate′, -at′ed,
 -at′ing

ob′vi•a′tion

ob′vi•a′tor

ob′vi•ous

oc′a•ri′na

oc•ca′sion

oc•ca′sion•al

oc′ci•dent *or*
 Oc′ci•dent

oc′ci•den′tal *or*
 Oc′ci•den′tal

oc•cip′i•tal

oc•clude′, -clud′ed,
 -clud′ing

oc•clu′sion

oc•cult′

oc′cul•ta′tion

oc•cult′ism

oc′cu•pan′cy

oc′cu•pant

oc′cu•pa′tion

oc′cu•pa′tion•al

oc′cu•pi′er

oc′cu•py′, -pied′,
 -py′ing

oc•cur′, -curred′,
 -cur′ring

oc•cur′rence

o′cean

o′ce•an′ic

o′cean•og′ra•pher

o′cean•o•graph′ic
 or o′cean•o•graph′-
 i•cal

o′cean•og′ra•phy

o•cel′lus *pl.* -li′

oc′e•lot′

o′cher *or* o′chre

o•clock′

oc′ta•gon′

oc•tag′o•nal

oc•ta•he′dron *pl.*
 -drons *or* -dra

oc′tal

oc′tane′

oc′tant

oc′tave

oc•ta′vo *pl.* -vos

oc•tet′

oc•til′lion

oc•til′lionth

Oc•to′ber

oc′to•ge•nar′i•an

oc′to•pus *pl.* -pus•es
 or -pi′

oc′u•lar

oc′u•list

o′da•lisque′ *also*
 o′da•lisk′

odd′ball′

odd′i•ty

odds

ode

o′di•ous

o′di•um

o•dom′e•ter

o′dor

o′dor•if′er•ous

o′dor•ous

od′ys•sey *pl.* -seys

oed′i•pal *also*
 Oed′i•pal

o′er *(over)*
 ✔ oar, or, ore

of

of′fal *(refuse)*
 ✔ awful

off′beat′
off′-Broad′way′
off′-col′or
of•fend′
of•fend′er
of•fense′ *(violation)*
of•fense′ *(act of attacking)*
of•fen′sive
of′fer
of′fer•ing
of′fer•er *or* of′fer•or
of′fer•to′ry
off′hand′
off′hand′ed•ly
off′-hour′
of′fice
of′fice•hold′er
of′fi•cer
of•fi′cial *(authorized)*
  ✔ officious
of•fi′ci•ate, -at′ed, -at′ing
of•fi′ci•a′tor
of•fi′cious *(meddlesome)*
  ✔ official
off′ing
off′-key′
off′-lim′its
off′-line′ *adj.*
off′load′ *or* off′-load′
off′-peak′
off′-price′
off′print′

off′-put′ting
off′-road′
off′-screen′ *or* off′screen′
off′-sea′son
off′set′, -set′, -set′ting
off′shoot′
off′shore′
off′side′ *also* off′sides′
off′-site′
off′spring′ *pl.* off′spring′
off′-stage′ *or* off′stage′
off′-the-cuff′ *adj.*
off′-the-rec′ord *adj.*
off′-the-wall′ *adj.*
off′-white′
oft
of′ten
of′ten•times′ *also* oft′times′
o′gle, o′gled, o′gling
o′gler
o′gre
oh *interj.*
  ✔ owe
O•hi′o•an
ohm
ohm′me′ter
oil
oil′cloth′
oil′i•ness

oil′skin′
oil′y
oink
oint′ment
O•jib′wa *pl.* -wa *or* -was
OK *or* o•kay′ *pl.* OK's *or* o•kays′
OK *or* o•kay′, OK'd *or* o•kayed′, OK'ing *or* o•kay′ing
o•ka′pi *pl.* -pi *or* -pis
O′kla•ho′man
o′kra
old
old′en
old′-fash′ioned
old′-time′
old′-tim′er
old′-world′ *also* Old′ World′ *adj.*
o′le•ag′i•nous
o′le•an′der
o′le•fin
o•le′ic
o′le•o′ *(margarine), pl.* -os′
  ✔ olio
o′le•o•res′in
ol•fac′to•ry
ol′i•garch′
ol′i•gar′chic *or* ol′i•gar′chi•cal
ol′i•gar′chy
Ol′i•go•cene′
o′li•o′ *(stew), pl.* -os′
  ✔ oleo

ol'ive
Ol'mec *pl.* -mec *or* -mecs
O•lym'pi•ad'
O•lym'pi•an
O•lym'pic
O•lym'pics
O'ma•ha' *pl.* -ha' *or* -has'
om'buds'man
om'buds•per'son
om'buds•wom'an
o•me'ga
om'e•let *also* om'e•lette
o'men
om'i•cron'
om'i•nous
o•mis'sion
o•mit', o•mit'ted, o•mit'ting
om'ni•bus' *pl.* -bus'es
om•nip'o•tence *or* om•nip'o•ten•cy
om•nip'o•tent
om'ni•pres'ence
om'ni•pres'ent
om•nis'cience *or* om•nis'cien•cy
om•nis'cient
om'ni•vore'
om•niv'o•rous
on•board' *adj.*
once
once'-o'ver *n.*
on'com'ing

one
O•nei'da *pl.* -da *or* -das
one'-lin'er
one'ness
one'-on-one'
on'er•ous
one•self' *also* one's self'
one'-sid'ed
one'time' *(former)*
one'-time' *(for one time)*
one'-to-one'
one'-track'
one-up'man•ship'
one'-way'
on'go'ing
on'ion
on'ion•skin'
on'-line' *adj.*
on'load'
on'look'er
on'ly
on'o•mat'o•poe'ia
on'o•mat'o•poe'ic *or* on'o•mat'o•po•et'ic
On'on•da'ga *pl.* -ga *or* -gas
on'rush'
on'rush'ing
on'-screen' *or* on'screen'
on'set'
on'shore'
on'side'

on'-site'
on'slaught'
on-stage' *or* on•stage'
on'-the-job' *adj.*
on'to'
on'to•log'i•cal
on•tol'o•gy
o'nus
on'ward *adj. & adv.*
on'wards *adv.*
on'yx
oo'dles
ooze, oozed, ooz'ing
ooz'y
o•pac'i•ty
o'pal
o'pal•es'cence
o'pal•es'cent
o•paque'
ope, oped, op'ing
op-ed' page' *or* Op-Ed' page'
o'pen
o'pen-air'
o'pen-and-shut' *adj.*
o'pen-end'ed
o'pen•er
o'pen-eyed'
o'pen•hand'ed
o'pen•heart'ed
o'pen•hearth'
o'pen-heart' sur'ger•y
o'pen•ing
o'pen-mind'ed

o'pen·work'
op'er·a
op'er·a·ble
op'er·and
op'er·ant
op'er·ate', -at'ed,
  -at'ing
op'er·at'ic
op'er·a'tion
op'er·a·tive
op'er·a'tor
o·per'cu·lum *pl.* -la
  or -lums
op'e·ret'ta
oph·thal'mic *(relating to the eye)*
oph·thal'mo·log'-
  ic *or* oph·thal'mo·
  log'i·cal *(relating to ophthalmology)*
oph'thal·mol'o·
  gist
oph'thal·mol'o·gy
o'pi·ate
o·pine', o·pined',
  o·pin'ing
o·pin'ion
o·pin'ion·at'ed
o'pi·um
o·pos'sum *pl.* -sum
  or -sums
op·po'nent
op'por·tune'
op'por·tun'ism
op'por·tun'ist
op'por·tun·is'tic
op'por·tu'ni·ty

op·pos'a·ble
op·pose' *(to contend against)*, -posed',
  -pos'ing
  ✔ appose
op'po·site *(altogether different)*
  ✔ apposite
op'po·si'tion
op·press'
op·pres'sion
op·pres'sive
op·pres'sor
op·pro'bri·ous
op·pro'bri·um
opt
op'ti·cal
op'ti·cian
op'tics
op'ti·mal
op'ti·mism
op'ti·mist
op'ti·mis'tic
op'ti·mi·za'tion
op'ti·mize',
  -mized', -miz'ing
op'ti·mum *pl.* -ma
  or -mums
op'tion
op'tion·al
op·tom'e·trist
op·tom'e·try
op'u·lence
op'u·lent
o'pus *pl.* o'per·a *or*
  o'pus·es
or *conj.*

✔ oar, o'er, ore
or'a·cle *(prophet)*
  ✔ auricle
o·rac'u·lar
o'ral *(relating to the mouth)*
  ✔ aural
or'ange
or'ange·ade'
o·rang'u·tan' *also*
  o·rang'ou·tang'
o·rate', o·rat'ed,
  o·rat'ing
o·ra'tion
or'a·tor
or'a·to'ri·o' *pl.* -os'
or'a·to'ry
orb
or'bit
or'bit·al
or'chard
or'ches·tra
or·ches'tral
or'ches·trate',
  -trat'ed, -trat'ing
or'ches·tra'tion
or'chid
or·dain'
or·deal'
or'der
or'der·ly
or'di·nal
or'di·nance *(command)*
  ✔ ordnance
or'di·nar'i·ly
or'di·nar'y

or'di·nate'
or'di·na'tion
ord'nance *(military supplies)*
  ✔ ordinance
Or'do·vi'cian
or'dure
ore *(mineral)*
  ✔ oar, o'er, or
o·reg'a·no
Or'e·go'ni·an
or'gan
or'gan·dy
or'gan·elle'
or·gan'ic
or'gan·ism
or'gan·ist
or'gan·i·za'tion
or'gan·ize', -ized',
  -iz'ing
or'gan·iz'er
or·gan'za
or'gasm
or'gi·as'tic
or'gy
o'ri·el
O'ri·ent *(to locate)*
O'ri·ent *(Asia)*
o'ri·en'tal *also*
  O'ri·en'tal
o'ri·en·tate',
  -tat'ed, -tat'ing
o'ri·en·ta'tion
or'i·fice
o'ri·ga'mi *pl.* -mis
or'i·gin
o·rig'i·nal

o·rig'i·nal'i·ty
o·rig'i·nate',
  -nat'ed, -nat'ing
o·rig'i·na'tor
o'ri·ole'
or'i·son
or'na·ment
or'na·men'tal
or'na·men·ta'tion
or·nate'
or'ner·y
or'ni·thol'o·gist
or'ni·thol'o·gy
o'ro·tund'
or'phan
or'phan·age
or'tho·clase'
or'tho·don'tia
or'tho·don'tics
or'tho·don'tist
or'tho·dox' *also*
  Or'tho·dox'
or'tho·dox'y
or·thog'o·nal
or'tho·graph'ic
or·thog'ra·phy
or'tho·pe'dics
or'tho·pe'dist
o'ryx *pl.* o'ryx *or*
  o'ryx·es
O'sage' *pl.* O'sage'
  or O'sag'es
os'cil·late', -lat'ed,
  -lat'ing
os'cil·la'tion
os'cil·la'tor
os·cil'lo·scope'

o'sier
os'mi·um
os·mo'sis *pl.* -ses
os·mot'ic
os'prey *pl.* -preys
os'si·fi·ca'tion
os'si·fy', -fied',
  -fy'ing
os·ten'si·ble
os·ten'si·bly
os'ten·ta'tion
os'ten·ta'tious
os'te·o·path'
os'te·op'a·thy
os'te·o·po·ro'sis
os'tra·cism
os'tra·cize', -cized',
  -ciz'ing
os'trich *pl.* -trich *or*
  -trich·es
oth'er
oth'er·wise'
Ot'ta·wa *pl.* -wa *or*
  -was
ot'ter *pl.* -ter *or* -ters
ot'to·man *(furniture)*, *pl.* -mans
Ot'to·man *(people)*,
  pl. -mans
ouch
ought *aux. v.*
  ✔ aught
ounce
our *pron.*
  ✔ hour
ours
our·selves'

oust′er
out′age
out′-and-out′ *adj.*
out′back′ *adv.*
out′back′ *n.*
out•bid′, -bid′,
 -bid′den *or* -bid′,
 -bid′ding
out′board′
out′bound′
out′break′
out′build′ing
out′burst′
out′cast′
out•class′
out′come′
out′crop′
out′cry′
out•dat′ed
out•dis′tance,
 -tanced, -tanc•ing
out•do′, -did′,
 -done′, -do′ing,
 -does′
out′door′ *adj.*
out•doors′ *adv. & n.*
out′er
out′er•most′
out′field′
out′field′er
out′fit′, -fit•ted,
 -fit•ting
out′fit′ter
out′flank′
out′flow′
out′fox′
out′go′ing

out•grow′, -grew′,
 -grown′, -grow′ing
out′growth′
out•guess′
out′house′
out′ing
out•land′ish
out•last′
out′law′
out′lay′
out′let′
out′line′, -lined′,
 -lin′ing
out•live′, -lived′,
 -liv′ing
out′look′
out′ly′ing
out•ma•neu′ver
out•mod′ed
out•num′ber
out′-of-bounds′
 adv.
out′-of-date′ *adj.*
out′-of-the-way′
 adj.
out′pa′tient
out′play′
out′post′
out′pour′ing
out′put′
out′rage′, -raged′,
 -rag′ing
out•ra′geous
out•rank′
out•reach′ *v.*
out′reach′ *n.*
out′rid′er

out′rig′ger
out′right′
out•run′, -ran′,
 -run′, -run′ning
out•sell′, -sold′,
 -sell′ing
out′set′
out•shine′, -shone′,
 -shin′ing
out•side′
out•sid′er
out•size′ *also*
 out′sized′
out′skirts′
out•smart′
out•spo′ken
out•spread′,
 -spread′,
 -spread′ing
out′spread′ *n.*
out•stand′ing
out•stay′
out•stretch′
out•strip′,
 -stripped′,
 -strip′ping
out′ward
out•wear′, -wore′,
 -worn′, -wear′ing
out•weigh′
out•wit′, -wit′ted,
 -wit′ting
out•work′ *v.*
out′work′ *n.*
o′val
o•var′i•an
o′va•ry

o·va′tion

ov′en

ov′en·bird′

o′ver

o′ver·a·bun′dance

o′ver·a·bun′dant

o′ver·a·chieve′,
-chieved′,
-chiev′ing

o′ver·a·chiev′er

o′ver·act′

o′ver·ac′tive

o′ver·age *n.*

o′ver·age′ *adj.*

o′ver·all′ *adj.*

o′ver·alls′

o′ver·arm′ *adj.*

o′ver·arm′ *v.*

o′ver·awe′, -awed′,
-aw′ing

o′ver·bal′ance,
-anced, -anc·ing

o′ver·bear′ing

o′ver·bid′, -bid′,
-bid′den *or* -bid′,
-bid′ding

o′ver·bid′ *n.*

o′ver·bite′

o′ver·board′

o′ver·book′

o′ver·bur′den

o′ver·buy′,
-bought′, -buy′ing

o′ver·call′ *v.*

o′ver·call′ *n.*

o′ver·ca·pac′i·ty

o′ver·cap′i·tal·ize′,

-ized′, -iz′ing

o′ver·cast′ *adj. & n.*

o′ver·cast′, -cast′,
-cast′ing

o′ver·charge′,
-charged′,
-charg′ing

o′ver·charge′ *n.*

o′ver·coat′

o′ver·come′,
-came′, -come′,
-com′ing

o′ver·com′pen·
sate′, -sat′ed,
-sat′ing

o′ver·com·pen·sa′-
tion

o′ver·con′fi·dence

o′ver·con′fi·dent

o′ver·crowd′

o′ver·de·vel′op

o′ver·do′ *(to do to
excess),* -did′,
-done′, -do′ing,
-does′
✔ *overdue*

o′ver·dose′,
-dosed′, -dos′ing

o′ver·draft′

o′ver·draw′,
-drew′, -drawn′,
-draw′ing

o′ver·dress′

o′ver·drive′ *n.*

o′ver·drive′,
-drove′, -driv′en,
-driv′ing

o′ver·due′ *(unpaid)*
✔ *overdo*

o′ver·eat′, -ate′,
-eat′en, -eat′ing

o′ver·es′ti·mate′,
-mat′ed, -mat′ing

o′ver·ex·ert′

o′ver·ex·pose′,
-posed′, -pos′ing

o′ver·ex·po′sure

o′ver·ex·tend′

o′ver·flow′ *v.*

o′ver·flow′ *n.*

o′ver·grow′, -grew′,
-grown′, -grow′ing

o′ver·growth′

o′ver·hand′ *also*
o′ver·hand′ed

o′ver·hang′,
-hung′, -hang′ing

o′ver·hang′ *n.*

o′ver·haul′ *v.*

o′ver·haul′ *n.*

o′ver·head′ *adj. & n.*

o′ver·head′ *adv.*

o′ver·hear′,
-heard′, -hear′ing

o′ver·heat′

o′ver·joyed′

o′ver·kill′

o′ver·land′

o′ver·lap′, -lapped′,
-lap′ping

o′ver·lap′ *n.*

o′ver·lay′, -laid′,
-lay′ing

o′ver·lay′ *n.*

o′ver•leaf′

o′ver•leap′,
  -leaped′ or -leapt′,
  -leap′ing

o′ver•lie′, -lay′,
  -lain′, -ly′ing

o′ver•load′ v.

o′ver•load′ n.

o′ver•long′

o′ver•look′ v.

o′ver•look′ n.

o′ver•lord′

o′ver•ly

o′ver•mas′ter

o′ver•much′

o′ver•night′ adj. &
  n.

o′ver•night′ adv.

o′ver•pass′ n.

o′ver•pass′,
  -passed′ or -past′,
  -pass′ing

o′ver•pay′, -paid′,
  -pay′ing

o′ver•play′

o′ver•pop′u•late′,
  -lat′ed, -lat′ing

o′ver•pop′u•la′tion

o′ver•pow′er

o′ver•print′ v.

o′ver•print′ n.

o′ver•pro•duce′,
  -duced′, -duc′ing

o′ver•pro•duc′tion

o′ver•qual′i•fied′

o′ver•rate′, -rat′ed,
  -rat′ing

o′ver•reach′

o′ver•ride′, -rode′,
  -rid′den, -rid′ing

o′ver•ripe′

o′ver•rule′, -ruled′,
  -rul′ing

o′ver•run′, -ran′,
  -run′, -run′ning

o′ver•run′ n.

o′ver•seas′

o′ver•see′, -saw′,
  -seen′, -see′ing

o′ver•se′er

o′ver•sell′, -sold′,
  -sell′ing

o′ver•set′, -set′,
  -set′ting

o′ver•shad′ow

o′ver•shoe′

o′ver•shoot′,
  -shot′, -shoot′ing

o′ver•shot′ adj.

o′ver•sight′

o′ver•sim′pli•fi•ca′-
  tion

o′ver•sim′pli•fy′,
  -fied′, -fy′ing

o′ver•size′ also
  o′ver•sized′

o′ver•sleep′, -slept′,
  -sleep′ing

o′ver•state′,
  -stat′ed, -stat′ing

o′ver•state′ment

o′ver•stay′

o′ver•step′,
  -stepped′,

-step′ping

o′ver•stock′ v.

o′ver•stuff′

o′ver•sub•scribe′,
  -scribed′, -scrib′ing

o′ver•sup•ply′ n.

o′ver•sup•ply′,
  -plied′, -ply′ing

o•vert′

o′ver•take′, -took′,
  -tak′en, -tak′ing

o′ver•tax′

o′ver•tax•a′tion

o′ver•the-count′er
  adj.

o′ver•the-hill′ adj.

o′ver•throw′,
  -threw′, -thrown′,
  -throw′ing

o′ver•throw′ n.

o′ver•time′

o′ver•tone′

o′ver•top′, -topped′,
  o•ver•top′ping

o′ver•ture′

o′ver•turn′

o′ver•use′, -used′,
  -us′ing

o′ver•view′

o′ver•ween′ing

o′ver•weight′

o′ver•whelm′

o′ver•whelm′ing

o′ver•work′ v.

o′ver•work′ n.

o′ver•wrought′

o′vi•duct′

o'vine'
o•vip'a•rous
o'vi•pos'i•tor
o'void'
o'vo•lac'to•veg'e•
tar'i•an
o'vo•vi•vip'a•rous
o'vu•lar
o'vu•late', -lat'ed,
-lat'ing
o'vu•la'tion
o'vule
o'vum *pl.* o'va
owe (*to be indebted*),
owed, ow'ing
✔ *oh*
owl'et
own
own'er
own'er•ship'
ox *pl.* ox'en
ox•al'ic ac'id
ox'blood' red'
ox'bow'
ox'ford
ox'i•dant
ox'i•da'tion
ox'ide'
ox'i•dize', -dized',
-diz'ing
ox'i•diz'er
ox'tail'
ox'y•a•cet'y•lene
ox'y•gen
ox'y•gen•ate',
-at'ed, -at'ing
ox'y•gen•a'tion

ox'y•gen'ic *also*
ox'yg'e•nous
ox'y•he'mo•glo'-
bin
ox'y•mo'ron *pl.* -ra
or -rons
o'yez'
oys'ter
o'zone'

P

pace paced, pac'ing
pace'mak'er
pac'er
pach'y•derm'
pa•cif'ic
pac'i•fi•ca'tion
pac'i•fi'er
pac'i•fism
pac'i•fist
pac'i•fy' -fied',
-fy'ing
pack
pack'age,
-aged, -ag•ing
pack'er
pack'et
pack'ing
pack'ing•house'
pack'sack'
pack'sad'dle
pact
pad, pad'ded,
pad'ding
pad'dle, -dled,

-dling
pad'dle•fish' *pl.*
-fish' *or* -fish'es
pad'dock
pad'dy
pad'lock'
pa'dre
pae'an (*praise*)
✔ *peon*
pa•el'la
pa'gan
pa'gan•ism
page, paged, pag'ing
pag'eant
pag'eant•ry
page'boy'
pag'er
pag'i•nate', -nat'ed,
-nat'ing
pag'i•na'tion
pa•go'da
pail (*bucket*)
✔ *pale*
pail'ful'
pain (*hurt*)
✔ *pane*
pain'ful
pain'kill'er
pain'less
pains'tak'ing
paint
paint'brush'
paint'ed
paint'er (*person who
paints*)
pain'ter (*rope*)
paint'ing

pair (set of two), pl.
   pair or pairs
   ✔ pare, pear
pais'ley
Pai·ute' pl. -ute' or
   -utes'
pa·ja'mas
Pak·i·stan'i
pal, palled, pal'ling
pal'ace
pal'an·quin'
pal'at·a·bil'i·ty
pal'at·a·ble
pal'a·tal
pal'ate (roof of the
   mouth)
   ✔ palette, pallet
pa·la'tial
pa·lav'er
pale (stake)
   ✔ pail
pale (lacking color),
   pal'er, pal'est
   ✔ pail
pale (to fence in, to
   lose color), paled,
   pal'ing
   ✔ pail
Pa'le·o·cene'
pa'le·og'ra·pher
pa'le·o·graph'ic or
   pa'le·o·graph'i·cal
pa'le·og'ra·phy
Pa'le·o·lith'ic
pa'le·on·tol'o·gist
pa'le·on·tol'o·gy
Pa'le·o·zo'ic

pal'ette (board for
   mixing paint)
   ✔ palate, pallet
pal'frey pl. -freys
pal'imp·sest
pal'in·drome'
pal'ing
pal'i·sade'
pall (covering for a
   coffin)
   ✔ pawl
pall (to grow tiresome)
   ✔ pawl
pal·la'di·um
pall'bear'er
pal'let (hard bed)
   ✔ palate, palette
pal'li·ate', -at·ed,
   -at·ing
pal'li·a'tion
pal'li·a·tive
pal'lid
pal'lor
palm
pal'mate' also
   pal'mat·ed
pal·met'to pl. -tos
   or -toes
palm'ist
palm'is·try
pal'o·mi'no pl.
   -nos
Pa·louse' pl. -louse'
   or -lous'es
palp
pal'pa·bil'i·ty
pal'pa·ble

pal'pa·bly
pal'pate' (to feel by
   touching), -pat·ed,
   -pat·ing
   ✔ palpitate
pal·pa'tion
pal'pa·tor
pal'pi·tate' (to
   throb), -tat·ed,
   -tat·ing
   ✔ palpate
pal'pi·ta'tion
pal'pus pl. -pi
pal'sy, -sied, -sy·ing
pal'tri·ness
pal'try
pam'pa pl. -pas
pam'per
pam'phlet
pam'phlet·eer'
pan, panned,
   pan'ning
pan·a·ce'a
pa·nache'
Pan·a·ma hat'
Pan·a·ma'ni·an
Pan'-A·mer'i·can
pan'cake'
pan'chro·mat'ic
pan'cre·as
pan'cre·at'ic
pan'da
pan·dem'ic
pan·de·mo'ni·um
pan'der
pan'der·er
pane (sheet of glass)

✔ pain
pan'e•gyr'ic
pan'e•gyr'i•cal
pan'e•gyr'ist
pan'el -eled *or*
-elled, -el•ing *or*
-el•ling
pan'el•ist
pang
pan'han'dle, -dled,
-dling
pan'ic, -icked,
-ick'ing
pan'ick•y
pan'ic-strick'en
pan'nier
pan'o•ply
pan'o•ram'a
pan'o•ram'ic
pan'pipe'
pan'sy
pant
pan'ta•lets' *also*
pan'ta•lettes'
pan'ta•loons'
pan'the•ism
pan'the•ist
pan'the•is'tic *or*
pan'the•is'ti•cal
pan'the•on'
pan'ther
pant'ies
pan'to•mime',
-mimed', -mim'ing
pan'to•mim'ist
pan'try
pants

pant'suit' *also*
pants' suit'
pant'y•hose' *or*
pant'y hose'
pap
pa'pa
pa'pa•cy
pa'pal
pa'pa•raz'zo *pl.* -zi
pa'paw' *also*
paw'paw'
pa•pa'ya
pa'per
pa'per•back'
pa'per•board'
pa'per•boy'
pa'per•girl'
pa'per•weight'
pa'per•work'
pa'per•y
pa'pier-mâ•ché'
pa•pil'la *pl.* -pil'lae
pa•poose'
pa•pri'ka
Pap'u•an
Pap'u•a New
Guin'e•an
pa•py'rus *pl.* -rus•es
or -ri'
par
par'a•ble
pa•rab'o•la
par'a•bol'ic *also*
par'a•bol'i•cal
par'a•chute',
-chut'ed, -chut'ing
par'a•chut'ist

pa•rade', -rad'ed,
-rad'ing
pa•rad'er
par'a•digm'
par'a•dise'
par'a•dox'
par'a•dox'i•cal
par•af•fin
par'a•gon'
par'a•graph'
Par'a•guay'an
par'a•keet'
par•al'de•hyde'
par•a•le'gal
par'al•lax'
par'al•lel', -leled'
also -lelled', -lel'ing
or -lel'ling
par•'al•lel•ism
par'al•lel'o•gram'
pa•ral'y•sis *pl.* -ses'
par'a•lyt'ic
par'a•lyze', -lyzed',
-lyz'ing
par'a•me'ci•um *pl.*
-ci•a *or* -ci•ums
par'a•med'ic
par'a•med'i•cal
pa•ram'e•ter *(con-
stant, limit)*
✔ perimeter
par'a•mil'i•tar'y
par'a•mount'
par'a•mour'
par'a•noi'a
par'a•noi'ac'
par'a•noid'

par'a·pet'
par'a·pher·na'lia
par'a·phrase',
  -phrased',
  -phras'ing
par'a·ple'gi·a
par'a·ple'gic
par'a·pro·fes'sion·
  al
par'a·psy·chol'o·gy
par'a·site'
par'a·sit'ic *also*
  par'a·sit'i·cal
par'a·sit·ism
par'a·sol'
par'a·sym'pa·
  thet'ic
par'a·thy'roid
par'a·troop'er
par'boil'
par'cel, -celed *also*
  -celled, -cel·ing *or*
  -cel·ling
parch
parch'ment
par'don
par'don·a·ble
pare *(to peel)*, pared,
  par'ing
  ✔ pair, pear
par'e·gor'ic
pa·ren'chy·ma
par'ent
par'ent·age
pa·ren'tal
pa·ren'the·sis *pl.*
  -ses'

par'en·thet'i·cal
  also par'en·thet'ic
par'ent·hood'
pa·re'sis
par·fait'
pa·ri'ah
pa·ri'e·tal bone'
par'i-mu'tu·el
par'ish
pa·rish'ion·er
Pa·ri'sian
par'i·ty
park
par'ka
Par'kin·son's
  dis·ease'
park'way'
par'lance
par'lay' *(to bet)*
par'ley *(conference)*,
  pl. -leys
par'lia·ment
par'lia·men·tar'-
  i·an
par'lia·men'ta·ry
par'lor
Par'me·san'
pa·ro'chi·al
pa·ro'chi·al·ism
par'o·dy -died,
  -dy'ing
pa·role',
  -roled', -rol'ing
pa·rol'ee'
pa·rot'id
par'ox·ysm
par'ox·ys'mal

par·quet'
par'quet·ry
par'ri·cid'al
par'ri·cide'
par'rot
par'ry -ried, -ry·ing
parse, parsed,
  pars'ing
par'sec'
Par'see *pl.* -sees
par'si·mo'ni·ous
par'si·mo'ny
pars'ley *pl.* -leys
pars'nip
par'son
par'son·age
part
par·take', -took',
  -tak'en, -tak'ing
par·tak'er
par'tial
par'ti·al'i·ty
par·tic'i·pant
par·tic'i·pate',
  -pat'ed, -pat'ing
par·tic'i·pa'tion
par·tic'i·pa'tor
par·tic'i·pa·to'ry
par·ti·cip'i·al
par·ti·ci·ple
par'ti·cle
par'ti-col'ored
par·tic'u·lar
par·tic'u·lar'i·ty
par·tic'u·lar·i·za'-
  tion
par·tic'u·lar·ize'

-ized', -iz'ing
par·tic'u·lar·ly
part'ing
par'ti·san
par·ti'tion
part'ner
part'ner·ship'
part' of speech' *pl.*
  parts' of speech'
par'tridge *pl.* -tridge
  or -tridg·es
part'-time' *adj.*
part'-time' *adv.*
par·tu·ri'tion
part'way'
par'ty
Pas·cal' *or* PAS·CAL'
pas'chal
pass
pass'a·ble *(capable*
  of being passed)
  ✔ passible
pass'a·bly
pas'sage
pas'sage·way'
pass'book'
pas·sé'
pas'sen·ger
pas'ser·by' *also*
  pas'ser-by' *pl.*
  pas'sers·by' *also*
  pas'sers-by'
pas'ser·ine'
pass'-fail'
pas'si·ble *(sensitive)*
  ✔ passable
pas'sim

pass'ing
pas'sion
pas'sion·ate
pas'sion·flow'er
pas'sive
pas·siv'i·ty
pass'key'
Pass'o'ver
pass'port'
pass'word'
past
pas'ta
paste, past'ed,
  past'ing
paste'board'
pas·tel'
pas'tern
pas·teur·i·za'tion
pas'teur·ize', -ized',
  -iz'ing
pas·tiche'
pas·tille' *also* pas'til
pas'time'
pas'tor
pas'tor·al
pas'tor·ate
pas·tra'mi *pl.* -mis
pas'try
pas'tur·age
pas'ture, -tured,
  -tur·ing
past'y *(resembling
  paste)*
pas'ty *(meat pie)*
pat, pat'ted, pat'ting
patch
patch'i·ness

patch·ou'li *also*
  patch·ou'ly *or*
  pach·ou'li *pl.* -lis
  also -lies
patch'work'
patch'y
pate *(head)*
pâ·té' *(meat paste)*
pa·tel'la *pl.* -tel'lae
pat'ent
pat'ent·ee'
pa·ter·fa·mil'i·as *pl.*
  pa·tres·fa·mil'i·as
pa·ter'nal
pa·ter'nal·ism
pa·ter'nal·is'tic
pa·ter'ni·ty
pa·ter'nos'ter
path
pa·thet'ic
path'find'er
path'o·gen
path'o·gen'ic
path'o·log'i·cal
  also path'o·log'ic
pa·thol'o·gist
pa·thol'o·gy
pa'thos'
path'way'
pa'tience
pa'tient
pat'i·o' *pl.* -os'
pat'ois' *pl.* pat'ois'
pa'tri·arch'
pa'tri·ar'chal
pa'tri·ar'chy
pa·tri'cian

pat'ri·cid'al
pat'ri·cide'
pat'ri·lin'e·al
pat'ri·mo'ni·al
pat'ri·mo'ny
pa'tri·ot
pa'tri·ot'ic
pa'tri·ot·ism
pa·trol', -trolled',
  -trol'ling
pa·trol'man
pa·trol'wom'an
pa'tron
pa'tron·age
pa'tron·ize', -ized',
  -iz'ing
pat'ro·nym'ic
pa·troon'
pat'sy
pat'ter
pat'tern
pat'ty
pau'ci·ty
paunch'y
pau'per
pause, paused,
  paus'ing
pa·vane' *also*
  pa·van'
pave, paved, pav'ing
pave'ment
pa·vil'ion
paw
pawl *(hinged device)*
  ✔ *pall*
pawn
pawn'bro'ker

Paw·nee' *pl.* -nee'
  or -nees'
pawn'shop'
pay, paid, pay'ing
pay'a·ble
pay'check'
pay'day'
pay'ee'
pay'load'
pay'mas'ter
pay'ment
pay'off' *n.*
pay'-per·view' *n.*
pay'roll'
pea
peace *(calm)*
  ✔ *piece*
peace'a·ble
peace'a·bly
peace'ful
peace'keep'ing
peace'mak'er
peace'time'
peach
peach'y
pea'cock'
pea'fowl' *pl.* -fowl'
  or -fowls'
pea'hen'
peak *(mountain top)*
  ✔ *peek, pique*
peaked *(pointed)*
peak'ed *(sickly)*
peal *(ringing)*
  ✔ *peel*
pea'nut
pear *(fruit)*

✔ *pair, pare*
pearl *(gem)*
  ✔ *purl*
pearl'y
peas'ant
peas'ant·ry
peat
peat' moss'
peb'ble, -bled, -bling
peb'bly
pe·can'
pec·ca·dil'lo *pl.*
  -loes *or* -los
pec'ca·ry
peck
pec'tin
pec'to·ral
pe·cu'liar
pe·cu'li·ar'i·ty
pe·cu'ni·ar'y
ped'a·gog'ic *also*
  ped'a·gog'i·cal
ped'a·gogue'
ped'a·go'gy
ped'al *(to operate a
  lever with the foot)*,
  -aled *or* -alled,
  -al'ing *or* -al·ling
  ✔ *peddle*
ped'ant
pe·dan'tic
ped'ant·ry
ped'dle *(to sell)*,
  -dled, -dling
  ✔ *pedal*
ped'dler
ped'es·tal

pe•des'tri•an
pe'di•at'ric
pe'di•a•tri'cian
pe'di•at'rics
ped'i•cel
ped'i•cure'
ped'i•gree'
ped'i•greed'
ped'i•ment
ped'lar
pe•dom'e•ter
ped'o•phile'
ped'o•phil'i•a
pe•dun'cle
peek *(glance)*
  ✔ *peak, pique*
peel *(skin or rind)*
  ✔ *peal*
peep
peep'er
peep'hole'
peer *(to look)*
  ✔ *pier*
peer *(equal)*
  ✔ *pier*
peer'age
peer'ess
peer'less
peeve, peeved,
  peev'ing
pee'vish
pee'wee *(small
  thing)*
  ✔ *pewee*
peg, pegged,
  peg'ging
peg'board'

peg'ma•tite'
pei•gnoir'
pe•jor'a•tive
Pe•'king•ese' *also*
  Pe'kin•ese' *pl.* -ese'
pe'koe *(tea)*
  ✔ *picot*
pe•lag'ic
pelf
pel'i•can
pe•lisse'
pel•lag'ra
pel'let
pell'-mell' *also*
  pell'mell'
pel•lu'cid
pelt
pel'vic
pel'vis *pl.* -vis•es *or*
  -ves
pem'mi•can
pen *(to write),*
  penned, pen'ning
pen *(to confine),*
  penned *or* pent,
  pen'ning
pe'nal
pe'nal•i•za'tion
pe'nal•ize', -ized',
  -iz'ing
pen'al•ty
pen'ance
pence
pen'chant
pen'cil, -ciled *also*
  -cilled, -cil•ing *also*
  -cil•ling

pen'dant *also*
  pen'dent *n.*
pen'dent *also*
  pen'dant *adj.*
pend'ing
pen'du•lous
pen'du•lum
pen'e•tra•bil'i•ty
pen'e•tra•ble
pen'e•trate',
  -trat'ed, -trat'ing
pen'e•tra'tion
pen'guin
pen'i•cil'lin
pen•in'su•la
pen•in'su•lar
pe'nis *pl.* -nis•es *or*
  -nes
pen'i•tence
pen'i•tent
pen'i•ten'tial
pen'i•ten'tia•ry
pen'knife'
pen'man
pen'man•ship'
pen' name' *or*
  pen'name'
pen'nant
pen'ne *pl.* pen'ne
pen'ni•less
pen'non
Penn'syl•va'nian
pen'ny *(U.S. coin),*
  pl. pen'nies
pen'ny *(British
  coin), pl.* pence *or*
  pen'nies

pen'ny-pinch'ing

pen'ny•roy'al

pen'ny•weight'

pen'ny-wise' *or*
 pen'ny•wise'

pen'ny•worth'

Pe•nob'scot *pl.*
 -scot *or* -scots

pe•nol'o•gist

pe•nol'o•gy

pen'sion *(retirement
 money)*

pen•sion' *(lodging)*

pen'sion•er

pen'sive

pen'stock'

pen'ta•cle

pen'ta•gon'

pen•tag'o•nal

pen•tam'e•ter

Pen'ta•teuch'

pen'tath'lon

pen'ta•ton'ic

Pen'te•cost'

Pen'te•cos'tal

pent'house'

pent'-up' *adj.*

pe•nu'che *also*
 pe•nu'chi

pe'nult'

pe•nul'ti•mate

pe•num'bra *pl.*
 -brae *or* -bras

pe•nu'ri•ous

pen'u•ry

pe'on *(menial
 worker)*

✔ *paean*

pe'on•age

pe'o•ny

peo'ple *pl.* -ple *or*
 -ples

peo'ple, -pled,
 -pling

pep, pepped,
 pep'ping

pep'per

pep'per•corn'

pep'per•mint'

pep'per•o'ni *pl.*
 -nis

pep'per•y

pep'py

pep'sin *also* pep'sine

pep'tic

Pe'quot' *pl.* -quot'
 or -quots'

per

per•am'bu•late',
 -lat'ed, -lat'ing

per•am'bu•la'tion

per•am'bu•la'tor

per an'num

per•cale'

per cap'i•ta

per•ceiv'a•ble

per•ceive', -ceived',
 -ceiv'ing

per•cent' *also*
 per cent'

per•cent'age

per•cen'tile'

per•cep'ti•bil'i•ty

per•cep'ti•ble

per•cep'ti•bly

per•cep'tion

per•cep'tive

per•cep'tu•al

perch *(roost)*

perch *(fish)*, *pl.*
 perch *or* perch'es

per•chance'

per'co•late', -lat'ed,
 -lat'ing

per'co•la'tion

per'co•la'tor

per•cus'sion

per di'em

per•di'tion

per'e•grine

per•emp'to•ri•ly

per•emp'to•ry

per•en'ni•al

per'fect *adj.*

per•fect' *v.*

per•fect'i•bil'i•ty

per•fect'i•ble

per•fec'tion

per•fec'tion•ism

per•fec'tion•ist

per•fid'i•ous

per'fi•dy

per'fo•rate', -rat'ed,
 -rat'ing

per'fo•ra'tion

per•force'

per•form'

per•form'er

per•form'ance

per'fume' *n.*

per•fume', -fumed',

-fum'ing
per·fum'er·y
per·func'to·ri·ly
per·func'to·ry
per·haps'
per·i·car'di·um *pl.*
-di·a
per·i·gee
per·i·he'li·on *pl.*
-li·a
per'il
per'il·ous
pe·rim'e·ter
(*boundary*)
✓ *parameter*
pe'ri·od
pe'ri·od'ic
pe'ri·od'i·cal
pe'ri·o·dic'i·ty
per·i·o·don'tal
per·i·pa·tet'ic
pe·riph'er·al
pe·riph'er·y
per'i·scope'
per'ish
per'ish·a·ble
per·i·stal'sis *pl.* -ses
per·i·stal'tic
per·i·to·ne'al
per·i·to·ne'um *pl.*
-ne'a
per·i·to·ni'tis
per'i·wig'
per'i·win·kle
per·jure, -jured,
-jur·ing
per'jur·er

per'ju·ry
perk (*to stick up*)
perk (*perquisite*)
perk'y
perm
per'ma·frost'
per'ma·nence
per'ma·nen·cy
per'ma·nent
per'ma·nent-
press' *adj.*
per·man'ga·nate'
per'me·a·bil'i·ty
per'me·a·ble
per'me·ate', -at'ed,
-at'ing
per'me·a'tion
Per'mi·an
per·mis'si·ble
per·mis'sion
per·mis'sive
per·mit', -mit'ted,
-mit'ting
per'mit *n.*
per'mu·ta'tion
per·mute', -mut'ed,
-mut'ing
per·ni'cious
per·nick'e·ty
per'o·rate', -rat'ed,
-rat'ing
per'o·ra'tion
per·ox'ide',
-id'ed, -id'ing
per'pen·dic'u·lar
per'pe·trate',
-trat'ed, -trat'ing

per'pe·tra'tion
per'pe·tra'tor
per·pet'u·al
per·pet'u·ate',
-at'ed, -at'ing
per·pet'u·a'tion
per'pe·tu'i·ty
per·plex'
per·plexed'
per·plex'i·ty
per'qui·site (*benefit*)
✓ *prerequisite*
per se'
per'se·cute' (*to ha-
rass*), -cut'ed,
-cut'ing
✓ *prosecute*
per'se·cu'tion
per'se·cu'tor
per'se·ver'ance
per'se·vere',
-vered', -ver'ing
Per'sian
per·sim'mon
per·sist'
per·sist'ence *or*
per·sist'en·cy
per·sist'ent
per·snick'e·ty
per'son
per·so'na *pl.* -nas *or*
-nae
per'son·a·ble
per'son·age
per'son·al (*private*)
✓ *personnel*
per'son·al'i·ty

per'son•al•ize',
  -ized', -iz'ing
per•so'na non
  gra'ta
per•son'i•fi•ca'tion
per•son'i•fy', -fied',
  -fy'ing
per•son•nel' *(em-
  ployees)*
  ✔ *personal*
per•spec'tive *(view)*
  ✔ *prospective*
per•spi•ca'cious
per•spi•cac'i•ty
per•spi•cu'i•ty
per•spi•ra'tion
per•spire', -spired',
  -spir'ing
per•suad'a•ble
per•suade',
  -suad'ed, -suad'ing
per•sua'sion
per•sua'sive
pert
per•tain'
per•ti•na'cious
per•ti•nac'i•ty
per'ti•nence *or*
  per'ti•nen•cy
per'ti•nent
per•turb'
per•tur•ba'tion
pe•ruke'
pe•rus'a•ble
pe•rus•al
pe•ruse', -rused',
  -rus'ing

Pe•ru'vi•an
per•vade', -vad'ed,
  -vad'ing
per•va'sion
per•va'sive
per•verse'
per•ver'sion
per•ver'si•ty
per•vert' *v.*
per'vert' *n.*
per•vert'ed
Pe'sach'
pe•se'ta
pes'ky
pe'so *pl.* -sos
pes'si•mism
pes'si•mist
pes'si•mis'tic
pest
pes'ter
pes'ti•cide'
pes•tif'er•ous
pes'ti•lence
pes'ti•lent
pes'ti•len'tial
pes'tle
pes'to
pet, pet'ted, pet'ting
pet'al
pe•tard'
pet'cock'
pe'ter
pet'i•ole'
pet'it *also* pet'ty
  (lesser)
  ✔ *petty*
pe•tite' *(small)*

pet'it four' *pl.*
  pet'its fours' *or*
  pet'it fours'
pe•ti'tion
pet'it point'
pet'rel *(bird)*
  ✔ *petrol*
pe'tri dish'
pet'ri•fac'tion *also*
  pet'ri•fi•ca'tion
pet'ri•fy', -fied',
  -fy'ing
pet'ro•chem'i•cal
pe•trog'ra•phy
pet'rol *(gasoline)*
  ✔ *petrel*
pet'ro•la'tum
pe•tro'le•um
pe•trol'o•gy
pet'ti•coat'
pet'ti•fog'ger
pet'tish
pet'ti•ness
pet'ty *(trivial)*
  ✔ *petit*
pet'ty of'fi•cer
pet'u•lance
pet'u•lant
pe•tu'nia
pew
pe'wee *also* pee'wee
  (bird)
  ✔ *peewee*
pew'ter
pfen'nig
pH
pha'e•ton

phag'o•cyte'
pha•lanx' *pl.*
　-lanx'es *or*
　pha•lan'ges
phal'lic
phal'lus
phan'tasm
phan•tas'mal *or*
　phan•tas'mic
phan'tom
Phar'aoh
phar'i•see
phar'ma•ceu'ti•cal
　also phar'ma•ceu'-
　tic
phar'ma•ceu'tics
phar'ma•cist
phar'ma•col'o•gy
phar'ma•co•poe'ia
　also phar'ma•co•
　pe'ia
phar'ma•cy
pha•ryn'ge•al
phar'ynx *pl.*
　phar•ryn'ges *or*
　phar'ynx•es
phase *(to plan in
　stages)*, phased,
　phas'ing
　✔ *faze*
pheas'ant *pl.* -ants
　or -ant
phe'no•bar'bi•tal'
phe'nol'
phe'nol•phthal'-
　ein'
phe•nom'e•nal

phe•nom'e•non'
　pl. -na *also* -nons'
phe'no•type'
phen'yl
phi
phi'al
Phil'a•del'phi•an
phi•lan'der
phil'an•throp'ic
phi•lan'thro•pist
phi•lan'thro•py
phil'a•tel'ic
phi•lat'e•list
phi•lat'e•ly
phil'har•mon'ic
　also Phil'har•
　mon'ic
phi•lip'pic
Phil'ip•pine'
Phil'is•tine
phil'o•den'dron *pl.*
　-drons *or* -dra
phi•lol'o•gist
phi•lol'o•gy
phi•los'o•pher
phil'o•soph'i•cal
　also phil'o•soph'ic
phi•los'o•phize',
　-phized', -phiz'ing
phi•los'o•phy
phil'ter *also* phil'tre
　(magic potion)
　✔ *filter*
phle•bi'tis
phle•bot'o•mist
phle•bot'o•my
phlegm

phleg•mat'ic
phlo'em
phlox *pl.* phlox *or*
　phlox'es
pho'bi•a
phoe'be
Phoe•ni'cian
phoe'nix
phone, phoned,
　phon'ing
pho'neme'
pho•ne'mic
pho•net'ic
pho•ne•ti'cian
pho•net'ics
phon'ic
phon'ics
pho'ni•ness
pho'no•graph'
pho'no•graph'ic
pho'ny *also*
　pho'ney *pl.* -nies
　also -neys
phooey
phos'phate'
phos'phor
phos'pho•res'-
　cence
phos'pho•res'cent
phos•phor'ic
phos'pho•rous *adj.*
phos'pho•rus *n.*
pho'to *pl.* -tos
pho'to•cell'
pho'to•cop'i•er
pho'to•cop'y,
　-cop'ied, -cop'y•ing

pho'to•e•lec'tric
also pho'to•e•lec'-
tri•cal

pho'to•e•lec'tron'

pho'to•en•grave',
-graved', -grav'ing

pho'to•es'say' also
pho'to•es'say'

pho'to•gen'ic

pho'to•graph'

pho•tog'ra•pher

pho'to•graph'ic

pho•tog'ra•phy

pho'to•gra•vure'

pho'to•jour'nal•
ism

pho'to•me•chan'-
i•cal

pho•tom'e•ter

pho•tom'e•try

pho'to•mi'cro•
graph'

pho'to•mon•tage'

pho'ton'

pho'to•re•cep'tive

pho'to•re•cep'tor

pho'to•sen'si•tive

pho'to•sen'si•tiv'-
i•ty

pho'to•sen'si•tize',
-tized', -tiz'ing

pho'to•sphere'

pho'to•syn'the•sis

pho'to•syn'the•
size', -sized',
-siz'ing

pho•tot'ro•pism

phras'al

phrase, phrased,
phras'ing

phra'se•ol'o•gy

phre•nol'o•gy

phy•lac'ter•y

phy'lum pl. -la

phys'ic (to act as a
cathartic), -icked,
-ick'ing
✔ physique, psychic

phys'i•cal

phy•si'cian

phys'i•cist

phys'ics

phys'i•og'no•my

phys'i•o•log'i•cal

phys'i•ol'o•gist

phys'i•ol'o•gy

phys'i•o•ther'-
a•py

phy•sique' (body)
✔ physic

pi (Greek letter), pl.
pis
✔ pie

pi'a•nis'si•mo'

pi•an'ist

pi•an'o (instrument),
pl. -os

pi•a'no (musical
direction)

pi•an'o•for'te

pi•az'za pl. -zas also
-ze

pi'ca (type size)
✔ pika

pic'a•dor' pl. -dors'
or pic'a•do'res

pic'a•resque'

pic'a•yune'

pic•ca•lil'li pl. -lis

pic'co•lo' pl. -los'

pick

pick'ax' or pick'axe'

pick'er•el pl. -el or
-els

pick'et

pick'le, -led, -ling

pick'-me-up' n.

pick'pock'et

pick'up' n.

pick'y

pic'nic, -nicked,
-nick•ing

pic'nick•er

pi'cot (loop)
✔ pekoe

pic'ric ac'id

Pict

pic'to•gram'

pic'to•graph'

pic•tog'ra•phy

pic•to'ri•al

pic'ture

pic'tur•esque'

pid'dling

pidg'in (form of
speech)
✔ pigeon

pie (pastry)
✔ pi

pie'bald'

piece (to join parts

of), pieced,
piec•ing
✔ *peace*
pièce de ré•sis•
tance′ *pl.* pièces
de ré•sis•tance′
piece′meal′
piece′ of eight′ *pl.*
piec′es of eight′
piece′work′
pied
pier *(dock)*
✔ *peer*
pierce, pierced,
pierc′ing
pi′e•ty
pi•e′zo•e•lec•tric′-
i•ty
pig
pi′geon *(bird)*
✔ *pidgin*
pi′geon•hole′,
-holed′, -hol′ing
pi′geon-toed′
pig′gish
pig′gy•back′
pig′gy bank′
pig′head•ed
pig′let
pig′ment
pig′men•ta′tion
Pig′my
pig′pen′
pig′skin′
pig′sty′
pig′tail′
pi′ka *(animal)*

✔ *pica*
pike *(spear, turnpike)*
pike *(fish), pl.* pike *or*
pikes
pike′staff′
pi′laf′ *or* pi′laff′
pi•las′ter
pile *(to heap),* piled,
pil′ing
pile *(beam, loop of*
yarn)
piles
pile′up′ *or*
pile′-up′ *n.*
pil′fer
pil′grim
pil′grim•age
pil′ing
pill
pil′lage, -laged,
-lag•ing
pil′lag•er
pil′lar
pill′box′
pil′lion
pil′lo•ry, -ried,
-ry•ing
pil′low
pil′low•case′
pil′low•slip′
pi′lot
pi′lot•house′
Pi′ma *pl.* -ma *or*
-mas
pi•mien′to *also*
pi•men′to *pl.* -tos
pim′per•nel′

pim′ple
pim′ply
pin, pinned,
pin′ning
pi′ña co•la′da
pin′a•fore′
pi•ña′ta
pin′ball′
pince′-nez′ *pl.*
pince′-nez′
pin′cers *also*
pinch′ers
pinch
pinch′-hit′, -hit′,
-hit′ting
pinch′ hit′ *n.*
pinch′ hit′ter
pin′cush′ion
pine, pined, pin′ing
pin′e•al
pine′ap′ple
pin′feath′er
pin′head′
pin′hole′
pin′ion *(wing, gear-*
wheel)
✔ *piñon*
pink′eye′
pink′ie *also* pink′y
pink′ing shears′
pin′nace
pin′na•cle
pin′nate′
pi′noch′le *or*
pi′noc′le *also*
pe′nuch′le *or*
pe′nuck′le

pi′ñon′ *also*
  pin′yon′ *(tree) pl.*
  -ñons′ *or* pi•ño′nes
  also -yons
  ✔ *pinion*

pin′point′

pin′prick′

pin′scher

pin′stripe′

pint

pin′to *pl.* -tos *or*
  -toes

pin′to bean′

pint′size′ *also*
  pint′sized′

pin′wale′

pin′wheel′

pin′worm′

pin′y *also* pine′y

Pin′yin′ *or* pin′yin′

pi′o•neer′

pi′ous

pip, pipped, pip′ping

pipe, piped, pip′ing

pipe′line′, -lined′,
  -lin′ing

pip′er

pi•pette′ *(glass tube)*

pip′it *(bird)*

pip′pin

pip′-squeak′

pi′quan•cy *or*
  pi′quant•ness

pi′quant

pique *(to provoke),*
  piqued, piqu′ing
  ✔ *peak, peek*

pi•qué′ *(fabric)*

pi•quet′ *also*
  pic•quet′ *(card
  game)*

pi′ra•cy

pi•ra′nha *also*
  pi•ra′ña

pi′rate, -rat•ed,
  -rat•ing

pi•rogue′

pir′ou•ette′, -et′ted,
  -et′ting

pis′ca•to′ri•al *or*
  pis′ca•to′ry

pis•ta′chi•o′ *pl.* -os′

pis′til *(flower organ)*
  ✔ *pistol*

pis′til•late′

pis′tol *(gun)*
  ✔ *pistil*

pis′ton

pit, pit′ted, pit′ting

pi′ta

pit′a•pat′, -pat′ted,
  -pat′ting

pitch

pitch′-black′

pitch′blende′

pitch′-dark′

pitch′er

pitch′fork′

pitch′out′

pit′e•ous

pit′fall′

pith

pith′ hel′met

pith′y

pit′i•a•ble

pit′i•ful

pit′i•less

pit′tance

pit′ter-pat′ter

pi•tu′i•tar′y

pit′y, -ied, -y•ing

piv′ot

piv′ot•al

pix′el

pix′y *or* pix′ie

piz′za

piz•zazz′ *or* piz•zaz′

piz′ze•ri′a

piz′zi•ca′to

plac′ard

pla•cate′, -cat′ed,
  -cat′ing

pla′cat′er

pla•ca′tion

place *(to set),* placed,
  plac′ing
  ✔ *plaice*

pla•ce′bo *pl.* -bos *or*
  -boes

place′hold′er

place′kick′ *v.*

place′-kick′er

place′ mat′

place′ment

pla•cen′ta *pl.* -tas *or*
  -tae

pla•cen′tal

plac′id

pla•cid′i•ty

plack′et

pla′gia•rism

pla'gia·rist

pla'gia·rize',
  -rized', -riz'ing

plague, plagued,
  plagu'ing

plaice (*fish*), pl.
  plaice or plaic'es
  ✔ place

plaid

plain (*clear, simple*)
  ✔ plane

plain (*flat, treeless
  area*)
  ✔ plane

plain'chant'

plain'clothes'
  man or
  plain'clothes'man

plain'song'

plain'spo'ken

plaint

plain'tiff

plain'tive

plait (*braid, to braid*)
  ✔ plat, plate

plan, planned
  plan'ning

pla'nar (*flat*)
  ✔ planer

pla·nar'i·an

plane (*surface, air-
  plane, tool, tree*)
  ✔ plain

plane (*to smooth
  with a plane*),
  planed, plan'ing
  ✔ plain

plan'er (*one that
  planes*)
  ✔ planar

plan'et

plan'e·tar'i·um pl.
  -i·ums or -i·a

plan'e·tar'y

plan'e·toid'

plank

plank'ton

plan'ner

plant

plan'tain

plan'tar (*relating to
  the sole of the foot*)
  ✔ planter

plan·ta'tion

plant'er (*one that
  plants*)
  ✔ plantar

plaque

plash

plas'ma also plasm

plas·mo'di·um pl.
  -di·a

plas'ter

plas'ter·board'

plas'ter·work'

plas'tic

plas·tic'i·ty

plas'tid

plat (*braid, to braid*),
  plat'ted, plat'ting
  ✔ plait

plate (*to coat*),
  plat'ed, plat'ing
  ✔ plait

pla·teau' pl. -teaus'
  or -teaux'

plate'ful'

plate'let

plat'en

plat'form'

plat'i·num

plat'i·tude'

plat'i·tu'di·nous

Pla·ton'ic

Pla'to·nism

pla·toon'

plat'ter

plat'y·pus pl.
  -pus·es

plau'dit

plau'si·ble

plau'si·bil'i·ty

plau'si·bly

play

pla'ya

play'a·ble

play'-act'

play'back' n.

play'bill'

play'book'

play'boy'

play'-by-play'

play'er

play'ful

play'girl'

play'go'er

play'ground'

play'house'

play'mate'

play'off' n.

play'pen'

play'room'
play'thing'
play'wright'
pla'za
plea
plea'-bar'gain v.
plead, plead'ed or
  pled, plead'ing
pleas'ant
pleas'ant•ry
please, pleased,
  pleas'ing
pleas'ur•a•ble
pleas'ur•a•bly
pleas'ure
pleat
plebe *also* pleb
ple•be'ian
pleb'i•scite'
plec'trum *pl.*
  -trums *or* -tra
pledge, pledged,
  pledg'ing
Pleis'to•cene'
ple'na•ry
plen'i•po•ten'ti•
  ar'y
plen'i•tude'
plen'te•ous
plen'ti•ful
plen'ty
ple'num *pl.* -nums
  or -na
ple'si•o•saur' *also*
  ple'si•o•sau'rus
pleth'o•ra
pleu'ra *pl.* -rae

pleu'ral
pleu'ri•sy
plex'us *pl.* -us *or*
  -us•es
pli'a•bil'i•ty *or*
  pli'a•ble•ness
pli'a•ble
pli'an•cy
pli'ant
pli•é'
pli'ers
plight
plinth
Pli'o•cene'
plod, plod'ded,
  plod'ding
plod'der
plop, plopped,
  plop'ping
plot, plot'ted,
  plot'ting
plot'ter
plov'er *pl.* -er *or* -ers
plow *also* plough
plow'man
plow'share'
ploy
pluck'y
plug, plugged,
  plug'ging
plug'ger
plum *(fruit)*
  ✔ *plumb*
plum'age
plumb *(weight)*
  ✔ *plum*
plumb'er

plumb'ing
plumb' line'
plume, plumed,
  plum'ing
plum'met
plump
plun'der
plun'der•er
plunge, plunged,
  plung'ing
plung'er
plunk
plu•per'fect
plu'ral
plu•ral'i•ty
plus *pl.* plus'es *or*
  plus'ses
plush
plu•toc'ra•cy
plu'to•crat'ic
Plu•to'ni•an *also*
  Plu•ton'ic *(relating
  to Pluto)*
plu•to'ni•um
  (element)
plu•vi•al
ply, plied, ply'ing
ply'wood'
pneu•mat'ic
pneu•mo'nia
poach
poach'er
pock *(pustule, scar)*
  ✔ *pox*
pock'et
pock'et•book'
pock'et•ful' *pl.*

pock′et•fuls′ *or*
pock′ets•ful′
pock′et-knife′
pock′et-sized′ *or*
pock′et•size′
pock′mark′
po′co
pod
po•di′a•trist
po•di′a•try
po′di•um *pl.* -di•a *or*
-di•ums
po′em
po′e•sy
po′et
po•et′ic
po•et′i•cal
po′et lau′re•ate *pl.*
po′ets lau′re•ate *or*
po′et lau′re•ates
po′et•ry
po′go stick′
po•grom′
poi
poign′an•cy
poign′ant
poin•set′ti•a
point
point′-blank′
point′ed
point′er
poin′til•lism
poin′til•list
point′less
poise, poised,
pois′ing
poi′son

poi′son•er
poi′son•ous
poke, poked, pok′ing
pok′er
pok′er•faced′
po′key *(jail), pl.*
-keys
pok′y *also* poke′y
(slow)
po′lar
po•lar′i•ty
po′lar•i•za′tion
po′lar•ize′, -ized′,
-iz′ing
pole *(axis point, rod)*
✔ poll
pole *(to propel with a*
pole), poled,
pol′ing
✔ poll
Pole *(inhabitant of*
Poland)
✔ poll
pole′ax′ *or* pole′axe′
pole′cat′
po•lem′ic
po•len′ta
pole′star′
pole′-vault′ *v.*
pole′-vault′er
po•lice′ *pl.* po•lice′
po•lice′, -liced′,
-lic′ing
po•lice′man
po•lice′wom′an
pol′i•cy
pol′i•cy•hold′er

po′li•o′
po′li•o•my′e•li′tis
pol′ish *(to shine)*
Po′lish *(relating to*
Poland)
po•lite′, -lit′er,
-lit′est
pol′i•tic *(shrewd)*
✔ politick
po•lit′i•cal
pol′i•ti′cian
pol′i•tick *(to talk*
politics)
✔ politic
pol′i•tics
pol′i•ty
pol′ka
poll *(casting of votes)*
✔ pole, Pole
pol′len
pol′li•nate′,
-li•nat′ed,
-li•nat′ing
pol′li•na′tion
pol′li•na′tor
pol′li•wog′ *also*
pol′ly•wog′
poll′ster
pol•lut′ant
pol•lute′, -lut′ed,
-lut′ing
pol•lu′tion
po′lo
pol′o•naise′
po•lo′ni•um
pol′ter•geist′
pol•troon′

pol′y·an′drous
pol′y·an′dry
pol′y·chro·mat′ic
  also pol′y·chro′mic
  or pol′y·chro′mous
pol′y·chrome′
pol′y·es′ter
pol′y·eth′yl·ene′
po·lyg′a·mist
po·lyg′a·mous
po·lyg′a·my
pol′y·glot′
pol′y·gon′
po·lyg′o·nal
pol′y·graph′
pol′y·he′dron *pl.*
  -drons *or* -dra
pol′y·mer
pol′y·mer′ic
po·lym′er·i·za′-
  tion
pol′y·mer·ize′,
  -ized′, -iz′ing
Pol′y·ne′sian
pol′y·no′mi·al
pol′yp
pol′y·phon′ic
po·lyph′o·ny
pol′y·sac′cha·ride′
  also pol′y·sac′cha·
  rid *or* pol′y·sac′-
  cha·rose′
pol′y·sty′rene
pol′y·syl·lab′ic
pol′y·syl′la·ble
pol′y·tech′nic
pol′y·the·ism

pol′y·the′ist
pol′y·the·is′tic
pol′y·un·sat′u·
  rat′ed
pol′y·u′re·thane′
pol′y·va′lence *or*
  pol′y·va′len·cy
pol′y·va′lent
po·made′
pome′gran′ate
Pom′er·a′ni·an
pom′mel *(to beat
  up),* -meled *also*
  -melled, -mel·ing
  also -mel·ling
  ✔ *pummel*
pom′mel *(part of
  saddle)*
  ✔ *pummel*
pomp
pom′pa·dour′
pom′pa·no′ *pl.* -no′
  or -nos′
pom′pon′ *or*
  pom′pom′
pom·pos′i·ty *or*
  pom′pous·ness
pom′pous
pon′cho *pl.* -chos
pond
pon′der
pon′der·ous
pon·gee′
pon′iard
pon′tiff
pon·tif′i·cal
pon·tif′i·cate′,

-cat′ed, -cat′ing
pon·toon′
po′ny
po′ny·tail′
pooch
poo′dle
pooh
pooh′-pooh′ *v.*
pool
pool′room′
pool′side′
poop
poor
poor′house′
pop, popped,
  pop′ping
pop′corn′
pope *or* Pope
pop′gun′
pop′in·jay′
pop′lar
pop′lin
pop′o′ver
pop′py
pop′py·cock′
pop′-top′
pop′u·lace *(general
  public)*
  ✔ *populous*
pop′u·lar
pop′u·lar′i·ty
pop′u·lar·i·za′tion
pop′u·lar·ize′,
  -ized′, -iz′ing
pop′u·late′, -lat′ed,
  -lat′ing
pop′u·la′tion

pop'u·list
pop'u·lous (*thickly settled*)
  ✔ populace
por'ce·lain
porch
por'cine'
por'cu·pine'
pore (*to study*),
  pored, por'ing
  ✔ pour
pore (*tiny opening*)
  ✔ pour
por'gy *pl.* -gy *or* -gies
pork
pork'er
pork'pie'
por·nog'ra·pher
por·no·graph'ic
por·nog'ra·phy
po·ros'i·ty
po'rous
por'phy·ry
por'poise *pl.* -poise
  or -pois·es
por'ridge
por'rin·ger
port
port'a·ble
port'age, -aged,
  -ag·ing
por'tal
port·cul'lis
por·tend'
por'tent'
por·ten'tous
por'ter

por'ter·house'
port·fo'li·o' *pl.* -os'
port'hole'
por'ti·co' *pl.* -coes'
  or -cos'
por'tion
port'li·ness
port'ly
por'trait
por'trait·ist
por'trai·ture'
por·tray'
por·tray'al
Por'tu·guese' *pl.*
  -guese'
pose, posed, pos'ing
pos'er (*one that
  poses, problem*)
po·seur' (*affected
  person*)
posh
pos'it
po·si'tion
pos'i·tive
pos'i·tiv·ism
pos'i·tiv·ist
pos'i·tron'
pose'se
pos·sess'
pos·sessed'
pos·ses'sion
pos·ses'sive
pos·ses'sor
pos·si·bil'i·ty
pos'si·ble
pos'si·bly
pos'sum

post
post'age
post'al
post' card' *also*
  post'card'
post·date', -dat'ed,
  -dat'ing
post'er
pos·te'ri·or
pos·ter'i·ty
pos'tern
post·grad'u·ate
post·haste'
post'hu·mous
post'hyp·not'ic
pos·til'ion *also*
  pos·til'lion
post'im·pres'sion·
  ism
post'im·pres'sion·
  ist
post'in·dus'tri·al
post'man
post'mark'
post'mas'ter
post'me·rid'i·an
  (*in the afternoon*)
post' me·rid'i·em
  (*after noon*)
post'mis'tress
post·mod'ern *or*
  post-mod'ern
post·mod'ern·ism
post·mod'ern·ist
post·mor'tem
post·na'sal
post·na'tal

post•op′er•a•tive

post′paid′

post•par′tum

post•pone′,
-poned′, -pon′ing

post•pone′ment

post′script′

post′trau•mat′ic

pos′tu•lant

pos′tu•late′, -lat′ed,
-lat′ing

pos′tu•la′tion

pos′tu•la′tor

pos′ture, -tured,
-tur•ing

post′war′

po′sy

pot, pot′ted, pot′ting

po′ta•ble

pot′ash′

po•tas′si•um

po•ta′tion

po•ta′to pl. -toes

Pot′a•wat′o•mi pl.
-mi or -mis

pot′bel′lied

pot′bel′ly

pot′boil′er

pot′bound′

po′ten•cy

po′tent

po′ten•tate′

po•ten′tial

po•ten′ti•al′i•ty

po•ten′ti•om′e•ter

pot′herb′

pot′hold′er

pot′hole′

pot′hook′

po′tion

pot′latch′

pot′luck′

pot′pie′

pot′pour•ri′ pl. -ris

pot′sherd′ also
pot′shard′

pot′shot′ also
pot′ shot′

pot′tage

pot′ted

pot′ter

pot′ter•y

pouch

poul′tice

poul′try

pounce, pounced,
pounc′ing

pound pl. pound or
pounds

pound v.

pound′-fool′ish

pour (to flow)
✔ pore

pout

pov′er•ty

pov′er•ty-strick′en

POW pl. POW's also
POWs

pow′der

pow′der•y

pow′er

pow′er•boat′

pow′er•ful

pow′er•house′

pow′er•less

Pow•ha•tan′ pl.
-tan′ or -tans′

pow′wow′

pox (disease)
✔ pock

prac′ti•ca•bil′i•ty

prac′ti•ca•ble
(possible)

prac′ti•cal (useful,
sensible)

prac′ti•cal′i•ty

prac′ti•cal•ly

prac′tice, -ticed,
-tic•ing

prac•ti′tion•er

prae′tor

prae•to′ri•an

prag•mat′ic

prag′ma•tism

prag′ma•tist

prai′rie

praise, praised,
prais′ing

praise′wor′thy

pra′line′

pram

prance, pranced,
pranc′ing

prank

prank′ster

pra′se•o•dym′i•um

prate, prat′ed,
prat′ing

prat′fall′

prat′tle, -tled, -tling

prawn

pray *(to say a prayer)*
  ✔ prey
prayer *(petition)*
pray'er *(person who prays)*
preach
preach'er
preach'y
pre•ad•o•les'cence
pre•ad•o•les'cent
pre•am'ble
pre•am'pli•fi•er
pre•ar•range',
  -ranged', -rang'ing
Pre•cam'bri•an
pre•car'i•ous
pre•cau'tion
pre•cau'tion•ar'y
pre•cede' *(to come before)*, -ced'ed,
  -ced'ing
  ✔ proceed
prec'e•dence
prec'e•dent *(prior example)*
  ✔ president
pre•ced'ing
pre'cept'
pre•cep'tor
pre•ces'sion *(precedence, axial movement)*
  ✔ procession
pre'cinct'
pre'cious
prec'i•pice
pre•cip'i•tate',

-tat'ed, -tat'ing
pre•cip'i•tate
  (hasty)
  ✔ precipitous
pre•cip'i•ta'tion
pre•cip'i•tous
  (steep)
  ✔ precipitate
pre•cise'
pre•ci'sion
pre•clude',
  -clud'ed, -clud'ing
pre•co'cious
pre•co'cious•ness
  or pre•coc'i•ty
pre'-Co•lum'bi•an
pre•con•ceive',
  -ceived', -ceiv'ing
pre'con•cep'tion
pre'con•di'tion
pre•cur'sor
pre•date', -dat'ed,
  -dat'ing
pred'a•tor
pred'a•to'ry
pre•de•cease',
  -ceased', -ceas'ing
pred'e•ces'sor
pre•des'ti•na'tion
pre•des'tine,
  -tined, -tin•ing
pre•de•ter'mi•na'-
  tion
pre•de•ter'mine,
  -mined, -min•ing
pre•dic'a•ment
pred'i•cate',

-cat'ed, -cat'ing
pred'i•ca'tion
pred'i•ca'tive
pre•dict'
pre•dict'a•ble
pre•dic'tion
pred'i•lec'tion
pre'dis•pose',
  -posed', -pos'ing
pre'dis•po•si'tion
pre•dom'i•nance
pre•dom'i•nant
pre•dom'i•nate',
  -nat'ed, -nat'ing
pree'mie
pre•em'i•nence
pre•em'i•nent *or*
  pre-em'i•nent
pre•empt' *or*
  pre-empt'
pre•emp'tion *or*
  pre-emp'tion
pre•emp'tive *or*
  pre-emp'tive
pre•emp'to•ry *or*
  pre-emp'to•ry
preen
pre'ex•ist' *or*
  pre'-ex•ist'
pre'fab'
pre•fab'ri•cate',
  -cat'ed, -cat'ing
pre•fab'ri•ca'tion
pref'ace, -aced,
  -ac'ing
pref'a•to'ry
pre'fect'

pre′fec′ture

pre•fer′, -ferred′, -fer′ring

pref′er•a•ble

pref′er•a•bly

pref′er•ence

pref′er•en′tial

pre•fer′ment

pre•fig′ure, -ured, -ur•ing

pre•fix′ v.

pre′fix′ n.

pre′flight′

preg′nan•cy

preg′nant

pre•heat′

pre•hen′sile

pre•his•tor′ic *also* pre′his•tor′i•cal

pre•his′to•ry

pre•judge′, -judged′, -judg′ing

prej′u•dice, -diced, -dic•ing

prej′u•di′cial

prel′ate

pre′law′

pre•lim′i•nar′y

prel′ude′, -ud′ed, -ud′ing

pre•mar′i•tal

pre′ma•ture′

pre′med′

pre•med′i•cal

pre•med′i•tate′, -tat′ed, -tat′ing

pre•med′i•ta′tion

pre•mier′ *(first in importance, prime minister)*

pre•miere′ *(first performance)*

prem′ise, -ised, -is•ing

pre′mi•um

pre•mo′lar

pre′mo•ni′tion

pre•na′tal

pre•nup′tial

pre•oc′cu•pa′tion

pre•oc′cu•py′, -pied′, -py′ing

pre′or•dain′

prep

pre•pack′age, -aged, -ag•ing

prep′a•ra′tion

pre•par′a•to′ry

pre•pare′, -pared′, -par′ing

pre•par′ed•ness

pre•pay′, -paid′, -pay′ing

pre•pon′der•ance

pre•pon′der•ant

pre•pon′der•ate′, -at′ed, -at•ing

prep′o•si′tion

prep′o•si′tion•al

pre•pos•sess′ing

pre•pos•ses′sion

pre•pos′ter•ous

prep′py *or* prep′pie *pl.* -pies

pre′puce′

Pre-Raph′a•el•ite′ *also* pre-Raph′a•el•ite′

pre•req′ui•site *(prior requirement)* ✔ perquisite

pre•rog′a•tive

pres′age n.

pre•sage′, -saged′, -sag′ing

pres′by•ter

Pres′by•te′ri•an

pres′by•te′ri•an•ism

pres′by•ter′y

pre′school′

pre′sci•ence

pre′sci•ent

pre•scribe′ *(to impose, to order),* -scribed′, -scrib′ing ✔ proscribe

pre•scrip′tion

pre•scrip′tive

pres′ence

pres′ent n.

pre•sent′ v.

pre•sent′a•bil′i•ty

pre•sent′a•ble

pres′en•ta′tion

pres′ent-day′

pre•sen′ti•ment *(premonition)* ✔ presentment

pres′ent•ly

pre•sent′ment *(presentation)*

✔ *presentiment*
pres′er•va′tion
pre•ser′va•tive
pre•serve′, -served′,
　-serv′ing
pre•serv′er
pre•set′, -set′,
　-set′ting
pre′shrunk′
pre•side′, -sid′ed,
　-sid′ing
pres′i•den•cy
pres′i•dent (*chief
　officer*)
　✔ *precedent*
pres′i•dent-e•lect′
　pl. pres′i•dents-
　e•lect′
pres′i•den′tial
pre•si′di•o′
pre•sid′i•um *pl.* -i•a
　or -i•ums
pre•soak′
pre•sort′
press
press′ing
press′room′
press′run′
pres′sure, -sured,
　-sur•ing
pres′sur•i•za′tion
pres′sur•ize′, -ized′,
　-iz′ing
pres′ti•dig′i•ta′tion
pres′ti•dig′i•ta′tor
pres•tige′
pres•ti′gious

pres•tis′si•mo′
pres′to
pre•sum′a•ble
pre•sum′a•bly
pre•sume′ (*to sup-
　pose, to dare*),
　-sumed′, -sum′ing
　✔ *assume*
pre•sum′ed•ly
pre•sump′tion
pre•sump′tive
pre•sump′tu•ous
pre′sup•pose′,
　-posed′, -pos′ing
pre′sup′po•si′tion
pre′teen′
pre•tend′
pre•tend′er
pre•tense′
pre•ten′sion
pre•ten′tious
pret′er•it *or*
　pret′er•ite
pre′term′
pre′ter•nat′u•ral
pre′text′
pre•tri′al
pret′ti•fy′, -fied′,
　-fy′ing
pret′ti•ly
pret′ti•ness
pret′ty, -tied, -ty•ing
pret′zel
pre•vail′
prev′a•lence
prev′a•lent
pre•var′i•cate′,

　-cat′ed, -cat′ing
pre•var′i•ca′tion
pre•var′i•ca′tor
pre•vent′
pre•vent′a•ble *or*
　pre•vent′i•ble
pre•ven′tion
pre•ven′tive *also*
　pre•ven′ta•tive
pre′view′ *also*
　pre′vue′
pre′vi•ous
pre′war′
prey (*quarry, victim*)
　✔ *pray*
price, priced,
　pric′ing
prick
prick′le, -led, -ling
prick′ly
pride, prid′ed,
　prid′ing
pri′er *also* pry′er
　(*one that pries*)
　✔ *prior*
priest
priest′ess
priest′hood′
prig
prig′gish
prim, prim′mer,
　prim′mest
pri′ma•cy
pri′ma don′na
pri′mal
pri′mar′i•ly
pri′mar′y

pri′mate′
pri′ma•ve′ra
prime, primed,
  prim′ing
prim′er *(elementary
  textbook)*
prim′er *(one that
  primes)*
prime′-time′ *adj.*
pri•me′val
prim′i•tive
pri′mo•gen′i•tor
pri′mo•gen′i•ture
pri•mor′di•al
primp
prim′rose′
prince
prince′dom
prince′ly
prin′cess
prin′ci•pal *(chief,
  money)*
  ✓ principle
prin′ci•pal′i•ty
prin′ci•ple *(doctrine)*
  ✓ principal
print
print′er
print′ing
print′out′
pri′or *(before)*
  ✓ prier
pri′or *(monk)*
  ✓ prier
pri′or•ess
pri•or′i•tize′,

-tized′, -tiz′ing
pri•or′i•ty
pri′or•y
prism
pris•mat′ic
pris′on
pris′on•er
pris′sy
pris′tine′
pri′va•cy
pri′vate
pri′va•teer′
pri•va′tion
priv′et
priv′i•lege
priv′i•leged
priv′i•ly
priv′y
prize, prized, priz′ing
prize′fight′
prize′fight′er
prize′win′ning
pro *pl.* pros
pro•ac′tive *or*
  pro-ac′tive
prob′a•bil′i•ty
prob′a•ble
prob′a•bly
pro′bate′, -bat′ed,
  -bat′ing
pro•ba′tion
pro•ba′tion•ar′y
probe, probed,
  prob′ing
pro′bi•ty
prob′lem

prob′lem•at′ic *also*
  prob′lem•at′i•cal
pro•bos′cis *pl.*
  -cis•es *or* -ci•des′
pro•caine′
pro•ce′dur•al
pro•ce′dure
pro•ceed′ *(to go for-
  ward)*
  ✓ precede
pro•ceed′ing
pro•ceeds′
proc′ess′
pro•ces′sion
  (parade)
  ✓ precession
pro•ces′sion•al
pro-choice′
pro•claim′
proc′la•ma′tion
pro•cliv′i•ty
pro•con′sul
pro•con′su•lar
pro•cras′ti•nate′,
  -nat′ed, -nat′ing
pro•cras′ti•na′tion
pro•cras′ti•na′tor
pro•cre•ate′, -at′ed,
  -at′ing
pro′cre•a′tion
proc•tol′o•gist
proc•tol′o•gy
proc′tor
proc′u•ra′tor
pro•cure′, -cured′,
  -cur′ing

pro•cure′ment
prod, prod′ded,
　prod′ding
prod′der
prod′i•gal
prod′i•gal′i•ty
pro•di′gious
prod′i•gy
pro•duce′, -duced′,
　-duc′ing
pro′duce′ *n.*
pro•duc′er
pro•duc′i•ble *or*
　pro•duce′a•ble
prod′uct
pro•duc′tion
pro•duc′tive
pro′duc•tiv′i•ty *or*
　pro•duc′tive•ness
prof′a•na′tion
pro•fane′, -faned′,
　-fan′ing
pro•fan′i•ty
pro•fess′
pro•fes′sion
pro•fes′sion•al
pro•fes′sor
pro′fes•so′ri•al
prof′fer
pro•fi′cien•cy
pro•fi′cient
pro′file′, -filed′,
　-fil′ing
prof′it *(gain)*
　✓ *prophet*
prof′it•a•ble

prof′it•eer′
prof′li•ga•cy
prof′li•gate
pro•found′
pro•fun′di•ty
pro•fuse′
pro•fu′sion
pro•gen′i•tor
prog′e•ny *pl.* -ny *or*
　-nies
pro•ges′ter•one′
prog•no′sis *pl.* -ses
prog•nos′tic
prog•nos′ti•cate′,
　-cat′ed, -cat′ing
prog•nos′ti•ca′tion
prog•nos′ti•ca′tor
pro′gram′,
　-grammed′ *or*
　-gramed′,
　-gram′ming *or*
　-gram′ing
pro′gram•mat′ic
pro′gram′mer *or*
　pro′gram′er
prog′ress *n.*
pro•gress′ *v.*
pro•gres′sion
pro•gres′sive
pro•hib′it
pro′hi•bi′tion
pro′hi•bi′tion•ist
pro•hib′i•tive *also*
　pro•hib′i•to′ry
proj′ect *n.*
pro•ject′ *v.*

pro•jec′tile
pro•jec′tion
pro•jec′tion•ist
pro•jec′tor
pro′le•tar′i•an
pro′le•tar′i•at
pro-life′
pro•lif′er•ate′,
　-at′ed, -at′ing
pro•lif′er•a′tion
pro•lif′ic
pro′lix′
pro•lix′i•ty
pro′logue′
pro•long′
pro′lon•ga′tion
prom
prom′e•nade′,
　-nad′ed, -nad′ing
pro•me′thi•um
prom′i•nence
prom′i•nent
prom′is•cu′i•ty
pro•mis′cu•ous
prom′ise, -ised,
　-is′ing
prom′is•so′ry
prom′on•to′ry
pro•mote′,
　-mot′ed, -mot′ing
pro•mo′tion
pro•mo′tion•al
prompt
prompt′er
prom′ul•gate′,
　-gat′ed, -gat′ing

prom'ul·ga'tion
prone
prong'horn' pl.
  -horn' or -horns'
pro·nom'i·nal
pro'noun'
pro·nounce',
  -nounced',
  -nounc'ing
pro·nounce'a·ble
pro·nounce'ment
pron'to
pro·nun'ci·a'tion
proof
proof'read', -read',
  -read'ing
proof'read'er
prop, propped,
  prop'ping
prop'a·gan'da
prop'a·gan'dist
prop'a·gan'dize',
  -dized', -diz'ing
prop'a·gate',
  -gat'ed, -gat'ing
prop'a·ga'tion
pro'pane'
pro·pel', -pelled',
  -pel'ling
pro·pel'lant also
  pro·pel'lent
pro·pel'ler
pro·pen'si·ty
prop'er
prop'er·tied'
prop'er·ty

pro'phase'
proph'e·cy n.
proph'e·sy', -sied',
  -sy'ing
proph'et (seer)
  ✔ profit
pro·phet'ic
pro'phy·lac'tic
pro·pin'qui·ty
pro·pi'ti·ate',
  -at'ed, -at'ing
pro·pi'tious
pro·po'nent
pro·por'tion
pro·por'tion·al
pro·por'tion·ate
pro·pos'al
pro·pose', -posed',
  -pos'ing
prop'o·si'tion
pro·pound'
pro·pri'e·tar'y
pro·pri'e·tor
pro·pri'e·ty
pro·pul'sion
pro·pul'sive
pro'pyl·ene'
pro·rate', -rat'ed,
  -rat'ing
pro·sa'ic
pro·sce'ni·um pl.
  -ni·ums or -ni·a
pro·scribe' (to for-
  bid), -scribed',
  -scrib'ing
  ✔ prescribe

pro·scrip'tion
pro·scrip'tive
prose
pros'e·cute' (to try
  by law), -cut'ed,
  -cut'ing
  ✔ persecute
pros'e·cu'tion
pros'e·cu'tor
pros'e·lyte', -lyt'ed,
  -lyt'ing
pros'e·ly·tize',
  -tized', -tiz'ing
pros'o·dy
pros'pect'
pro·spec'tive
  (likely to be or
  become)
  ✔ perspective
pros'pec'tor
pro·spec'tus
pros'per
pros·per'i·ty
pros'per·ous
pros'ta·glan'din
pros'tate' (gland)
  ✔ prostrate
pros·the'sis pl. -ses
pros·thet'ic
pros'ti·tute',
  -tut'ed, -tut'ing
pros'ti·tu'tion
pros'trate' (to throw
  down flat), -trat'ed,
  -trat'ing
  ✔ prostate

pros•tra′tion
pro′tac•tin′i•um
pro•tag′o•nist
pro′te•an
pro•tect′
pro•tec′tion
pro•tec′tive
pro•tec′tor *also*
  pro•tect′er
pro•tec′tor•ate
pro′té•gé′
pro′tein′
pro′test′ *v.*
pro′test′ *n.*
Prot′es•tant
Prot′es•tant•ism
prot′es•ta′tion
pro′to•col′
pro′toc′tist
pro′ton′
pro′to•plasm
pro′to•plas′mic *or*
  pro′to•plas′mal *or*
  pro′to•plas•mat′ic
pro′to•typ′al *or*
  pro′to•typ′ic *or*
  pro′to•typ′i•cal
pro′to•type′
pro′to•zo′an *also*
  pro′to•zo′on′ *pl.*
  -zo′ans *or* -zo′a *also*
  -zo′ons′
pro′to•zo′an *or*
  pro′to•zo′al *or*
  pro′to•zo′ic
pro•tract′

pro•trac′tion
pro•trac′tor
pro•trude′,
  -trud′ed, -trud′ing
pro•tru′sion
pro•tu′ber•ance
pro•tu′ber•ant
proud
prov′a•ble
prove, proved,
  proved *or* prov′en
  prov′ing
prov′e•nance
Pro′ven•çal′
prov′en•der
prov′erb′
pro•ver′bi•al
pro•vide′, -vid′ed,
  -vid′ing
pro•vid′er
prov′i•dence
prov′i•dent
prov′i•den′tial
prov′ince
pro•vin′cial
pro•vin′ci•al′i•ty
pro•vi′sion
pro•vi′sion•al
pro•vi′so *pl.* -sos *or*
  -soes
prov′o•ca′tion
pro•voc′a•tive
pro•voke′, -voked′,
  -vok′ing
pro′vo•lo′ne
pro′vost′

prow
prow′ess
prowl
prowl′er
prox′i•mal
prox′i•mate
prox•im′i•ty
prox′y
prude
pru′dence
pru′dent
pru•den′tial
prud′er•y
prud′ish
prune *(fruit)*
prune *(to trim)*,
  pruned, prun′ing
pru′ri•ence
pru′ri•ent
Prus′sian
prus′sic ac′id
pry, pried, pry′ing
psalm
psalm′o•dy
Psal′ter *also* psal′ter
psal′ter•y
pseu′do•nym′
pseu′do•pod′
pseu′do•sci′ence
pshaw
psi
psit′ta•co′sis
pso•ri′a•sis
psych *(to inspirit)*
psy′che *(soul or*
  spirit)

psy'che•del'ic
psy'chi•at'ric
psy•chi'a•trist
psy•chi'a•try
psy'chic *(relating to the mind)*
  ✔ *physic*
psy'cho•a•nal'y•sis
  pl. -ses'
psy'cho•an'a•lyst
psy'cho•an'a•lyt'ic
  or psy'cho•an'a•lyt'i•cal
psy'cho•an'a•lyze', -lyzed', -lyz'ing
psy'cho•bi•ol'o•gy
psy'cho•dra'ma
psy'cho•log'i•cal
psy•chol'o•gist
psy•chol'o•gy
psy'cho•path'
psy'cho•path'ic
psy•cho'sis *pl.* -ses
psy'cho•so•mat'ic
psy'cho•ther'a•pist
psy'cho•ther'a•py
psy•chot'ic
ptar'mi•gan *pl.* -gan *or* -gans
pter'o•dac'tyl
pter'o•saur'
Ptol'e•ma'ic
pto'maine'
pty'a•lin
pub
pu'ber•ty

pu•bes'cence
pu•bes'cent
pu'bic
pu'bis *pl.* -bes
pub'lic
pub'li•can
pub'li•ca'tion
pub'li•cist
pub•lic'i•ty
pub'li•cize', -cized', -ciz'ing
pub'lic-spir'it•ed
pub'lish
pub'lish•er
puce
puck
puck'er
pud'ding
pud'dle
pudg'i•ness
pudg'y
pueb'lo *(community)*, *pl.* -los
Pueb'lo *(people)*, *pl.* -lo *or* -los
pu'er•ile
pu•er'per•al
Puer'to Ri'can
puff'ball'
puff'er
puff'in
puff'i•ness
puff'y
pug
pu'gi•lism
pu'gi•list
pug•na'cious

pug•nac'i•ty
puis'sance
puis'sant
puke, puked, puk'ing
pul'chri•tude'
pul'chri•tu'di•nous
pule, puled, pul'ing
pull
pul'let
pul'ley *pl.* -leys
Pull'man
pull'o'ver *n.*
pull'-up' *n.*
pul'mo•nar'y
pulp
pul'pit
pulp'wood'
pulp'y
pul'sar'
pul'sate', -sat'ed, -sat'ing
pul•sa'tion
pulse, pulsed, puls'ing
pul'ver•i•za'tion
pul'ver•ize', -ized', -iz'ing
pu'ma
pum'ice
pum'mel *(to beat)*, -meled *also* -melled, -mel•ing *or* -mel•ling
  ✔ *pommel*
pump

pum'per•nick'el

pump'kin

pun, punned,
  pun'ning

pun'cheon

punch'y

punc•til'i•o' *pl.* -os'

punc•til'i•ous

punc'tu•al

punc•tu•al'i•ty

punc'tu•ate',
  -at'ed, -at'ing

punc•tu•a'tion

punc'ture, -tured,
  -tur•ing

pun'dit

pun'gen•cy

pun'gent

pun'ish

pun'ish•a•ble

pu'ni•tive

punk

pun'ster

punt'er

pu'ny

pu'pa *pl.* -pae *or*
  -pas

pu'pal *(relating to a
  pupa)*
  ✔ *pupil*

pu'pate', -pat'ed,
  -pat'ing

pu•pa'tion

pu'pil *(student)*
  ✔ *pupal*

pup'pet

pup'pet•eer'

pup'pet•ry

pup'py

pur'blind'

pur'chas•a•ble

pur'chase, -chased,
  -chas•ing

pure, pur'er, pur'est

pure'bred'

pu•rée' -réed',
  -ré'ing

pur'ga•tive

pur'ga•to'ri•al

pur'ga•to'ry

purge, purged,
  purg'ing

pu'ri•fi•ca'tion

pu'ri•fi'er

pu'ri•fy', -fied',
  -fy'ing

Pu'rim

pu'rine'

pur'ist

Pu'ri•tan

pu'ri•tan'i•cal

Pu'ri•tan•ism

pu'ri•ty

purl *(to flow, knitting
  stitch)*
  ✔ *pearl*

pur•loin'

pur'ple

pur•port' *v.*

pur'port' *n.*

pur'pose

purr

purse, pursed,
  purs'ing

purs'er

pur•su'a•ble

pur•su'ance

pur•su'ant

pur•sue', -sued',
  -su'ing

pur•suit'

pu'ru•lence

pu'ru•lent

pur•vey'

pur•vey'ance

pur•vey'or

pus *(yellowish
  fluid)*
  ✔ *puss*

push'-but'ton
  also push'but'ton
  adj.

push'cart'

push'o'ver *n.*

push'pin'

push'up' *n.*

push'y

pu'sil•lan'i•mous

puss *(cat, mouth)*
  ✔ *pus*

puss'y *(cat)*

pus'sy *(full of pus)*

puss'y•foot'

pus'tule

put *(to place)*, put,
  put'ting
  ✔ *putt*

pu'ta•tive

put'down' *or*
  put'-down' *n.*

put'-on' *adj. & n.*

pu'tre•fac'tion

pu'tre•fy', -fied',
  -fy'ing

pu'trid

putsch

putt *(to hit a golf
  ball)*, putt'ed,
  putt'ing
  ✔ put

putt'er *(golf club)*

put'ter *v.*

put'ty, -tied, -ty•ing

puz'zle, -zled,
  -zling

puz'zle•ment

puz'zler

Pyg'my *also* Pig'my
  pl. -mies

py•ja'mas

py'lon'

py•lo'rus *pl.* -ri

py'or•rhe'a

pyr'a•mid

py•ram'i•dal

pyre

pyr'i•dine'

pyr'i•dox'ine'

py'rite'

py•ri'tes *pl.* -tes

py'ro•ma'ni•a

py'ro•ma'ni•ac'

py'ro•tech'nic *also*
  py'ro•tech'ni•cal

py'ro•tech'nics

Pyr'rhic vic'to•ry

Py•thag'o•re'an

py'thon'

Q

quack

quack'er•y

quad

quad'ran'gle

quad'rant

quad'ra•phon'ic
  also quad'ri•
  phon'ic

quad•rat'ic

quad•ren'ni•al

quad'ri•ceps'

quad'ri•lat'er•al

qua•drille'

quad•ril'lion

quad•ril'lionth

quad'ri•ple'gia

quad'ri•ple'gic

quad'ru•ped'

quad•ru'ple, -pled,
  -pling

quad•ru'plet

qua•dru'pli•cate',
  -cat'ed, -cat'ing

quaff

quag'mire'

qua'hog'

quail *pl.* quail *or*
  quails

quail *v.*

quaint

quake, quaked,
  quak'ing

Quak'er

Quak'er•ism

qual'i•fi•ca'tion

qual'i•fi'er

qual'i•fy', -fied',
  -fy'ing

qual'i•ta'tive

qual'i•ty

qualm

quan'da•ry

quan'ta

quan'ti•fi•ca'tion

quan'ti•fy', -fied',
  -fy'ing

quan'ti•ta'tive

quan'ti•ty

quan'tum *pl.* -ta

Qua'paw *pl.* -paw *or*
  -paws

quar'an•tine',
  -tined', -tin'ing

quark

quar'rel, -reled *or*
  -relled, -rel'ing *or*
  -rel•ling

quar'rel•er *or*
  quar'rel•ler

quar'rel•some

quar'ry *(object of
  pursuit, excavation)*

quar'ry *(to excavate
  stone)*, -ried,
  -ry'ing

quart

quar'ter

quar'ter•back'

quar'ter•deck'

quar'ter•fi'nal

quar'ter•fi'nal•ist

quar'ter-hour' *also*

quar'ter hour'
quar'ter•ly
quar'ter•mas'ter
quar'ter•staff' *pl.*
   -staves'
quar•tet' *also*
   quar•tette'
quar'to *pl.* -tos
quartz
quartz'ite'
qua'sar'
quash
qua'si
qua'si-stel'lar
   ob'ject'
quat'er•nar'y *(in
   fours)*
Qua'ter•nar'y *(geo-
   logic period)*
quat'rain'
qua'ver
quay *(wharf)*
   ✔ *cay, key*
quea'si•ness
quea'sy
que•bra'cho *pl.*
   -chos
Quech'ua *pl.* -ua *or*
   -uas
queen
queen'li•ness
queen'ly
queer
quell
quench
quench'a•ble
quer'u•lous

que'ry, -ried, -ry•ing
quest
ques'tion
ques'tion•a•ble
ques'tion•a•bly
ques'tion•er
ques'tion•naire'
quet•zal' *pl.* -zals' *or*
   -za'les
queue *(to get in line),*
   queued, queu'ing
   ✔ *cue*
quib'ble, -bled,
   -bling
quib'bler
quiche
quick
quick'en
quick'-freeze',
   -froze', -fro'zen,
   -freez'ing
quick'lime'
quick'sand'
quick'sil'ver
quick'step'
quick'-tem'pered
quick'-wit'ted
quid *(piece of chew-
   ing tobacco)*
quid *(money), pl.*
   quid *or* quids
qui•es'cence
qui•es'cent
qui'et
qui'e•tude'
quill
quilt'ing

quince
qui'nine'
quin•quen'ni•al
quin'sy
quin•tes'sence
quin•tes•sen'tial
quin•tet' *also*
   quin•tette'
quin•til'lion
quin•til'lionth
quin•tu'ple, -pled,
   -pling
quin•tu'plet
quip, quipped,
   quip'ping
quip'ster
quire *(unit of paper)*
   ✔ *choir*
quirk
quirt
quis'ling
quit, quit *or*
   quit'ted, quit'ting
quit'claim'
quite
quit'ter
quiv'er
quix•ot'ic *also*
   quix•ot'i•cal
quiz *pl.* quiz'zes
quiz, quizzed,
   quiz'zing
quiz'zi•cal
quoin *(corner)*
   ✔ *coin*
quoit
quon'dam

quo′rum
quo′ta
quot′a•bil′i•ty
quot′a•ble
quo•ta′tion
quote, quot′ed,
 quot′ing
quo•tid′i•an
quo′tient

R

rab′bet *also* re′bate′
 (groove)
 ✔ *rabbit*
rab′bi *pl.* -bis
rab′bi•nate′
rab•bin′i•cal
rab′bit *(animal), pl.*
 -bits *or* -bit
 ✔ *rabbet*
rab′ble
rab′ble-rous′er
Rab′e•lai′si•an
rab′id
ra′bies
rac•coon′ *pl.*
 -coons′ *or* -coon′
race, raced, rac′ing
race′course′
race′horse′
ra•ceme′
rac′er
race′track′
race′way′
ra′cial

rac′ism
rac′ist
rack *(frame)*
 ✔ *wrack*
rack′et *also* rac′quet
 *(device for striking a
 ball)*
rack′et *(uproar)*
rack′et•eer′
rac′on•teur′
rac′quet•ball′
rac′y
rad
ra′dar
ra′dar•scope′
ra′di•al
ra′di•ance *also*
 ra′di•an•cy
ra′di•ant
ra′di•ate′, -at′ed,
 -at′ing
ra′di•a′tion
ra′di•a′tor
rad′i•cal
rad′i•cal•ism
rad′i•cand′
ra•dic′chi•o *pl.* -os
ra′di•o *pl.* -os
ra′di•o, -oed, -o•ing
ra′di•o•ac′tive
ra′di•o•ac•tiv′i•ty
ra′di•o•car′bon
ra′di•o•gram′
ra′di•o•graph′
ra′di•og′ra•pher
ra′di•o•graph′ic
ra′di•og′ra•phy

ra′di•o•i′so•tope′
ra′di•o•log′i•cal *or*
 ra′di•o•log′ic
ra′di•ol′o•gist
ra′di•ol′o•gy
ra′di•om′e•ter
ra′di•om′e•try
ra′di•o•pac′i•ty
ra′di•o•paque′
ra′di•o•phone′
ra′di•o•sonde′
ra′di•o•tel′e•
 phone′
rad′ish
ra′di•um
ra′di•us *pl.* -di•i′ *or*
 -di•us•es
ra′dix *pl.* rad′i•ces′
 or ra′dix•es
ra′don
raf′fi•a
raff′ish
raf′fle
raft
raft′er
rag, ragged, rag′ging
rag′a•muf′fin
rage, raged, rag′ing
rag′ged
rag′ged•y
rag′lan
ra•gout′
rag′tag′
rag′time′
rag′weed′
rah
raid

raid'er
rail
rail'ing
rail'ler•y
rail'road'
rail'way'
rai'ment
rain *(precipitation)*
  ✔ reign, rein
rain'bow'
rain' check'
rain'coat'
rain'drop'
rain'fall'
rain'storm'
rain'wa'ter
rain'wear'
rain'y
raise *(to lift)*, raised,
  rais'ing
  ✔ raze
rais'er *(one that
  raises)*
  ✔ razor
rai'sin
rai'son d'ê'tre
ra'jah *or* ra'ja
rake, raked, rak'ing
rak'ish
ral'li•er
ral'ly, -lied, -ly•ing
ram, rammed,
  ram'ming
Ram'a•dan
ram'ble, -bled,
  -bling
ram'bler

ram•bunc'tious
ram'ie
ram'i•fi•ca'tion
ram'i•fy', -fied',
  -fy'ing
ra'mose'
ramp
ram'page, -paged,
  -pag•ing
ram'pant
ram'part
ram'rod'
ram'shack'le
ranch
ranch'er
ran•che'ro *pl.* -ros
ran'cho *pl.* -chos
ran'cid
ran'cor
ran'cor•ous
ran'dom
rang
range, ranged,
  rang'ing
rang'er
rang'y
ra'ni *also* ra'nee *pl.*
  -nis *also* -nees
rank'ing
ran'kle, -kled, -kling
ran'sack'
ran'som
rant
rant'er
rap *(to knock)*,
  rapped, rap'ping
  ✔ wrap

ra•pa'cious
ra•pa'cious•ness *or*
  ra•pac'i•ty
rape, raped, rap'ing
rap'id
ra•pid'i•ty *or*
  rap'id•ness
rap'id-fire'
ra'pi•er
rap'ine
rap'ist
rap•pel', -pelled',
  -pel'ling
rap•port'
rap'proche•ment'
rap•scal'lion
rapt
rap'ture
rap'tur•ous
rare, rar'er, rar'est
rare'ness
rare'bit
rare' earth'
rare'-earth'
  el'e•ment
rar'e•fac'tion
rar'e•fi'a•ble
rar'e•fy', -fied',
  -fy'ing
rar'i•ty
ras'cal
ras•cal'i•ty
rash'er
rasp
rasp'ber'ry
rasp'y
Ras'ta•far'i•an

Ras'ta·far'i·an·ism
rat, rat'ted, rat'ting
rat'a·touille'
ratch'et
rate, rat'ed, rat'ing
rath'er
rat'i·fi·ca'tion
rat'i·fy', -fied',
  -fy'ing
ra'tio *pl.* -tios
ra'ti·oc'i·nate',
  -nat'ed, -nat'ing
ra'ti·oc'i·na'tion
ra'ti·oc'i·na'tive
ra'tion
ra'tion·al *adj.*
ra'tion·ale' *n.*
ra'tion·al·ism
ra'tion·al·ist
ra'tion·al·is'tic
ra'tion·al'i·ty
ra'tion·al·i·za'tion
ra'tion·al·ize',
  -ized', -iz'ing
rat'line *also* rat'lin
rat·tan'
rat'ter
rat'tle, -tled, -tling
rat'tler
rat'tle·snake'
rau'cous
raun'chy
rav'age, -aged,
  -ag·ing
rav'ag·er
rave, raved, rav'ing
rav'el, -eled *also*

-elled, -el·ing *also*
  -el·ling
ra'ven
rav'en·ing
rav'en·ous
ra·vine'
rav'i·o'li *pl.* -li *or* -lis
rav'ish
rav'ish·ing
raw
raw'boned'
raw'hide'
ray *(beam, fish)*
  ✔ re
ray'on
raze *also* rase *(to de-
  molish)*, razed,
  raz'ing
  ✔ raise
ra'zor *(cutting instru-
  ment)*
  ✔ raiser
ra'zor·blade' *also*
  ra'zor blade'
razz
re *(musical tone)*
  ✔ ray
re *(concerning)*
reach
re·act'
re·ac'tant
re·ac'tion
re·ac'tion·ar'y
re·ac'ti·vate',
  -vat'ed, -vat'ing
re·ac'ti·va'tion
re·ac'tive

re·ac'tor
read *(to examine
  something written)*,
  read, read'ing
  ✔ reed
read'a·bil'i·ty *or*
  read'a·ble·ness
read'a·ble
read'er
read'er·ship'
read'i·ly
read'i·ness
re·ad·just'
re·ad·just'ment
read'y, -ied, -y·ing
read'y-made' *or*
  read'y·made'
re·af·firm'
re·af·fir·ma'tion
re·a'gent
re·al *(actual)*
  ✔ reel
re·al es·tate'
re'al·ism
re'al·ist
re'al·is'tic
re'al·is'ti·cal·ly
re·al'i·ty *(actuality)*
  ✔ realty
re·al·iz'a·ble
re'al·i·za'tion
re'al·ize', -ized',
  -iz'ing
re'al·ly
realm
real'-time'
Re'al·tor

re'al•ty *(property)*
  ✔ reality
ream *(unit of paper)*
ream *(to form a hole)*
ream'er
reap
reap'er
re'ap•por'tion
re'ap•prais'al
re'ap•praise',
  -praised', -prais'ing
rear
re'ar•range',
  -ranged', -rang'ing
re'ar•range'ment
rear'-view' mir'ror
  or rear'view'
  mir'ror
rear'ward *adv. &*
  adj.
rear'wards *adv.*
rea'son
rea'son•a•ble
rea'son•a•bly
rea'son•ing
re'as•sem'ble,
  -bled, -bling
re'as•sur'ance
re'as•sure', -sured',
  -sur'ing
re'bate', -bat'ed,
  -bat'ing
re•bel', -belled',
  -bel'ling
reb'el *n.*
re•bel'lion
re•bel'lious

re•birth'
re•born'
re•bound' *v.*
re'bound' *n.*
re•buff'
re•build', -built',
  -build'ing
re•buke', -buked',
  -buk'ing
re'bus *pl.* -bus•es
re•but', -but'ted,
  -but'ting
re•but'tal
re•cal'ci•trance *or*
  re•cal'ci•tran•cy
re•cal'ci•trant
re•call' *v.*
re'call' *n.*
re•cant'
re'can•ta'tion
re•cap' *(to replace a*
  cap), -capped',
  -cap'ping
re'cap' *(recapped tire,*
  summary)
re•cap' *(to summa-*
  rize), -capped',
  -cap'ping
re'ca•pit'u•late',
  -lat'ed, -lat'ing
re'ca•pit'u•la'tion
re•cap'ture, -tured,
  -tur•ing
re•cast', -cast',
  -cast'ing
re'cast' *n.*
re•cede' *(to ebb),*

  -ced'ed, -ced'ing
re-cede' *(to cede*
  back), -ced'ed,
  -ced'ing
re•ceipt'
re•ceiv'a•ble
re•ceive', -ceived',
  -ceiv'ing
re•ceiv'er
re•ceiv'er•ship'
re'cent
re•cep'ta•cle
re•cep'tion
re•cep'tion•ist
re•cep'tive
re'cep•tiv'i•ty
re•cep'tor
re•cess'
re•ces'sion *(with-*
  drawal)
re-ces'sion *(restora-*
  tion)
re•ces'sion•al
re•ces'sive
re•charge',
  -charged',
  -charg'ing
re'charge' *n.*
re•cid'i•vism
re•cid'i•vist
rec'i•pe'
re•cip'i•ent
re•cip'ro•cal
re•cip'ro•cate',
  -cat'ed, -cat'ing
re•cip'ro•ca'tion
rec'i•proc'i•ty

re•cit′al
rec′i•ta′tion
rec′i•ta′tive *adj.*
rec′i•ta•tive′ *n.*
re•cite′, -cit′ed,
  -cit′ing
reck′less
reck′on
reck′on•ing
re•claim′ *(to make
  usable)*
re-claim′ *(to claim
  again)*
re•claim′a•ble
rec′la•ma′tion
re•cline′, -clined′,
  -clin′ing
re•clin′er
re•cluse′ *adj.*
rec′luse′ *n.*
re•clu′sive
rec′og•ni′tion
rec′og•niz′a•ble
re•cog′ni•zance
re•cog′ni•zant
rec′og•nize′,
  -nized′, -niz′ing
re•coil′ *v.*
re′coil′ *n.*
rec′ol•lect′ *(to re-
  member)*
re′-col•lect′ *(to col-
  lect again)*
rec′ol•lec′tion
re•com′bi•nant
rec′om•mend′
rec′om•men•da′-
tion
rec′om•pense′,
  -pensed′, -pens′ing
rec′on•cil′a•ble
rec′on•cile′, -ciled′,
  -cil′ing
rec′on•cil′i•a′tion
rec′on•dite′
re′con•di′tion
re•con′nais•sance
re′con•noi′ter
re′con•sid′er
re′con•sid′er•a′-
tion
re′con•struct′
re′con•struc′tion
re′con•struc′tive
re•cord′ *v.*
rec′ord *n.*
re•cord′er
re•cord′ing
re•count′ *(to nar-
  rate)*
re-count′ *(to count
  again)*
re′-count′ *(another
  count)*
re•coup′
re′course′
re•cov′er *(to regain)*
re-cov′er *(to cover
  again)*
re•cov′er•a•ble
re•cov′er•y
rec′re•ant
rec′re•ate′ *(to re-
  fresh)*, -at′ed,
-at′ing
re′-cre•ate′ *(to create
  again)*, -at′ed,
-at′ing
rec′re•a′tion *(re-
  freshment)*
re′-cre•a′tion *(new
  creation)*
rec′re•a′tion•al
re•crim′i•nate′,
  -nat′ed, -nat′ing
re•crim′i•na′tion
re•crim′i•na•to′ry
re′cru•desce′,
  -desced′, -desc′ing
re′cru•des′cence
re′cru•des′cent
re•cruit′
re•cruit′er
rec′tal
rec′tan•gle
rec•tan′gu•lar
rec′ti•fy′, -fied′,
  -fy′ing
rec′ti•lin′e•ar
rec′ti•tude′
rec′to *pl.* -tos
rec′tor
rec′to•ry
rec′tum *pl.* -tums *or*
  -ta
re•cum′bent
re•cu′per•ate′,
  -at′ed, -at′ing
re•cu′per•a′tion
re•cu′per•a′tive *or*
  re•cu′per•a•to′ry

re•cur′, -curred′,
-cur′ring

re•cur′rence

re•cur′rent

re•cuse′, -cused′,
-cus′ing

re•cy′cle, -cled,
-cling

red, red′der, red′dest

re•dact′

re•dac′tion

red′bird′

red′-blood′ed

red′breast′

red′coat′

red′den

red′dish

re•deem′

re•deem′a•ble

re•demp′tion

red′-hand′ed

red′head′

red′head′ed

red′-hot′

red′-let′ter

re•do′, -did′, -done′,
-do′ing, -does′

red′o•lence

red′o•lent

re•dou′ble, -bled,
-bling

re•doubt′a•ble

re•dound′

re•dress′

re•dress′er *or*
re•dres′sor

red′start′

re•duce′, -duced′,
-duc′ing

re•duc′i•bil′i•ty

re•duc′i•ble

re•duc′tion

re•duc′tive

re•dun′dan•cy

re•dun′dant

re•dux′

red′wing′

red′wood′

re•ech′o *also*
re-ech′o, -oed,
-o•ing

reed *(grass, musical
instrument)*
✔ read

reef

reek *(to smell badly)*
✔ wreak

reel *(spool, whirling,
dance)*
✔ real

re•e•lect′ *also*
re′-e•lect′

re•e•lec′tion

re•en•act′ *also*
re′-en•act′

re•en′ter *also*
re-en′ter

re•en′trance

re•en′try *also*
re-en′try

re′es•tab′lish

re′es•tab′lish•
ment

re′ex•am′ine,

-ined, -in•ing

re•fec′to•ry

re•fer′, -ferred′,
-fer′ring

ref′er•a•ble

ref′er•ee′, -reed′,
-ree′ing

ref′er•ence

ref′er•en′dum *pl.*
-dums *or* -da

ref′er•ent

ref′er•en′tial

re•fer′ral

re•fill′ *v.*

re′fill′ *n.*

re•fine′, -fined′,
-fin′ing

re•fine′ment

re•fin′er•y

re•fit′, re•fit′ted,
re•fit′ting

re•flect′

re•flec′tion

re•flec′tive

re•flec′tor

re•flex′ *adj. & n.*

re•flex′ *v.*

re•flex′ive

re•for′est

re′for•es•ta′tion

re•form′ *(to improve)*

re-form′ *(to form
again)*

ref′or•ma′tion

re•for′ma•tive

re•for′ma•to′ry

re•form′er

re•fract'
re•frac'tion
re•frac'tive
re•frac'tive•ness or
  re'frac•tiv'i•ty
re•frac'tor
re•frac'to•ry
re•frain'
re•fresh'
re•fresh'er
re•fresh'ing
re•fresh'ment
re'fried' beans'
re•frig'er•ant
re•frig'er•ate',
  -at'ed, -at'ing
re•frig'er•a'tion
re•frig'er•a'tor
ref'uge
ref'u•gee'
re•ful'gence or
  re•ful'gen•cy
re•ful'gent
re•fund' *v.*
re'fund' *n.*
re•fund'a•ble
re•fur'bish
re•fus'al
re•fuse' (to decline),
  -fused', -fus'ing
ref'use (trash)
re•fut'a•ble
ref'u•ta'tion *also*
  re•fut'al
re•fute', -fut'ed,
  -fut'ing
re•gain'

re'gal (royal)
re•gale' (to delight),
  -galed', -gal'ing
re•ga'lia
re•gard'
re•gard'ing
re•gard'less
re•gat'ta
re'gen•cy
re•gen'er•ate',
  -at'ed, -at'ing
re•gen'er•a'tion
re•gen'er•a'tive
re'gent
reg'gae
reg'i•cid'al
reg'i•cide'
re•gime' *also*
  ré•gime'
reg'i•men
reg'i•ment
reg'i•men'tal
reg'i•men•ta'tion
re'gion
re'gion•al
reg'is•ter (record)
  ✔ registrar
reg'is•tered
reg'is•trar' (official)
  ✔ register
reg'is•tra'tion
reg'is•try
re•gress'
re•gres'sion
re•gres'sive
re•gret', -gret'ted,
  -gret'ting

re•gret'ful
re•gret'ta•ble
re•group'
reg'u•lar
reg'u•lar'i•ty
reg'u•lar•ize',
  -ized', -iz'ing
reg'u•late', -lat'ed,
  -lat'ing
reg'u•la'tion
reg'u•la'tive
reg'u•la'tor
reg'u•la•to'ry
re•gur'gi•tate',
  -tat'ed, -tat'ing
re•gur'gi•ta'tion
re'ha•bil'i•tate',
  -tat'ed, -tat'ing
re'ha•bil'i•ta'tion
re'ha•bil'i•ta'tive
re•hash' *v.*
re'hash' *n.*
re•hears'al
re•hearse',
  -hearsed',
  -hears'ing
reign (rule)
  ✔ rain, rein
re'im•burs'a•ble
re'im•burse',
  -bursed', -burs'ing
re'im•burse'ment
rein (strap, to hold
  back)
  ✔ rain, reign
re'in•car'nate',
  -nat'ed, -nat'ing

re'in•car•na'tion
rein'deer' *pl.* -deer'
  or -deers'
re'in•force'a•ble
re'in•force' *or*
  re'en•force'
  -forced', -forc'ing
re'in•force'ment
re'in•state',
  -stat'ed, -stat'ing
re'in•state'ment
re•it'er•ate', -at'ed,
  -at'ing
re•it'er•a'tion
re•it'er•a'tive
re•ject' *v.*
re'ject' *n.*
re•jec'tion
re•joice', -joiced',
  -joic'ing
re•join' *(to reply)*
re-join' *(to join*
  again)
re•join'der
re•ju've•nate',
  -nat'ed, -nat'ing
re•ju've•na'tion
re•lapse', -lapsed',
  -laps'ing
re•lapse' *n.*
re•late', -lat'ed,
  -lat'ing
re•la'tion
re•la'tion•ship'
rel'a•tive
rel'a•tiv'i•ty
re•lax'

re'lax•a'tion
re•laxed'
re'lay' *n.*
re'lay' *(to pass along)*
re-lay' *(to lay again),*
  -laid', -lay'ing
re•lease' *(to let go),*
  -leased', -leas'ing
re-lease' *(to lease*
  again), -leased',
  -leas'ing
rel'e•gate', -gat'ed,
  -gat'ing
rel'e•ga'tion
re•lent'
re•lent'less
rel'e•vance *or*
  rel'e•van•cy
rel'e•vant
re•li'a•bil'i•ty *or*
  re•li'a•ble•ness
re•li'a•ble
re•li'a•bly
re•li'ance
re•li'ant
rel'ic
re•lief'
re•liev'a•ble
re•lieve', -lieved',
  -liev'ing
re•liev'er
re•lig'ion
re•lig'ious
re•lin'quish
rel'ish
re•live', -lived',
  -liv'ing

re•lo•cate', -cat'ed,
  -cat'ing
re'lo•ca'tion
re•luc'tance
re•luc'tant
re•ly', -lied', -ly'ing
re•main'
re•main'der
re•mains'
re•make', -made',
  -mak'ing
re'make' *n.*
re•mand'
re•mark'
re•mark'a•ble
re•mark'a•bly
re'match' *n.*
re•me'di•a•ble
re•me'di•a•bly
re•me'di•al
rem'e•dy, -died,
  -dy•ing
re•mem'ber
re•mem'brance
re•mind'
re•mind'er
rem'i•nisce',
  -nisced', -nisc'ing
rem'i•nis'cence
rem'i•nis'cent
re•miss'
re•mis'sion
re•mit', -mit'ted,
  -mit'ting
re•mit'tance
re•mit'ter
rem'nant

re•mod′el, -eled
  also -elled, -el′ing
  also -el•ling
re•mod′el•er
re•mon′strance′
re•mon′strate′,
  -strat′ed, -strat′ing
re′mon•stra′tion
re•mon′stra•tive
rem′o•ra′
re•morse′
re•morse′ful
re•mote′, -mot′er,
  -mot′est
re•mov′a•ble
re•mov′al
re•move′, -moved′,
  -mov′ing
re•mu′ner•ate′,
  -at′ed, -at′ing
re•mu′ner•a′tion
re•mu′ner•a•tive
ren′ais•sance′
  (rebirth)
  ✔ *renascence*
re′nal
re•nas′cence
  (renaissance)
  ✔ *renaissance*
re•nas′cent
rend, rent *or*
  rend′ed, rend′ing
ren′der
ren′dez•vous′ *pl.*
  -vous′
ren′dez•vous′,
  -voused′, -vous′ing

ren•di′tion
ren′e•gade′
re•nege′, -neged′,
  -neg′ing
re•new′
re•new′a•ble
re•new′al
ren′net
ren′nin
re•nounce′,
  -nounced′,
  -nounc′ing
re•nounce′ment
ren′o•vate′, -vat′ed,
  -vat′ing
ren′o•va′tion
ren′o•va′tor
re•nown′
re•nowned′
rent *(payment)*
rent *(tear)*
rent′al
rent′er
re•nun′ci•a′tion
re•o′pen
re•or′gan•i•za′tion
re•or′gan•ize′,
  -ized′, -iz′ing
re•or′gan•iz′er
re•pair′ *(to fix)*
re•pair′ *(to go)*
re•pair′a•ble
re•pair′man
re•pair′wom′an
rep′a•ra•ble
rep′a•ra′tion
re•par′a•tive *also*

re•par′a•to′ry
rep′ar•tee′
re•past′
re•pa′tri•ate′,
  -at′ed, -at′ing
re•pa′tri•a′tion
re•pay′, -paid′,
  -pay′ing
re•pay′a•ble
re•pay′ment
re•peal′
re•peat′
re•peat′ed
re•peat′er
re•pel′, -pelled′,
  -pel′ling
re•pel′lence *or*
  re•pel′len•cy
re•pel′lent
re•pent′
re•pen′tance
re•pen′tant
re′per•cus′sion
rep′er•toire′ *(group
  of works)*
rep′er•to′ry *(theatri-
  cal company)*
rep′e•ti′tion
rep′e•ti′tious
re•pet′i•tive
re•place′, -placed′,
  -plac′ing
re•place′a•ble
re•place′ment
re•play′ *v.*
re′play′ *n.*
re•plen′ish

re·plete′
re·ple′tion
rep′li·ca
rep′li·cate′, -cat′ed,
  -cat′ing
rep′li·ca′tion
re·pli′er
re·ply′, -plied′,
  -ply′ing
re·port′
re·port′ed·ly
re·port′er
re·pose′, -posed′,
  -pos′ing
re·pos′i·to′ry
re′pos·sess′
re′pos·ses′sion
rep′re·hend′
rep′re·hen′si·ble
rep′re·hen′si·bil′-
  i·ty
rep′re·hen′si·bly
rep′re·hen′sion
rep′re·sent′
rep′re·sen·ta′tion
rep′re·sen·ta′tion·
  al
rep′re·sen′ta·tive
re·press′
re·press′i·ble
re·pres′sion
re·pres′sive
re·prieve′,
  -prieved′,
  -priev′ing
rep′ri·mand′
re′print′ *n.*

re·print′ *v.*
re·pri′sal
re·prise′, -prised′,
  -pris′ing
re·proach′
re·proach′ful
rep′ro·bate′
rep′ro·ba′tion
re′pro·duce′,
  -duced′, -duc′ing
re′pro·duc′i·ble
re′pro·duc′tion
re′pro·duc′tive
re·proof′
re·prove′, -proved′,
  -prov′ing
rep′tile
rep·til′i·an
re·pub′lic
re·pub′li·can
re·pu′di·ate′,
  -at′ed, -at′ing
re·pu′di·a′tion
re·pu′di·a′tive
re·pu′di·a′tor
re·pug′nance
re·pug′nant
re·pulse′, -pulsed′,
  -puls′ing
re·pul′sion
re·pul′sive
rep′u·ta·ble
rep′u·ta·bly
rep′u·ta′tion
re·pute′, -put′ed,
  -put′ing
re·quest′

req′ui·em
re·quire′, -quired′,
  -quir′ing
re·quire′ment
req′ui·site
req′ui·si′tion
re·quit′al
re·quite′, -quit′ed,
  -quit′ing
re′run′ *n.*
re·run′, -ran′, -run′,
  -run′ning
re′sale′
re·scind′
re·scind′a·ble
re·scis′sion
res′cue, -cued,
  -cu·ing
res′cu·er
re·search′
re·search′er
re·sem′blance
re·sem′ble, -bled,
  -bling
re·sent′
re·sent′ful
re·sent′ment
res′er·va′tion
re·serve′, -served′,
  -serv′ing
re·serv′ed·ly
re·serv′ist
res′er·voir′
re·side′, -sid′ed,
  -sid′ing
res′i·dence
res′i·den·cy

res•i•dent
res•i•den′tial
re•sid′u•al
res′i•due′
re•sign′ *(to give up)*
re-sign′ *(to sign again)*
res′ig•na′tion
re•sil′ience
re•sil′ien•cy
re•sil′ient
res′in
res′in•ous
re•sist′
re•sis′tance
re•sis′tant
re•sist′er *(one that resists)*
re•sis′tor *(electrical device)*
res′o•lute′
res′o•lu′tion
re•solv′a•ble
re•solve′, -solved′, -solv′ing
res′o•nance
res′o•nant
res′o•nate′, -nat′ed, -nat′ing
res′o•na′tion
re•sort′
re•sound′
re′source′
re•source′ful
re•spect′
re•spect′a•bil′i•ty
re•spect′a•ble

re•spect′a•bly
re•spect′ful
re•spec′tive
re•spell′, -spelled′ or -spelt′, -spell′ing
res′pi•ra′tion
res′pi•ra′tor
res′pi•ra•to′ry
re•spire′, -spired′, -spir′ing
res′pite
re•splen′dence or re•splen′den•cy
re•splen′dent
re•spond′
re•sponse′
re•spon′si•bil′i•ty
re•spon′si•ble
re•spon′si•bly
re•spon′sive
rest *(quiet, remainder)*
 ✔ wrest
re•state′, -stat′ed, -stat′ing
re•state′ment
res′tau•rant
res′tau•ra•teur′
rest′ful
res′ti•tu′tion
res′tive
rest′less
res′to•ra′tion
re•stor′a•tive
re•store′, -stored′, -stor′ing
re•strain′
re•straint′

re•strict′
re•stric′tion
re•stric′tive
rest′room′
re•sult′
re•sul′tant
re•sume′ *(to begin again)*, -sumed′, -sum′ing
ré′su•mé′ or re′su•me′ or re′su•mé′ *(summary)*
re•sump′tion
re•sur′gence
re•sur′gent
res′ur•rect′
res′ur•rec′tion
re•sus′ci•tate′, -tat′ed, -tat′ing
re•sus′ci•ta′tion
re•sus′ci•ta′tor
re′tail′
re′tail′er
re•tain′
re•tain′er
re•tal′i•ate′, -at′ed, -at′ing
re•tal′i•a′tion
re•tal′i•a•to′ry
re•tard′
re•tar′dant
re′tar•da′tion
re•tard′ed
retch *(to vomit)*
 ✔ wretch
re•ten′tion

re•ten′tive
ret′i•cence
ret′i•cent
re•tic′u•lar
re•tic′u•late
re•tic′u•la′tion
ret′i•na *pl.* -nas *or*
 -nae′
ret′i•nal
ret′i•nol′
ret′i•nue′
re•tire′, -tired′,
 -tir′ing
re•tir•ee′
re•tire′ment
re•tort′
re•touch′
re•trace′, -traced′,
 -trac′ing
re•tract′
re•tract′a•ble *or*
 re•tract′i•ble
re•trac′tile
re•trac′tion
re•trac′tor
re•tread′ *(to fit a
 new tire tread)*
re′tread′ *n.*
re-tread′ *(to tread
 again)*, -trod′,
 -trod′den, -tread′-
 ing
re•treat′
re•trench′
re•tri′al
ret′ri•bu′tion
re•trib′u•tive

re•trib′u•to′ry
re•triev′a•ble
re•triev′al
re•trieve′, -trieved′,
 -triev′ing
re•triev′er
ret′ro•ac′tive
ret′ro•grade′
ret′ro•gress′
ret′ro•gres′sion
ret′ro•gres′sive
ret′ro•rock′et
ret′ro•spect′
ret′ro•spec′tive
ret′ro•vi′rus *pl.*
 -rus•es
re•turn′
re•turn′a•ble
re•turn•ee′
re•un′ion
re′u•nite′, -nit′ed,
 -nit′ing
re•us′a•ble
re•use′, -used′,
 -us′ing
rev, revved, rev′ving
re•vamp′
re•veal′
rev′eil•le
rev′el, -eled *also*
 -elled, -el•ing *or*
 -el•ling
rev′e•la′tion
rev′el•er *or*
 rev′el•ler
rev′el•ry
re•venge′, -venged′,

 -veng′ing
re•venge′ful
rev′e•nue
re•verb′
re•ver′ber•ate′,
 -at′ed, -at′ing
re•ver′ber•a′tion
re•vere′, -vered′,
 -ver′ing
rev′er•ence
rev′er•end
rev′er•ent
rev′er•en′tial
rev′er•ie
re•ver′sal
re•verse′, -versed′,
 -vers′ing
re•vers′i•ble
re•ver′sion
re•vert′
re•vert′i•ble
re•view′ *(to examine)*
 ✔ *revue*
re•view′er
re•vile′, -viled′,
 -vil′ing
re•vis′a•ble
re•vise′, -vised′,
 -vis′ing
re•vis′er *or* re•vi′sor
re•vi′sion
re•vi′tal•i•za′tion
re•vi′tal•ize′, -ized′,
 -iz′ing
re•viv′al
re•vive′, -vived′,
 -viv′ing

rev'o·ca·ble
rev'o·ca'tion
re·voke', -voked',
  -vok'ing
re·volt'
re·volt'ing
rev'o·lu'tion
rev'o·lu'tion·ar'y
rev'o·lu'tion·ist
rev'o·lu'tion·ize',
  -ized', -iz'ing
re·volve', -volved',
  -volv'ing
re·volv'er
re·vue' *(show)*
  ✔ *review*
re·vul'sion
re·ward'
re·wind', -wound',
  -wind'ing
re'wind' *n.*
re·word'
re·work'
re·write', -wrote',
  -writ'ten, -writ'ing
re'write' *n.*
re·writ'er
Reye's' syn'drome
rhap·sod'ic *also*
  rhap·sod'i·cal
rhap'so·dize',
  -dized', -diz'ing
rhap'so·dy
rhe'a
Rhen'ish
rhe'ni·um
rhe'o·stat'

rhe'sus mon'key
rhet'o·ric
rhe·tor'i·cal
rhet'o·ri'cian
rheum *(mucus)*
  ✔ *room*
rheu·mat'ic
rheu'ma·tism
rheu'ma·toid'
Rh fac'tor
rhine'stone'
rhi'no *pl.* -nos
rhi·noc'er·os *pl.* -os
  or -os·es
rhi'zome'
rho *(Greek letter)*
  ✔ *roe, row*
Rhode' Is'land·er
Rho·de'sian
rho'di·um
rho'do·den'dron
rhom'boid'
rhom·boi'dal
rhom'bus *pl.*
  -bus·es *or* -bi
rhu'barb'
rhyme *also* rime *(to
  compose verse)*,
  rhymed *also* rimed,
  rhym'ing *also*
  rim'ing
  ✔ *rime*
rhythm
rhyth'mic *also*
  rhyth'mi·cal
rib, ribbed, rib'bing
rib'ald

rib'ald·ry
rib'bon
ri'bo·fla'vin
ri'bo·nu·cle'ic
  ac'id
ri'bose'
ri'bo·some'
rice
rich
rich'es
Rich'ter scale'
rick
rick'ets
rick'et·y
rick'rack'
rick'sha *or*
  rick'shaw
ric'o·chet'
ri·cot'ta
rid, rid *or* rid'ded,
  rid'ding
rid'dance
rid'dle, -dled, -dling
ride, rode, rid'den,
  rid'ing
rid'er
ridge, ridged,
  ridg'ing
ridge'pole'
rid'i·cule', -culed',
  -cul'ing
ri·dic'u·lous
rife, rif'er, rif'est
rif'fle *(to shuffle)*,
  -fled, -fling
  ✔ *rifle*
riff'raff'

ri′fle *(firearm)*

ri′fle *(to plunder)*,
-fled, -fling
✔ *riffle*

ri′fle•man

rift

rig, rigged, rig′ging

rig′a•to′ni

rig′ger *(one who rigs)*
✔ *rigor*

right *(correct, opposite of left)*
✔ *rite, wright, write*

right′-an′gled

right′eous

right′ful

right′-hand′ *adj.*

right′-hand′ed

right′-hand′er

right′ist

right′-mind′ed

right′ of way′ *also*
right′-of-way′ *pl.*
rights′ of way′ *or*
right′ of ways′ *also*
rights′-of-way′ *or*
right′-of-ways′

right′-side′ up′

right′-to-life′ *adj.*

right′wing′ *adj.*

right′wing′er

right′y

rig′id

ri•gid′i•ty

rig′ma•role′ *also*
rig′a•ma•role′

rig′or *(severity)*

✔ *rigger*

rig′or mor′tis

rig′or•ous

rile, riled, ril′ing

rill

rim, rimmed,
rim′ming

rime *(to cover with frost)*, rimed,
rim′ing
✔ *rhyme*

rind

ring *(circle)*
✔ *wring*

ring *(to encircle)*,
ringed, ring′ing
✔ *wring*

ring *(to sound)*, rang,
rung, ring′ing
✔ *wring*

ring′er

ring′lead′er

ring′let

ring′mas′ter

ring′side′

ring′worm′

rink

rin′ky-dink′

rinse, rinsed, rins′ing

ri′ot

ri′ot•er

ri′ot•ous

rip, ripped, rip′ping

rip′cord′

ripe, rip′er, rip′est

rip′en

rip′-off′

rip′ple, -pled, -pling

rip′-roar′ing

rip′saw′

rise, rose, ris′en,
ris′ing

ris′er

ris′i•ble

risk′y *(dangerous)*
✔ *risqué*

ri•sot′to

ris•qué′ *(suggestive)*
✔ *risky*

ri′tar•dan′do

rite *(ceremony)*
✔ *right, wright, write*

rit′u•al

rit′u•al•ism

rit′u•al•is′tic

ritz′y

ri′val, -valed *or*
-valled, -val′ing *or*
-val•ling

ri′val•ry

riv′er

riv′er•bank′

riv′er•bed′

riv′er•boat′

riv′er•side′

riv′et, -et•ed, -et•ing

riv′et•er

riv′u•let

ri•yal′

RNA

roach *(fish)*, *pl.*
roach *or* roach′es

roach (cockroach), pl.
  roach'es
road
road'bed'
road'block'
road'house'
road'ie also road'y
road'run'ner
road'side'
road'ster
road'way'
road'work'
roam
roam'er
roan
roar
roar'ing
roast
roast'er
rob, robbed,
  rob'bing
rob'ber
rob'ber•y
robe, robed, rob'ing
rob'in
ro'bot
ro•bot'ics
ro•bust'
roc (legendary bird)
rock (stone, to move
  back and forth)
rock'er
rock'et
rock'et•eer'
rock'et•ry
rock'fish' pl. -fish'
  or -fish'es

rock'ing chair'
rock'ing horse'
rock'′n'roll' or
  rock'-and-roll'
rock'-ribbed'
rock'y
ro•co'co
rod
ro'dent
ro•de'o' pl. -os'
roe (fish eggs)
  ✔ rho, row
roe (small deer), pl.
  roe or roes
  ✔ rho, row
roe'buck'
roent'gen
rog'er interj.
rogue
rogu'er•y
rogu'ish
roil
rois'ter
role also rôle (part in
  a play)
roll (to revolve)
roll (list of names,
  bread)
roll'a•way' adj.
roll'back' n.
roll'er
roll'er coast'er
roll'er skate' n.
roll'er-skate',
  -skat'ed, -skat'ing
roll'er skat'er
rol'lick

rol'lick•ing
rol'lick•some or
  rol'lick•y
roll'-on' adj. & n.
roll'out' n.
roll'o'ver n.
ro'ly-po'ly
ro•maine'
ro'man (type)
Ro'man (relating to
  Rome)
ro•mance' (to woo),
  -manced',
  -manc'ing
Ro•mance'
  (languages)
Ro'man•esque'
Ro•ma'ni•an also
  Ru•ma'ni•an
ro•man'tic
ro•man'ti•cism
ro•man'ti•cist
ro•man'ti•cize',
  -cized', -ciz'ing
Rom'a•ny
Ro'me•o' pl. -os'
romp
romp'ers
ron'do pl. -dos
rood (cross)
  ✔ rude
roof
roof'er
roof'ing
roof'top'
roof'tree'
rook

rook'er•y
rook'ie
room *(space)*
  ✔ rheum
room'er *(lodger)*
  ✔ rumor
room'ful'
room'i•ness
room'mate'
room'y
roost
roost'er
root *(plant part, origin)*
  ✔ route
root *(to dig, to cheer)*
  ✔ route
root' beer'
root'less
root'let
root'stock'
rope, roped, rop'ing
rop'er
rop'y
Ror'schach test'
ro'sa•ry
rose *(flower)*
ro•sé' *(wine)*
ro'se•ate
rose'bud'
rose'bush'
rose'-col'ored
rose'mar'y
ro•sette'
rose'wood'
Rosh' Ha•sha'nah
  also Rosh'

Ha•sha'na
Ro'si•cru'cian
ros'in
ros'i•ness
ros'ter
ros'trum *pl.* -trums
  or -tra
ros'y
rot, rot'ted, rot'ting
Ro•tar'i•an
ro'ta•ry
ro'tate', -tat'ed,
  -tat'ing
ro•ta'tion
ro'ta'tor
ro'ta•to'ry
rote *(memorizing by repetition)*
  ✔ wrote
ro'ti•fer
ro•tis'se•rie
ro'tor
ro'to•till'er
rot'ten
ro•tund'
ro•tun'da
ro•tun'di•ty
rouge, rouged,
  roug'ing
rough *(not smooth)*
  ✔ ruff
rough'age
rough'en
rough'house',
  -housed', -hous'ing
rough'neck'
rough'ness

rough'shod'
rou•lette'
round
round'a•bout'
round'ed
roun'de•lay'
round'house'
round'-the-clock'
round'trip' *or*
  round'-trip'
round'up' *n.*
round'worm'
rouse, roused,
  rous'ing
roust'a•bout'
rout *(to defeat, to dig up)*
route *(to direct)*,
  rout'ed, rout'ing
  ✔ root
rou•tine'
roux *(thickener)*
  ✔ rue
rove, roved, rov'ing
rov'er *(wanderer)*
ro'ver *(pirate)*
row *(line)*
  ✔ rho, roe
row *(to propel with oars)*
  ✔ rho, roe
row *(brawl)*
row'boat'
row'di•ness
row'dy
row'el
row'lock'

roy'al
roy'al•ist
roy'al•ty
rub, rubbed,
  rub'bing
rub'ber
rub'ber band'
rub'ber•ize', -ized',
  -iz'ing
rub'ber-neck'
rub'ber stamp' *also*
  rub'ber•stamp' *n.*
rub'ber-stamp' *v.*
rub'ber•y
rub'bish
rub'ble
rub'down' *n.*
ru•bel'la
ru•bi'cund
ru•bid'i•um
ru'ble *also* rou'ble
ru'bric
ru'by
ruck'sack'
ruck'us
rud'der
rud'dy
rude *(ill-mannered),*
  rud'er, rud'est
  ✔ *rood*
ru'di•ment
ru'di•men'ta•ry
rue *(to feel regret for),*
  rued, ru'ing
  ✔ *roux*
rue'ful
ruff *(collar)*

✔ *rough*
ruf'fi•an
ruf'fle, -fled, -fling
rug
Rug'by
rug'ged
ru'in
ru'in•a'tion
ru'in•ous
rule, ruled, rul'ing
rul'er
rum
rum'ba *also*
  rhum'ba
rum'ble, -bled,
  -bling
rum•bus'tious
ru'men *pl.* -mi•na *or*
  -mens
ru'mi•nant
ru'mi•nate',
  -nat'ed, -nat'ing
ru'mi•na'tion
ru'mi•na'tive
ru'mi•na'tor
rum'mage, -maged,
  -mag•ing
rum'my
ru'mor *(gossip)*
  ✔ *roomer*
ru'mor•mon'ger
rump
rum'ple, -pled,
  -pling
rum'pus
run, ran, run,
  run'ning

run'a•bout' *n.*
run'a•round' *n.*
run'a•way' *n. & adj.*
run'down' *n.*
run'-down' *adj.*
rune
rung *(rod)*
  ✔ *wrung*
run'ic
run'-in' *n.*
run'ner
run'ner-up' *pl.*
  run'ners-up'
run'ning
run'ny
run'off' *n.*
run'-of-the-mill'
run'-on' sen'tence
runt
run'-through' *n.*
run'way'
ru•pee'
ru•pi'ah
rup'ture, -tured,
  -tur•ing
ru'ral
ruse
rush
rush' hour' *n.*
rush'-hour' *adj.*
rus'set
Rus'sian
rust
rus'tic
rus'ti•cate', -cat'ed,
  -cat'ing
rus'ti•ca'tion

rus·tic′i·ty
rust′i·ness
rus′tle, -tled, -tling
rus′tler
rust′y
rut, rut′ted, rut′ting
ru′ta·ba′ga
ru·the′ni·um
ruth′er·ford′i·um
ruth′less
rye (grain)
  ✔ wry

S

Sab′bath
sab·bat′i·cal
sa′ber
sa′ber-toothed′
  ti′ger
sa′ble
sa·bot′
sab′o·tage′, -taged′,
  -tag′ing
sab′o·teur′
sac (body part)
  ✔ sack
sac′cha·rin n.
sac′cha·rine adj.
sac′er·do′tal
sa′chem
sa·chet′ (perfumed
  bag)
  ✔ sashay
sack (bag, loot, wine)
  ✔ sac

sack (to fire, to rob)
  ✔ sac
sack′cloth′
sack′ing
sac′ra·ment
sac′ra·men′tal
sa′cred
sac′ri·fice′, -ficed′,
  -fic′ing
sac′ri·fi′cial
sac′ri·lege
sac′ri·le′gious
sac′ris·tan
sac′ris·ty
sac′ro·sanct′
sa′crum pl. -cra
sad, sad′der, sad′dest
sad′den
sad′dle, -dled, -dling
sad′dle·bag′
sad′dler
sa′dism
sa′dist
sa·dis′tic
sa·fa′ri pl. -ris
safe, saf′er, saf′est
safe′-con′duct
safe′-de·pos′it
  box′
safe′guard′
safe′keep′ing
safe′ty
saf′flow′er
saf′fron
sag, sagged, sag′ging
sa′ga
sa·ga′cious

sa·gac′i·ty
sag′a·more′
sage, sag′er, sag′est
sage′brush′
sa′go pl. -gos
sa·gua′ro pl. -ros
Sa·hap′ti·an
Sa·hap′tin pl. -tin
  or -tins
sa′hib
said
sail (canvas)
  ✔ sale
sail′board′
sail′boat′
sail′cloth′
sail′fish′ pl. -fish′ or
  -fish′es
sail′ing
sail′or
saint
Saint′ Ber·nard′
saint′ed
saint′hood′
saint′li·ness
sake (purpose)
sa′ke also sa′ki
  (liquor)
sal
sa·laam′
sal′a·bil′i·ty
sal′a·ble also
  sale′a·ble
sa·la′cious
sal′ad
sal′a·man′der
sa·la′mi

sal'a·ried'
sal'a·ry
sale (act of selling)
  ✔ sail
sales'clerk'
sales'man
sales'man·ship'
sales'peo'ple
sales'per'son
sales'wom'an
sa·lic'y·late'
sal'i·cyl'ic ac'id
sa·li·ence also
  sa'li·en·cy
sa'li·ent
sa'line'
sa·lin'i·ty
Sa'lish
sa·li'va
sal'i·var'y
sal'i·vate', -vat'ed,
  -vat'ing
sal'i·va'tion
sal'low
sal'ly, -lied, -ly·ing
sal'ma·gun'di pl.
  -dis
salm'on pl. -on or
  -ons
sal'mo·nel'la pl.
  -nel'lae or -nel'las
  -nel'la
sa·lon' (room, gath-
  ering)
sa·loon' (tavern)
sal'sa
sal' so'da

salt
salt'box'
salt'cel'lar
sal·tine'
salt'i·ness
salt'pe'ter
salt'shak'er
salt'wa'ter or
  salt'-wa'ter adj.
salt'y
sa·lu'bri·ous
sa·lu'ki pl. -kis
sal'u·tar'y
sal'u·ta'tion
sa·lu'ta·to'ri·an
sa·lu'ta·to'ry
sa·lute', -lut'ed,
  -lut'ing
sal'va·ble
Sal'va·do'ran or
  Sal'va·do'ri·an
sal'vage, -vaged,
  -vag·ing
sal'vage·a·ble
sal'vag·er
sal·va'tion
salve, salved,
  salv'ing
sal'ver
sal'vo pl. -vos or
  -voes
Sa·mar'i·tan
sa·mar'i·um
sam'ba
sam·bu'ca
same
same'ness

Sa·mo'an
sam'o·var'
Sam'o·yed' also
  Sam'o·yede'
sam'pan'
sam'ple, -pled,
  -pling
sam'pler
sam'u·rai' pl. -rai'
  or -rais'
San pl. San or Sans
san'a·to'ri·um also
  san'i·tar'i·um pl.
  -to'ri·ums or
  -to'ri·a also
  -tar'i·ums or
  -tar'i·a
sanc'ti·fi·ca'tion
sanc'ti·fy', -fied',
  -fy'ing
sanc'ti·mo'ni·ous
sanc'ti·mo'ny
sanc'tion
sanc'ti·ty
sanc'tu·ar'y
sanc'tum pl. -tums
  or -ta
sand
san'dal
san'dal·wood'
sand'bag', -bagged',
  -bag'ging
sand'bank'
sand'bar'
sand'blast'
sand'blast'er
sand'box'

sand'er
sand'lot'
sand'man
sand'pa'per
sand'pi'per
sand'stone'
sand'storm'
sand'wich
sand'y
sane (of sound mind),
  san'er, san'est
  ✔ seine
sang-froid'
san·gri'a
san'gui·nar'y
san'guine
san·guin'i·ty
san'i·tar'y
san'i·ta'tion
san'i·tize', -tized',
  -tiz'ing
san'i·ty
sans
San'sei' pl. -sei' or
  -seis
San'skrit'
San'ta Claus'
San·tee' pl. -tee' or
  -tees
sap, sapped,
  sap'ping
sa'pi·ence
sa'pi·ent
sap'ling
sap'o·dil'la
sa·pon'i·fi'a·ble
sa·pon'i·fi'er

sa·pon'i·fi·ca'tion
sa·pon'i·fy', -fied',
  -fy'ing
sap'phire
sap'py
sap'suck'er
sap'wood'
Sar'a·cen
sa·ran'
sar'casm
sar·cas'tic
sar·co'ma pl. -mas
  also -ma·ta
sar·coph'a·gus pl.
  -gi' or -gus·es
sar·dine'
Sar·din'i·an
sar·don'ic
sa'ri pl. -ris
sa·rong'
sar'sa·pa·ril'la
sar·to'ri·al
sash
sa·shay' (walk
  casually)
  ✔ sachet
sa·shi'mi
sass
sas'sa·fras'
sas'sy
sa·tan'ic or
  sa·tan'i·cal
satch'el
sate, sat'ed, sat'ing
sa·teen'
sat'el·lite'
sa·tia·bil'i·ty

sa'tia·ble
sa'ti·ate', -at'ed,
  -at'ing
sa'ti·a'tion
sa·ti'e·ty
sat'in
sat'in·y
sat'ire
sa·tir'i·cal or
  sa·tir'ic
sat'i·rist
sat'i·rize', -rized',
  -riz'ing
sat'is·fac'tion
sat'is·fac'to·ri·ly
sat'is·fac'to·ry
sat'is·fi'er
sat'is·fy', -fied',
  -fy'ing
sa'trap'
sa'tra·py
sat'u·ra·ble
sat'u·rate', -rat'ed,
  -rat'ing
sat'u·ra'tion
Sat'ur·day'
sat'ur·na'li·a
sat'ur·nine'
sa'tyr
sauce, sauced,
  sauc'ing
sauce'pan'
sau'cer
sauc'y
Sau'di or Sau'di
  A·ra'bi·an
sau'er·kraut'

Sauk *pl.* Sauk *or*
  Sauks
sau'na
saun'ter
sau'ri•an
sau'sage
sau•té', -téed',
  -té'ing
Sau•ternes' *or*
  sau•ternes'
sav'a•ble *or*
  save'a•ble
sav'age
sav'age•ry
sa•van'na *also*
  sa•van'nah
sa•vant'
save, saved, sav'ing
sav'ior
sa'voir-faire'
sa'vor
sa'vor•y
sav'vy, -vied, -vy•ing
saw, sawed, sawed *or*
  sawn, saw'ing
saw'buck'
saw'dust'
sawed'-off'
saw'fish' *pl.* -fish' *or*
  -fish'es
saw'horse'
saw'mill'
saw'yer
sax
sax'i•frage
Sax'on
sax'o•phone'

sax'o•phon'ist
say, said, say'ing
say'-so' *pl.* -sos'
scab, scabbed,
  scab'bing
scab'bard
sca'bies
scads
scaf'fold
scaf'fold•ing
scal'a•wag' *also*
  scal'ly•wag'
scald
scale, scaled, scal'ing
sca'lene'
scal'i•ness
scal'lion
scal'lop *also*
  scol'lop
sca'lop•pi'ne *also*
  sca'lop•pi'ni
scalp
scal'pel
scalp'er
scal'y
scam
scamp
scam'per
scam'pi *pl.* -pi
scan, scanned,
  scan'ning
scan'dal
scan'dal•ize',
  -ized', -iz'ing
scan'dal•mon'ger
scan'dal•ous
Scan'di•na'vi•an

scan'di•um
scan'ner
scan'sion
scant
scant'i•ly
scant'y
scape
scape'goat'
scape'grace'
scap'u•la *pl.* -las *or*
  -lae'
scar, scarred,
  scar'ring
scar'ab
scarce, scarc'er,
  scarc'est
scar'ci•ty
scare, scared,
  scar'ing
scare'crow'
scarf *pl.* scarfs *or*
  scarves
scar'let
scar'y
scat, scat'ted,
  scat'ting
scathe, scathed,
  scath'ing
scat'o•log'i•cal
sca•tol'o•gy
scat'ter
scat'ter•brain'
scat'ter•brained'
scav'enge, -enged,
  -eng•ing
scav'en•ger
sce•nar'i•o' *pl.* -os'

sce•nar'ist

scene

scen'er•y

sce'nic

scent *(odor)*

  ✔ *cent, sent*

scep'ter

scep'tic

scep'ti•cal

scep'ti•cism

sched'ule, -uled,

  -ul•ing

sche'ma *pl.* -ma•ta

  or -mas

sche•mat'ic

sche'ma•tize',

  -tized', -tiz'ing

scheme, schemed,

  schem'ing

schem'er

scher•zan'do *pl.*

  -dos

scher'zo *pl.* -zos *or*

  -zi

schil'ling *(monetary*

  unit of Austria)

  ✔ *shilling*

schism

schis•mat'ic

schist

schiz'oid'

schiz'o•phre'ni•a

schiz'o•phren'ic

schlep *or* schlepp

  also shlep,

  schlepped *also*

  shlepped,

schlep'ping *or*

  schlepp'ing *also*

  shlep'ping

schlock *also* shlock

schmaltz *also*

  schmalz

schmaltz'y *also*

  schmalz'y

schmo *pl.* schmoes

  or schmos

schmooze *or*

  schmoose,

  schmoozed *or*

  schmoosed,

  schmooz'ing *or*

  schmoos'ing

schmuck *also*

  shmuck

schnapps *pl.*

  schnapps

schnau'zer

schol'ar

scho•las'tic

scho•las'ti•cism

school

school'book'

school'boy'

school' bus'

school'child' *also*

  school' child'

school'girl'

school'house'

school'ing

school'marm'

school'mas'ter

school'mate'

school'mis'tress

school'room'

school'teach'er

school'work'

school'yard'

schoo'ner

schot'tische

schwa

sci•at'ic

sci•at'i•ca

sci'ence

sci'en•tif'ic

sci'en•tist

sci'en•tol'o•gy

scim'i•tar

scin•til'la

scin'til•late',

  -lat'ed, -lat'ing

scin'til•la'tion

sci'on *(descendant or*

  heir)

sci'on *also* ci'on

  (shoot or twig)

scis'sile

scis'sion

scis'sors

scle'ra

scle•ro'sis *pl.* -ses

scle•rot'ic

scoff

scoff'law'

scold

sco•li•o'sis

sconce

scone

scoop'ful'

scoot'er

scope

scor•bu′tic *also*
  scor•bu′ti•cal
scorch
scorch′er
score, scored,
  scor′ing
score′board′
score′card′
score′keep′er
scor′er
sco′ri•a *pl.* -ri•ae′
scorn
scorn′ful
scor′pi•on
Scot
scotch *(to stifle or
  wound)*
Scotch *(people,
  whisky)*
Scotch′man
Scotch′wom′an
scot′-free′
Scots
Scots′man
Scots′wom′an
Scot′tie
Scot′tish
scoun′drel
scour
scourge, scourged,
  scourg′ing
scourg′er
scout
scout′ing
scout′mas′ter
scow
scowl

scrab′ble, -bled,
  -bling
scrag
scrag′gy
scram, scrammed,
  scram′ming
scram′ble, -bled,
  -bling
scram′bler
scrap, scrapped,
  scrap′ping
scrap′book′
scrape, scraped,
  scrap′ing
scrap′er
scrap′pi•ness
scrap′ple
scrap′py
scratch
scratch′i•ly
scratch′i•ness
scratch′y
scrawl
scraw′ni•ness
scraw′ny
scream
scream′er
screech
screech′ing
screed
screen
screen′ing
screen′play′
screen′ test′ *n.*
screen′-test′ *v.*
screen′writ′er
screen′writ′ing

screw
screw′ball′
screw′driv′er
screw′y
scrib′al
scrib′ble, -bled,
  -bling
scrib′bler
scribe, scribed,
  scrib′ing
scrim
scrim′mage,
  -maged, -mag•ing
scrimp
scrim′shaw′ *pl.*
  -shaw′ *or* -shaws′
scrip *(paper money)*
script *(writing, text)*
Scrip′tur•al
Scrip′ture
script′writ′er
script′writ′ing
scriv′en•er
scrod
scrof′u•la
scrof′u•lous
scroll
Scrooge
scro′tal
scro′tum *pl.* -ta *or*
  -tums
scrounge,
  scrounged,
  scroung′ing
scroung′y
scrub, scrubbed,
  scrub′bing

scrub'ber
scrub'bi·ness
scrub'by
scruff
scruff'y
scrump'tious
scrunch
scru'ple, -pled,
  -pling
scru'pu·los'i·ty *or*
  scru'pu·lous·ness
scru'pu·lous
scru'ti·nize',
  -nized', -niz'ing
scru'ti·niz'er
scru'ti·ny
scu'ba
scud, scud'ded,
  scud'ding
scuff
scuf'fle, -fled, -fling
scuf'fler
scull (*oar, boat*)
  ✔ *skull*
scul'ler·y
scul'lion
sculpt
sculp'tor
sculp'tur·al
sculp'ture, -tured,
  -tur'ing
scum
scup *pl.* scup *or*
  scups
scup'per
scurf
scur·ril'i·ty

scur'ri·lous
scur'ry, -ried,
  -ry·ing
scur'vy
scutch'eon
scut'tle, -tled, -tling
scut'tle·butt'
scythe, scythed,
  scyth'ing
sea (*body of water*)
  ✔ *see, si*
sea'bed'
sea'bird'
sea'board'
sea'coast'
sea'far'er
sea'far'ing
sea'food'
sea'go'ing
sea' green'
sea' gull' *also*
  sea'gull'
sea' horse'
seal
sea'-lane'
seal'ant
seal'er
seal'ing wax'
seal'skin'
seam (*junction*)
  ✔ *seem*
sea'man (*sailor*)
  ✔ *semen*
sea'man·ship'
seam'stress
seam'y
sé'ance'

sea'plane'
sea'port'
sear (*to scorch*)
  ✔ *seer, sere*
search
search'light'
sea'scape'
sea'shell'
sea'shore'
sea'sick'
sea'side'
sea'son
sea'son·a·ble
sea'son·a·bly
sea'son·al
sea'son·ing
seat
seat'ing
sea'ward *adv. & adj.*
sea'wards *adv.*
sea'way'
sea'weed'
sea'wor'thi·ness
sea'wor'thy
se·ba'ceous
se'cant'
se·cede', -ced'ed,
  -ced'ing
se·ces'sion
se·ces'sion·ism
se·ces'sion·ist
se·clude', -clud'ed,
  -clud'ing
se·clu'sion
sec'ond
sec'on·dar'i·ly
sec'ond·ar'y

sec′ond-class′ *adj.*
  & *adv.*

sec′ond-de•gree′
  burn′

sec′ond-guess′ *v.*

sec′ond•hand′ *adj.*
  & *adv.*

sec′ond-rate′ *adj.*

se′cre•cy

se′cret (*hidden*)
  ✔ secrete

sec′re•tar′i•al

sec′re•tar′i•at

sec′re•tar′y

sec′re•tar′y-
  gen′er•al *pl.*
  sec′re•tar′ies-
  gen′er•al

se•crete′ (*to produce
  a substance, to
  hide*), -cret′ed,
  -cret′ing
  ✔ secret

se•cre′tion

se•cre′tive

se•cre′tor

se•cre′to•ry

sect

sec•tar′i•an

sec•tar′i•an•ism

sec′tion

sec′tion•al

sec′tion•al•ism

sec′tion•al•ist

sec′tor

sec′u•lar

sec′u•lar•i•za′tion

sec′u•lar•ize′,
  -ized′, -iz′ing

se•cur′a•ble

se•cure′, -cur′er,
  -cur′est

se•cure′, -cured′,
  -cur′ing

se•cu′ri•ty

se•dan′

se•date′, -dat′ed,
  -dat′ing

se•da′tion

sed′a•tive

sed′en•tar′i•ly

sed′en•tar′y

Se′der *pl.* -ders *or*
  Se•dar′im

sedge

sed′i•ment

sed′i•men′ta•ry

sed′i•men•ta′tion

se•di′tion

se•di′tious

se•duce′, -duced′,
  -duc′ing

se•duce′a•ble *or*
  se•duc′i•ble

se•duc′er

se•duc′tion

se•duc′tive

sed′u•lous

see (*to perceive with
  the eye*), saw, seen,
  see′ing
  ✔ sea, si

see (*bishop's position*)
  ✔ sea, si

seed (*plant part*), *pl.*
  seeds *or* seed
  ✔ cede

seed′ling

seed′y

seek, sought,
  seek′ing

seem (*to appear to be*)
  ✔ seam

seep

seep′age

seer (*person who fore-
  sees*)
  ✔ sear, sere

seer′suck′er

see′saw′

seethe, seethed,
  seeth′ing

see′-through′ *adj.*

seg′ment

seg•men′tal

seg′men•ta′tion

se′go lil′y

seg′re•gate′,
  -gat′ed, -gat′ing

seg′re•ga′tion

seg′re•ga′tion•ist

seine (*to fish with a
  net*), seined,
  sein′ing
  ✔ sane

seis′mic

seis′mo•gram′

seis′mo•graph′

seis•mog′ra•pher

seis′mo•graph′ic
  also seis′mo•graph′-

i•cal
seis•mog′ra•phy
seis•mo•log′ic *also*
    seis′mo•log′i•cal
seis•mol′o•gist
seis•mol′o•gy
seiz′a•ble
seize, seized, seiz′ing
sei′zure
sel′dom
se•lect′
se•lec′tion
se•lec′tive
se•lec′tiv′i•ty
se•lect′man
se•lec′tor
se•lect′wom′an
se•le′ni•um
self *pl.* selves
self′-ab•sorbed′
self′-ad•dressed′
self′-ap•point′ed
self′-as•sur′ance
self′-as•sured′
self′-cen′tered
self′-con•fessed′
self′-con•fi•dence
self′-con•fi•dent
self′-con•scious
self′-con•tained′
self′-con•trol′
self′-con•trolled′
self′-de•fense′
self′-de•ni′al
self′-de•struct′
self′-de•ter′mi•na′•
    tion

self′-dis′ci•pline
self′-ed′u•cat′ed
self′-ef•fac′ing
self′-em•ployed′
self′-es•teem′
self′-ev′i•dent
self′-ex•plan′a•
    to′ry
self′-ex•pres′sion
self′-ful•fill′ing
self′-gov′ern•ing
self′-gov′ern•ment
self′-help′
self′-im•por′tance
self′-im•por′tant
self′-im•prove′-
    ment
self′-in•dul′gence
self′-in•dul′gent
self′-in′ter•est
self′ish
self′-knowl′edge
self′less
self′-made′
self′-pit′y
self′-pol′li•na′tion
self′-por′trait
self′-pos•sessed′
self′-pos•ses′sion
self′-pres•er•va′tion
self′-pro•pelled′
self′-re•gard′
self′-re•li′ance
self′-re•li′ant
self′-re•spect′
self′-re•straint′
self′-right′eous

self′-rule′
self′-sac′ri•fice′
self′same′
self′-sat′is•fac′tion
self′-sat′is•fied′
self′-seek′ing
self′-serv′ice
self′-serv′ing
self′-start′er
self′-styled′
self′-suf•fi′cien•cy
self′-suf•fi′cient
self′-sup•port′ing
self′-sus•tain′ing
self′-taught′
self′-will′
self′-willed′
self′-wind′ing
sell (*to exchange for
    money*), sold,
    sell′ing
    ✔ cell
sell′er (*person who
    sells*)
    ✔ cellar
sell′out′ *n.*
selt′zer
sel′vage *also*
    sel′vedge
se•man′ti•cist
se•man′tics
sem′a•phore′
sem′blance
se′men (*whitish
    fluid*)
    ✔ seaman
se•mes′ter

sem'i·an'nu·al
(twice a year)
✔ biannual, biennial,
biyearly, semiyearly
sem'i·ar'id
sem'i·a·rid'i·ty
sem'i·au'to·mat'ic
sem'i·cir'cle
sem'i·cir'cu·lar
sem'i·co'lon
sem'i·con·duc'tor
sem'i·con'scious
sem'i·de·tached'
sem'i·dry'
sem'i·fi'nal n.
sem'i·fi'nal adj.
sem'i·fi'nal·ist
sem'i·for'mal
sem'i·gloss'
sem'i·month'ly
(twice a month)
✔ bimonthly
sem'i·nal
sem'i·nar
sem'i·nar'i·an
sem'i·nar'y
Sem'i·nole' pl.
-nole' or -noles'
sem'i·of·fi'cial
sem'i·pre'cious
sem'i·pri'vate
sem'i·pro·fes'sion·al
sem'i·skilled'
sem'i·sol'id
Sem'ite'
Se·mit'ic
sem'i·tone'

sem'i·trail'er
sem'i·trop'i·cal
sem'i·vow'el
sem'i·week'ly
(twice a week)
✔ biweekly
semiyearly (twice a
year)
✔ biannual, biennial,
biyearly, semiannual
sen'ate also Sen'ate
sen'a·tor
sen'a·to'ri·al
send, sent, send'ing
send'off' n.
Sen'e·ca pl. -ca or
-cas
sen'e·schal
se'nile'
se·nil'i·ty
sen'ior
sen·ior'i·ty
sen'na
se·ñor' pl. -ño'res
se·ño'ra
se·ño·ri'ta
sen'sate' also
sen'sat'ed
sen·sa'tion
sen·sa'tion·al
sen·sa'tion·al·ism
sen·sa'tion·al·ize',
-ized', -iz'ing
sense, sensed,
sens'ing
sense'less
sen·si·bil'i·ty

sen'si·ble
sen'si·bly
sen'si·tive
sen'si·tiv'i·ty or
sen'si·tive·ness
sen'si·ti·za'tion
sen'si·tize', -tized',
-tiz'ing
sen'sor
sen'so·ry
sen'su·al
sen'su·al'i·ty
sen'su·ous
sent past tense and
past participle of
send
✔ cent, scent
sen'tence, -tenced,
-tenc'ing
sen·ten'tial (relating
to a sentence)
sen·ten'tious
(pithy, pompous)
sen'tience
sen'tient
sen'ti·ment
sen'ti·men'tal
sen'ti·men·tal'i·ty
sen'ti·men·tal·ize',
-ized', -iz'ing
sen'ti·nel
sen'try
se'pal
sep'a·ra·ble
sep'a·rate', -rat'ed,
-rat'ing
sep'a·rate·ly

sep'a·ra'tion

sep'a·ra·tism

sep'a·ra·tist

sep'a·ra'tor

se'pi·a

sep'sis

Sep·tem'ber

sep·ten'ni·al

sep·tet' *also*
  sep'tette'

sep'tic

sep'ti·ce'mi·a

sep·til'lion

sep·til'lionth

sep·tu·a·ge·nar'-
  i·an

sep'tum *pl.* -ta

sep'ul·cher

se·pul'chral

se'quel

se'quence

se·quen'tial

se·ques'ter

se'ques·tra'tion

se'quin

se'quined

se·quoi'a

se·ra'glio *pl.* -glios

se·ra'pe *also*
  sa·ra'pe

ser'aph *pl.* -a·phim
  or -aphs

se·raph'ic

Serb

Ser'bi·an

Ser'bo-Cro·a'tian

sere *(withered)*

  ✔ *sear, seer*

ser'e·nade',
  -nad'ed, -nad'ing

ser'en·dip'i·tous

ser'en·dip'i·ty

se·rene'

se·ren'i·ty

serf *(laborer)*

  ✔ *surf*

serf'dom

serge *(cloth)*

  ✔ *surge*

ser'geant

ser'geant at arms'
  pl. ser'geants at
  arms'

ser'geant ma'jor
  pl. ser'geants
  ma'jor *or* ser'geant
  ma'jors

se'ri·al *(of or in a se-
ries)*

  ✔ *cereal*

se'ri·al·i·za'tion

se'ri·al·ize', -ized',
  -iz'ing

se'ries *pl.* -ries

ser'if

se'ri·ous

ser'mon

ser'mon·ize',
  -ized', -iz'ing

ser'mon·iz'er

se'rous

ser'pent

ser'pen·tine'

ser'rate' *or* ser'rat'ed

se'rum *pl.* -rums *or*
  -ra

ser'vant

serve, served,
  serv'ing

serv'er

serv'ice, -iced,
  -ic·ing

serv'ice·a·bil'i·ty

serv'ice·a·ble

serv'ice·man

serv'ice·per'son

serv'ice·wom'an

ser'vile

ser·vil'i·ty

ser'vi·tor

ser'vi·tude'

ses'a·me

ses'qui·cen·ten'-
  ni·al

ses'sile'

ses'sion *(meeting)*

  ✔ *cession*

set, set, set'ting

set'back' *n.*

set·tee'

set'ter

set'ting

set'tle, -tled, -tling

set'tle·ment

set'tler

set'-to' *pl.* -tos'

set'up' *n.*

sev'en

sev'en·teen'

sev'en·teenth'

sev'enth

Sev'enth-day'
  Ad'ven'tist
sev'en·ti·eth
sev'en·ty
sev'er
sev'er·al
sev'er·ance
se·vere', -ver'er,
  -ver'est
se·ver'i·ty
sew (to stitch),
  sewed, sewn or
  sewed, sew'ing
  ✔ so, sow
sew'age
sew'er
sew'er·age
sex
sex'a·ge·nar'i·an
sex'ism
sex'ist
sex'-linked'
sex'tant
sex·tet'
sex·til'lion
sex·til'lionth
sex'ton
sex·tu'ple, -pled,
  -pling
sex·tup'let
sex'u·al
sex'u·al'i·ty
shab'bi·ly
shab'bi·ness
shab'by
shack
shack'le, -led, -ling

shad pl. shad or
  shads
shade, shad'ed,
  shad'ing
shad'i·ness
shad'ow
shad'y
shaft
shag
shag'bark'
shag'gy
shah
shak'a·ble or
  shake'a·ble
shake, shook,
  shak'en, shak'ing
shake'down'
shake'out'
shak'er (one that
  shakes)
Shak'er (member of
  a religious group)
Shake·spear'e·an
  or Shake·spear'i·an
shake'up' n.
shak'i·ly
shak'o pl. -os or -oes
shak'y
shale
shall
shal'lop
shal'lot
shal'low
sham, shammed,
  sham'ming
sha'man
sham'ble, -bled,

-bling
sham'bles
shame, shamed,
  sham'ing
shame'faced'
shame'fac'ed·ly
shame'ful
shame'less
sham·poo' pl.
  -poos
sham'rock'
shang·hai', -haied',
  -hai'ing
shank
shan·tung'
shan'ty (shack)
  ✔ chantey
shape, shaped,
  shap'ing
shape'less
shape'li·ness
shape'ly
shard also sherd
  (potsherd)
  ✔ chard
share, shared,
  shar'ing
share'crop'per
share'hold'er
shark
sharp'en
sharp'en·er
sharp'shoot'er
shat'ter
shat'ter·proof'
shave, shaved,
  shaved or shav'en,

shav′ing
shav′er
Sha•vi′an
Sha•vu′ot′
shawl
Shaw•nee′ *pl.* -nee′
  or -nees′
she
sheaf *pl.* sheaves
shear *(to clip)*,
  sheared, sheared *or*
  shorn, shear′ing
  ✔ *sheer*
shears
sheath *pl.* sheaths
sheathe, sheathed,
  sheath′ing
shed, shed, shed′-
  ding
shed′der
sheen
sheep *pl.* sheep
sheep′dog′ *also*
  sheep′ dog′
sheep′fold′
sheep′herd′er
sheep′ish
sheep′skin′
sheer *(to swerve)*
  ✔ *shear*
sheer *(transparent,*
  complete)
  ✔ *shear*
sheet
sheet′ing
sheik *also* sheikh
  (Arab leader)

✔ *chic*
shek′el
shel′duck′
shelf *pl.* shelves
shell
shel•lac′, -lacked,
  -lack′ing
shelled
shell′fish′
shell′-shocked′
shel′ter
shel′tie *also* shel′ty
shelve, shelved
  shelv′ing
she•nan′i•gan
shep′herd
shep′herd•ess
sher′bet
sher′iff
sher′ry
Shet′land′ po′ny
shib′bo•leth
shield
shift′i•ly
shift′less
shift′y
Shi′ite′
shil•le′lagh *also*
  shil•la′lah
shil′ling *(British*
  coin)
  ✔ *schilling*
shil′ly-shal′ly,
  -lied, -ly•ing
shim′mer
shim′my, -mied,
  -my•ing

shin, shinned,
  shin′ning
shin′bone′
shin′dig′
shine, shone *or*
  shined, shin′ing
shin′er
shin′gle, -gled,
  -gling
shin′gles
shin′i•ness
shin′ny, -nied,
  -ny•ing
shin′ splints′ *also*
  shin′splints′
Shin′to
Shin′to•ism
Shin′to•ist
shin′y
ship, shipped,
  ship′ping
ship′board′
ship′build′er
ship′build′ing
ship′load′
ship′mas′ter
ship′mate′
ship′ment
ship′per
ship′shape′
ship′wreck′
ship′yard′
shire
shirk
shirr
shirt
shirt′ing

shirt′tail′
shirt′waist′
shish′ ke•bab′ *also*
  shish′ ke•bob′ *or*
  shish′ ka•bob′
shiv′er
shiv′er•y
shoal
shoat *also* shote
shock
shock′er
shock′ing
shod′dy
shoe *(to cover the
  foot)*, shod, shod *or*
  shod′den, shoe′ing
  ✔ *shoo*
shoe′horn′
shoe′lace′
shoe′mak′er
shoe′string′
shoe′tree′
sho′far′ *pl.* -fars *or*
  sho•froth′
sho′gun
shoo *(to scare away)*,
  shooed, shoo′ing
  ✔ *shoe*
shoo′-in′
shook-up′ *adj.*
shoot *(to fire a
  weapon)*, shot,
  shoot′ing
  ✔ *chute*
shoot′er
shoot′out′ *also*
  shoot′-out′ *n.*

shop, shopped,
  shop′ping
shop′keep′er
shop′lift′
shop′lift′er
shop′per
shop′talk′
shop′worn′
shore *(land along a
  body of water)*
shore *(to support)*,
  shored, shor′ing
shore′ bird′
shore′line′
short
short′age
short′bread′
short′cake′
short′change′,
  -changed′,
  -chang′ing
short′chang′er
short′ cir′cuit *n.*
short′-cir′cuit *v.*
short′com′ing
short′cut′
short′en
short′en•ing
short′fall′
short′hand′
short′-hand′ed
short′horn′
short′-lived′
short′-or′der *adj.*
short′-range′
short′sight′ed
short′stop′

short′-tem′pered
short′wave′ *adj.*
short′-wind′ed
Sho•sho′ne *pl.* -ne
  or -nes
shot
shot′gun′
shot′ put′
shot′-put′er
should
shoul′der
should′n't
shout
shove, shoved,
  shov′ing
shov′el, -eled *also*
  -elled, -el•ing *also*
  -el•ling
shov′el•er *also*
  shov′el•ler
show, showed,
  shown *or* showed,
  show′ing
show′boat′
show′case′
show′down′
show′er *(one that
  shows)*
show′er *(rainfall)*
show′girl′
show′i•ness
show′man
show′man•ship′
show′off′ *n.*
show′piece′
show′ room′
show′time′ *or*

show′time′
show′y
shrap′nel *pl.* -nel
shred, shred′ded *or*
  shred, shred′ding
shred′der
shrew
shrewd
shrew′ish
shriek
shrike
shrill
shrimp *pl.* shrimp *or*
  shrimps
shrine
shrink, shrank *or*
  shrunk, shrunk *or*
  shrunk′en,
  shrink′ing
shrink′a•ble
shrink′age
shrink′er
shrink′-wrap′,
  -wrapped′,
  -wrap′ping
shrive, shrove *or*
  shrived, shriv′en *or*
  shrived, shriv′ing
shriv′el, -eled *or*
  -elled, -el•ing *or*
  -el•ling
shriv′er
shroud
shrub
shrub′ber•y
shrub′by
shrug, shrugged,

shrug′ging
shuck
shucks
shuck′er
shud′der
shuf′fle, -fled, -fling
shuf′fle•board′
shul
shun, shunned,
  shun′ning
shun′ner
shunt
shush
shut, shut, shut′ting
shut′down′ *n.*
shut′eye′
shut′-in′ *n.*
shut′off′ *n.*
shut′out′ *n.*
shut′ter
shut′ter•bug′
shut′tle, -tled, -tling
shut′tle•cock′
shy, shi′er *or* shy′er,
  shi′est *or* shy′est
shy, shied, shy′ing
shy′ster
si *(musical tone)*
  ✔ sea, see
Si′a•mese′ *pl.* -mese′
Si•be′ri•an
sib′i•lance *or*
  sib′i•lan•cy
sib′i•lant
sib′ling
sib′yl
sic *(thus)*

✔ sick
sic *also* sick *(to at-*
  tack), sicced *also*
  sicked, sic′cing *also*
  sick′ing
  ✔ sick
Si•cil′ian
sick *(ill)*
  ✔ sic
sick′bay′
sick′bed′
sick′en
sick′en•ing
sick′le
sick′li•ness
sick′ly
sid′dur *pl.*
  sid•du′rim
side, sid′ed, sid′ing
side′arm′ *adj. & adv.*
side′ arm′ *n.*
side′board′
side′burns′
side′car′
sid′ed
side′kick′
side′light′
side′line′
side′long′
si•de′re•al
side′sad′dle
side′show′
side′split′ting
side′step′,
  -stepped′, -step′ping
side′step′per
side′stroke′

side'swipe',
-swiped', -swip'ing
side'track'
side'walk'
side'wall'
sideward *adv. & adj.*
sidewards *adv.*
side'ways' *also*
side'way'
side'wind'er
sid'ing
si'dle, -dled, -dling
siege
si•en'na
si•er'ra
si•es'ta
sieve, sieved, siev'ing
sift
sift'er
sigh
sight *(ability to see)*
✔ *cite, site*
sight'ed
sight'less
sight'-read', -read',
-read'ing
sight'see'ing
sight'se'er
sig'ma
sign *(indication)*
✔ *sine*
sig'nal, -naled *or*
-nalled, -nal•ing *or*
-nal•ling
sig'nal•er *or*
sig'nal•ler
sig'nal•i•za'tion

sig'nal•ize', -ized',
-iz'ing
sig'na•to'ry
sig'na•ture
sign'board'
sig'net *(seal)*
✔ *cygnet*
sig•nif'i•cance
sig•nif'i•cant
sig•nif'i•ca'tion
sig'ni•fy, -fied,
-fy'ing
si•gnor' *pl.* -gno'ri
also -gnors'
si•gno'ra *pl.* -gno're
or -gno'ras
si•gno're *pl.* -gno'ri
si'gno•ri'na *pl.* -ne
or -nas
sign'post'
Sikh
si'lage
si'lence, -lenced,
-lenc•ing
si'lent
sil'hou•ette',
-et'ted, -et'ting
sil'i•ca
sil'i•cate'
sil'i•con *(element)*
sil'i•cone' *(polymer)*
silk'en
silk'i•ness
silk'-screen' *or*
silk'screen' *n.*
silk'-screen' *v.*
silk'worm'

silk'y
sill
sil'li•ness
sil'ly
si'lo *pl.* -los
silt
Si•lu'ri•an
sil'ver
sil'ver•fish' *pl.* -fish'
or -fish'es
sil'ver•smith'
sil'ver-tongued'
sil'ver•ware'
sil'ver•y
sim'i•an
sim'i•lar
sim'i•lar'i•ty
sim'i•le
si•mil'i•tude'
sim'mer
si'mo•ny
sim'per
sim'ple, -pler, -plest
sim'ple-mind'ed
or sim'ple•mind'ed
sim'ple•ton
sim•plic'i•ty
sim'pli•fi•ca'tion
sim'pli•fi'er
sim'pli•fy', -fied',
-fy'ing
sim'ply
sim'u•late', -lat'ed,
-lat'ing
sim'u•la'tion
sim'u•la'tive
sim'u•la'tor

si′mul·cast′
si′mul·ta·ne′i·ty
si′mul·ta′ne·ous
sin, sinned, sin′ning
since
sin·cere′, -cer·er,
   -cer′est
sin·cere′ly
sin·cer′i·ty
sine *(mathematical*
   function)
   ✔ *sign*
si′ne·cure′
sin′ew
sin′ew·y
sin′ful
sing, sang *or* sung,
   sung, sing′ing
singe, singed,
   singe′ing
sing′er
Sin′gha·lese′ *or*
   Sin′ha·lese′ *pl.*
   -lese′
sin′gle, -gled, -gling
sin′gle-breast′ed
sin′gle-hand′ed
sin′gle-mind′ed
sin′gle-space′,
   -spaced′, -spac′ing
sin′gly
sing′song′
sin′gu·lar
sin′gu·lar′i·ty
sin′is·ter
sin′is·tral
sink, sank *or* sunk,

sunk, sink′ing
sink′a·ble
sink′hole′
sin′ner
sin′u·os′i·ty
sin′u·ous
si′nus
si′nus·i′tis
Siou′an
Sioux *pl.* Sioux
sip, sipped, sip′ping
si′phon *also*
   sy′phon
si′phon·al *or*
   si·phon′ic
sir
sire, sired, sir′ing
si′ren
sir′loin′
si·roc′co *pl.* -cos
sis
si′sal
sis′sy
sis′ter
sis′ter·hood′
sis′ter-in-law′ *pl.*
   sis′ters-in-law′
sis′ter·li·ness
sis′ter·ly
sit, sat, sit′ting
si·tar′
sit′com′ *also*
   sit′-com′
sit′-down′ strike′
site *(location)*
   ✔ *cite, sight*
sit′-in′ *n.*

sit′ter
sit′ting
sit′u·ate′, -at′ed,
   -at′ing
sit′u·a′tion
sit′-up′ *n.*
sitz′ bath′
six
six′-gun′
six′-pack′
six′pence
six′-shoot′er
six′teen′
six′teenth′
sixth
six′ti·eth
six′ty
siz′a·ble *also*
   size′a·ble
siz′a·bly
size, sized, siz′ing
siz′zle, -zled, -zling
skate, skat′ed,
   skat′ing
skate′board′
skate′board′er
skate′board′ing
skat′er
skeet
skein
skel′e·tal
skel′e·ton
skep′tic *also* scep′tic
skep′ti·cal *also*
   scep′ti·cal
skep′ti·cism *also*
   scep′ti·cism

sketch
sketch'book'
sketch'i•ly
sketch'i•ness
sketch'pad'
sketch'y
skew
skew'er
ski *pl.* skis
ski, skied, ski'ing
skid, skid'ded,
  skid'ding
ski'er
skiff
skill
skilled
skil'let
skill'ful
skim, skimmed,
  skim'ming
skim'mer
skimp'i•ness
skimp'y
skin, skinned,
  skin'ning
skin'-deep'
skin'-dive', -dived',
  -div'ing
skin' div'er
skin' div'ing *n.*
skin'flint'
skin'ner
skin'ni•ness
skin'ny
skin'tight'
skip, skipped,
  skip'ping

skip'per
skir'mish
skirt
skit
skit'ter
skit'tish
skit'tles
skoal
skulk
skull *(head bones)*
  ✔ scull
skull'cap'
skull•dug'ger•y *or*
  skul•dug'ger•y
skunk
sky
sky' blue'
sky'box'
sky'dive', -dived',
  -div'ing
sky'div'er
Skye' ter'ri•er
sky'-high'
sky'jack'
sky'jack'er
sky'lark'
sky'light'
sky'line'
sky'rock'et
sky'scrap'er
sky'ward *adv. & adj.*
sky'wards *adv.*
sky'writ'er
sky'writ'ing
slab
slack
slack'en

slack'er
slag
slake, slaked,
  slak'ing
sla'lom
slam, slammed,
  slam'ming
slam'-dunk' *or*
  slam' dunk'
slan'der
slan'der•ous
slang
slang'y
slant
slant'wise'
slap, slapped,
  slap'ping
slap'dash'
slap'hap'py
slap'stick'
slash
slat
slate, slat'ed, slat'ing
slath'er
slat'tern
slaugh'ter
slaugh'ter•house'
Slav
slave, slaved,
  slav'ing
slave' driv'er
slave'hold'er
slav'er *(to drool)*
slav'er *(ship engaged
  in slave traffic)*
slav'er•y
Slav'ic

slav′ish
slaw
slay *(to kill)*, slew,
 slain, slay′ing
 ✔ *sleigh*
slea′zi•ness
slea′zy
sled, sled′ded,
 sled′ding
sledge
sledge′ham′mer
sleek
sleep, slept, sleep′ing
sleep′i•ly
sleep′i•ness
sleep′o′ver
sleep′walk′ing
sleep′walk′er
sleep′y
sleep′y•head′
sleet
sleeve, sleeved,
 sleev′ing
sleigh *(sledge)*
 ✔ *slay*
sleight *(dexterity,*
 trick)
 ✔ *slight*
slen′der
sleuth
slew *also* slue *(large*
 amount)
 ✔ *slough, slue*
slice, sliced, slic′ing
slice′a•ble
slic′er
slick

slick′er
slide, slid, slid′ing
slight *(small)*
 ✔ *sleight*
slight *(to snub)*
 ✔ *sleight*
slim, slim′mer,
 slim′mest
slim, slimmed,
 slim′ming
slime
slim′i•ness
slim′y
sling, slung,
 sling′ing
sling′shot′
slink, slunk *also*
 slinked, slink′ing
slip, slipped,
 slip′ping
slip′case′
slip′cov′er
slip′knot′
slip′-on′ *n. & adj.*
slip′o′ver
slip′page
slip′per
slip′per•i•ness
slip′per•y
slip′shod′
slip′-up′ *n.*
slit, slit, slit′ting
slith′er
slit′ter
sliv′er
slob
slob′ber

sloe *(fruit)*
 ✔ *slow*
slog, slogged,
 slog′ging
slo′gan
slog′ger
sloop
slop, slopped,
 slop′ping
slope, sloped,
 slop′ing
slop′pi•ly
slop′pi•ness
slop′py
slosh
slot, slot′ted,
 slot′ting
sloth
sloth′ful
slouch
slouch′y
slough *also* slew
 (hollow, swamp)
 ✔ *slew, slue*
slough *(to shed)*
Slo′vak′
slov′en
Slo′vene′
slov′en•li•ness
slov′en•ly
slow *(not quick)*
 ✔ *sloe*
slow′down′ *n.*
slow′-mo′tion *adj.*
slow′poke′
slow′-wit′ted *or*
 slow′wit′ted

sludge
sludg'y
slue *also* slew *(to turn),* slued *also* slewed, slu'ing *or* slew'ing
✓ slew, slough
slug, slugged, slug'ging
slug'gard
slug'ger
slug'gish
sluice, sluiced, sluic'ing
slum
slum'ber
slum'ber·er
slum'ber·ous *or* slum'brous
slump
slur, slurred, slur'ring
slurp
slush'i·ness
slush'y
slut
sly, sli'er *also* sly'er, sli'est *or* sly'est
sly'ness
smack
smack'-dab' *adv.*
small
small'ish
small'-mind'ed
small'pox'
small'-scale' *adj.*
small'time' *or* small'-time' *adj.*

smarm'y
smart
smart' al'eck *n.*
smart'-al'eck *or* smart'-al'eck·y *adj.*
smart'en
smash
smash'ing
smash'up' *n.*
smat'ter·ing
smear
smell, smelled *or* smelt, smell'ing
smell'y
smelt *(to melt)*
smelt *(fish), pl.* smelts *or* smelt
smelt'er
smid'gen *also* smid'geon *or* smid'gin
smile, smiled, smil'ing
smil'er
smirch
smirk
smite, smote, smit'ten *or* smote, smit'ing
smith
smith'er·eens'
smith'y
smock
smock'ing
smog
smog'gy
smoke, smoked,

smok'ing
smoke'house'
smoke'less
smok'er
smoke' screen' *or* smoke'screen'
smoke'stack'
smok'i·ness
smok'y
smol'der *also* smoul'der
smooth
smooth'bore' *also* smooth' bore'
smor'gas·bord'
smoth'er
smudge, smudged, smudg'ing
smudg'y
smug, smug'ger, smug'gest
smug'gle, -gled, -gling
smug'gler
smut
smut'ty
snack
snaf'fle, -fled, -fling
snag, snagged snag'ging
snail
snake
snake'bite'
snake'root'
snake'skin'
snak'y
snap, snapped,

snap'ping
snap'drag'on
snap'per
snap'pi·ly
snap'pi·ness
snap'pish
snap'py
snap'shot'
snare, snared,
 snar'ing
snarl
snatch
sneak, sneaked *also*
 snuck, sneak'ing
sneak'er
sneak'i·ly
sneak'i·ness
sneak'y
sneer
sneeze, sneezed,
 sneez'ing
snick'er
snide, snid'er,
 snid'est
sniff
snif'fle, -fled, -fling
snif'ter
snig'ger
snip, snipped,
 snip'ping
snipe *pl.* snipe *or*
 snipes
snipe, sniped,
 snip'ing
snip'er
snip'pet
snip'py

snit
snitch
sniv'el, -eled *or*
 -elled, -el·ing *or*
 -el·ling
sniv'el·er *or*
 sniv'el·ler
snob
snob'ber·y
snob'bish
snob'bism
snood
snook'er
snoop
snoop'y
snoot'i·ly
snoot'i·ness
snoot'y
snooze, snoozed,
 snooz'ing
snore, snored,
 snor'ing
snor'kel
snort
snout
snow
snow'ball'
snow'bird'
snow'-blind' *or*
 snow'-blind'ed
snow'bound'
snow'cap'
snow'capped'
snow'drift'
snow'drop'
snow'fall'
snow'flake'

snow'man'
snow'mo·bile'
snow'plow'
snow'shoe',
 -shoed', -shoe'ing
snow'storm'
snow'suit'
snow'y
snub, snubbed,
 snub'bing
snub'-nosed'
snuff
snuff'box'
snuf'fle, -fled, -fling
snug, snug'ger,
 snug'gest
snug'gle, -gled,
 -gling
so *(thus)*
 ✔ sew, sow
soak
so'-and-so' *pl.* -sos'
soap
soap'box'
soap'i·ness
soap'stone'
soap'suds'
soap'y
soar *(to rise)*
 ✔ sore
sob, sobbed,
 sob'bing
so'ber
so·bri'e·ty
so'bri·quet'
so'-called'
soc'cer

so·cia·bil'i·ty *or*
  so'cia·ble•ness
so'cia·ble
so'cia·bly
so'cial
so'cial·ism
so'cial·ist
so'cial·is'tic
so'cial·ite'
so'cial·i·za'tion
so'cial·ize', -ized',
  -iz'ing
so·ci'e·tal
so·ci'e·ty
so'ci·o·cul'tur·al
so'ci·o·ec'o·nom'ic
so'ci·o·log'ic *or*
  so'ci·o·log'i·cal
so'ci·ol'o·gist
so'ci·ol'o·gy
so'ci·o·path'
so'ci·o·po·lit'i·cal
sock *pl.* socks *or* sox
sock'et
sock'eye' salm'on
So·crat'ic
sod, sod'ded,
  sod'ding
so'da
so·dal'i·ty
sod'den
so'di·um
so'di·um-va'por
  lamp'
sod'om·y
so'fa
soft

soft'ball'
soft'-boiled'
soft'-core'
soft'cov'er
soft'en
soft'en·er
soft'heart'ed
soft'-ped'al, -aled
  or -alled, -al·ing *or*
  -al·ling
soft'-shell' *also*
  soft'-shelled'
soft'-shoe' *n.*
soft'-soap' *v.*
soft'-spo'ken
soft'ware'
soft'wood'
soft'y *or* soft'ie *pl.*
  -ies
sog'gi·ness
sog'gy
soil
soi·ree' *also* soi·rée'
so'journ'
so'journ'er
sol *also* so (*musical
  tone*)
  ✔ sole, soul
sol'ace, -aced,
  -ac·ing
so'lar
so·lar'i·um *pl.* -i·a
  or -i·ums
sol'der
sol'dier
sole (*bottom of a
  shoe*)

✔ sol, soul
sole (*to put a sole on*),
  soled, sol'ing
  ✔ sol, soul
sole (*single*)
  ✔ sol, soul
sole (*fish*), *pl.* sole *or*
  soles
  ✔ sol, soul
sol'e·cism
sole'ly
sol'emn
so·lem'ni·ty
sol'em·ni·za'tion
sol'em·nize',
  -nized', -niz'ing
so'le·noid'
so·lic'it
so·lic'i·ta'tion
so·lic'i·tor
so·lic'i·tous
so·lic'i·tude'
sol'id
sol'i·dar'i·ty
so·lid'i·fi·ca'tion
so·lid'i·fy', -fied',
  -fy'ing
so·lid'i·ty
sol'id-state' *adj.*
so·lil'o·quize',
  -quized', -quiz'ing
so·lil'o·quy *pl.*
  -quies
sol'ip·sism
sol'ip·sis'tic
sol'i·taire'
sol'i·tar'y

sol'i·tude'
so'lo *pl.* -los
so'lo·ist
sol'stice
sol'u·bil'i·ty
sol'u·ble
sol'ute
so·lu'tion
solv'a·ble
solve, solved,
 solv'ing
sol'ven·cy
sol'vent
So·ma'li *pl.* -li *or* -lis
so·mat'ic
som'ber
som·bre'ro *pl.* -ros
some *(a few)*
 ✔ sum
some'bod'y
some'day'
some'how'
some'one'
some'place'
som'er·sault' *also*
 sum'mer·sault'
some'thing'
some'time'
some'times'
some'way' *also*
 some'ways'
some'what'
some'where'
som·nam'bu·late',
 -lat'ed, -lat'ing
som·nam'bu·lism
som·nam'bu·list

som·nam'bu·lis'-
 tic *also* som·nam'-
 bu·lar
som'no·lence
som'no·lent
son *(male child)*
 ✔ sun
so'nar'
so·na'ta
song
song'bird'
song'writ'er
son'ic
son'-in-law' *pl.*
 sons'-in-law'
son'net
son'net·eer'
son'ny *(boy)*
 ✔ sunny
so·nor'i·ty
so·no'rous
soon
soot
sooth *(truth)*
soothe *(to calm)*,
 soothed, sooth'ing
sooth'say'er
soot'y
sop, sopped,
 sop'ping
soph'ism
soph'ist
so·phis'ti·cate',
 -cat'ed, -cat'ing
so·phis'ti·ca'tion
soph'is·try
soph'o·more'

soph'o·mor'ic
sop'o·rif'ic
sop'py
so·pran'o *pl.* -os
sor'cer·er
sor'cer·ess
sor'cer·y
sor'did
sore *(painful)*, sor'er,
 sor'est
 ✔ soar
sor'ghum
so·ror'i·ty
sor'rel
sor'row
sor'row·ful
sor'ry
sort'er
sor'tie
so'-so'
sot
sou
souf·flé'
sough
soul *(spirit)*
 ✔ sol, sole
soul'ful
soul'less
soul'-search'ing
sound
sound'ing
sound'proof'
sound'track'
soup
soup'spoon'
soup'y
sour

source
sour'dough'
sou'sa•phone'
souse, soused,
  sous'ing
south
South' Af'ri•can
South' A•mer'i•
  can
south'bound'
South' Car'o•
  lin'i•an
South' Da•ko'tan
south•east'
south•east'er
south•east'er•ly
south•east'ern
south•east'ward
  adj. & adv.
south•east'wards
  adv.
south'er•ly
south'ern
south'ern•er
south'ern•most'
south'paw
south'ward *adv. &*
  adj.
south'wards *adv.*
south•west'
south•west'er *also*
  sou'•west'er
south•west'er•ly
south•west'ern
south•west'ward
  adv. & adj.
south•west'wards

adv.
sou've•nir'
sov'er•eign
sov'er•eign•ty
so'vi•et'
sow *(to plant),*
  sowed, sown *or*
  sowed, sow'ing
  ✔ *sew, so*
sow *(female pig)*
soy
soy'a
soy'bean'
soy' sauce'
spa
space, spaced,
  spac'ing
space'craft' *pl.*
  -craft'
space'ship'
space'-time'
spa'cious
spade, spad'ed,
  spad'ing
spa'dix *pl.* -di•ces'
spa•ghet'ti
span, spanned,
  span'ning
span'dex
span'gle, -gled,
  -gling
Span'iard
span'iel
Span'ish
Span'ish
  A•mer'i•can *n.*
Span'ish-

A•mer'i•can *adj.*
spank'ing
span'ner
spar *(pole)*
spar *(to box),*
  sparred, spar'ring
spare, spared,
  spar'ing
spare, spar'er,
  spar'est
spare'ribs'
spark
spar'kle, -kled,
  -kling
spar'kler
spar'row
sparse, spars'er,
  spars'est
spar'si•ty
Spar'tan
spasm
spas•mod'ic
spas'tic
spat *(oyster spawn),*
  pl. spat *or* spats
spat *(to spawn, to*
  quarrel), spat'ted,
  spat'ting
spat *(shoe covering)*
spate
spa'tial
spat'ter
spat'u•la
spav'in
spav'ined
spawn
spay

speak, spoke,
spo'ken, speak'ing
speak'eas'y
speak'er
speak'er•phone'
spear
spear'fish' v.
spear'head'
spear'mint'
spe'cial
spe'cial•ist
spe•ci•al'i•ty (distin-
guishing feature)
✔ specialty
spe'cial•i•za'tion
spe'cial•ize', -ized',
-iz'ing
spe'cial•ty (special
occupation or skill)
✔ speciality
spe'cie (coin)
spe'cies (kind), pl.
-cies
spe•cif'ic
spe•cif'i•cal•ly
spec'i•fi•ca'tion
spec'i•fy', -fied',
-fy'ing
spec'i•men
spe'cious
speck
speck'le
speck'led
spec'ta•cle
spec•tac'u•lar
spec'ta'tor
spec'ter

spec'tral
spec'tro•gram'
spec'tro•graph'
spec'tro•graph'ic
spec•trog'ra•phy
spec'trom'e•ter
spec•trom'e•try
spec'tro•scope'
spec'tro•scop'ic or
spec'tro•scop'i•cal
spec•tros'co•py
spec'trum pl. -tra or
-trums
spec'u•late', -lat'ed,
-lat'ing
spec'u•la'tion
spec'u•la•tive
spec'u•la•tor
speech'less
speech'mak'er
speech'mak'ing
speech'writ'er
speech'writ'ing
speed, sped or
speed'ed,
speed'ing
speed'boat'
speed'er
speed•om'e•ter
speed'-read'ing
speed'up' n.
speed'way'
speed'well'
speed'y
spe'le•ol'o•gist
spe'le•ol'o•gy
spell, spelled or

spelt, spell'ing
spell'bind',
-bound', -bind'ing
spell'er
spell'ing bee'
spe•lunk'er
spe'lunk'ing
spend, spent,
spend'ing
spend'thrift'
sperm pl. sperm or
sperms
sper'ma•ce'ti pl.
-tis
sper•mat'o•phyte'
sper•mat'o•zo'on'
pl. -zo'a
spew
sphag'num
sphe'noid'
sphe•noi'dal
sphere
spher'i•cal
sphe'roid'
sphinc'ter
sphinx pl. sphinx'es
or sphin'ges'
sphyg'mo•ma•
nom'e•ter
spice, spiced,
spic'ing
spic'i•ness
spick'-and-span'
spic'ule
spic'y
spi'der
spiel

spiff′y
spig′ot
spike, spiked,
  spik′ing
spike′nard′
spik′i•ness
spik′y
spill, spilled *or* spilt,
  spill′ing
spill′age
spill′o•ver
spill′way′
spin, spun,
  spin′ning
spin′ach
spi′nal
spin′dle, -dled,
  -dling
spin′dly
spin′drift′
spine
spine′less
spin′et
spin′na•ker
spin′ner
spin′ner•et′
spin′off′ *or*
  spin′-off′
spin′ster
spin′y
spir′a•cle
spi′ral, -raled *also*
  -ralled, -ral•ing *also*
  -ral•ling
spire
spi•ril′lum *pl.* -la
spir′it

spir′it•ed
spir′it•less
spir′i•tu•al
spir′i•tu•al•ism
spir′i•tu•al•ist
spir′i•tu•al′i•ty
spi′ro•chete′
spi′ro•gy′ra
spit *(to eject from the mouth)*, spat *or* spit,
  spit′ting
spit *(to place on a rod)*, spit′ted,
  spit′ting
spit′ball′
spite, spit′ed,
  spit′ing
spite′ful
spit′fire′
spit′tle
spit•toon′
spitz
splash
splash′down′
splash′y
splat′ter
splay
splay′foot′
splay′foot′ed
spleen
splen′did
splen′dor
splice, spliced,
  splic′ing
splic′er
splint
splin′ter

split, split, split′ting
split′-lev′el
split′ter
splotch
splotch′y
splurge, splurged,
  splurg′ing
splut′ter
spoil, spoiled *or*
  spoilt, spoil′ing
spoil′age
spoil′er
spoil′sport′
spoke, spoked,
  spok′ing
spo′ken
spokes′man
spokes′per′son
spokes′wom′an
spo′li•a′tion
spo′li•a′tor
spon′dee′
sponge, sponged,
  spong′ing
spong′i•ness
spong′y
spon′sor
spon′sor•ship′
spon′ta•ne′i•ty
spon•ta•ne•ous
spoof
spook
spook′i•ness
spook′y
spool
spoon
spoon′bill′

spoon'-feed', -fed',
-feed'ing
spoon'ful'
spoor *(animal track)*
✔ *spore*
spo•rad'ic
spo•ran'gi•um *pl.*
-gi•a
spore *(reproductive
organ)*
✔ *spoor*
spo'ro•phyte'
spo'ro•zo'an
spor'ran
sport
sport'ing
spor'tive
sports'man
sports'man•like'
sports'man•ship'
sports'wear'
sports'wom'an
sports'writ'er
sport'y
spot, spot'ted,
spot'ting
spot'-check' *v.*
spot'less
spot'light', -light'ed
or -lit', -light'ing
spot'ti•ness
spot'ty
spouse
spout
spout'er
sprain
sprat

sprawl
spray
spread, spread,
spread'ing
spread'a•bil'i•ty
spread'a•ble
spread'-ea'gle,
-gled, -gling
spread'er
spread'sheet'
spree
sprig, sprigged,
sprig'ging
spright'li•ness
spright'ly
spring, sprang *or*
sprung, sprung,
spring'ing
spring'board'
spring'bok' *pl.* -bok'
or -boks'
spring'time'
spring'y
sprin'kle, -kled,
-kling
sprin'kler
sprint
sprint'er
sprit
sprite
sprit'sail
spritz
spritz'er
sprock'et
sprout
spruce *(tree)*
spruce *(neat),*

spruc'er, spruc'est
spruce *(to make
neat)*, spruced,
spruc'ing
spry, spri'er *or*
spry'er, spri'est *or*
spry'est
spry'ly
spry'ness
spud
spume, spumed,
spum'ing
spu•mo'ni *or* -ne
spunk
spunk'y
spur, spurred,
spur'ring
spu'ri•ous
spurn
spurt
sput'nik
sput'ter
spu'tum *pl.* -ta
spy, spied, spy'ing
spy'glass'
squab
squab'ble, -bled,
-bling
squab'bler
squad
squad'ron
squal'id
squall
squall'y
squal'or
squa'mous *also*
squa'mose'

squan'der

square, squar'er,
  squar'est

square, squared,
  squar'ing

square' dance' n.

square'-dance',
  -danced', -danc'ing

square'-rigged'

square'-rig'ger

squash

squash'y

squat, squat'ted,
  squat'ting

squat, squat'ter,
  squat'test

squat'ter

squawk

squeak

squeak'y

squeal

squea'mish

squee'gee

squeez'a•ble

squeeze, squeezed,
  squeez'ing

squeez'er

squelch

squib

squid *pl.* squids *or*
  squid

squig'gle, -gled,
  -gling

squint

squire, squired,
  squir'ing

squirm

squir'rel, -reled *or*
  -relled, -rel•ing *or*
  -rel•ling

squirt

squish

stab, stabbed,
  stab'bing

stab'ber

sta•bil'i•ty

sta'bi•li•za'tion

sta'bi•lize', -lized',
  -liz'ing

sta'bi•liz'er

sta'ble, -bler, -blest

sta'ble, -bled, -bling

sta'bly

stac•ca'to

stack

sta'di•um *pl.*
  -di•ums *or* -di•a

staff (*rod*), *pl.* staffs
  or staves

staff (*group of assis-
  tants*), *pl.* staffs

staff'er

stag

stage, staged,
  stag'ing

stage'coach'

stage'hand'

stage'-struck'

stag'ger

stag'ger•ing

stag'ing

stag'nan•cy

stag'nant

stag'nate', -nat'ed,
  -nat'ing

stag•na'tion

stag'y *also* stag'ey

staid

stain

stain'less

stair (*steps*)
  ✔ stare

stair'case'

stair'way'

stair'well'

stake (*to mark the
  limits of, to gamble*),
  staked, stak'ing
  ✔ steak

stake'out'

sta•lac'tite' (*down-
  ward deposit*)

sta•lag'mite' (*up-
  ward deposit*)

stale, stal'er, stal'est

stale'mate',
  -mat'ed, -mat'ing

Sta'lin•ism

Sta'lin•ist

stalk'er

stall

stal'lion

stal'wart

sta'men *pl.* -mens *or*
  -mi•na

stam'i•na

sta'mi•nate'

stam'mer

stamp

stam•pede',
  -ped'ed, -ped'ing

stance

stanch *also* staunch
   (to check the flow)
   ✔ staunch

stan'chion

stand, stood,
   stand'ing

stand'-a·lone' *adj.*

stan'dard

stan'dard-bear'er

stan'dard·i·za'tion

stan'dard·ize',
   -ized', -iz'ing

stand'by' *pl.* -bys'

stand·ee'

stand'-in' *n.*

stand'ing

stand'off' *n.*

stand·off'ish

stand'out' *n.*

stand'pipe'

stand'point'

stand'still'

stand'up' *or*
   stand'-up' *adj.*

stan'nic

stan'nous

stan'za

sta'pes' *pl.* -pes *or*
   -pe·des'

staph'y·lo·coc'cus
   pl. -coc'ci

sta'ple, -pled, -pling

sta'pler

star, starred,
   star'ring

star'board

starch'y

star'-crossed'

star'dom

stare (to gaze fixedly),
   stared, star'ing
   ✔ stair

star'fish' *pl.* -fish' *or*
   -fish'es

star'gaze', -gazed',
   -gaz'ing

stark

star'let

star'light'

star'ling

star'lit'

star'ry

star'ry-eyed'

star'struck' *or*
   star'-struck'

start'er

star'tle, -tled, -tling

star·va'tion

starve, starved,
   starv'ing

starve'ling

stash

sta'sis *pl.* -ses

state, stat'ed, stat'ing

state'hood'

state'house' *also*
   state' house'

state'li·ness

state'ly

state'ment

state'-of-the-art'
   adj.

state'room'

state'side'

states'man

states'man·ship'

states'wom'an

stat'ic

stat'ics

sta'tion

sta'tion·ar'y (not
   moving)
   ✔ stationery

sta'tion·er

sta'tion·er'y (paper
   and envelopes)
   ✔ stationary

sta'tion·mas'ter

sta·tis'tic

sta·tis'ti·cal

stat'is·ti'cian

sta·tis'tics

sta'tor

stat'u·ar'y

stat'ue

stat'u·esque'

stat'u·ette'

stat'ure

sta'tus

stat'us quo'

stat'ute

stat'u·to'ry

staunch *also* stanch
   (steadfast)
   ✔ stanch

stave, staved *or*
   stove, stav'ing

stay

stay'sail'

stead

stead'fast' also
 sted'fast'
stead'i•ly
stead'i•ness
stead'y, -ied, -y•ing
stead'y-state'
 theo'ry
steak *(meat)*
 ✔ stake
steal *(to take without*
 permission), stole,
 sto'len, steal'ing
 ✔ steel
stealth
stealth'i•ly
stealth'y
steam
steam'boat'
steam'er
steam'fit'ter
steam'roll'er
steam'ship'
steam'y
ste'a•tite'
steed
steel *(metal)*
 ✔ steal
steel'work'
steel'work'er
steel'y
steel'yard'
steep
steep'en
stee'ple
stee'ple•chase'
stee'ple•jack'
steer

steer'age
steers'man
steg'o•saur' also
 steg'o•sau'rus
stein
stel'lar
stem, stemmed,
 stem'ming
stem'ware'
stem'wind'er
stench
sten'cil, -ciled or
 -cilled, -cil•ing or
 -cil•ling
ste•nog'ra•pher
sten'o•graph'ic or
 sten'o•graph'i•cal
ste•nog'ra•phy
sten•to'ri•an
step *(to walk)*,
 stepped, step'ping
 ✔ steppe
step'broth'er
step'child'
step'daugh'ter
step'-down' adj. &
 n.
step'fa'ther
step'-in' adj. & n.
step'lad'der
step'moth'er
step'par'ent
steppe *(plain)*
 ✔ step
stepped'-up' adj.
step'ping•stone'
step'sis'ter

step'son'
step'-up' adj. & n.
ster'e•o' pl. -os'
ster'e•o•phon'ic
ster'e•o•scope'
ster'e•o•scop'ic
ster'e•o•type',
 -typed', -typ'ing
ster'e•o•typ'ic or
 ster'e•o•typ'i•cal
ster'ile
ste•ril'i•ty
ster'il•i•za'tion
ster'il•ize', -ized',
 -iz'ing
ster'il•iz'er
ster'ling
stern
ster'num pl. -nums
 or -na
stern'-wheel'er
ster'oid n.
ster'oid' or
 ste•roi'dal adj.
ster'ol'
steth'o•scope'
ste've•dore'
stew
stew'ard
stew'ard•ship'
stewed
stick, stuck, stick'ing
stick'ball'
stick'er
stick'i•ness
stick'le, -led, -ling
stick'le•back'

stick'ler
stick'pin'
stick'up' *n.*
stick'y
stiff
stiff'en
stiff'-necked'
sti'fle, -fled, -fling
stig'ma *pl.*
  stig•ma'ta *or*
  stig'mas
stig'ma•ti•za'tion
stig'ma•tize',
  -tized', -tiz'ing
stile *(steps)*
  ✔ *style*
sti•let'to *pl.* -tos *or*
  -toes
still
still'birth'
still'born'
still' life' *pl.* still'
  lifes'
still'-life' *adj.*
stilt
stilt'ed
stim'u•lant
stim'u•late', -lat'ed,
  -lat'ing
stim'u•lat'er *or*
  stim'u•la'tor
stim'u•la'tion
stim'u•la'tive
stim'u•lus *pl.* -li'
sting, stung,
  sting'ing
stin'gi•ness

sting'ray'
stin'gy
stink, stank *or* stunk,
  stunk, stink'ing
stint
sti'pend
stip'ple, -pled,
  -pling
stip'u•late', -lat'ed,
  -lat'ing
stip'u•la'tion
stip'u•la'tor
stip'ule
stir, stirred, stir'ring
stir'rer
stir'rup
stitch
stoat *pl.* stoat *or*
  stoats
stock
stock•ade'
stock'bro'ker
stock'hold'er
stock'i•ness
stock'i•nette' *also*
  stock'i•net'
stock'ing
stock'man
stock'pile', -piled',
  -pil'ing
stock'room' *also*
  stock' room'
stock'-still'
stock'y
stock'yard'
stodg'i•ly
stodg'i•ness

stodg'y
sto'gy *or* sto'gie *pl.*
  -gies
sto'ic *also* sto'i•cal
sto'i•cism
stoke, stoked,
  stok'ing
stok'er
stole
stol'id
sto•lid'i•ty
sto'lon'
sto'ma *pl.* -ma•ta *or*
  -mas
stom'ach
stom'ach•ache'
stomp
stone, stoned,
  ston'ing
stone'-blind'
stone'cut'ter
stone'-deaf'
stone'ma'son
stone'wall'
stone'ware'
stone'work'
stone'work'er
ston'i•ness
ston'y
stooge
stool
stool' pi'geon
stoop *(to bend for-*
  ward)
  ✔ *stoup*
stoop *(staircase)*
  ✔ *stoup*

stop, stopped,
  stop′ping
stop′gap′
stop′light′
stop′o′ver
stop′page
stop′per
stop′watch′
stor′age
store, stored, stor′ing
store′-bought′ adj.
store′front′
store′house′
store′keep′er
store′room′
sto′ried
stork
storm
storm′i•ness
storm′y
sto′ry
sto′ry•book′
sto′ry•tell′er
stoup (basin)
  ✔ stoop
stout
stout′heart′ed
stove
stove′pipe′
stow
stow′a•way′ n.
strad′dle, -dled,
  -dling
strad′dler
strafe, strafed,
  straf′ing
strag′gle, -gled,

-gling
strag′gler
strag′gly
straight (erect)
  ✔ strait
straight′a•way′
straight′edge′
straight′en (to make
  straight)
  ✔ straiten
straight•for′ward
  adj. & adv.
straight•for′wards
  adv.
straight′way′
strain
strained
strain′er
strait (channel)
  ✔ straight
strait′en (to make
  narrow)
  ✔ straighten
strait′jack′et also
  straight′jack′et
strait′-laced′
strand
strange, strang′er,
  strang′est
stran′gle, -gled,
  -gling
stran′gler
stran′gu•late′,
  -lat′ed, -lat′ing
stran′gu•la′tion
strap, strapped,
  strap′ping

strat′a•gem
stra•te′gic
strat′e•gist
strat′e•gy
strat′i•fi•ca′tion
strat′i•fy′, -fied′,
  -fy′ing
stra′to•cu′mu•lus
  pl. -li′
strat′o•sphere′
strat′o•spher′ic
stra′tum pl. -ta or
  -tums
stra′tus pl. -ti
straw
straw′ber′ry
stray
streak′y
stream′er
stream′let
stream′line′,
  -lined′, -lin′ing
street′car′
street′-smart′
strength
strength′en
stren′u•ous
strep′to•coc′cal
strep′to•coc′cus pl.
  -coc′ci
strep′to•my′cin
stress
stretch
stretch′a•ble
stretch′er
streu′sel
strew, strewed,

strewn *or* strewed,
strew'ing
stri'a *pl.* -ae
stri'ate' *also*
stri'at'ed
stri•a'tion
strick'en
strict
stric'ture
stride, strode,
strid'den, strid'ing
stri'dence *or*
stri'den•cy
stri'dent
strife
strike, struck, struck
or strick'en,
strik'ing
strike'break'er
strike'out'
strik'er
string, strung,
string'ing
strin'gen•cy
strin'gent
string'er
string'i•ness
string'y
strip, stripped,
strip'ping
stripe, striped,
strip'ing
strip'ling
strip'-mine',
-mined', -min'ing
strip'-search' *v.*
strip'tease' *also*

strip' tease' *n.*
strive, strove,
striv'en *or* strived,
striv'ing
strobe
stro'ga•noff'
stroke, stroked,
strok'ing
stroll
stroll'er
strong'-arm'
adj. & v.
strong'box'
strong'hold'
stron'ti•um
strop, stropped,
strop'ping
stro'phe
struc'tur•al
struc'ture, -tured,
-tur•ing
stru'del
strug'gle, -gled,
-gling
strum, strummed,
strum'ming
strut, strut'ted,
strut'ting
strych'nine'
stub, stubbed,
stub'bing
stub'bi•ness
stub'ble
stub'born
stub'by
stuc'co *pl.* -coes *or*
-cos

stuck'-up' *adj.*
stud, stud'ded,
stud'ding
stu'dent
stu'di•o' *pl.* -os
stu'di•ous
stud'y, -ied, -y•ing
stuff'i•ness
stuff'ing
stuff'y
stul'ti•fi•ca'tion
stul'ti•fy', -fied',
-fy'ing
stum'ble, -bled,
-bling
stum'bler
stump'y
stun, stunned,
stun'ning
stunt'man'
stunt'wom'an
stu'pe•fac'tion
stu'pe•fy', -fied',
-fy'ing
stu•pen'dous
stu'pid
stu•pid'i•ty
stu'por
stur'di•ness
stur'dy
stur'geon
stut'ter
stut'ter•er
sty *(pigpen), pl.* sties
sty *also* stye *(inflam-*
mation), pl. sties
also styes

style *(to design)*,
  styled, styl'ing
  ✔ stile
styl'ish
styl'ist
sty·lis'tic
styl'ize', -ized',
  -iz'ing
sty'lus *pl.* -lus·es *or*
  -li
sty'mie, -mied,
  -mie·ing *also*
  -my'ing
styp'tic
sty'rene'
sua'sion
suave, suav'er,
  suav'est
suav'i·ty *or*
  suave'ness
sub, subbed,
  sub'bing
sub·al'tern
sub'a·tom'ic
sub'cen'ter
sub'class'
sub·com·mit'tee
sub·com'pact'
sub·con'scious
sub·con'ti·nent
sub·con'tract'
sub·con'trac'tor
sub'cu·ta'ne·ous
sub'di·vide',
  -vid'ed, -vid'ing
sub'di·vi'sion
sub·dom'i·nant

sub·due', -dued',
  -du'ing
sub'fam'i·ly
sub'ge'nus *pl.*
  -gen'er·a
sub'group'
sub'head'
sub·hu'man
sub'ject *adj. & n.*
sub·ject' *v.*
sub·jec'tion
sub·jec'tive
sub'jec·tiv'i·ty
sub·join'
sub'ju·gate',
  -gat'ed, -gat'ing
sub'ju·ga'tion
sub'ju·ga'tor
sub·junc'tive
sub'king'dom
sub'lease', -leased',
  -leas'ing
sub'lease' *n.*
sub'let', -let',
  -let'ting
sub'let' *n.*
sub'li·mate',
  -mat'ed, -mat'ing
sub'li·ma'tion
sub·lime'
sub·lim'i·nal
sub·lim'i·ty
sub'ma·chine'
  gun'
sub'ma·rine'
sub·merge',
  -merged',

  -merg'ing
sub·mer'gence
sub·mer'gi·bil'i·ty
sub·mer'gi·ble
sub·merse',
  -mersed', -mers'ing
sub·mers'i·ble
sub·mer'sion
sub·mis'sion
sub·mis'sive
sub·mit', -mit'ted,
  -mit'ting
sub·mit'tal
sub'or'der
sub·or'di·nate',
  -nat'ed, -nat'ing
sub·or'di·na'tion
sub·orn'
sub'or·na'tion
sub'phy'lum
sub'plot'
sub·poe'na, -naed,
  -na'ing
sub'rou·tine'
sub·scribe',
  -scribed', -scrib'ing
sub·scrib'er
sub'script'
sub·scrip'tion
sub'se·quence
sub'se·quent
sub·serve', -served',
  -serv'ing
sub·ser'vi·ence
sub·ser'vi·ent
sub'set'
sub·side', -sid'ed,

-sid′ing
sub·si′dence
sub·sid′i·ar′y
sub·si·dize′, -dized′,
 -diz′ing
sub·si·diz′er
sub′si·dy
sub·sist′
sub·sis′tence
sub·soil′
sub·son′ic
sub·spe′cies *pl.* -cies
sub′stance
sub·stan′dard
sub·stan′tial
sub·stan′ti·al′i·ty
sub·stan′ti·ate′,
 -at′ed, -at′ing
sub·stan′ti·a′tion
sub′stan·tive
sub·sta′tion
sub·sti·tut′a·bil′i·ty
sub·sti·tut′a·ble
sub·sti·tute′,
 -tut′ed, -tut′ing
sub·sti·tu′tion
sub·stra′tum *pl.* -ta
 or -tums
sub·struc′ture
sub·sum′a·ble
sub·sume′,
 -sumed′, -sum′ing
sub′ter·fuge′
sub′ter·ra′ne·an
sub′text′
sub′ti′tle
sub′tle, sub′tler,

sub′tlest
sub′tle·ty
sub′tly
sub·ton′ic
sub·to′tal, -taled
 also -talled, -tal·ing
 also -tal′ling
sub·tract′
sub·trac′tion
sub·trac′tive
sub·tra·hend′
sub·trop′i·cal
sub·trop′ics
sub·urb′
sub·ur′ban
sub·ur′ban·ite′
sub·ur′bi·a
sub·ver′sion
sub·ver′sive
sub·vert′
sub′way′
suc·ceed′
suc·cess′
suc·cess′ful
suc·ces′sion
suc·ces′sive
suc·ces′sor
suc·cinct′
suc′cor *(relief)*
 ✔ *sucker*
suc′co·tash′
Suc′coth *also*
 Suk′koth
suc′cu·lence *or*
 suc′cu·len·cy
suc′cu·lent
suc·cumb′

such
suck
suck′er *(one that
 sucks, lollipop, dupe)*
 ✔ *succor*
suck′le, -led, -ling
suck′ling
su′cre
su′crose′
suc′tion
Su′da·nese′ *pl.*
 -nese′
sud′den
sud′sy
sue, sued, su′ing
suede *also* suède
su′et
suf′fer
suf′fer·a·ble
suf′fer·ance
suf·fice′, -ficed′,
 -fic′ing
suf·fi′cien·cy
suf·fi′cient
suf′fix
suf′fo·cate′, -cat′ed,
 -cat′ing
suf′fo·ca′tion
suf′frage
suf′fra·gette′
suf′fra·gist
suf·fuse′, -fused′,
 -fus′ing
suf·fu′sion
sug′ar
sug′ar·coat′ *v.*
sug′ar·plum′

sug'ar•y
sug•gest'
sug•gest'i•bil'i•ty
sug•gest'i•ble
sug•ges'tion
sug•ges'tive
su'i•cid'al
su'i•cide'
suit (*set of clothes,
   playing cards, legal
   action*)
   ✔ *suite*
suit'a•bil'i•ty
suit'a•ble
suit'a•bly
suit'case'
suite (*series of rooms*)
   ✔ *suit, sweet*
suit'or
su'ki•ya'ki
sul'fate'
sul'fide'
sul'fite'
sul'fur *also* sul'phur
sul•fu'ric
sul'fur•ous *also*
   sul'phur•ous
sulk'y
sul'len
sul'ly, -lied, -ly•ing
sul'tan
sul•tan'a
sul'tan•ate'
sul'try
sum (*to add*),
   summed,
   sum'ming

✔ *some*
su'mac *also*
   su'mach
Su•me'ri•an
sum'ma cum
   lau'de
sum•mar'i•ly
sum'ma•ri•za'tion
sum'ma•rize',
   -rized', -riz'ing
sum'ma•ry (*brief
   statement*)
   ✔ *summery*
sum•ma'tion
sum'mer
sum'mer•house'
sum'mer•time'
sum'mer•y (*of
   summer*)
   ✔ *summary*
sum'mit
sum'mon
sum'mons *pl.*
   -mons•es
sump'tu•ous
sun (*star*)
   ✔ *son*
sun (*to bask in the
   sun*), sunned,
   sun'ning
   ✔ *son*
sun'bathe',
   -bathed', -bath'ing
sun'beam'
sun'bon•net
sun'burn', -burned'
   or -burnt',

-burn'ing
sun'burst'
sun'dae (*ice cream
   dessert*)
Sun'day (*day of the
   week*)
sun'der
sun'di'al
sun'down'
sun'dress'
sun'dries
sun'dry
sun'fish' *pl.* -fish' *or*
   -fish'es
sun'flow'er
sun'glass'es
sunk'en
sun'light'
sun'lit'
Sun'na
Sun'ni
Sun'nite'
sun'ny (*full of sun-
   shine, cheerful*)
   ✔ *sonny*
sun'rise'
sun'room'
sun'screen'
sun'set'
sun'shade'
sun'shine'
sun'spot'
sun'stroke'
sun'tan'
sun'tanned'
sun'up'
sun'ward *adv. &*

adj.
sun'wards *adv.*
sup, supped,
  sup'ping
su'per
su'per·a·bun'-
  dance
su'per·a·bun'dant
su'per·an'nu·at'ed
su·perb'
su'per·charge'
  -charged',
  -charg'ing
su'per·cil'i·ous
su'per·com·put'er
su'per·con·duc·
  tiv'i·ty
su'per·con·duc'tor
su'per·con'ti·nent
su'per·cool' *v.*
su'per·e'go
su'per·e·rog'a·
  to'ry
su'per·fi'cial
su'per·fi'ci·al'i·ty
su'per·fine'
su'per·flu·i·ty
su·per·flu'ous
su'per·heat'
su'per·high'
  fre'quen·cy
su'per·high'way'
su'per·hu'man
su'per·im·pose',
  -posed', -pos'ing
su'per·im·po·si'-
  tion

su'per·in·tend'
su'per·in·ten'-
  dence
su'per·in·ten'dent
su·pe'ri·or
su·pe'ri·or'i·ty
su·per'la·tive
su'per·man'
su'per·mar'ket
su·per'nal
su'per·nat'u·ral
su'per·no'va *pl.*
  -vae *or* -vas
su'per·nu'mer·ar'y
su'per·pow'er
su'per·sat'u·rate',
  -rat'ed, -rat'ing
su'per·sav'er
su'per·script'
su'per·scrip'tion
su'per·sede',
  -sed'ed, -sed'ing
su'per·sen'si·tive
su'per·son'ic
su'per·star'
su'per·sti'tion
su'per·sti'tious
su'per·store'
su'per·struc'ture
su'per·tank'er
su'per·ton'ic
su'per·vene',
  -vened', -ven'ing
su'per·vise', -vised',
  -vis'ing
su'per·vi'sion
su'per·vi'sor

su'per·vi'so·ry
su·pine'
sup'per
sup·plant'
sup'ple, -pler, -plest
sup'ple·ment
sup'ple·men'ta·ry
  or sup'ple·men'tal
sup'pli·ant
sup'pli·cant
sup'pli·cate',
  -cat'ed, -cat'ing
sup'pli·ca'tion
sup·pli'er
sup·ply', -plied',
  -ply'ing
sup·port'
sup·port'a·ble
sup·por'tive
sup·pos'a·ble
sup·pose', -posed',
  -pos'ing
sup·pos'ed·ly
sup'po·si'tion
sup·pos'i·to'ry
sup·press'
sup·press'er *also*
  sup·pres'sor
sup·press'i·ble
sup·pres'sion
sup'pu·rate',
  -rat'ed, -rat'ing
sup'pu·ra'tion
su'pra·re'nal
su·prem'a·cist
su·prem'a·cy
su·preme'

sur'cease', -ceased',
   -ceas'ing
sur'charge',
   -charged',
   -charg'ing
sur'coat'
surd
sure, sur'er, sur'est
sure'-fire'
sure'-foot'ed *or*
   sure'foot'ed
sur'e•ty
surf *(waves)*
   ✔ serf
sur'face, -faced,
   -fac•ing
surf'board'
sur'feit
surge *(to move with
   gathering force)*,
   surged, surg'ing
   ✔ serge
sur'geon
Sur'geon
   Gen'er•al *pl.*
   Sur'geons
   Gen'er•al
sur'ger•y
sur'gi•cal
sur'li•ness
sur'ly
sur•mise', -mised',
   -mis'ing
sur•mount'
sur•mount'a•ble
sur'name'

sur•pass'
sur'plice *(robe)*
sur'plus *(excess)*
sur•prise', -prised',
   -pris'ing
sur•re'al
sur•re'al•ism
sur•re'al•ist
sur•re'al•is'tic
sur•ren'der
sur'rep•ti'tious
sur'rey *pl.* -reys
sur'ro•ga•cy
sur'ro•gate
sur•round'
sur•round'ings
sur'tax'
sur•veil'lance
sur•vey' *v.*
sur'vey' *pl.* -veys
sur•vey'ing
sur•vey'or
sur•viv'al
sur•viv'al•ist
sur•vive', -vived',
   -viv'ing
sur•vi'vor
sus•cep'ti•bil'i•ty
sus•cep'ti•ble
sus•cep'tive
su'shi
sus•pect' *v.*
sus•pect' *n. & adj.*
sus•pend'
sus•pend'ers
sus•pense'

sus•pen'sion
sus•pi'cion
sus•pi'cious
sus•tain'
sus•tain'able
sus'te•nance
su'ture, -tured,
   -tur•ing
su'ze•rain
su'ze•rain•ty
svelte, svelt'er,
   svelt'est
swab *also* swob,
   swabbed *also*
   swobbed,
   swab'bing *also*
   swob'bing
swad'dle, -dled,
   -dling
swag
swag'ger
Swa•hi'li *pl.* -li *or*
   -lis
swain
swal'low
swal'low•tail'
swal'low-tailed'
swa'mi *pl.* -mis
swamp'land'
swamp'y
swan
swank
swank'y
swan's'-down' *also*
   swans'down'
swap *also* swop,

swapped *also*
swopped,
swap'ping *also*
swop'ping
sward *(turf)*
✔ *sword*
swarm
swarth'y
swash'buck'ler
swash'buck'ling
swas'ti·ka
swat, swat'ted,
swat'ting
swatch
swath *also* swathe
(width, strip)
swathe *(to wrap)*,
swathed, swath'ing
swat'ter
sway
sway'back'
sway'backed'
swear, swore, sworn,
swear'ing
sweat, sweat'ed *or*
sweat, sweat'ing
sweat'er
sweat'pants'
sweat'shirt'
sweat'shop'
sweat'y
swede *(rutabaga)*
Swede *(inhabitant of*
Sweden)
Swed'ish
sweep, swept,

sweep'ing
sweep'stakes'
sweet *(sugary)*
✔ *suite*
sweet'bread'
sweet'bri·er *also*
sweet'bri·ar
sweet'en
sweet'en·er
sweet'heart'
sweet'ie
sweet'meat'
swell, swelled,
swelled *or* swol'len,
swell'ing
swel'ter
swept'back'
swerve, swerved,
swerv'ing
swift
swig, swigged,
swig'ging
swill
swim, swam, swum,
swim'ming
swim'mer
swim'mer·et'
swim'suit'
swim'wear'
swin'dle, -dled,
-dling
swin'dler
swine *pl.* swine
swine'herd'
swing, swung,
swing'ing

swin'ish
swipe, swiped,
swip'ing
swirl
swish
Swiss *pl.* Swiss
Swiss' chard'
Swiss' cheese'
switch
switch'blade'
switch'board'
switch'er
switch'man
switch'o·ver *n.*
switch'yard'
swiv'el, -eled *or*
-elled, -el·ing *or*
-el·ling
swoon
swoop
swoosh
sword *(weapon)*
✔ *sward*
sword'fish' *pl.* -fish'
or -fish'es
sword'play'
swords'man
swords'man·ship'
sword'tail'
Syb'a·rite' *also*
syb'a·rite'
syb'a·rit'ic *also*
Syb'a·rit'ic
syc'a·more'
syc'o·phan·cy
syc'o·phant

syc'o•phan'tic *or*
  syc'o•phan'ti•cal
syl•lab'ic
syl•lab'i•ca'tion
syl•lab'i•fi•ca'tion
syl•lab'i•fy' *or*
  syl•lab'i•cate',
  -fied' *or* -cat'ed,
  -fy'ing *or* -cat'ing
syl'la•ble
syl'la•bus *pl.* -bus•es
  or s-bi'
syl'lo•gism
sylph
syl'van *also* sil'van
sym'bi•o'sis *pl.* -ses
sym'bi•ot'ic
sym'bol *(sign)*
  ✔ *cymbal*
sym•bol'ic *also*
  sym•bol'i•cal
sym'bol•ism
sym'bol•i•za'tion
sym'bol•ize', -ized',
  -iz'ing
sym•met'ri•cal *also*
  sym•met'ric
sym'me•try
sym'pa•thet'ic
sym'pa•thize',
  -thized', -thiz'ing
sym'pa•thiz'er
sym'pa•thy
sym•phon'ic
sym'pho•ny
sym•po'si•um *pl.*
  -si•ums *or* -si•a

symp'tom
symp'to•mat'ic
syn'a•gogue' *also*
  syn'a•gog'
syn'apse'
sync *or* synch
syn•chron'ic
syn'chro•nic'i•ty
syn'chro•ni•za'-
  tion
syn'chro•nize',
  -nized', -niz'ing
syn'chro•nous
syn'chro•tron'
syn•cli'nal
syn'cline'
syn'co•pate',
  -pat'ed, -pat'ing
syn'co•pa'tion
syn'co•pe
syn'cre•tism
syn'cre•tize',
  -tized', -tiz'ing
syn'di•cate',
  -cat'ed, -cat'ing
syn'di•ca'tion
syn'drome'
syn'er•gism
syn'er•gis'tic
syn'er•gy
syn'fu'el
syn'od
syn'o•nym'
syn•on'y•mous
syn•on'y•my
syn•op'sis *pl.* -ses'
syn•op'size',

-sized', -siz'ing
syn•tac'tic *or*
  syn•tac'ti•cal
syn'tax'
syn'the•sis *pl.* -ses'
syn'the•size',
  -sized', -siz'ing
syn'the•siz'er
syn•thet'ic
syph'i•lis
syph'i•lit'ic
Syr'i•an
sy•rin'ga
sy•ringe'
syr'inx' *pl.*
  sy•rin'ges *or*
  syr'inx'es
syr'up *also* sir'up
syr'up•y
sys'tem
sys'tem•at'ic *also*
  sys'tem•at'i•cal
sys'tem•a•ti•za'tion
sys'tem•a•tize',
  -tized', -tiz'ing
sys•tem'ic
sys'to•le
sys•tol'ic

T

tab, tabbed, tab'bing
tab'ard
tab•bou'leh
tab'by
tab'er•na'cle

ta'ble, -bled, -bling
tab•leau' *pl.* -leaux'
  or -leaus'
ta'ble•cloth'
ta'ble•land'
ta'ble•spoon'
ta'ble•spoon•ful'
tab'let
ta'ble•top'
ta'ble•ware'
tab'loid'
ta•boo' *also* ta•bu'
  pl. -boos' *also* -bus'
ta'bor
tab'u•lar
tab'u•late', -lat'ed,
  -lat'ing
tab'u•la'tion
tab'u•la'tor
ta•chom'e•ter
tac'it
tac'i•turn'
tac'i•tur'ni•ty
tack
tack'le, -led, -ling
tack'ler
tack'y
ta'co *pl.* -cos
tac'o•nite'
tact
tact'ful
tac'tic
tac'ti•cal
tac•ti'cian
tac'tile
tact'less
tad'pole'

taf'fe•ta
taf'fy
tag, tagged, tag'ging
Ta•ga'log *pl.* -log *or*
  -logs
Ta•hi'tian
tail *(hind part)*
  ✔ tale
tail *(to follow)*
  ✔ tale
tail'board'
tail'coat'
tail'gate', -gat'ed,
  -gat'ing
tail'light'
tai'lor
tail'pipe'
tail'spin'
Tai'no *pl.* -no *or*
  -nos
taint
take, took, tak'en,
  tak'ing
take'down' *adj. & n.*
take'off' *n.*
take'out' *also*
  take'-out' *n.*
take'o'ver *also*
  take'-o'ver *n.*
tak'er
talc
tal'cum
tale *(story)*
  ✔ tail
tale'bear'er
tal'ent
tal'ent•ed

tale'tell'er
tal'is•man
tal'is•man'ic
talk
talk'a•tive
talk'back' *n.*
talk'ie *(movie)*
  ✔ talky
talk'ing-to' *pl.* -tos'
talk'y *(talkative)*
  ✔ talkie
tall
tal'lith *pl.* -liths *or*
  tal•lith'im
tal'low
tal'ly, -lied, -ly•ing
tal'ly•ho'
Tal'mud
Tal•mu'dic *also*
  Tal•mu'di•cal
tal'on
ta'lus *(bone),* *pl.* -li'
ta'lus *(debris), pl.*
  -lus•es
tam
ta•ma'le
tam'a•rack'
tam'a•rind'
tam'a•risk'
tam'bour'
tam'bou•rine'
tame, tam'er,
  tam'est
tame, tamed,
  tam'ing
tam'er
Tam'il *pl.* -il *or* -ils

tam'-o'-shan'ter

tamp

tam'per *(to interfere)*

tamp'er *(neutron reflector)*

tam'pon'

tan, tanned, tan'ning

tan, tan'ner, itan'nest

tan'a•ger

Ta•nakh'

tan'bark'

tan'dem

tang

tan'ge•lo' *pl.* -los'

tan'gent

tan•gen'tial

tan'ger•ine'

tan'gi•bil'i•ty

tan'gi•ble

tan'gi•bly

tan'gle, -gled, -gling

tan'go *pl.* -gos

tan'go, -goed, -go•ing

tang'y

tank'ard

tank'er

tan'ner

tan'ner•y

tan'nic

tan'nin

tan'ning

tan'sy

tan'ta•lite'

tan'ta•lize', -lized',

-liz'ing

tan'ta•lum

tan'ta•mount'

tan'trum

Tao'ism

Tao'ist

tap, tapped, tap'ping

ta'pa

tap'-dance', -danced', -danc'ing

tap' danc'er

tape, taped, tap'ing

ta'per *(candle, to diminish)*

✔ *tapir*

tape'-re•cord' *v.*

tape' re•cord'er

tap'es•try

tape'worm'

tap'i•o'ca

ta'pir *(animal)*

✔ *taper*

tap'root'

taps

tar, tarred, tar'ring

tar'an•tel'la

ta•ran'tu•la *pl.* -las or -lae'

tar'di•ness

tar'dy

tare *(weed, weight)*

✔ *tear*

tar'get

tar'iff

tar'mac'

tar'nish

ta'ro *(plant), pl.* -ros

tar'ot *(card)*

tarp

tar'pa'per

tar'pau•lin

tar'pon *pl.* -pon *or* -pons

tar'ra•gon'

tar'ry *(to delay)*, -ried, -ry•ing

tar'ry *(like tar)*

tar'sal

tar'sus *pl.* -si

tart

tar'tan

tar'tar *(deposit on the teeth, acid compound, violent person)*

Tar'tar *also* Ta'tar *(people)*

tar•tar'ic

tar'tar sauce'

task

task'mas'ter

Tas•ma'ni•an

tas'sel, -seled *or* -selled, -sel•ing *or* -sel•ling

taste, tast'ed, tast'ing

taste'ful *(showing good taste)*

✔ *tasty*

taste'less

tast'y *(having good flavor)*

✔ *tasteful*
tat, tat′ted, tat′ting
tat′ter
tat′tle, -tled, -tling
tat′tler
tat′tle•tale′
tat•too′ *pl.* -toos′
tat•too′, -tooed′,
  -too′ing
tau *(Greek letter)*
  ✔ *taw*
taunt
taupe *(color)*
  ✔ *tope*
taut
tau′to•log′i•cal *or*
  tau′to•log′ic
tau•tol′o•gy
tav′ern
taw *(marble)*
  ✔ *tau*
taw′dry
taw′ny
tax′a•ble
tax•a′tion
tax′-de•duct′i•ble
tax′-ex•empt′
tax′i *pl.* -is *or* -ies
tax′i, -ied, -i•ing *or*
  -y•ing
tax′i•cab′
tax′i•der′mist
tax′i•der′my
tax′i•me′ter
tax′o•nom′ic *also*
  tax′o•nom′i•cal
tax•on′o•my

tax′pay′er
T′-ball′ *also*
  tee′-ball′
tea *(beverage)*
  ✔ *tee, ti*
teach, taught,
  teach′ing
teach′a•ble
teach′er
tea′cup′
tea′house′
teak
tea′ket′tle
teal *pl.* teal *or* teals
team *(group)*
  ✔ *teem*
team′mate′
team′ster
team′work′
tea′pot′
tear *(to pull apart)*,
  tore, torn, tear′ing
  ✔ *tare*
tear *(drop of liquid)*
  ✔ *tier*
tear′drop′
tear′ful
tear′jerk′er
tea′room′
tease, teased,
  teas′ing
tea′sel
tea′spoon′
tea′spoon•ful′
teat
tea′time′
tech•ne′ti•um

tech′ni•cal
tech′ni•cal′i•ty
tech•ni′cian
tech•nique′
tech′no•log′i•cal
  also tech′no•log′ic
tech•nol′o•gist
tech•nol′o•gy
ted′dy bear′ *also*
  Ted′dy bear′
Te′ De′um
te′di•ous
te′di•um
tee *(small peg)*
  ✔ *tea, ti*
teem *(to abound)*
  ✔ *team*
teen′age′ *or* teen′-
  age′ *also* teen′aged′
  or teen′-aged′
teen′ag′er *also*
  teen′-ag′er
tee′ny *also* teen′sy
tee′ter
tee′ter-tot′ter
teethe, teethed,
  teeth′ing
tee′to′tal•er *or*
  tee′to′tal•ler
tek′tite′
tel′e•cast′, -cast′ *or*
  -cast′ed, -cast′ing
tel′e•com•mu′ni•
  ca′tion
tel′e•com•mut′ing
tel′e•gram′
tel′e•graph′

te·leg'ra·pher *or*
  te·leg'ra·phist
tel'e·graph'ic *also*
  tel'e·graph'i·cal
te·leg'ra·phy
tel'e·ki·ne'sis
tel'e·ki·net'ic
tel'e·mar'ket·ing
tel'e·me'ter
te·lem'e·try
tel'e·path'ic
te·lep'a·thy
tel'e·phone',
  -phoned',
  -phon'ing
tel'e·phon'ic
te·leph'o·ny
tel'e·pho'to·
  graph'
tel'e·pho·tog'ra·
  phy
tel'e·pho'to lens'
tel'e·scope',
  -scoped', -scop'ing
tel'e·scop'ic
tel'e·thon'
tel'e·type'writ'er
tel'e·vise', -vised',
  -vis'ing
tel'e·vi'sion
tell, told, tell'ing
tell'er
tell'tale'
tel'lu·ride'
tel·lu'ri·um
tel'o·phase'
te·mer'i·ty

tem'per
tem'per·a
tem'per·a·ment
tem'per·a·men'tal
tem'per·ance
tem'per·ate
tem'per·a·ture
tem'pered
tem'pest
tem·pes'tu·ous
tem'plate *also*
  tem'plet
tem'ple
tem'po *pl.* -pos *or*
  -pi
tem'po·ral
tem'po·rar'y
tem'po·ri·za'tion
tem'po·rize',
  -rized', -riz'ing
temp·ta'tion
tempt'ing
tem'pu·ra
ten
ten'a·bil'i·ty
ten'a·ble
te·na'cious
te·nac'i·ty
ten'an·cy
ten'ant
tend
ten'den·cy
ten·den'tious *also*
  ten·den'cious
ten'der *(fragile)*
ten'der *(to offer)*
tend'er *(one that*
  tends)

ten'der·foot' *pl.*
  -foots' *or* -feet'
ten'der·heart'ed
ten'der·ize', -ized',
  -iz'ing
ten'der·iz'er
ten'der·loin'
ten'don
ten'dril
ten'e·ment
ten'et
ten'-gal'lon hat'
Ten'nes·se'an
ten'nis
ten'on
ten'or
ten'pin'
tense, tens'er,
  tens'est
tense, tensed,
  tens'ing
ten'sile
ten'sion
ten'sor
tent
ten'ta·cle
ten'ta·tive
ten'ter
ten'ter·hook'
tenth
ten'u·ous
ten'ure
te'pee *also* tee'pee
tep'id
te·qui'la
ter'a·byte'

ter'bi•um
ter'i•ya'ki
term
ter'ma•gant
ter'mi•na•ble
ter'mi•nal
ter'mi•nate',
  -nat'ed, -nat'ing
ter'mi•na'tion
ter'mi•na'tive
ter'mi•na'tor
ter'mi•nol'o•gy
ter'mi•nus *pl.*
  -nus•es *or* -ni'
ter'mite'
tern *(bird)*
  ✔ *turn*
ter'race, -raced,
  -rac•ing
ter'ra cot'ta *n.*
ter'ra-cot'ta *adj.*
ter'ra fir'ma
ter•rain'
ter'ra•pin
ter•rar'i•um *pl.*
  -i•ums *or* -i•a
ter•res'tri•al
ter'ri•ble
ter'ri•bly
ter'ri•er
ter•rif'ic
ter'ri•fy', -fied',
  -fy'ing
ter'ri•to'ri•al
ter'ri•to'ri•al'i•ty
ter'ri•to'ry
ter'ror

ter'ror•ism
ter'ror•ist
ter'ror•ize', -ized',
  -iz'ing
ter'ry
terse, ters'er, ters'est
ter'ti•ar'y *(third)*
Ter'ti•ar'y *(geologic*
  period)
tes'se•late', -lat'ed,
  -at'ing
tes'se•la'tion
test
tes'ta•ment
tes'tate'
tes'ta•tor
test'-drive', -drove',
  -driv'en, -driv'ing
test'er *(one that*
  tests)
tes'ter *(canopy)*
tes'ti•cle
tes'ti•fy', -fied',
  -fy'ing
tes'ti•mo'ni•al
tes'ti•mo'ny
tes'tis *pl.* -tes
tes•tos'ter•one'
test'-tube' ba'by
tes'ty
tet'a•nus
tetch'y *also* tech'y
tête'-à-tête'
teth'er
teth'er•ball'
Te'ton' *pl.* -ton' *or*
  -tons'

tet'ra
tet'ra•cy'cline'
tet'rad'
tet'ra•he'dron *pl.*
  -drons *or* -dra
te•tram'e•ter
tet'rarch'
tet'rar'chy
Teu'ton
Teu•ton'ic
Tex'an
text
text'book'
tex'tile'
tex'tu•al
tex'tur•al
tex'ture
Thai *pl.* Thai *or*
  Thais
thal'a•mus *pl.* -mi'
thal'li•um
thal'lo•phyte'
thal'lus *pl.*-li *or*
  -lus•es
than
thane
thank'ful
thank'less
thanks
thanks•giv'ing
that *pl.* those
thatch
thaw
the *article*
  ✔ *thee*
the'a•ter *or*
  the'a•tre

the•at'ri•cal *also*
  the•at'ric
the•at'rics
thee *pron.*
  ✔ the
theft
their *possessive form*
  of they
  ✔ there, they're
theirs
them
the•mat'ic
theme
them•selves'
then
thence
thence•forth'
thence•for'ward
  also thence•
  for'wards
the•oc'ra•cy
the'o•crat'ic *or*
  the'o•crat'i•cal
the'o•lo'gi•an
the'o•log'i•cal *also*
  the'o•log'ic
the•ol'o•gy
the'o•rem
the'o•ret'i•cal *also*
  the'o•ret'ic
the'o•re•ti'cian
the'o•rist
the'o•rize', -rized',
  -riz'ing
the'o•ry
the'o•soph'i•cal
the•os'o•phist

the•os'o•phy
ther'a•peu'tic *also*
  ther'a•peu'ti•cal
ther'a•peu'tics
ther'a•pist
ther'a•py
there *(at that place)*
  ✔ their, they're
there'a•bouts' *also*
  there'a•bout'
there•af'ter
there•at'
there•by'
there'fore'
there•from'
there•in'
there•of'
there•on'
there•to'
there'to•fore'
there•un'der
there•un•to'
there•up•on'
there•with'
ther'mal
ther'mic
therm'i'on
ther'mo•cou'ple
ther'mo•dy•nam'ic
ther'mo•e•lec'tric
  also ther'mo•e•lec'-
  tri•cal
ther'mo•e•lec•tric'-
  i•ty
ther'mo•graph'
ther'mom'e•ter
ther'mo•nu'cle•ar

ther'mo•plas'tic
ther'mo•sphere'
ther'mo•stat'
the•sau'rus *pl.*
  -sau'rus•es *or*
  -sau'ri
these *sing.* this
the'sis *pl.* -ses
thes'pi•an
the'ta
thew
they
they're *contraction of*
  they are
  ✔ their, there
thi'a•mine *also*
  thi'a•min
thick
thick'en
thick'en•er
thick'et
thick'set'
thick'-skinned'
thief *pl.* thieves
thieve, thieved,
  thiev'ing
thiev'er•y
thigh'bone'
thim'ble
thin, thin'ner,
  thin'nest
thin, thinned,
  thin'ning
thine
thing
thing'a•ma•bob' *or*
  thing'u•ma•bob'

also thing′um•bob′
thing′a•ma•jig′ *also*
  thing′u•ma•jig′
think, thought,
  think′ing
think′a•ble
thin′-skinned′
third′-class′ *adv. &*
  adj.
third′-de•gree′
  burn′
thirst′y
thir•teen′
thir•teenth′
thir′ti•eth
thir′ty
this *pl.* these
this′tle
this′tle•down′
thith′er
thole′ pin′
thong
tho•rac′ic
tho•rax′ *pl.* -rax′es
  or -ra•ces′
tho′ri•um
thorn′y
thor′ough
thor′ough•bred′
thor′ough•fare′
thor′ough•go′ing
those *sing.* that
thou
though
thought
thought′ful
thought′less

thou′sand
thou′sandth
thrash
thread
thread′bare′
thread′y
threat
threat′en
three
three′-
  di•men′sion•al
three′-piece′ *adj.*
three′-ply′ *adj.*
three′score′
three′some
thren′o•dy
thresh′er
thresh′old′
thrice
thrift′i•ly
thrift′y
thrill′er
thrive, thrived *or*
  throve, thrived *or*
  thriv′en, thriv′ing
throat
throat′y
throb, throbbed,
  throb′bing
throe *(pang)*
  ✔ *throw*
throm′bin
throm•bo′sis *pl.*
  -ses
throm′bus *pl.* -bi
throne
throng

throt′tle, -tled,
  -tling
through
through•out′
throw *(to hurl),*
  threw, thrown,
  throw′ing
  ✔ *throe*
throw′a•way′ *adj.*
  & n.
throw′back′
thrum, thrummed,
  thrum′ming
thrush
thrust
thru′way′ *also*
  through′way′
thud, thud′ded,
  thud′ding
thug
thu′li•um
thumb′nail′
thumb′screw′
thumb′tack′
thump
thun′der
thun′der•bird′
thun′der•bolt′
thun′der•clap′
thun′der•cloud′
thun′der•head′
thun′der•ous
thun′der•show′er
thun′der•storm′
thun′der•struck′
Thurs′day
thus

thwack
thwart
thy
thyme *(plant)*
  ✓ time
thy'mine'
thy'mus *pl.* -mus•es
thy'roid'
thy•rox'ine' *also*
  thy•rox'in
thy•self'
ti *(musical tone)*
  ✓ tea, tee
ti•ar'a
Ti•bet'an
tib'i•a *pl.* -i•ae' *or*
  -i•as
tic *(muscle contraction)*
tick *(clicking sound, mark, arachnid, cloth case)*
tick'bird'
tick'er
tick'et
tick'ing
tick'le, -led, -ling
tick'ler
tick'lish
tick'tack'toe' *also*
  tick'-tack'-toe'
tid'al
tid'bit'
tid'dly•winks'
tide, tid'ed, tid'ing
tide'land'
tide'wa'ter

ti'di•ly
tid'ings
ti'dy, -died, -dy•ing
tie, tied, ty•ing
tie'back' *n.*
tie'break'er
tie'-dye', -dyed',
  -dye'ing
tie'-in' *n.*
tier *(row)*
  ✓ tear
tie'-up' *n.*
tiff
ti'ger
ti'ger-eye' *also*
  ti'ger's-eye'
tight
tight'en
tight'fist'ed
tight'lipped' *also*
  tight'-lipped'
tight'rope'
tights
tight'wad'
ti'gress
til'de
tile, tiled, til'ing
till *(to prepare land)*
till *(until)*
till *(drawer, glacial deposit)*
till'a•ble
till'age
till'er *(one that tills)*
til'ler *(lever)*
tilt
tilth

tim'ber *(trees)*
  ✓ timbre
tim'ber•land'
tim'ber•line'
tim'bre *(sound quality)*
  ✓ timber
tim'brel
time *(to clock)*,
  timed, tim'ing
  ✓ thyme
time'card'
timed'-re•lease'
  also time'-re•lease'
time'-hon'ored
time'keep'er
time'-lapse' *adj.*
time'less
time'ly
time'-out' *also*
  time' out'
time'piece'
tim'er
time'sav'ing
time'serv'er *also*
  time'-serv'er
time'-share'
time'-shar'ing
time'ta'ble
time'-test'ed
time'worn'
tim'id
ti•mid'i•ty
tim'or•ous
tim'o•thy
tim'pa•ni *also*
  tym'pa•ni

tin, tinned, tin′ning
tinc′ture
tin′der
tin′der•box′
tine
tin′foil′ *also*
tin′ foil′
ting *(to make a light*
metallic sound),
tinged, ting′ing
tinge *(to tint),*
tinged, tinge′ing *or*
ting′ing
tin′gle, -gled, -gling
tin′ker
tin′kle, -kled, -kling
tin′ny
tin′-plate′, -plat′ed,
-plat′ing
tin′sel, -seled *or*
-selled, -sel•ing *or*
-sel•ling
tin′smith′
tint
tin′tin•nab′u•la′-
tion
ti′ny
tip, tipped, tip′ping
tip′-off′ *n.*
tip′per
tip′pet
tip′ple, -pled, -pling
tip′pler
tip′sy
tip′toe′, -toed′,
-toe′ing
tip′top′

ti′rade′
tire, tired, tir′ing
tire′less
tire′some
'tis
tis′sue
tit
ti′tan *(great person)*
Ti′tan *(giant)*
ti•tan′ic
ti•ta′ni•um
tithe, tithed,
tith′ing
ti′tian
tit′il•late′, -lat′ed,
-lat′ing
tit′il•la′tion
ti′tle, -tled, -tling
tit′mouse′
tit′ter
tit′tle
tit′tle-tat′tle, -tled,
-tling
tit′u•lar
tiz′zy
Tlin′git *pl.* -git *or*
-gits
to *(toward)*
✔ too, two
toad *(animal)*
✔ toed
toad′stool′
toad′y, -ied, -y•ing
toast
toast′er
toast′mas′ter
toast′mis′tress

to•bac′co *pl.* -cos *or*
-coes
to•bac′co•nist
to•bog′gan
toc•ca′ta
toc′sin *(alarm)*
✔ toxin
to•day′
tod′dle, -dled,
-dling
tod′dler
tod′dy
to-do′ *pl.* -dos′
toe *(digit)*
✔ tow
toed *(having toes)*
✔ toad
toe′hold′
toe′nail′
tof′fee
to′fu
tog, togged, tog′ging
to′ga
to•geth′er
tog′gle, -gled, -gling
toil *(labor)*
toile *(fabric)*
toi′let
toi′let•ry
toi•lette′
toil′some
to′ken
to′ken•ism
tol′er•a•ble
tol′er•a•bly
tol′er•ance
tol′er•ant

tol'er•ate', -at'ed,
   -at'ing
tol'er•a'tion
toll'booth'
toll'gate'
Tol'tec' *pl.* -tec or
   -tecs'
Tol•tec'an
tol'u•ene'
tom'a•hawk'
to•ma'to *pl.* -toes
tomb
tom'boy'
tomb'stone'
tom'cat'
tome
tom•fool'er•y
to•mor'row
tom'tit'
tom'-tom' *also*
   tam'-tam'
ton *(unit of weight)*
   ✔ *tun*
ton'al
to•nal'i•ty
tone, toned, ton'ing
Ton'gan
tongs
tongue, tongued,
   tongu'ing
tongue'-in-cheek'
tongue'-lash'ing
tongue'-tied'
ton'ic
to•night'
ton'nage
ton'sil

ton'sil•lec'to•my
ton'sil•li'tis
ton•so'ri•al
ton'sure, -sured,
   -sur•ing
ton'tine'
too *(also)*
   ✔ *to, two*
tool *(device)*
   ✔ *tulle*
tool'box'
tool'ing
toot
tooth *pl.* teeth
tooth'ache'
tooth'brush'
toothed
tooth'paste'
tooth'pick'
tooth'pow'der
tooth'some
tooth'y
top, topped,
   top'ping
to'paz'
top'coat'
top'drawer' *adj.*
tope *(to drink)*,
   toped, top'ing
   ✔ *taupe*
top'flight' *adj.*
top•gal'lant
top'-heav'y
to'pi•ar'y
top'ic
top'i•cal
top'knot'

top'mast'
top'most'
top'notch'
to•pog'ra•pher
top'o•graph'ic *or*
   top'o•graph'i•cal
to•pog'ra•phy
top'o•log'ic *or*
   top'o•log'i•cal
to•pol'o•gy
top'ping
top'ple, -pled,
   -pling
top'sail
top'-se'cret *adj.*
top'side'
top'soil'
top'spin'
top'stitch'
top'sy-tur'vy
toque
To'rah *also* to'rah
torch
tor'e•a•dor'
tor'ment' *n.*
tor•ment' *v.*
tor•men'tor *also*
   tor•ment'er
tor•na'do *pl.* -does
   or -dos
tor•pe'do *pl.* -does
tor'pid
tor'por
torque
tor'rent'
tor•ren'tial
tor'rid

tor'sion

tor'so *pl.* -sos *or* -si

tort *(wrongful act)*

torte *(cake)*

tor·til'la

tor'toise

tor'toise·shell'

tor·tu·ous *(winding)*

  ✔ *torturous*

tor'ture, -tured,

  -tur·ing

tor'tur·ous *(painful)*

  ✔ *tortuous*

To'ry

toss'up' *n.*

tos·ta'da *or*

  tos·ta'do *pl.* -das *or*

  -dos

tot

to'tal, -taled *or*

  -talled, -tal·ing *or*

  -tal·ling

to·tal'i·tar'i·an

to·tal'i·tar'i·an·

  ism

to·tal'i·ty

tote, tot'ed, tot'ing

to'tem

to·tem'ic

tot'ter

tou'can'

touch

touch'-and-go'

  adj.

touch'back' *n.*

touch'down' *n.*

tou·ché'

touch'ing

touch'-me-not'

touch'stone'

touch'-tone'

touch'-type',

  -typed', -typ'ing

touch'-up' *n.*

touch'y

tough *(rugged)*

  ✔ *tuff*

tough'en

tou·pee'

tour

tour' de force' *pl.*

  tours' de force'

tour'ism

tour'ist

tour'ma·line *also*

  tur'ma·line

tour'na·ment

tour'ne·dos' *pl.*

  -dos'

tour'ney *pl.* -neys

tour'ni·quet

tou'sle, -sled, -sling

tout

tow *(to pull along)*

  ✔ *toe*

tow *(flax)*

  ✔ *toe*

to·ward' *also*

  to·wards'

tow'el, -eled *or*

  -elled, -el·ing *or*

  -el·ling

tow'er

tow'head'

tow'head'ed

tow'hee

town

towns'folk'

town'ship'

towns'peo'ple

tow'path'

tox·e'mi·a

tox'ic

tox·ic'i·ty

tox'i·co·log'i·cal *or*

  tox'i·co·log'ic

tox'i·col'o·gist

tox'i·col'o·gy

tox'in *(poison)*

  ✔ *tocsin*

toy

trace, traced,

  trac'ing

trace'a·ble

trac'er

trac'er·y

tra'che·a *pl.*

  -che·ae' *or* -che·as

tra'che·ot'o·my

tra·cho'ma

track *(path)*

  ✔ *tract*

track'-and-field'

  adj.

track'ball'

tract *(area, pamphlet)*

  ✔ *track*

trac'ta·ble

trac'ta·bly

trac'tion

trac'tor

trade, trad′ed,
  trad′ing
trade′-in′ *n.*
trade′mark′
trade′off′ *n.*
trades′man
trades′peo′ple
tra•di′tion
tra•di′tion•al
tra•duce′, -duced′,
  -duc′ing
traf′fic, -ficked,
  -fick′ing
traf′fick•er
tra•ge′di•an
tra•ge′di•enne′
trag′e•dy
trag′ic
trag′i•cal
trag′i•com′e•dy
trag′i•com′ic *or*
  trag′i•com′i•cal
trail′blaz′er
trail′er
train
train•ee′
train′er
train′load′
train′man
traipse, traipsed,
  traips′ing
trait
trai′tor
trai′tor•ous
tra•jec′to•ry
tram
tram′mel, -meled *or*

-melled, -mel•ing
  or -mel•ling
tramp
tram′ple, -pled,
  -pling
tram′po•line′
trance
tran′quil
tran′quil•ize′ *also*
  tran′quil•lize′,
  -quil•ized′ *also*
  -quil•lized′,
  -quil•iz′ing *also*
  -quil•liz′ing
tran′quil•iz′er
tran•quil′li•ty *or*
  tran•quil′i•ty
trans•act′
trans•ac′tion
trans′at•lan′tic
tran•scend′
tran•scen′dent
tran′scen•den′tal
trans′con•ti•nen′-
  tal
tran•scribe′,
  -scribed′, -scrib′ing
tran′script′
tran•scrip′tion
tran′sept′
trans•fer′, -ferred′,
  -fer′ring
trans′fer *also*
  trans•fer′al *n.*
trans•fer′a•ble
trans•fer′ence
trans•fig′u•ra′tion

trans•fig′ure, -ured,
  -ur•ing
trans•fi′nite′
trans•fix′
trans•form′ *v.*
trans′form′ *n.*
trans′for•ma′tion
trans′for•ma′tion•
  al
trans•form′a•tive
trans•form′er
trans•fuse′, -fused′,
  -fus′ing
trans•fu′sion
trans•gress′
trans•gres′sion
trans•gres′sor
tran′sience *or*
  tran′sien•cy
tran′sient
tran•sis′tor
tran•sis′tor•ize′,
  -ized′, -iz′ing
tran′sit
tran•si′tion
tran•si′tion•al
tran′si•tive
tran′si•to′ry
trans•lat′a•ble
trans•late′, -lat′ed,
  -lat′ing
trans•la′tion
trans•la′tor
trans•lit′er•ate′,
  -at′ed, -at′ing
trans•lit′er•a′tion
trans•lu′cence *or*

trans•lu•cen•cy
trans•lu'cent
trans•mi'grate',
  -grat'ed, -grat'ing
trans'mi•gra'tion
trans•mis'si•ble
trans•mis'sion
trans•mit',
  -mit'ted, -mit'ting
trans•mit'ta•ble
trans•mit'tal
trans•mit'ter
trans•mut'a•ble
trans'mu•ta'tion
trans•mute',
  -mut'ed, -mut'ing
trans'o•ce•an'ic
tran'som
tran•son'ic
trans'pa•cif'ic
trans•par'en•cy
  also trans•par'ence
trans•par'ent
tran'spi•ra'tion
tran•spire', -spired',
  -spir'ing
trans•plant' *v.*
trans'plant' *n.*
trans'plan•ta'tion
trans•po'lar
trans•port' *v.*
trans'port' *n.*
trans'por•ta'tion
trans•pos'a•ble
trans•pose',
  -posed', -pos'ing
trans'po•si'tion

trans•sex'u•al
trans•ship',
  -shipped',
  -ship'ping
trans•ship'ment
tran'sub•stan'ti•
  ate', -at'ed, -at'ing
tran'sub•stan'ti•
  a'tion
trans'u•ran'ic
trans•ver'sal
trans•verse'
trans•ves'tite'
trap, trapped,
  trap'ping
tra•peze'
tra•pe'zi•um *pl.*
  -zi•ums *or* -zi•a
trap'e•zoid'
trap'e•zoi'dal
trap'per
trap'ping
Trap'pist
trap'shoot'ing
trash'i•ness
trash'y
trau'ma *pl.* -mas *or*
  -ma•ta
trau•mat'ic
trau'ma•tize',
  -tized', -tiz'ing
tra•vail'
trav'el, -eled *or*
  -elled, -el'ing *or*
  -el'ling
trav'el•er *or*
  trav'el•ler

trav'e•logue' *also*
  trav'e•log'
tra•verse', -versed',
  -vers'ing
trav'erse *n.*
trav'es•ty, -tied,
  -ty•ing
tra•vois' *pl.* -vois'
  also -vois'es
trawl'er
tray
treach'er•ous
treach'er•y
trea'cle
tread, trod, trod'den
  or trod, tread'ing
tread'le, -led, -ling
tread'mill'
trea'son
trea'son•a•ble
trea'son•ous
treas'ure, -ured,
  -ur•ing
treas'ur•er
treas'ure-trove'
treas'ur•y
treat
treat'a•ble
trea'tise
treat'ment
trea'ty
treb'le, -led, -ling
treb'ly
tree, treed, tree'ing
tree'-of-heav'en
tree'top'
tre'foil'

trek, trekked,
  trek′king
trel′lis
trem′a•tode′
trem′ble, -bled,
  -bling
tre•men′dous
trem′o•lo′ *pl.* -los′
trem′or
trem′u•lous
trench
trench′an•cy
trench′ant
trend′y
tre•pan′, -panned′,
  -pan′ning
trep′a•na′tion
treph′i•na′tion
tre•phine′,
  -phined′, -phin′ing
trep′i•da′tion
tres′pass
tres′pass•er
tress
tres′tle
tri′ad′
tri′age′
tri′al
tri•an′gle
tri•an′gu•lar
tri•an′gu•late′
  -lat′ed, -lat′ing
tri•an′gu•la′tion
Tri•as′sic
tri•ath′lon
trib′al
tribe

trib′u•la′tion
tri•bu′nal
trib′une′
trib′u•tar′y
trib′ute
trice
tri′ceps′ *pl.* -ceps′es
  also -ceps′
tri•cer′a•tops′
tri•chi′na *pl.* -nae *or*
  -nas
trich′i•no′sis
trick′er•y
trick′le, -led, -ling
trick′ster
trick′y
tri′col′or
tri′cot
tri•cus′pid
tri•cus′pi•dal *or*
  tri•cus′pi•date′
tri′cy′cle
tri′dent
tried
tri•en′ni•al
tri′fle, -fled, -fling
tri•fo′cal
tri•fo′li•ate *also*
  tri•fo′li•at′ed
tri•fur′cate *also*
  tri•fur′cat′ed
trig′ger
trig′o•no•met′ric *or*
  trig′o•no•met′ri•cal
trig′o•nom′e•try
trill
tril′lion

tril′lionth
tril′li•um
tri•lo′bate′
tri′lo•bite′
tril′o•gy
trim, trimmed,
  trim′ming
trim, trim′mer,
  trim′mest
tri•mes′ter
tri•ni′tro•tol′u•ene′
trin′i•ty
trin′ket
tri•no′mi•al
tri′o *pl.* -os
tri′ode′
tri•ox′ide′
trip, tripped,
  trip′ping
tri•par′tite′
tripe
tri′ple, -pled, -pling
trip′let
trip′li•cate *adj.*
trip′li•cate′, -cat′ed,
  -cat′ing
tri′pod′
trip′tych′
tri′sect′
tri•sec′tion
trite, trit′er, trit′est
trit′i•um
tri′ton
tri′umph
tri•um′phal
tri•um′phant
tri•um′vir *pl.* -virs

or -vi•ri'
tri•um'vi•rate
tri•va'lent
triv'et
triv'i•a
triv'i•al
triv'i•al'i•ty
tRNA
tro'che *(lozenge)*
tro'chee *(metrical foot in poetry)*
trog'lo•dyte'
Tro'jan
troll
trol'ley *pl.* -leys
trol'lop
trom•bone'
trom•bon'ist
troop *(group, group of soldiers)*
  ✔ *troupe*
troop'er
troop'ship'
trope
tro'phy
trop'ic
trop'i•cal
tro'pism
tro'po•pause'
tro'po•sphere'
trot, trot'ted, trot'ting
troth
trot'ter
trou'ba•dour'
trou'ble, -led, -ling
trou'ble•mak'er

trou'ble•shoot'er
trou'ble•some
trough
trounce, trounced, trounc'ing
troupe *(group of actors)*
  ✔ *troop*
trou'sers
trous'seau *pl.* -seaux *or* -seaus
trout *pl.* trout *or* trouts
trow'el
troy
tru'an•cy
tru'ant
truce
truck'er
truck'le, -led, -ling
truck'load'
truc'u•lence
truc'u•lent
trudge, trudged, trudg'ing
true, tru'er, tru'est
true, trued, tru'ing *or* true'ing
true'-blue'
true'-life' *adj.*
true'love' *n.*
truf'fle
tru'ism
tru'ly
trump'er•y
trum'pet
trum'pet•er

trun'cate', -cat'ed, -cat'ing
trun•ca'tion
trun'cheon
trun'dle, -dled, -dling
trunk
truss
trust
trus•tee' *(guardian)*
  ✔ *trusty*
trust'ful
trust'wor'thy
trust'y *(dependable)*
  ✔ *trustee*
truth
truth'ful
try, tried, try'ing
try'out' *n.*
try•pan'o•some'
tryp'sin
tryst
tset'se fly'
T'-shirt' *also* tee' shirt'
T'-square'
tsu•na'mi *pl.* -mis
tu'ba
tub'by
tube
tu'ber
tu'ber•cle
tu•ber'cu•lar
tu•ber'cu•late'
tu•ber'cu•lin
tu•ber'cu•lo'sis
tu•ber'cu•lous

tube′rose′
tu′ber·ous
tub′ing
tu′bu·lar
tu′bule
tuck′er
Tu′dor
Tues′day
tu′fa
tuff (rock)
  ✔ tough
tuft
tug, tugged,
  tug′ging
tug′boat′
tu·i′tion
tu·la·re′mi·a
tu′lip
tulle (net)
  ✔ tool
tum′ble, -bled,
  -bling
tum′ble·down′ adj.
tum′bler
tum′ble·weed′
tum′brel or
  tum′bril
tu·mes′cence
tu·mes′cent
tu′mid
tum′my
tu′mor
tu′mult′
tu·mul′tu·ous
tun (cask)
  ✔ ton
tu′na pl. -na or -nas

tun′a·ble also
  tune′a·ble
tun′dra
tune, tuned, tun′ing
tune′ful
tun′er
tune′-up′ n.
tung′sten
tu′nic
Tu·ni′sian
tun′nel, -neled or
  -nelled, -nel·ing or
  -nel·ling
tun′ny pl. -ny or
  -nies
tu′pe·lo′ pl. -los′
Tu′pi pl. -pi or -pis
tur′ban (headdress)
  ✔ turbine
tur′bid
tur′bid·ness or
  tur·bid′i·ty
tur′bine (engine)
  ✔ turban
tur′bo·charg′er
tur′bo·jet′
tur′bo·prop′
tur′bot pl. -bot or
  -bots
tur′bu·lence
tur′bu·lent
tu·reen′
turf pl. turfs also
  turves
tur′gid
tur·gid′i·ty or
  tur′gid·ness

Turk
tur′key pl. -keys
Turk′ic
Turk′ish
tur′mer·ic
tur′moil′
turn (to rotate)
  ✔ tern
turn′a·bout′ n.
turn′a·round′ n.
turn′buck′le
turn′coat′
tur′nip
turn′key′ pl. -keys′
turn′off′ n.
turn′out′ n.
turn′o′ver n.
turn′pike′
turn′stile′
turn′ta′ble
tur′pen·tine′
tur′pi·tude′
tur′quoise′
tur′ret
tur′tle
tur′tle·dove′
tur′tle·neck′
Tus′ca·ro′ra pl.
  -ra or -ras
tusk
tus′sle
tus′sock
tu′te·lage
tu′tor
tu·to′ri·al
tut′ti-frut′ti pl. -tis
tu′tu

tux
tux•e′do *pl.* -dos *or*
 -does
TV *pl.* TVs *or* TV's
twad′dle, -dled,
 -dling
twain
twang
'twas
tweak
tweed
tweet′er
tweez′ers
twelfth
twelve
twelve′month′
twelve′-tone′ *adj.*
twen′ti•eth
twen′ty
twerp
twice
twice′-told′
twid′dle, -dled,
 -dling
twig
twi′light′
twill
twin
twine, twined,
 twin′ing
twinge, twinged,
 twing′ing
twin′kle, -kled,
 -kling
twirl′er
twist′a•ble
twist′er

twit, twit′ted,
 twit′ting
twitch
twit′ter
two *(number)*
 ✔ to, too
two′-bit′
two′-by-four′
two′-di•men′-
 sion•al
two′-faced′
two′-fist′ed
two′-hand′ed
two′-ply′
two′-seat′er
two′some
two′-step′
two′-time′, -timed′,
 -tim′ing
two′-tim′er
two′-way′
two′-wheel′er
ty•coon′
tyke *also* tike
tym•pan′ic
tym′pa•num *also*
 tim′pa•num *pl.* -na
 or -nums
type, typed, typ′ing
type′cast′, -cast′,
 -cast′ing
type′face′
type′script′
type′set′, -set′,
 -set′ting
type′set′ter
type′write′, -wrote′,

 -writ′ten, -writ′ing
type′writ′er
ty′phoid′
ty•phoon′
ty′phous *adj.*
ty′phus *n.*
typ′i•cal
typ′i•fy′, -fied′,
 -fy′ing
typ′ist
ty′po *pl.* -pos
ty•pog′ra•pher
ty′po•graph′i•cal
 or ty′po•graph′ic
ty•pog′ra•phy
ty•pol′o•gy
ty•ran′ni•cal *also*
 ty•ran′nic
tyr′an•nize′,
 -nized′, -niz′ing
ty•ran′no•saur′ *also*
 ty•ran′no•saur′us
tyr′an•nous
tyr′an•ny
ty′rant
ty′ro *pl.* -ros

U

u•biq′ui•tous
u•biq′ui•ty
ud′der
UFO *pl.* UFOs *or*
 UFO's
ugh
ug′li•ness

ug'ly
uh
uh-huh'
U·krain'i·an
u'ku·le'le
ul'cer
ul'cer·ate', -at·ed,
  -at'ing
ul'cer·a'tion
ul'cer·a·tive
ul'cer·ous
ul'na pl. -nas or -nae
ul'nar
ul·te'ri·or
ul'ti·mate
ul'ti·ma'tum pl.
  -tums or -ta
ul'tra·con·ser'va·
  tive
ul'tra·high'
ul'tra·lib'er·al
ul'tra·light' n. &
  adj.
ul'tra·ma·rine'
ul'tra·mod'ern
ul'tra·son'ic
ul'tra·sound'
ul'tra·vi'o·let
ul'u·late', -lat·ed,
  -lat'ing
ul'u·la'tion
um'bel
um'ber
um·bil'i·cal
um·bil'i·cus pl. -ci'
um'bra pl. -bras or
  -brae

um'brage
um·brel'la
u'mi·ak'
um'laut'
um'pire', -pired',
  -pir'ing
ump'teen'
ump'teenth'
un'a·bashed'
un·a'ble
un'a·bridged'
un·ac·cent·ed
un'ac·cept'a·ble
un'ac·com'pa·nied
un'ac·count'a·ble
un'ac·cus'tomed
un'ac·quaint'ed
un'a·dorned'
un'a·dul'ter·at·ed
un'af·fect'ed
un·al'ien·a·ble
un'a·ligned'
un'al·loyed'
un·al'ter·a·ble
un'-A·mer'i·can
u'na·nim'i·ty
u·nan'i·mous
un·an'swer·a·ble
un'an·tic'i·pat·ed
un'ap·peal'ing
un'ap·pre'ci·at·ed
un'ap·proach'a·ble
un·apt'
un·armed'
un'a·shamed'
un'as·sail'a·ble
un'as·sem'bled

un'as·sist'ed
un'as·sum'ing
un'at·tached'
un'at·tain'a·ble
un'at·test'ed
un'a·vail'a·ble
un'a·vail'ing
un'a·void'a·ble
un'a·void'a·bly
un'a·ware'
un'a·wares'
un·bal'anced
un·bar', -barred',
  -bar'ring
un·bear'a·ble
un·bear'a·bly
un·beat'a·ble
un·beat'en
un'be·com'ing
un'be·known'
un'be·knownst'
un'be·lief'
un'be·liev'a·ble
un'be·liev'a·bly
un'be·liev'er
un·bend', -bent',
  -bend'ing
un·bi'ased also
  un·bi'assed
un·bid'den
un·bind', -bound',
  -bind'ing
un·blessed' also
  un·blest'
un·blink'ing
un·blush'ing
un·bolt'

un·born'
un·bos'om
un·bound'
un·bound'ed
un·bowed'
un·bri'dled
un·bro'ken
un·buck'le, -led,
  -ling
un·bur'den
un·but'ton
un·called'-for'
un·can'ni·ly
un·can'ny
un·cap', -capped',
  -cap'ping
un·car'ing
un·ceas'ing
un·cer'e·mo'ni·ous
un·cer'tain
un·cer'tain·ty
un·chain'
un·change'a·ble
un·char'i·ta·ble
un·chart'ed
un·chris'tian
un'cial
un'ci·form'
un·cir'cum·cised'
un·civ'il
un·civ'i·lized'
un·clad'
un·clasp'
un'cle
un·clean'
un·clear'
un·clog', -clogged',

-clog'ging
un·close', -closed',
  -clos'ing
un·clothe',
  -clothed',
  -cloth'ing
un·coil'
un·com'fort·a·ble
un·com'fort·a·bly
un'com·mit'ted
un·com'mon
un'com·mu'ni·ca'-
  tive
un·com'pro·
  mis'ing
un'con·cern'
un'con·cerned'
un'con·di'tion·al
un'con·di'tioned
un'con·quer·a·ble
un'con·scion·a·ble
un'con·scious
un'con·sid'ered
un'con·sti·tu'tion·
  al
un'con·sti·tu'tion·
  al'i·ty
un'con·trol'la·ble
un'con·trol'la·bly
un'con·trolled'
un'con·ven'tion·al
un'con·ven'tion·
  al'i·ty
un'co·or'di·nat'ed
un·cork'
un·count'ed
un·coup'le, -pled,

-pling
un·couth'
un·cov'er
un·cross'
unc'tion
unc'tu·ous
un·cul'ti·vat'ed
un·cul'tured
un·cut'
un·daunt'ed
un'de·cid'ed
un'de·clared'
un'de·mon'stra·
  tive
un'de·ni'a·ble
un'de·ni'a·bly
un'der
un'der·a·chieve',
  -chieved',
  -chiev'ing
un'der·act'
un'der·age'
un'der·arm'
un'der·bel'ly
un'der·bid', -bid',
  -bid'ding
un'der·brush'
un'der·buy',
  -bought', -buy'ing
un'der·cap'i·tal·
  ize', -ized', -iz'ing
un'der·car'riage
un'der·charge',
  -charged',
  -charg'ing
un'der·charge' *n.*
un'der·clothes'

un'der·cloth'ing
un'der·coat'
un'der·cov'er
un'der·cur'rent
un'der·cut', -cut',
  -cut'ting
un'der·de·vel'oped
un'der·dog'
un'der·done'
un'der·dressed'
un'der·em·ployed'
un'der·es'ti·mate',
  -mat'ed, -mat'ing
un'der·ex·pose',
  -posed', -pos'ing
un'der·ex·po'sure
un'der·feed', -fed',
  -feed'ing
un'der·foot'
un'der·gar'ment
un'der·go', -went',
  -gone', -go'ing,
  -goes'
un'der·grad'u·ate
un'der·ground'
  adj.
un'der·ground'
  adv.
un'der·growth'
un'der·hand' also
  un'der·hand'ed
un'der·lay', -laid',
  -lay'ing
un'der·lie', -lay',
  -lain', -ly'ing
un'der·line',
  -lined', -lin'ing

un'der·ling
un'der·mine',
  -mined', -min'ing
un'der·most'
un'der·neath'
un'der·nour'ished
un'der·pants'
un'der·pass'
un'der·pin'ning
un'der·priv'i·leged
un'der·rate',
  -rat'ed, -rat'ing
un'der·score',
  -scored', -scor'ing
un'der·sea' adj.
un'der·sea' also
  un'der·seas' adv.
un'der·sec're·tar'y
un'der·sell', -sold',
  -sell'ing
un'der·shirt'
un'der·shoot',
  -shot', -shoot'ing
un'der·shot' adj.
un'der·side'
un'der·signed' pl.
  -signed'
un'der·sized' also
  un'der·size'
un'der·staffed'
un'der·stand',
  -stood', -stand'ing
un'der·stand'a·ble
un'der·stand'a·bly
un'der·state',
  -stat'ed, -stat'ing
un'der·state'ment

un'der·stud'y, -ied,
  -y·ing
un'der·take',
  -took', -tak'en,
  -tak'ing
un'der·tak'er
un'der·tak'ing n.
un'der-the-
  count'er adj.
un'der-the-ta'ble
  adj.
un'der·tone'
un'der·tow'
un'der·val'ue,
  -ued, -u·ing
un'der·wa'ter adj.
un'der·wa'ter adv.
un'der way' or
  un'der·way'
un'der·wear'
un'der·weight'
un'der·world'
un'der·write',
  -wrote', -writ'ten,
  -writ'ing
un'der·writ'er
un'de·sir'a·bil'i·ty
un'de·sir'a·ble
un'de·ter'mined
un'dies
un·dig'ni·fied'
un'dis·crim'i·nat'-
  ing
un'dis·tin'guished
un·do' (to reverse),
  -did', -done',
  -do'ing, -does'

✔ *undue*
un·doc'u·ment'ed
un·doubt'ed
un·dreamed' *also*
  un·dreamt'
un·dress'
un·due' (*excessive*)
  ✔ *undo*
un'du·lant
un'du·late', -lat'ed,
  -lat'ing
un'du·la'tion
un·du'ly
un·dy'ing
un·earned'
un·earth'
un·earth'ly
un·eas'y
un·ed'u·cat'ed
un'em·ploy'a·ble
un'em·ployed'
un'em·ploy'ment
un·e'qual
un·e'qualed *also*
  un·e'qualled
un'e·quiv'o·cal
un·err'ing
un'es·sen'tial
un·e'ven
un'e·vent'ful
un'ex·am'pled
un'ex·cep'tion·
  a·ble
un'ex·cep'tion·al
un'ex·pect'ed
un·fail'ing
un·fair'

un·faith'ful
un'fa·mil'iar
un'fa·mil·iar'i·ty
un·fas'ten
un·fa'vor·a·ble
un·fa'vor·a·bly
un·feel'ing
un·feigned'
un·fet'ter
un·fin'ished
un·fit'
un·flap'pa·ble
un·fledged'
un·flinch'ing
un·fold'
un'fore·seen'
un'for·get'ta·ble
un·formed'
un'for·tu·nate
un·found'ed
un·fre'quent·ed
un·friend'ly
un·frock'
un·fruit'ful
un·furl'
un·gain'ly
un·glued'
un·god'ly
un·gov'ern·a·ble
un·gra'cious
un'gram·mat'i·cal
un·grate'ful
un·guard'ed
un'guent
un'gu·late
un·hal'lowed
un·hand'

un·hap'py
un·har'ness
un·health'y
un·heard'
un·heard'-of'
un·hes'i·tat'ing
un·hinge',
  -hinged', -hing'ing
un·hitch'
un·ho'ly
un·hook'
un·horse', -horsed',
  -hors'ing
u'ni·cam'er·al
u'ni·cel'lu·lar
u'ni·corn'
u'ni·cy'cle
u'ni·den'ti·fied'
u'ni·di·rec'tion·al
u'ni·fi·ca'tion
u'ni·form'
u'ni·for'mi·ty
u'ni·fy', -fied',
  -fy'ing
u'ni·lat'er·al
un'im·peach'a·ble
un'im·por'tance
un'im·por'tant
un'im·proved'
un'in·formed'
un'in·hab'it·ed
un'in·hib'it·ed
un'in·spired'
un·in·tel'li·gent
un'in·tel'li·gi·bil'-
  i·ty
un'in·tel'li·gi·ble

un'in·tel'li·gi·bly
un'in·tend'ed
un'in·ten'tion·al
un·in'ter·est·ed
un'in·vit'ed
un'ion
un'ion·i·za'tion
un'ion·ize', -ized',
  -iz'ing
u·nique'
u'ni·sex'
u'ni·son
u'nit
U'ni·tar'i·an
U'ni·tar'i·an·ism
U'ni·tar'i·an
  U'ni·ver'sal·ism
u'ni·tar'y
u·nite', u·nit'ed,
  u·nit'ing
u'ni·ty
u'ni·va'lent
u'ni·valve'
u'ni·ver'sal
U'ni·ver'sal·ist
u'ni·ver·sal'i·ty
u'ni·verse'
u'ni·ver'si·ty
un·just'
un·jus'ti·fi'a·ble
un·kempt'
un·kind'
un·know'a·ble
un·know'ing
un·known'
un·lace', -laced',

-lac'ing
un·latch'
un·law'ful
un·lead'ed
un·learn', -learned'
  also -learnt',
  -learn'ing
un·learn'ed *adj.*
un·leash'
un·leav'ened
un·less'
un·let'tered
un·li'censed
un·like'
un·like'ly
un·lim'ber
un·lim'it·ed
un·list'ed
un·load'
un·lock'
un·looked'-for'
un·loose', -loosed',
  -loos'ing
un·loos'en
un·love'ly
un·luck'y
un·made'
un·man'age·a·ble
un·man'ly
un·manned'
un·man'nered
un·man'ner·ly
un·mar'ried
un·mask'
un·men'tion·a·ble
un·mer'ci·ful

un·mind'ful
un·mis·tak'a·ble
un·mis·tak'a·bly
un·mit'i·gat·ed
un·mor'al
un·moved'
un·nat'u·ral
un·nec'es·sar'i·ly
un·nec'es·sar'y
un·nerve',
  -nerved', -nerv'ing
un·num'bered
un·ob·served'
un·ob·tru'sive
un·oc'cu·pied'
un·of·fi'cial
un·op·posed'
un·or'gan·ized'
un·or'tho·dox'
un·pack'
un·paid'
un·par'al·leled'
un·pin', -pinned',
  -pin'ning
un·pleas'ant
un·plug', -plugged',
  -plug'ging
un·pop'u·lar
un·prac'ticed
un·prec'e·dent'ed
un'pre·dict'a·ble
un'pre·dict'a·bly
un·prej'u·diced
un'pre·med'i·
  tat'ed
un'pre·pared'

un'pre•pos•sess'ing
un'pre•ten'tious
un•prin'ci•pled
un•print'a•ble
un'pro•duc'tive
un'pro•fes'sion•al
un•prof'it•a•ble
un'pro•voked'
un•quote'
un•qual'i•fied'
un•ques'tion•a•ble
un•ques'tion•a•bly
un•ques'tioned
un•quote'
un•rav'el, -eled *or*
  -elled, -el•ing *or*
  -el•ling
un•read'
un•read'a•ble
un•read'y
un•re'al
un're•al•is'tic
un•rea'son•a•ble
un•rea'son•a•bly
un're•con•struct'ed
un•reel'
un're•gen'er•ate
un're•hearsed'
un're•lent'ing
un're•li'a•bil'i•ty
un're•li'a•ble
un're•mit'ting
un're•pent'ant
un're•quit'ed
un're•served'
un're•serv'ed•ly
un•rest'

un're•strained'
un•ripe'
un•ri'valed *or*
  un•ri'valled
un•roll'
un•ruf'fled
un•ru'ly
un•sad'dle, -dled,
  -dling
un•safe'
un•said'
un•san'i•tar'y
un•sat'is•fac'to•ry
un•sat'u•rat'ed
un•sa'vor•y
un•scathed'
un•schooled'
un'sci•en•tif'ic
un•scram'ble,
  -bled, -bling
un•screw'
un•scru'pu•lous
un•seal'
un•sea'son•a•ble
un•sea'soned
un•seat'
un•seem'ly
un•seen'
un•self'ish
un•set'tle, -tled,
  -tling
un•shack'le, -led,
  -ling
un•shak'a•ble
un•shak'a•bly
un•sheathe',

  -sheathed',
  -sheath'ing
un•shod'
un•sight'ly
un•skilled'
un•skill'ful
un•snap',
  -snapped',
  -snap'ping
un•snarl'
un•so'cia•bil'i•ty *or*
  un•so'cia•ble•ness
un•so'cia•ble
un'so•phis'ti•cat'ed
un•sound'
un•spar'ing
un•speak'a•ble
un•speak'a•bly
un•spoiled'
un•spo'ken
un•sta'ble
un•stead'y
un•stop', -stopped',
  -stop'ping
un•stressed'
un•struc'tured
un•strung'
un•stud'ied
un'sub•stan'tial
un'suc•cess'ful
un•suit'a•bil'i•ty
un•suit'a•ble
un•suit'a•bly
un•sung'
un'sus•pect'ed
un'sus•pect'ing

un•tan'gle, -gled,
-gling
un•tapped'
un•taught'
un•ten'a•ble
un•think'a•ble
un•think'ing
un•ti'dy
un•tie', -tied',
-ty'ing
un•til'
un•time'ly
un•tir'ing
un'to
un•told'
un•touch'a•ble
un•to•ward'
un•tried'
un•trod'den
un•true'
un•truth'
un•truth'ful
un•tu'tored
un•used'
un•u'su•al
un•ut'ter•a•ble
un•ut'ter•a•bly
un•var'nished
un•veil'
un•voiced'
un•war'rant•ed
un•war'y
un•well'
un•whole'some
un•wield'y
un•will'ing
un•wind', -wound',

-wind'ing
un•wise', -wis'er,
-wis'est
un•wit'ting
un•wont'ed
un•world'ly
un•wor'thy
un•wrap',
-wrapped',
-wrap'ping
un•writ'ten
un•yield'ing
un•yoke', -yoked',
-yok'ing
un•zip', -zipped',
-zip'ping
up, upped, up'ping
up'-and-com'ing
up'beat'
up•braid'
up•bring'ing
up'com'ing
up'coun'try n. &
adj.
up•coun'try adv.
up•date', -dat'ed,
-dat'ing
up'date' n.
up'draft'
up•end'
up'-front' or
up'front'
up'grade', -grad'ed,
-grad'ing
up•heav'al
up'hill'
up•hold', -held',

-hold'ing
up•hol'ster
up•hol'ster•y
up'keep'
up'land
up•lift' v.
up'lift' n.
up'load'
up'mar'ket
up•on'
up'per
up'per•case'
up'per-class' adj.
up'per•cut'
up'per•most'
up'pi•ty
up•raise', -raised',
-rais'ing
up'right'
up'ris'ing
up'riv'er
up'roar'
up•roar'i•ous
up•root'
up'scale', -scaled',
-scal'ing
up•set', -set',
-set'ting
up'set' n.
up'shot'
up'side' down'
up'si•lon
up'stage' adv. & adj.
up•stage', -staged',
-stag'ing
up'stairs' adv.
up'stairs' adj. & n.

up·stand'ing
up'start'
up'state'
up'stream'
up'surge', -surged',
  -surg'ing
up'surge' *n.*
up'sweep', -swept',
  -sweep'ing
up'swing'
up'take'
up'tight'
up'-to-date'
up'town' *n.*
up'town' *adv. &
  adj.*
up'turn'
up'ward *adv. & adj.*
up'wards *adv.*
up'wind' *adv.*
u'ra·cil
u·ra'ni·um
ur'ban *(relating to a
  city)*
ur·bane' *(refined)*
ur'chin
Ur'du
u·re'a
u·re'ter
u·re'thra *pl.* -thras
  or -thrae
urge, urged, urg'ing
ur'gen·cy
ur'gent
u'ric
u'ri·nal
u'ri·nal'y·sis *pl.*

-ses'
u'ri·nar'y
u'ri·nate', -nat'ed,
  -nat'ing
u'ri·na'tion
u'rine
urn *(vase)*
  ✔ earn
us
us'a·ble *also*
  use'a·ble
us'age
use, used, us'ing
use'ful
us'er
us'er-friend'ly
ush'er
u'su·al
u'su·rer
u·su'ri·ous
u·surp'
u'sur·pa'tion
u'su·ry
U'tah·an
Ute *pl.* Ute *or* Utes
u·ten'sil
u'ter·ine
u'ter·us *pl.* u'ter·i *or*
  u'ter·us·es
u·til'i·tar'i·an
u·til'i·ty
u'til·i·za'tion
u'til·ize', -ized',
  -iz'ing
ut'most'
U'to-Az'tec'an
u·to'pi·a

u·to'pi·an
ut'ter
ut'ter·ance
ut'ter·most'
U'-turn'
u'vu·la
u'vu·lar

V

va'can·cy
va'cant
va'cate', -cat'ed,
  -cat'ing
va·ca'tion
vac'ci·nate',
  -nat'ed, -nat'ing
vac'ci·na'tion
vac·cine'
vac'il·late', -lat'ed,
  -lat'ing
vac'il·la'tion
vac'il·la'tor
va·cu'i·ty
vac'u·o'lar
vac'u·ole'
vac'u·ous
vac'u·um *pl.*
  -u·ums *or* -u·a
vac'u·um-packed'
vag'a·bond'
va'ga·ry
va·gi'na *pl.* -nas *or*
  -nae
vag'i·nal
va'gran·cy

va′grant

vague, vagu′er,
vagu′est

vain *(fruitless,
conceited)*
✔ vane, vein

vain·glo′ri·ous

vain′glo′ry

val′ance *(drapery)*
✔ valence

vale *(valley)*
✔ veil

val′e·dic′tion

val′e·dic′to·ri·an

val′e·dic′to·ry

va′lence *also*
va·len·cy *(capacity
to combine)*
✔ valance

val′en·tine′

val′et

val′e·tu·di·nar′i·an

val′iant

val′id

val′i·date′, -dat′ed,
-dat′ing

val′i·da′tion

va·lid′i·ty

va·lise′

val′ley *pl.* -leys

val′or

val′or·ous

val′u·a·ble

val′u·a′tion

val′ue, -ued, -u·ing

valve

val′vu·lar

va·moose′,
-moosed′,
-moos′ing

vamp

vam′pire′

vam′pir·ism

van

va·na′di·um

Van Al′len belt′

van′dal *(person who
defaces)*

Van′dal *(tribe
member)*

van′dal·ism

van′dal·ize′, -ized′,
-iz′ing

Van·dyke′ beard′

vane *(weathervane)*
✔ vain, vein

van′guard′

va·nil′la

va·nil′lin

van′ish

van′i·ty

van′quish

van′tage

vap′id

va·pid′i·ty

va′por

va′por·iz′a·ble

va′por·i·za′tion

va′por·ize′, -ized′,
-iz′ing

va′por·iz′er

va′por·ous

va·que′ro *pl.* -ros

var′i·a·bil′i·ty *or*

var′i·a·ble·ness

var′i·a·ble

var′i·a·bly

var′i·ance

var′i·ant

var′i·a′tion

var′i·cel′la

var′i·col′ored

var′i·cose′

var′ied

var′i·e·gat′ed

va·ri′e·ty

var′i·ous

var′let

var′mint

var′nish

var′si·ty

var′y *(to change)*,
-ied, -y′ing
✔ very

vas′cu·lar

vase

va·sec′to·my

vas′sal

vas′sal·age

vast

vat

Vat′i·can

vaude′ville′

vault

vault′er

vaunt

VCR *pl.* VCRs *or*
VCR's

VDT *pl.* VDTs *or*
VDT's

veal

vec′tor

veer

veg′e•ta•ble

veg′e•tal

veg′e•tar′i•an

veg′e•tar′i•an•ism

veg′e•tate′, -tat′ed,
-tat′ing

veg′e•ta′tion

veg′e•ta′tive *also*
veg′e•tive

ve′he•mence *or*
ve′he•men•cy

ve′he•ment

ve′hi•cle

ve•hic′u•lar

veil *(covering)*
✔ vale

vein *(blood vessel,
strip)*
✔ vain, vane

ve′lar

veldt *also* veld

vel′lum *(parchment)*
✔ velum

ve•loc′i•ty

ve•lour′

ve′lum *(membrane,
soft palate), pl.* -la
✔ vellum

vel′vet

vel′vet•een′

vel′vet•y

ve′nal *(open to
bribery)*
✔ venial

ve•na′tion

vend

vend′er *or* ven′dor

ven•det′ta

ve•neer′

ven′er•a•ble

ven′er•a•bly

ven′er•ate′, -at′ed,
-at′ing

ven′er•a′tion

ven′er•a′tor

ve•ne′re•al

ve•ne′tian blind′
or Ve•ne′tian
blind′

ven′geance

venge′ful

ve′ni•al *(minor)*
✔ venal

ven′i•son

Venn′ di′a•gram′

ven′om

ven′om•ous

ve′nous

vent

ven′ti•late′, -lat′ed,
-lat′ing

ven′ti•la′tion

ven′ti•la′tor

ven′tral

ven′tri•cle

ven•tric′u•lar

ven′tril′o•quism
also ven•tril′o•quy

ven•tril′o•quist

ven′ture, -tured,
-tur′ing

ven′ture•some

ven′ue

Ve•nu′sian

Ve′nus's-fly′trap′

ve•ra′cious *(truthful)*
✔ voracious

ve•rac′i•ty

ve•ran′da *or*
ve•ran′dah

verb

ver′bal

ver′bal•i•za′tion

ver′bal•ize′, -ized′,
-iz′ing

ver•ba′tim

ver•be′na

ver′bi•age

ver•bose′

ver•bos′i•ty

ver′dant

ver′dict

ver′di•gris′

ver′dure

verge, verged,
verg′ing

ver′i•fi′a•ble

ver′i•fi•ca′tion

ver′i•fy′, -fied′,
-fy′ing

ver′i•ly

ver′i•si•mil′i•tude′

ver′i•ta•ble

ver′i•ty

ver′mi•cel′li

ver′mi•form′

ver•mil′ion *also*
ver•mil′lion

ver'min *pl.* -min
ver'min•ous
Ver•mont'er
ver•mouth'
ver•nac'u•lar
ver'nal
ver'sa•tile
ver'sa•til'i•ty
verse
versed
ver'si•fi•ca'tion
ver'si•fi'er
ver'si•fy', -fied',
    -fy'ing
ver'sion
ver'sus
ver'te•bra *pl.* -brae'
    or -bras
ver'te•bral
ver'te•brate'
ver'tex' *pl.* -tex'es *or*
    -ti•ces'
ver'ti•cal
ver•tig'i•nous
ver'ti•go' *pl.* -goes'
    or -gos'
verve
ver'y *(extremely)*
    ✔ *vary*
ves'i•cle
ve•sic'u•lar
ves'per *(bell)*
Ves'per *(star)*
ves'pers *also*
    Ves'pers
ves'sel
vest

ves'tal
vest'ed
ves'ti•bule'
ves'tige
ves•tig'i•al
vest'ment
ves'try
ves'try•man
ves'try•wom'an
vet, vet'ted, vet'ting
vetch
vet'er•an
vet'er•i•nar'i•an
vet'er•i•nar'y
ve'to *pl.* -toes
ve'to, -toed, -to•ing
vex•a'tion
vex•a'tious
vexed
vi'a
vi'a•bil'i•ty
vi'a•ble
vi'a•duct'
vi'al *(glass container)*
    ✔ *viol*
vi'and
vi'brant
vi'bra•phone'
vi'bra•phon'ist
vi'brate', -brat'ed,
    -brat'ing
vi•bra'tion
vi•bra'to *pl.* -tos
vi'bra'tor
vi'bra•to'ry
vi•bur'num
vic'ar

vic'ar•age
vi•car'i•ous
vice *(wickedness)*
    ✔ *vise*
vice'-pres'i•den•cy
vice' pres'i•dent *or*
    vice'-pres'i•dent
vice'-pres'i•den'-
    tial
vice'roy'
vi'ce ver'sa
vi'chys•soise'
Vi'chy wa'ter
vic'i•nage
vi•cin'i•ty
vi'cious
vi•cis'si•tude'
vic'tim
vic'tim•i•za'tion
vic'tim•ize', -ized',
    -iz'ing
vic'tim•iz'er
vic'tor
vic•to'ri•a
Vic•to'ri•an
vic•to'ri•ous
vic'to•ry
vict'ual
vi•cu'ña *also*
    vi•cu'na
vid'e•o' *pl.* -os'
vid'e•o•cas•sette'
vid'e•o•disk' *also*
    vid'e•o•disc'
vid'e•og'ra•pher
vid'e•og'ra•phy
vid'e•o•tape',

-taped', -tap'ing
vie, vied, vy'ing
Vi·en·nese' *pl.*
  -nese'
Vi·et'cong' *also*
  Vi·et' Cong'
Vi·et'minh' *also*
  Vi·et' Minh'
Vi·et'nam·ese' *pl.*
  -ese'
view
view'find'er
view'point'
vig'il
vig'i·lance
vig'i·lant
vig'i·lan'te
vi·gnette'
vig'or
vig'or·ous
Vi'king
vile, vil'er, vil'est
vil'i·fi·ca'tion
vil'i·fi'er
vil'i·fy', -fied',
  -fy'ing
vil'la
vil'lage
vil'lag·er
vil'lain (*wicked*
  person)
  ✔ *villein*
vil'lain·ous
vil'lain·y
vil'lein *also* vil'lain
  (*serf*)
  ✔ *villain*

vil'lus *pl.* -li
vim
vin'ai·grette'
vin'di·cate',
  -cat'ed, -cat'ing
vin'di·ca'tion
vin'di·ca'tor
vin·dic'tive
vine
vin'e·gar
vin'e·gar·y *also*
  vin'e·gar·ish
vine'yard'
vin'i·cul'ture
vin'tage
vint'ner
vi'nyl
vi'ol (*musical instru-*
  ment)
  ✔ *vial*
vi·o'la
vi'o·la·bil'i·ty *or*
  vi'o·la·ble·ness
vi'o·la·ble
vi'o·late', -lat'ed,
  -lat'ing
vi'o·la'tion
vi'o·la'tor
vi'o·lence
vi'o·lent
vi'o·let
vi'o·lin'
vi'o·lin'ist
vi·o'list
vi'o·lon·cel'list
vi'o·lon·cel'lo *pl.*
  -los

VIP *pl.* VIPs *or* VIP's
vi'per
vi'per·ous
vi·ra'go *pl.* -goes *or*
  -gos
vi'ral
vir'gin
vir'gin·al
Vir·gin'ian
vir·gin'i·ty
vir'gule
vir'ile
vi·ril'i·ty
vi·rol'o·gist
vi·rol'o·gy
vir·tu' *also* ver·tu'
  (*fine arts*)
  ✔ *virtue*
vir'tu·al
vir'tue (*goodness*)
  ✔ *virtu*
vir'tu·os'i·ty
vir'tu·o'so *pl.* -sos
  or -si
vir'tu·ous
vir'u·lence *or*
  vir'u·len·cy
vir'u·lent
vi'rus *pl.* -rus·es
vi'sa
vis'age
vis-'à-vis'
vis'cer·a
vis'cer·al
vis'cid
vis·cos'i·ty
vis'count'

vis'count'ess
vis'cous
vise *also* vice *(clamp)*
  ✔ **vice**
vis'i·bil'i·ty
vis'i·ble
vis'i·bly
Vis'i·goth'
vi'sion
vi'sion·ar'y
vis'it
vis'i·tant
vis'i·ta'tion
vis'i·tor
vi'sor *also* vi'zor
vis'ta
vi'su·al
vi'su·al·i·za'tion
vi'su·al·ize', -ized',
  -iz'ing
vi'ta *pl.* -tae
vi'tal
vi·tal'i·ty
vi'tal·i·za'tion
vi'tal·ize', -ized',
  -iz'ing
vi'tals
vi'ta·min
vi'ti·ate', -at'ed,
  -at'ing
vi'ti·a'tion
vit'i·cul'ture
vit'i·cul'tur·ist
vit're·ous
vit'ri·fi'a·ble
vit'ri·fi·ca'tion
vit'ri·fy', -fied',

  -fy'ing
vit'ri·ol'
vit'ri·ol'ic
vi·tu'per·ate',
  -at'ed, -at'ing
vi·tu'per·a'tion
vi·tu'per·a·tive
vi'va
vi·va'cious
vi·vac'i·ty
viv'id
viv'i·fi·ca'tion
viv'i·fy', -fied',
  -fy'ing
vi·vip'a·rous
viv'i·sect'
viv'i·sec'tion
vix'en
viz'ard *also* vis'ard
vi·zier'
vo·cab'u·lar'y
vo'cal
vo·cal'ic
vo'cal·ist
vo'cal·i·za'tion
vo'cal·ize', -ized',
  -iz'ing
vo·ca'tion
voc'a·tive
vo·cif'er·ate',
  -at'ed, -at'ing
vo·cif'er·a'tion
vo·cif'er·ous
vod'ka
vogue
voice, voiced,
  voic'ing

voice'less
voice' mail'
voice'-o'ver *or*
  voice'o'ver
void
voi·là'
voile
vol'a·tile
vol'a·til'i·ty
vol·can'ic
vol·ca'no *pl.* -noes
  or -nos
vole
vo·li'tion
vol'ley *pl.* -leys
vol'ley·ball'
volt'age
vol·ta'ic
volt·am'me'ter
volt'-am'pere'
volt'me'ter
vol'u·bil'i·ty
vol'u·ble
vol'u·bly
vol'ume
vol'u·met'ric
vo·lu'mi·nous
vol'un·tar'i·ly
vol'un·tar'y
vol'un·teer'
vo·lup'tu·ar'y
vo·lup'tu·ous
vo·lute'
vol'vox'
vom'it
voo'doo *pl.* -doos
voo'doo·ism

vo•ra′cious
  (ravenous)
  ✔ veracious
vo•rac′i•ty *or*
  vo•ra′cious•ness
vor′tex′ *pl.* -tex′es *or*
  -ti•ces′
vo′ta•ry
vote, vot′ed, vot′ing
vot′er
vo′tive
vouch
vouch′er
vouch•safe′,
  -safed′, -saf′ing
vow
vow′el
voy′age, -aged,
  -ag•ing
voy′ag•er
voy•eur′
voy•eur′ism
voy′eur•is′tic
vul′ca•nite′
vul′can•i•za′tion
vul′ca•nize′,
  -nized′, -niz′ing
vul′gar
vul•gar′i•an
vul′gar•ism
vul•gar′i•ty
vul′gar•i•za′tion
vul′gar•ize′, -ized′,
  -iz′ing
vul′gate′ *(vernac-
  ular)*
Vul′gate′ *(Bible)*

vul′ner•a•ble
vul′ner•a•bil′i•ty
vul′ner•a•bly
vul′pine′
vul′ture
vul′va *pl.* -vae

W

wack′y *also*
  whack′y
wad, wad′ded,
  wad′ding
wad′dle, -dled,
  -dling
wade, wad′ed,
  wad′ing
wad′ers
wa′di *pl.* -dis *also*
  -dies
wa′fer
waf′fle, -fled, -fling
waft
wag, wagged,
  wag′ging
wage, waged,
  wag′ing
wa′ger
wag′gish
wag′gle, -gled,
  -gling
wag′on
wag′on•er
waif
wail *(cry)*
  ✔ wale, whale

wain *(wagon)*
  ✔ wane
wain′scot
wain′scot•ing
waist *(body part)*
  ✔ waste
waist′band′
waist′coat
waist′line′
wait *(to remain)*
  ✔ weight
wait′er
wait′ing
wait′per′son
wait′ress
wait′ staff′ *also*
  wait′staff′
waive *(to relinquish),*
  waived, waiv′ing
  ✔ wave
waiv′er *(relinquish-
  ment)*
  ✔ waver
wake, woke *or*
  waked, waked *or*
  wok′en, wak′ing
wake′ful
wak′en
wale *(to mark with
  ridges),* waled,
  wal′ing
  ✔ wail, whale
walk
walk′ie-talk′ie *pl.*
  -ies
walk′-in′ *adj. & n.*
walk′-on′ *n.*

walk'out' *n.*

walk'o'ver *n.*

walk'-through' *n.*

walk'up' *also*
    walk'-up' *n.*

walk'way'

wall

wal'la•by *pl.* -bies *or*
    -by

wall'board'

wal'let

wall'eye'

wall'eyed'

wall'flow'er

Wal•loon'

wal'lop

wal'low

wall'pa'per

wall'-to-wall'

wal'nut

wal'rus *pl.* -rus *or*
    -rus•es

waltz

Wam'pa•no'ag *pl.*
    -ag *or* -ags

wam'pum

wan, wan'ner,
    wan'nest

wand

wan'der

wan'der•lust'

wane *(to decrease)*,
    waned, wan'ing
    ✔ *wain*

wan'gle, -gled,
    -gling

Wan'kel en'gine

wan'ly

want *(lack)*
    ✔ *wont*

wan'ton

wap'i•ti *pl.* -ti *or* -tis

war, warred,
    war'ring

war'ble, -bled,
    -bling

war'bler

ward

war'den

ward'er

ward'robe'

ware *(goods)*
    ✔ *wear, where*

ware'house'

war'fare'

war'head'

war'horse' *also*
    war'-horse'

war'like'

war'lock'

war'lord'

warm

warm'-blood'ed

warm'-heart'ed

war'mon'ger

warmth

warm'-up' *or*
    warm'up'

warn

warn'ing

warp

war'path'

war'rant

war'ran•ty

war'ren

war'ri•or

wart

wart' hog'

war'time'

war'y

wa•sa'bi

wash'a•ble

wash'-and-wear'

wash'ba'sin

wash'board'

wash'bowl'

wash'cloth'

washed'-out'

washed'-up'

wash'er

wash'ing

Wash'ing•to'ni•an

wash'out'

wash'rag'

wash'room'

wash'stand'

wash'tub'

was'n't

wasp'ish

was'sail

waste *(to squander)*,
    wast'ed, wast'ing
    ✔ *waist*

waste'bas'ket

waste'ful

waste'land'

waste'pa'per

wast'rel

watch

watch'band'

watch'dog'

watch′ful
watch′mak′er
watch′man
watch′tow′er
watch′word′
wa′ter
wa′ter•borne′
wa′ter•buck′ *pl.*
  -buck′ *or* -bucks′
wa′ter•col′or
wa′ter•cool′
wa′ter•course′
wa′ter•craft′
wa′ter•cress′
wa′ter•fall′
wa′ter•fowl′ *pl.*
  -fowl′ *or* -fowls′
wa′ter•front′
wa′ter•logged′
wa′ter•mark′
wa′ter•mel′on
wa′ter•pow′er
wa′ter•proof′
wa′ter•proof′ing
wa′ter•re•pel′lent
wa′ter•re•sis′tant
wa′ter•shed′
wa′ter ski′ *n.*
wa′ter-ski′, -skied′,
  -ski′ing
wa′ter•spout′
wa′ter•tight′
wa′ter•way′
wa′ter•works′
wa′ter•y
watt
watt′age

watt′-hour′
wat′tle
wave (*to move back
  and forth*), waved,
  wav′ing
  ✔ waive
wave′length′
wave′let
wav′er (*one that
  waves*)
  ✔ waiver
wa′ver (*to vacillate*)
  ✔ waiver
wav′i•ness
wav′y
wax
wax′en
wax′wing′
wax′work′
wax′y
way (*course*)
  ✔ weigh, whey
way′far′er
way′far′ing
way′lay′, -laid′,
  -lay′ing
way′-out′ *adj.*
way′side′
way′ward
we *pron.*
  ✔ wee
weak (*feeble*)
  ✔ week
weak′en
weak′fish′ *pl.* -fish′
  or -fish′es
weak′ling

weak′ly (*sickly*)
  ✔ weekly
weak′-mind′ed
weal (*prosperity, welt*)
  ✔ wheal, wheel
wealth
wealth′y
wean
weap′on
weap′on•ry
wear (*to have on, to
  erode*), wore, worn,
  wear′ing
  ✔ ware, where
wear′a•ble
wea′ri•ly
wea′ri•ness
wea′ri•some
wea′ry, -ried,
  -ry•ing
wea′sel, -seled *also*
  -selled, -sel•ing *also*
  -sel•ling
weath′er (*climate*)
  ✔ wether, whether
weath′er-beat′en
weath′er•cock′
weath′ered
weath′er•glass′
weath′er•ing
weath′er•proof′
weath′er-strip′,
  -stripped′,
  -strip′ping
weath′er
  strip′ping *n.*
weath′er•vane′

weave, wove *also*
weaved, wo'ven,
weav'ing
weav'er
weav'er•bird'
web, webbed,
web'bing
web'-foot'ed
wed, wed'ded, wed
or wed'ded,
wed'ding
wedge, wedged,
wedg'ing
wed'lock'
Wednes'day
wee (*tiny*), we'er,
we'est
✔ *we*
weed
weed'y
week (*calendar
period*)
✔ *weak*
week'day'
week'end'
week'long'
week'ly (*once a
week*)
✔ *weakly*
ween'ie
weep, wept,
weep'ing
wee'vil
weft
weigh (*to determine
weight*)
✔ *way, whey*

weight (*measure of
heaviness*)
✔ *wait*
weight'less
weight'lift'ing
weight'y
weir
weird
weird'o *pl.* -oes
welch
wel'come, -comed,
-com•ing
weld
weld'er
wel'fare'
wel'kin
well (*deep hole*)
well (*to rise up*)
well (*in a good man-
ner*), bet'ter, best
well'-ap•point'ed
well'-bal'anced
well'-be•ing
well'born'
well'-bred'
well'-de•fined'
well'-done'
well'-fa'vored
well'-fed'
well'-fixed'
well'-found'ed
well'-groomed'
well'-ground'ed
well'head'
well'-heeled'
well'-known'
well'-man'nered

well'-mean'ing
well'-nigh'
well'-off'
well'-read'
well'-round'ed
well'-spo'ken
well'spring'
well-thought'-of'
well'-timed'
well'-to-do'
well'-wish'er
well'-worn'
welsh *also* welch (*to
swindle*)
Welsh (*relating to
Wales*)
Welsh' cor'gi
Welsh'man
Welsh' rab'bit *also*
Welsh' rare'bit
Welsh'wom'an
welt
wel'ter
wel'ter•weight'
wen (*cyst*)
✔ *when*
wench
wend
were'n't
were'wolf'
west
west'bound'
west'er•ly
west'ern
west'ern•er
west'ern•ize',
-ized', -iz'ing

west′ern·most′
West′ In′di·an
West′ Vir·gin′ian
west′ward *adv. &*
  adj.
west′wards *adv.*
wet *(damp)*, wet′ter,
  wet′test
  ✔ **whet**
wet *(to dampen)*, wet
  or wet′ted, wet′ting
  ✔ **whet**
weth′er *(sheep)*
  ✔ **weather, whether**
wet′land′
whack
whale *(mammal)*
  ✔ **wail, wale**
whale′boat′
whale′bone′
whal′er
whal′ing
wham, whammed,
  wham′ming
wharf *pl.* wharves *or*
  wharfs
what
what·ev′er
what′not′
what′so·ev′er
wheal *(swelling)*
  ✔ **weal, wheel**
wheat
wheat′en
whee′dle, -dled,
  -dling
wheel *(circular*

frame)
  ✔ **weal, wheal**
wheel′bar′row
wheel′base′
wheel′chair′ *also*
  wheel′ chair′
wheeled
wheel′er-deal′er
wheel′house′
wheel′wright′
wheeze, wheezed,
  wheez′ing
wheez′y
whelk
whelm
whelp
when *(at what*
  time)
  ✔ **wen**
whence
when·ev′er
when′so·ev′er
where *(at what place)*
  ✔ **ware, wear**
where′a·bouts′
where·as′
where·at′
where·by′
where′fore′
where·in′
where·of′
where·on′
where′so·ev′er
where′to′
where′up·on′
wher·ev′er
where′with′

where′with·al′
whet *(to hone)*,
  whet′ted,
  whet′ting
  ✔ **wet**
wheth′er *(if)*
  ✔ **weather, wether**
whet′stone′
whew
whey *(watery part of*
  milk)
  ✔ **way, weigh**
which *pron.*
  ✔ **witch**
which·ev′er
whiff
whif′fle·tree′
Whig
while *(period of time)*
  ✔ **wile**
while *(to spend time*
  idly), whiled,
  whil′ing
  ✔ **wile**
whim
whim′per
whim′si·cal
whim′si·cal′i·ty
whim′sy *also*
  whim′sey *pl.* -sies
  or -seys
whine *(to complain)*,
  whined, whin′ing
  ✔ **wine**
whin′ny, -nied,
  -ny′ing
whin′y *or* whin′ey

whip, whipped *or*
  whipt, whip′ping
whip′cord′
whip′lash′
whip′per•snap′per
whip′pet
whip′poor•will′
whip′stitch′
whir, whirred,
  whir′ring
whirl
whirl′i•gig′
whirl′pool′
whirl′wind′
whirl′y•bird′
whisk
whisk′broom′
whisk′er
whis′key *also*
  whis′ky *pl.* -keys
  also -kies
whis′per
whist
whis′tle, -tled,
  -tling
whis′tle stop′ *n.*
whis′tle-stop′,
  -stopped′,
  -stop′ping
whit *(particle)*
  ✔ *wit*
white, whit′er,
  whit′est
white′cap′
white′-col′lar *adj.*
white′fish′ *pl.* -fish′
  or -fish′es

white′head′
white′-hot′
whit′en
whit′en•er
white′ness
white′out′ *n.*
white′-tailed′
  deer′
white′wall′
white′wash′
whith′er *(where)*
  ✔ *wither*
whit′ing *(chalk)*
whit′ing *(fish), pl.*
  -ing *or* -ings
whit′ish
Whit′sun•day
Whit′sun•tide′
whit′tle, -tled,
  -tling
whit′tler
whiz *also* whizz,
  whizzed, whiz′zing
who
whoa
who•dun′it
who•ev′er
whole *(complete)*
  ✔ *hole*
whole′heart′ed
whole′sale′
whole′sal′er
whole′some,
  -som•er, -som•est
whole′-wheat′
whol′ly *(totally)*
  ✔ *holey, holy*

whom
whom•ev′er
whom′so•ev′er
whoop *(cry, cough)*
  ✔ *hoop*
whoop′ing cough′
whoop′ing crane′
whoops
whop′per
whore *(prostitute)*
  ✔ *hoar*
whorl
whose
who′so•ev′er
why *pl.* whys
Wich′i•ta′ *pl.* -ta′
wick
wick′ed
wick′er
wick′et
wick′i•up′
wide, wid′er, wid′est
wide′-an′gle *adj.*
wide′-a•wake′
wide′-bod′ied
wide′-eyed′
wid′en
wide′-o′pen
wide′spread′
wid′geon *pl.* -geon
  or -geons
wid′ow
wid′ow•er
wid′ow's peak′
wid′ow's walk′
width
wield

wie′ner
Wie′ner schnit′zel
wie′ner•wurst′
wife *pl.* wives
wife′ly
wig
wig′gle, -gled,
 -gling
wig′gler
wig′wag′, -wagged′,
 -wag′ging
wig′wam′
wild
wild′cat′
wil′de•beest′ *pl.*
 -beests′ *or* -beest′
wil′der•ness
wild′-eyed′
wild′fire′
wild′flow′er *also*
 -flow′er
wild′fowl′ *pl.* -fowl′
 or -fowls′
wild′-goose′
 chase′
wild′life′
wild′wood′
wile *(to lure),* wiled,
 wil′ing
 ✔ *while*
will *(volition)*
will *aux. v., past tense*
 would
will′ful *also* wil′ful
will′ing
will′-o′-the-wisp′
wil′low

wil′low•y
will′pow′er *or* will′
 pow′er
wil′ly-nil′ly
wilt
wi′ly
wimp
wim′ple
win, won, win′ning
wince, winced,
 winc′ing
winch
wind *(to cause to be
 out of breath),*
 wind′ed, wind′ing
wind *(to wrap
 around),* wound,
 wind′ing
wind′bag′
wind′blown′
wind′break′
wind′burn′
wind′-chill′ fac′-
 tor
wind′fall′
wind′flow′er
wind′jam′mer
wind′lass
wind′mill′
win′dow
win′dow-dress′ing
 also win′dow
 dress′ing
win′dow•pane′
win′dow-shop′,
 -shopped′,
 -shop′ping

win′dow•sill′
wind′pipe′
wind′row′
wind′shield′
wind′sock′
Wind′sor chair′
wind′storm′
wind′surf′ing
wind′swept′
wind′-up′ *or*
 wind′up′ *n. & adj.*
wind′ward
wind′y
wine *(beverage)*
 ✔ *whine*
wine′ cel′lar
wine′press′
win′er•y
wing
winged
wing′span′
wing′spread′
wink
win′ner
win′ning
win′now
win′some
win′ter
win′ter•green′
win′ter•ize′, -ized′,
 -iz′ing
win′ter•time′
win′try *also*
 win′ter•y
wipe, wiped,
 wip′ing
wiped′-out′ *adj.*

wipe'out' *n.*

wip'er

wire, wired, wir'ing

wire'haired'

wire'less

wire'tap', -tapped',
  -tap'ping

wire'worm'

wir'i•ness

wir'ing

wir'y

wis'dom

wise, wis'er, wis'est

wise'a'cre

wise'crack'

wish'bone'

wish'ful

wish'y-wash'y

wisp

wist

wis•ter'i•a *also*
  wis•tar'i•a

wist'ful

wit *(intelligence,
  humor)*
  ✔ whit

witch *(woman with
  supernatural powers)*
  ✔ which

witch'craft'

witch'-hunt'

with

with•al'

with•draw', -drew',
  -drawn', -draw'ing

with•draw'al

with'er *(to shrivel)*

✔ whither

with'ers

with•hold', -held',
  -hold'ing

with•in'

with'-it' *adj.*

with•out'

with•stand',
  -stood', -stand'ing

wit'less

wit'ness

wit'ti•cism

wit'ti•ly

wit'ti•ness

wit'ting

wit'ty

wiz'ard

wiz'ard•ry

wiz'ened

wob'ble, -bled,
  -bling

wob'bly

woe

woe'be•gone'

woe'ful

wok

wolf *pl.* wolves

wolf'hound'

wolf'ram

wolfs'bane'

Wo'lof'

wol'ver•ine'

wom'an *pl.* wom'en

wom'an•hood'

wom'an•ish

wom'an•ize',
  -ized', -iz'ing

wom'an•iz'er

wom'an•kind'

womb

wom'bat'

wom'en•folk' *also*
  wom'en•folks'

won'der

won'der•ful

won'der•land'

won'der•ment

won'drous

wont *(accustomed)*
  ✔ want

wont'ed *(usual)*

won' ton' *or*
  won'ton'

woo

wood *(lumber)*
  ✔ would

wood'bine'

wood'carv'ing

wood'chuck'

wood'cock' *pl.*
  -cock' *or* -cocks'

wood'craft'

wood'cut'

wood'cut'ter

wood'ed

wood'en

wood'land

wood'man

wood'peck'er

wood'pile'

wood'shed'

woods'man

woods'y

wood'wind'

wood′work′
wood′work′ing
wood′y
woo′er
woof
woof′er
wool
wool′en *also*
  wool′len
wool′gath′er•er
wool′gath′er•ing
wool′ly
wooz′i•ness
wooz′y
word′book′
word′ for word′
  adv.
word′-for-word′
  adj.
word′i•ness
word′ing
word′-of-mouth′
  adj.
word′ proc′ess′ing
word′ proc′es′sor
word′y
work, worked *also*
  wrought, work′ing
work′a•bil′i•ty *or*
  work′a•ble•ness
work′a•ble
work′a•day′
work′bench′
work′book′
work′day′
work′er
work′ force′ *or*

work′force′
work′horse′
work′house′
work′ing class′ *n.*
work′ing-class′ *adj.*
work′ing•man′
work′ing•wom′an
work′load′
work′man
work′man•ship′
work′out′ *n.*
work′place′ *also*
  work′ place′
work′room′
work′shop′
work′space′
work′ta′ble
work′week′
world
world′li•ness
world′ly
world′ly-wise′
world′wide′
worm
worm′-eat′en
worm′wood′
worm′y
worn′-out′
wor′ri•er
wor′ri•some
wor′ry, -ried, -ry•ing
wor′ry•wart′
worse
wors′en
wor′ship, -shiped *or*
  -shipped, -ship•ing
  or -ship•ping

wor′ship•er *or*
  wor′ship•per
wor′ship•ful
worst *(most inferior)*
  ✔ *wurst*
wor′sted
worth
wor′thi•ness
worth′while′
wor′thy
would *past tense of*
  will
  ✔ *wood*
would′-be′
would′n′t
wound
wow
wrack *(ruin, wreck-*
  age)
  ✔ *rack*
wraith *(ghost)*
  ✔ *wrath*
wran′gle, -gled,
  -gling
wrang′ler
wrap *(to enclose),*
  wrapped *or* wrapt,
  wrap′ping
  ✔ *rap*
wrap′a•round′ *adj.*
wrap′per
wrap′-up′ *n.*
wrath *(anger)*
  ✔ *wraith*
wrath′ful
wreak *(to inflict)*
  ✔ *reek*

wreath *n.*

wreathe, wreathed,
wreath'ing

wreck

wreck'age

wren

wrench

wrest *(to obtain by
force)*
✔ rest

wres'tle, -tled, -tling

wres'tler

wretch *(miserable
person)*
✔ retch

wretch'ed

wrig'gle, -gled,
-gling

wright *(person who
constructs)*
✔ right, rite, write

wring *(to squeeze)*,
wrung, wring'ing
✔ ring

wring'er

wrin'kle, -kled,
-kling

wrist

wrist'band'

wrist'watch'

writ *(order)*

write *(to compose)*,
wrote *also* writ,
writ'ten *also* writ,
writ'ing
✔ right, rite, wright

write'-in' *n.*

write'-off' *n.*

writ'er

write'-up' *n.*

writhe, writhed,
writh'ing

wrong

wrong'do'er

wrong'do'ing

wrong'ful

wrong'-head'ed

wrought' i'ron

wry *(ironic, twisted)*,
wri'er *or* wry'er,
wri'est *or* wry'est
✔ rye

wry'ly

wun'der·kind' *pl.*
-kind'er

wurst *(sausage)*
✔ worst

X

Xan'a·du'

x'-ax'is *pl.* -ax'es

X'-chro'mo·some'

xe'bec'

xe'non'

xen'o·phobe'

xen'o·pho'bi·a

xen'o·pho'bic

xe·rog'ra·pher

xer'o·graph'ic

xe·rog'ra·phy

Xho'sa *pl.* -sa

xi

X'mas

x'-ra'di·a'tion

X'-rat'ed

x'-ray' *also* X'-ray'
also x' ray' *or*
X' ray'

xy'lem

xy'lo·phone'

Y

yacht

yacht'ing

yachts'man

yachts'wom'an

ya'hoo *pl.* -hoos

yak *(animal)*

yak *(talk)*, yakked,
yak'king

yam'mer

yank *(to jerk)*

Yank *(Yankee)*

Yan'kee

yap, yapped,
yap'ping

Ya'qui *pl.* -qui *or*
-quis

yard'age

yard'arm'

yard'mas'ter

yard'stick'

yar'mul·ke *also*
yar'mel·ke

yarn

yar'row

yaw

yawl

yawn

yawp

yaws

y'-ax'is *pl.* -ax'es

Y'-chro'mo•some'

ye

yea

yeah

year

year'book'

year'-end' *also*
   year'end'

year'ling

year'long'

yearn

yearn'ing

year'-round'

yeast

yell

yel'low

yel'low•ham'mer

yel'low•ish

yel'low•legs' *pl.*
   -legs'

yelp

yen *(longing)*

yen *(monetary unit),*
   pl. yen

yeo'man

yeo'man•ry

yer'ba ma•té'

yes *pl.* yes'es

ye•shi'va *or*
   ye•shi'vah

yes'ter•day'

yes'ter•year'

yet

ye'ti *pl.* -tis

yew *(tree)*
   ✔ ewe, you

Yid'dish

yield

yield'ing

yip, yipped,
   yip'ping

yip'pee

yo'del, -deled *or*
   -delled, -del'ing *or*
   -del'ling

yo'ga

yo'gi *pl.* -gis

yo'gurt *also*
   yo'ghurt

yoke *(to join)*, yoked,
   yok'ing
   ✔ yolk

yo'kel

yolk *(yellow of an
   egg)*
   ✔ yoke

Yom' Kip•pur'

yon

yon'der

yore

York'shire pud'-
   ding

you *pron.*
   ✔ ewe, yew

you'-all' *also* y'all

young

young'ish

young'ster

your *possessive form*

of you

you're *contraction of*
   you are

yours

your•self' *pl.*
   -selves'

youth

youth'ful

yowl

yo'-yo' *pl.* -yos'

yt•ter'bi•um

yt'tri•um

yu•an' *pl.* -an' *or*
   -ans'

yuc'ca

Yu'go•sla'vi•an

Yule

Yule'tide'

Yu'ma *pl.* -ma *or*
   -mas

Yu'man

yum'my

yup'pie

yurt

Z

za'ny

zap, zapped,
   zap'ping

Za'po•tec' *pl.* -tec'
   or -tecs'

z'-ax'is *pl.* -ax'es

zeal

zeal'ot

zeal'ous

ze′bra
ze′bu *pl.* -bus
zed
Zen′ Bud′dhism
Zen′ Bud′dhist
ze′nith
zeph′yr
zep′pe•lin *also*
  Zep′pe•lin
ze′ro *pl.* -ros *or*
  -roes
zest′ful
ze′ta
zig′gu•rat′
zig′zag′, -zagged′,
  -zag′ging
zil′lion
Zim•bab′we•an
zinc
zin′fan•del *also*

Zin′fan•del′
zing
zing′er
zin′ni•a
Zi′on *also* Si′on
Zi′on•ism
Zi′on•ist
zip, zipped, zip′ping
zip′per
zip′py
zir′con′
zir•co′ni•um
zith′er
zlo′ty *pl.* -ty *or* -tys
zo′di•ac′
zom′bie *also* zom′bi
  pl. -bies *also* -bis
zon′al
zone, zoned,
  zon′ing

zoo *pl.* zoos
zoo′keep′er
zo′o•log′i•cal *also*
  zo′o•log′ic
zo•ol′o•gist
zo•ol′o•gy
zoom
zo′o•phyte′
Zo′ro•as′tri•an
Zo′ro•as′tri•an•ism
zounds
zuc•chi′ni *pl.* -ni *or*
  -nis
Zu′lu *pl.* -lu *or* -lus
Zu′ni *also* Zu′ñi *pl.*
  -ni *or* -nis *also* -ñi
  or -ñis
zwie′back′
zy′gote′
zy•got′ic